A Flash of Golden Fire

Number Twenty-Two

CAROLYN AND ERNEST FAY SERIES IN ANALYTICAL PSYCHOLOGY

Michael Escamilla, General Editor

The Carolyn and Ernest Fay book series, based on the Fay Lecture Series in Analytical Psychology, was established to further the ideas of C. G. Jung among students, faculty, therapists, and other citizens and to enhance scholarly activities related to analytical psychology. The lecture and book series address topics of importance to the individual and to society. Both series were generously endowed by Carolyn Grant Fay, the founding president of the C. G. Jung Educational Center in Houston, Texas. The series are in part a memorial to her husband, Ernest Bel Fay. Carolyn Fay has planted a Jungian tree carrying both her name and that of her husband, which will bear fruitful ideas and stimulate creative works from this time forward. The Jung Center, Houston, and all those who come in contact with the growing Fay Jungian tree are extremely grateful to Carolyn Grant Fay for what she has done. The Frank N. McMillan Jr. Scholar at the Jung Center, Houston, functions as the general editor of the Fay book series.

A Flash of Golden Fire

The Birth, Death, and Rebirth of the Modern Soul
in Coleridge's *The Rime of the Ancient Mariner*

Thomas Elsner

Foreword by Michael Escamilla

Texas A&M University Press
College Station

First edition

∞ This paper meets the requirements of ANSI/NISO Z39.48–1992 (Permanence of Paper).
Binding materials have been chosen for durability.

Library of Congress Cataloging-in-Publication Data
Library of Congress Control Number: 2024039551
Identifiers: LCCN: 2024039551 | ISBN 9781648432286 (cloth) | ISBN 9781648432293 (ebook)
LC record available at https://lccn.loc.gov/2024039551

If you just have a dream and let it pass by you, nothing has happened at all, even if it is the most amazing dream; but if you look at it with the purpose of trying to understand it, and succeed in understanding it, then you have taken it into the here and now, the body being a visible expression of the here and now.

—C. G. Jung, *Visions*

Contents

Series Editor's Foreword, by Michael Escamilla xi

Acknowledgments xix

Introduction: *The Rime of the Ancient Mariner*: An Epic Poem for the Modern World 1

PART 1: SAMUEL TAYLOR COLERIDGE

CHAPTER 1
"Alone on a Wide Wide Sea": Coleridge's Biography 23

CHAPTER 2
Psycho-analytical: Coleridge as a Proto-Depth Psychologist 44

PART 2: DEPARTURE

CHAPTER 3
"It Is an Ancient Mariner": Confrontation with Some Other Consciousness 57

CHAPTER 4
"Below the Kirk, below the Hill, below the Light-House Top": Setting Off from Shore 87

CHAPTER 5
"And Now the Storm-Blast Came": The Great Wind Takes Control 99

CHAPTER 6
"The Land of Mist and Snow": Trauma and Transcendence 107

CHAPTER 7
"At Length Did Cross an Albatross": Spirit from Above 114

PART 3: INITIATION

CHAPTER 8
"I Shot the Albatross": The Birth of the Modern Soul 135

CHAPTER 9
"Water, Water Every where, nor Any Drop to Drink": From Enlightenment to Wasteland 160

CHAPTER 10
"The Water, like a Witch's Oils, Burnt Green, and Blue and White": Soul from Below 166

CHAPTER 11
"Instead of the Cross, the Albatross about My Neck Was Hung": The Transitus of Modern Man 177

CHAPTER 12
"The Night-mare LIFE-IN-DEATH Was She": The Return of the Feminine and the Death of the Modern Soul 193

CHAPTER 13
Celebrating a Last Supper with Oneself: A Dream 216

CHAPTER 14
"And Straight the Sun Was Flecked with Bars": The Eclipse of the Sun 225

CHAPTER 15
"The Hornèd Moon with One Bright Star": Into the Belly of the Goddess 229

CHAPTER 16
"A Spring of Love Gushed from My Heart, and I Blessed Them Unaware": Blessing the Water-Snakes: The Rebirth of the Modern Soul 241

CHAPTER 17
Turning Lead to Gold: Alchemy, Romanticism, Depth Psychology, and the Contemporary Enigma of Consciousness 264

CHAPTER 18
"To Mary Queen the Praise Be Given": The Union of Spirit from Above with Soul from Below 279

CHAPTER 19
"The Upper Air Burst into Life!": Nature and Supernature Come Alive 305

PART 4: RETURN

CHAPTER 20
"A Frightful Fiend Doth Close behind Him Tread": The Challenge of Consciously Facing the Unconscious 313

CHAPTER 21
"Full Plain I See the Devil Knows How to Row": The Agonizing Conflict between Sea and Land 330

CHAPTER 22
"O Sweeter Than the Marriage-Feast, 'Tis Sweeter Far to Me, to Walk Together to the Church": Individuation and the Regressive Restoration of the Persona 352

Conclusion: An Epic Poem for the Modern World Revisited: A Fourfold Consciousness in the Fourth Industrial Revolution 382

Afterword: On a Personal Note 391

Notes 405

Bibliography 457

Index 469

Series Editor's Foreword

Michael Escamilla

Riding along on the crest of the wave
Getting rid of the albatross
Another will not forget
I know you very well . . .

—"Albatross," Public Image Ltd

In November of 1979, Public Image Ltd (PiL), a British group led by John Lydon (formerly known as Johnny Rotten of the Sex Pistols), released their second album, *Metal Box*. The album begins with a disturbing song over ten minutes in length called "Albatross," with ominous, metallic guitar-scraping sounds and a hypnotic rhythm section, over which Lydon moaned the lyrics "Getting rid of the Albatross." Lydon reportedly made up the lyrics on the spot in the studio, in a somewhat trancelike state. The song broke with the expectations of the short, rapid-fire punk rock movement Lydon had been instrumental in founding just a few years before, instead referring obliquely to suffering and dissolution ("sowing the seeds of discontent") and failed social revolutions ("still the spirit of '68" refers to antiwar riots that occurred in London in 1968), looking unflinchingly at the shadow aspects of people, all held together by the musical vision of the protagonist trying to, through the sacrament of art, free himself from an "Albatross."[1]

The "Albatross" in this song is certainly drawn from one of the central images (symbols) from the English poet Samuel Coleridge's *Rime of the Ancient Mariner*.[2] Coleridge's *Rime*, published in 1798, almost two centuries before PiL's "Albatross," had resurfaced here in a bracing and compelling musical form. I recall listening, the week PiL's album was released, to this hypnotic and disturbing music with my college friend Ignacio Magaloni, who had in turn recently been expounding to me about Coleridge's poem (which he had discovered in a literature class he was taking). Ignacio, in his first semester at Harvard at the time (he is now a poet and a professor of English literature), had been under the spell of learning about the Romantic poets and, in particular, had been moved by Coleridge's *Rime* (I in turn had been embedded in studying the sciences and had no idea what he was talking about, falsely assuming the Romantic poets wrote aesthetically pleasing poetry about romantic love). Although I hadn't yet read Coleridge's poem, now listening to this new music, as chills ran down my back, I felt I had entered an artistic space of great depth, where the unsavory and repressed elements of life were forcing themselves to be seen and responded to. This was not a space of pleasant rhymes and pastoral images, of business as usual and well-functioning societies, but one of hard, mysterious, and unpleasant truths which were coexistent (just under the surface, in fact) with our modern, capitalist society. The "albatross" of Coleridge's poem, a symbolic image from a Romantic poet from the turn of the nineteenth century, was present and alive in the room. English culture (and its transatlantic offspring, the culture of the United States) had still not been able to "get rid" of the albatross back in 1979. I would say, in our current state of worldwide pandemics and climate change devastating our current socioeconomic systems, the albatross and whatever mysteries Coleridge's poem had conjured up are still ever present, beneath the surface, or breaking through, even as we move through the third decade of the twenty-first century. Our world culture and each of us as individuals (once opened to this "other" world) are still under the spell of the Ancient Mariner and his tortured story.

When I heard that the Fay Lecture Series in 2016 would be given by Thomas Elsner on the topic of Coleridge and his *Rime of the Ancient Mariner*, I found a copy of the poem (I had probably only briefly glanced at it back in my college days) and began reading it in earnest. I found myself frightened and disturbed by the imagery of the poem and remember calling my old friend, Ignacio, to "process" what I was reading. In preparation for the lecture series, Thomas was also very helpful in helping me learn about the Romantic poets. Through reading *Lyrical Ballads*,[3] the collection of poems *Rime* was first published in, I began to appreciate both the artistic endeavor of these poets (moving the subject matter of poetry from Greek myths and classical aesthetic artifices to direct experiences of "nature") and the strange mix of their styles (*Lyrical Ballads* was a collection of poems by William Wordsworth and Samuel Taylor Coleridge, with a preface establishing what their new poetic movement was all about). Both were exploring nature as it presented itself to them in the here and now, but whereas Wordsworth wrote about the environment he observed and the feelings it evoked in him, the "nature" which Coleridge explored, through poems like *Rime*, went into his deeper self—examining our inner, imaginal creative process and dream worlds, which are equally a part of nature. As explicated in Thomas's lectures (and now this book), Coleridge was an early explorer of our psychic inner world, and, no doubt aided by laudanum and the fractured nature of his psychological state, he helped bring to light aspects of the collective unconscious and symbols of this inner world in a way that anticipated the work of Carl Jung and the depth psychiatrists and psychologists of the twentieth century. Coleridge and his journeys (both his life journey and the journeys he went on in his poems) make for a compelling and emotional portrait of the psyche each of us have within us, and, most importantly, the collective issues which we as a culture must face, as a consequence of the scientific and materialistic developments Western culture (and now the entire world) has experienced since the "age of enlightenment." Coleridge's *Rime* and Thomas's book are vital and emotionally compelling works which help us to better understand ourselves as individuals, and as members of our species and the world we live in currently.

Thomas also does a wonderful job in this book of integrating aspects of his own life journey in a way that further illuminate the themes of the *Rime* and of the journey of "individuation" which is a central component of Jung's theory of psychological development. The process of individuation has, as a core element, a process (paralleling the principles seen in alchemy) in which one's ego (our everyday sense of the "I") encounters the different archetypal structures which lie within our unconscious and guide our psychological development. Thomas illustrates how this process unfolded in his own life, aided by his discovery of Jung and analytical psychology, but he also shows how the same type of individuation process (as Jungians, we hypothesize that the drive to individuate is innate in human psychology) unfolded in the life of Coleridge and (aesthetically) in the story of the Mariner. For Coleridge, dipping directly into the realms of the unconscious, in a time when there was no understanding or support available from psychologists or therapists, this was undoubtedly an overwhelming process, and one which he had to retreat from in order to survive psychologically in his place and time. This inability to fully individuate (to integrate the encounter with the deep unconscious) is, as Thomas points out, also reflected in the journey of the Ancient Mariner character himself. As Thomas proposes, the Mariner moves into direct contact with elements of the deep psyche but is unable to integrate this fully on his return from his night-sea journey, leading, in a sense, to a failed individuation process. I would venture to say, there was little other possibility for the "depth" explorers prior to the era when Jung and his colleagues developed a framework in which to explore these depths and integrate them through the work of depth analysis. Coleridge and his Mariner may have "failed," in some sense, to complete their individuation process (but aren't we all works in progress?), but they have succeeded in giving our world an enduring gift—forever after, the Mariner wanders through our own cultural and spiritual landscape, carrying his albatross around his neck or wandering from town to town telling his story of his "night journey," asking us as individuals and as a species to resolve the unfinished individuation process our culture (and, by extension, each of us, if we are psychologically aware) seems to be mired in. As Elsner writes in this book, during the Covid pandemic which has wreaked havoc on the entire world, a group of esteemed actors formed to record a reading of *The Rime of the Ancient Mariner*, realizing instinctively that this story is alive and has something to say to all of us in the here and now.

While Thomas and his partner, Monika Wikman, were here in Texas for his Fay Lectures at the Jung Center of Houston, we were able, one night, to visit a blues music bar and hear local music from several of Houston's great blues musicians. I didn't realize at the time that Thomas had his own story of learning and playing blues music, which he mentions in this book, as part of his own individuation process. Hearing the blues in Houston, where this type of music had been developed by great musicians such as Lightnin' Hopkins, seemed an appropriate balance to the bright lights, industry, hospitals, and museums of Houston. Blues musicians take one on a journey into suffering, sadness, poverty, and depression, into "night journeys" of the soul if you will, and, through the performing musician, bring the story back to the audience. For Houston, a city built, among other things, on the wealth of the US oil industry and state-of-the-art medical centers, the "blues" undercurrent helps to balance the culture and "soul" of the city and its wealth and materialism. It was a great experience, getting to hear and see these blues musicians at night with Thomas and Monika (and Frank McMillan III, who accompanied us), in between daytime lectures where Thomas took us through a depth analysis of Coleridge and *The Rime of the Ancient Mariner*. I am grateful for the opportunity of working with Thomas over the last few years as he shaped his lectures into this book form, and to many illuminating conversations (verbal and email) we had during this time.

It would be remiss of me not to mention, in this introduction to Thomas's excellent book, that his lectures constituted the first of the Fay Lecture Series to take place at the Jung Center of Houston. The Fay Lectures have been an important ongoing set of annual lectures for over two decades, later published as books by Texas A&M Press.[4] The entire series of lectures and books began in the 1980s in College Station, Texas, under the leadership of David Rosen, who was the first Frank McMillan Jr. Professor. Frank McMillan Jr. created this faculty position at Texas A&M University, the first of its kind, for a Jungian analyst to teach and do research on Jungian psychology.[5] Carolyn Fay, one of the founders of the Jung Center in Houston, also contributed to an endowment that supported the annual Fay Lecture Series and book publication—first at Texas A&M University and now at the Jung Center in Houston. On Dr. Rosen's retirement from Texas A&M, the Fay Lectures were moved to the

Jung Center in Houston, and, as the first Frank McMillan Jr. Scholar there, I have had the good fortune to continue to arrange the lectures and edit the books as the Fay Lecture Series entered this new era. The tradition of the Fay Lectures and books, set in place by McMillan Jr. and Fay, will hopefully continue to bear fruit as we move forward in the twenty-first century, and Thomas's lectures were an auspicious way to start this process. In making all this possible, we owe many thanks personally to Frank McMillan III, who helped create the McMillan Institute at the Jung Center in Houston, and to David Rosen, who has been a wonderful mentor to myself and many others over the years. I am very thankful to Frank and David for the many conversations I have had with each over the past decade. Lastly, I thank Sean Fitzpatrick, Michael Craig, Elissa Davis, and the staff of the Jung Center in Houston for their impeccable and dedicated work in hosting the Fay Lecture Series, and Thomas Lemmons at Texas A&M Press for his dedication and skill in publishing these lectures in book form.

MAE
Mission, Texas
December 2021

Acknowledgments

This book has been a long time in the making. Along the way, many people have offered support, guidance, dialogue, and patience as I traveled with the Ancient Mariner and sought to retell his story. First, I must thank an analysand of mine who started it all off many years ago when he told me he had an albatross around his neck and that there was water everywhere but not a drop to drink. I also thank all the people I have worked with over the years in my analytic practice whose dreams and stories contributed to this book.

My gratitude to C. G. Jung and Marie-Louise von Franz, whom I feel are part of an unbroken lineage stretching back to the Romantics and into the present day, is beyond words; theirs is the foundation stone of this book. I am grateful to the Center for Depth Psychology according to C. G. Jung and Marie-Louise von Franz and my teachers there, Theodor Abt, Hansueli Etter, Gotthilf Isler, Brigitte Jacobs, Regina Schweizer, and Eva Wertenshlag-Birkhäuser. Robert Romanyshyn's support and many memorable conversations about the Mariner and Frankenstein's Monster are much appreciated. I would like to remember other elders who offered invaluable contributions and who have, sadly, passed on. Dianne Cordic recognized the importance of Coleridge's *Rime* and its connection to Jung from the very start and graciously supported my efforts. Julian David invited me to present my work on Coleridge at the unforgettable conferences he held at his wild, ensouled home in Devon, so close to Coleridge's birthplace. Julian's presence was, for me, a living link to Coleridge. In dialogues with Nathan Schwartz-Salant it was clear to me that I was in the presence of a wise and well-traveled personality who intimately recognized Coleridge's connection to madness as his connection to soul. Nathan's understanding of the Attis-Cybele myth is central to *The Rime of the Ancient Mariner* and to my own journey. Finally, I want to say to Ross Woodman in the beyond: Ancient Mariner and alchemist, your work, conversation, and mentorship was a once-in-a-lifetime gift. The communion I found with Ross came through what he told me was the primary source material of the Romantic poets, the great Dream.

I wish to dedicate this book to my beloved Monika Wikman, who has graciously supported, and endured, the writing process over many years. Our days and nights of communion with the depths opened by Coleridge's visions are unforgettable. Through, death, re-death, and new birth, through life shared on land and at sea, from the beginning Monika has held the pregnant darkness with me. Her many valuable suggestions are a contrapuntal melody to my own, and I am blessed for the music of Monika's soul that is interwoven throughout this book.

Gratitude goes out to David Rosen, the first Frank McMillan Jr. Professor at Texas A&M, who invited me to the Fay Lecture and Book Series after hearing my presentation on the Ancient Mariner at the North-South Conference for Jungian analysts in San Francisco. Michael Escamilla, the current Carol and Ernest Fay Lecture and Book Series Scholar at the Houston Jung Center, was host and guide during these lectures. Michael also offered valuable suggestions with the preparation of the manuscript and memorable dialogue, especially our joint conversation to start my presentation.

It is an honor and privilege to be invited as a Fay Lecturer and to participate in this historic series.

A Flash of Golden Fire

Introduction

The Rime of the Ancient Mariner: An Epic Poem for the Modern World

This book was conceived in my consulting room as a Jungian analyst. Although I studied English literature at the University of California, San Diego and became fascinated with Romantic poetry, enjoying its delicious wildness as well as the unique blend of mind and heart I discovered in its pages, strangely, my real engagement with Coleridge's *Ancient Mariner* began not in the academy but early on in my psychotherapy practice.

I was working one day with a man in his late fifties who suddenly described his experience of depression as "like water, water, everywhere, but not a drop to drink." Then, about ten minutes later, he confessed to a pathological sense of guilt that was, he said, "like an albatross around my neck." My patient was not aware that both these lines come from *The Rime of the Ancient Mariner*; for him they were just common expressions, part of the vernacular. But I recognized their source and reread Coleridge's poem to see if it had anything to say about depression and guilt.

In rereading *The Ancient Mariner* I was instantly struck by the relevance of this poem to my patient's psychological process. Yet when I brought up the poem in the next session my patient politely feigned interest and quickly moved on to another subject. My description of the relationship between Coleridge's poetry and his symptoms failed to impress him in the slightest. But I was gripped! I felt transfixed, like the Wedding Guest in the poem hypnotized by the Mariner's "glittering eye." That psychotherapy session took place over twenty years ago and still today I am unable to wrest myself from the mystery of the leviathan that Coleridge dragged to shore, a mystery that continues to haunt me personally, professionally, and culturally.

In my training as a Jungian analyst at the Center for Depth Psychology in Zurich, my involvement with *The Ancient Mariner* deepened as I explored this topic thoroughly in my thesis. After completing that thesis, my Jungian training, and many chapters in my own analytic process, and lecturing on this topic for various Jungian groups, my interest in this poem was further reinforced through my teaching at Pacifica Graduate Institute in Santa Barbara where I met the visiting lecturer Ross Woodman. Woodman was a professor emeritus at the University of Western Ontario, a scholar of Romanticism, the recipient of the 1993 Distinguished Scholar Award by the Keats-Shelley Association, and the husband of the well-known Jungian analyst Marion Woodman. In our first meeting, Ross told me that his first published article was on Coleridge and *The Rime of the Ancient Mariner*,[1] in which he interpreted *The Ancient Mariner* as a symbolic depiction of initiation akin to that found in shamanism. Woodman's relationship with Romanticism was a revelation to me and one we shared. I had never met another person who shared my interests, let alone a scholar who had pondered over these topics for decades and written extensively on them from a depth psychological perspective in the Jungian tradition, probably more so than anyone else in the world. Woodman's presence and insight, as well as his book *Sanity, Madness, Transformation: The Psyche in Romanticism*, were fateful. Woodman and I would continue over the next few years to communicate about

Romantic poetry and dreams before his death in 2014 at the age of ninety-one. The relationship between poetry and dream was essential to my dialogues with Woodman; it was also essential for Coleridge, as we shall see.

After Woodman's death, the dialogue with the mysteries in Romanticism, and *The Ancient Mariner*, continued to deepen for me. I found the leviathan I wrestled with in this visionary poem to be the alchemical myth of our times, the resonant meaning of which fatefully seemed mine to try to bring to shore.

For over two decades as this opus has been cooking me, and vice versa, I have found that Coleridge's visionary poetry, and the Romantics in general, reveals the roots of Jungian depth psychology in the ground of the psyche-matter mysteries the Romantics were working. And in fact, there is intricate, detailed evidence in this current opus illuminating the fact that the depth psychological tradition owes key elements of its conception to Coleridge himself and the Romantics, a priori to Carl Gustav Jung's work and life. For example, in the early twentieth century, Jung survived an intense encounter with the unconscious. He did this by giving expression to his inner world in the paintings and dialogues found in *The Red Book*. Yet Jung felt alone in this work, unable to find a precedent or cultural parallel, until he discovered alchemy. This ancient "proto-science" became the bridge Jung had been seeking between the remote past and the present. Yet between the downfall of alchemy in the eighteenth century and Jung's *Red Book* in the twentieth, it seems there was a gap in the tradition. Samuel Taylor Coleridge's great visionary poem *The Rime of the Ancient Mariner* is a link in a golden chain that bridges the alchemical past with the depth psychological present.

Coleridge's night-sea journey can today be understood as a symbolic self-portrait of the collective unconscious, a self-portrait that, like *The Red Book*, finds its historical context and continuity in the alchemical tradition and is, as such, an invitation into the richness of the transformative modern roots of Western alchemy. In this book, I describe that process of transformation as the birth, death, and rebirth of the modern soul. Insofar as Coleridge's *Ancient Mariner* symbolically describes the birth of the modern soul, it is grounded in the factual knowledge of European history. Insofar as it describes the death and rebirth of the modern soul, *The Ancient Mariner* is prophecy and revelation.

Where We Are Heading

This book consists of four parts. Part 1 is introductory; it includes some background on the genesis of *The Ancient Mariner* and Romanticism, Coleridge's biography, and a brief illustration of some of the fascinating parallels between Coleridge and Jung. Parts 2, 3, and 4 are extended deep dive into the symbolic dynamics of *The Rime of the Ancient Mariner*.

Each of the chapters in parts 2, 3, and 4 brings a psychoanalytical understanding to bear upon a specific stage in the Mariner's journey—apropos, I believe, insofar as Coleridge invented the term "psycho-analytic" in an 1805 journal entry in which he calls for a psychoanalytic understanding of mythology. In this sense, all the psychologically oriented interpreters of myth in the twentieth century, from Freud and Jung to Joseph Campbell and Bruno Bettelheim, to Clarissa Pinkola-Estes and Martin Shaw, owe a debt of gratitude to their spiritual ancestor Coleridge, who broke open the semblance of myth and discovered, for the first time in a modern form, the psychological mana hidden within. I place myself solidly within this tradition of psychoanalytic mythologizers.

The way this book is organized can be compared to the stations of the cross in Catholicism, that is, as illustrative of stages that play a role in a larger story—in our case, not the death of Christ but the birth, death, and rebirth of the modern soul. The twenty chapters that track the Mariner's journey each take on a specific symbol or dynamic of this process in the poem. We will go slowly and deliciously through each of these chapters; they will become increasingly deep as the poem itself deepens. The disadvantage of going through the poem in this way—following the text step by step—is that it makes it impossible to say everything all at once. And so, because of this, I ask the reader for patience as we trek into the wilderness of the archetypal psyche and explore together the numinous secret of what the psyche is seeking in the Mariner's night-sea voyage, what *it* wants.

As mentioned above, this book is about Coleridge's *Ancient Mariner* as a history and prophecy of the Western soul. For example, the central image in this poem is the shooting of the Albatross. Why does the Mariner do this? The poem does not say. What are the consequences of killing the sacred white bird? Every child is taught that if you do something wrong, something bad is going to happen to you. We know this moralism; we do not need Coleridge's magnificent and enigmatic visionary night-sea journey to tell us *that*. When it comes to tracking the historical dimensions of what it means to the development of the Western soul to "shoot the Albatross," I hope to re-create the context of Coleridge's time and place as much as possible and thereby understand what *his* imagination is communicating to us about the spirit of his times as distinct from projecting what I already know, or what is today collectively well known, onto the poem. Not only does the Mariner shoot the Albatross as the "hellish" crime in this poem, but he also blesses the water-snakes, in the moonlight, in the shadow of the ship. This act is his redemption, at least briefly, and he accomplishes it "unaware." What is the wisdom of this redemptive imagery in Mariner's tale? What is the message of hope? Such questions touch on the prophetic dimension of Coleridge's imagination. To understand this dimension, we need to learn to interpret and understand the symbolism. The symbol is a bridge to the unknown, a doorway to something new from the spirit of the depths that does not merely confirm what our collective consciousness already knows about the spirit of the times.

There are, therefore, some red threads that weave throughout my analysis of the tale. Some threads are Coleridge's own associations to the imagery and dynamics in the poem. Others are amplifications drawn from the writings of other Romantic artists and philosophers, as well as broader parallels from myth, alchemy, and folklore that give us a feel for the deeper layers of meaning in this poem, layers of meaning that Coleridge may or may not have been aware of. Other threads are dreams, my own, those of my patients, and others. Yet more threads are the interpretations drawn from psychoanalysis and Jungian psychology. And a final thread is found in the afterword where I recount my own experience of the night-sea journey in the hope of bridging sea and land so to speak, of linking the archetypal-symbolic dreamworld with everyday life—the goal of every Jungian analysis.

"What manner of man art thou?" a Christian Hermit asks the Mariner late in the poem. If Coleridge appeared in my consulting room, a ghost with *The Rime of the Ancient Mariner* in hand, as a Jungian analyst I would work with him in much the same way as I approach the tale of the Ancient Mariner in this book. For those interested primarily in Coleridge, or Romantic poetry in general, I hope you will find in this approach a generative perspective on Coleridge's poetic masterpiece. Those interested in Jung will, I believe, be amazed to discover in Coleridge not only a poet but a proto-depth psychologist who anticipates Jung. Above all, my hope is to bring all of us a step closer to the mystery of our being by understanding Coleridge's visionary poem as expressive of the phenomenology of patterns and structures present in our inward nature.

Welcome to my attempt to comprehend the incomprehensible. I hope it sparks your own.

"This Riddle of This Sphinx of Modern Literature"

As mentioned earlier, Samuel Taylor Coleridge's (1772–1834) *Rime of the Ancient Mariner* was first published in 1798, in a collection of poems authored by Coleridge and William Wordsworth entitled *Lyrical Ballads*. Although this volume is now generally recognized as the genesis of English Romantic poetry, at the time the poem's readership consisted mostly of sailors who bought the *Lyrical Ballads* by accident thinking it was a collection of sea hymns. For those who did read *Lyrical Ballads* on purpose, most found Coleridge's night-sea journey to be bizarre. Many called the poem insane or immoral. There was one critic, a friend of Coleridge's, who acknowledged the poem's deep feeling, but he was an exception. It seemed nobody understood or appreciated the Mariner's strange tale, just as in the poem itself nobody understands the Mariner; those who encounter him call him a "grey beard loon," "the devil," and go "crazy" in his presence.

Coleridge, acknowledging that his poem was apparently incomprehensible and yet retaining his characteristic good humor, published a self-deprecating anonymous poem entitled "To the Author of the Ancient Mariner" in the London *Morning Post*.

To the Author of the Ancient Mariner
Your poem must eternal be,
Dear sir! it cannot fail,
For 'tis incomprehensible,
And without head or tail.[2]

This little poem is, of course, the tongue-in-cheek way that Coleridge acknowledges the lack of public appreciation for his visionary opus.

The sense of the enigmatic and mysterious that accompanied *The Ancient Mariner* over two centuries ago continues to this day, so much so that one contemporary commentator calls the poem "this riddle of this sphinx of modern literature."[3] Many literary critics have attempted to address this riddle of Coleridge's *The Ancient Mariner* by tracking down its origins. The poem has its sources, of course; Coleridge was, in his own words, a self-described "library cormorant" who had "read practically everything." Thus, he has given scholars much to do in tracking those sources down. John Livingston Lowes, in his brilliant and classic work *The Road to Xanadu* (1927), collects them in the most loving way and with thorough attention to detail.[4] However, as Lowes himself acknowledges, the essentially Coleridgean question, the question of *meaning*, remains even after all the sources have been accurately catalogued.

For example, in Coleridge's time, European sea exploration was in high gear, and Coleridge was entranced with the various published accounts of ships' logs describing circumnavigations of the globe. However, at the time he completed *The Rime of the Ancient Mariner* at the age of twenty-five, Coleridge had never set foot on a ship. The factual sea voyages that Coleridge read passed through the amplifier of his immense imagination, where they were boosted with symbolic resonances. In chapter 14 of his *Biographia Literaria* (1817), Coleridge takes us back to his intentions as he wrote *The Ancient Mariner* for *Lyrical Ballads* twenty years earlier.

> The thought suggested itself (to which of us [Wordsworth or Coleridge] I do not recollect) that a series of poems might be composed of two sorts. In the one, the incidents and agents were to be, in part at least, supernatural; and the excellence aimed at was to consist in the interesting of the affections by

> the dramatic truth of such emotions as would naturally accompany such situations, supposing them real. And real in this sense they have been to every human being who, from whatever source of delusion, has at any time believed himself under supernatural agency . . . it was agreed, that my endeavours should be directed to persons and characters supernatural, or at least romantic, yet so as to transfer from our inward nature a human interest and a semblance of truth sufficient to procure for these shadows of imagination that willing suspension of disbelief for the moment, which constitutes poetic faith. . . . With this view I wrote the "Ancient Mariner."[5]

In writing the *Ancient Mariner*, Coleridge's focus was not on historical fact or fundamentalist faith but on "poetic faith" in the "dramatic truth of such emotions" that take over once one believes that he or she is under the power of supernatural agency "from whatever source of delusion." For, as Coleridge himself tells us, *The Rime of the Ancient Mariner* is a poem of "pure imagination."

The Rime of the Ancient Mariner and the Great Dream

Coleridge often compared poetry to dreams. The 1800 version of *The Rime of the Ancient Mariner* is subtitled *A Poets Reverie*. Another of Coleridge's famous poems, "Kubla Khan," is subtitled, "A Vision in a Dream."[6] For Coleridge, poetry is a dream that has been worked on by the conscious mind, a "rationalized Dream." The poet's "Pen is the Tongue of a systematic Dream": "But the Pen is the Tongue of a systematic Dream—a Somnoloquist! . . . During this state of continuous not single-mindedness, but *one*-SIDE-mindedness. Writing is manual Somnambulism—the somnial Magic superinduced on, without suspending, the active powers of the mind."[7] Poetry is a "waking dream"[8] and all great works of art, Shakespeare for example, have their primary source in "a divine Dream" that expresses feelings that are ours and yet not ours. "Poetry [is] a rationalized Dream, dealing [out] to manifold forms our own Feelings, that never perhaps were attached to us consciously to our own personal Selves.—What is the Lear, the Othello, but a divine Dream/ all Shakespeare, & nothing Shakespeare."[9] Coleridge's notes on the manuscript of his 1796 poem "The Destiny of Nations," written a year before he began the *Ancient Mariner*, are further evidence that, for him, the composition of poetry involves interactions with an internal process that lies outside conscious control and rational understanding: "These are very fine Lines, tho' I say it, that should not: but, hang me, if I know or ever did know the meaning of them, tho' my own composition."[10] Many of the lines in "The Destiny of Nations" that Coleridge confesses he admires but does not know the meaning of appear in *The Rime of the Ancient Mariner*: the bird flying with "gorgeous wings" over the watery abyss becomes the Albatross; the "slimy shapes and miscreated life / Poisoning the vast Pacific" in "The Destiny of Nations" are the "thousand, thousand slimy things" and the "water-snakes" of *The Ancient Mariner*; and the "fresh breeze" which wakens new movement is the breeze that blows on the Mariner alone and sends him home.

Throughout Coleridge's many descriptions of dreams, the ocean is a steady metaphor. For instance, in a *Notebook* entry that is strikingly meaningful to our analysis of *The Ancient Mariner*, dreams emerge spontaneously from an inner ocean, "as if Sleep had indeed a material realm," and, bringing to mind *The Rime of the Ancient Mariner*, Coleridge's consciousness is analogized as a ship that sails over a sea of "Sleep and Dreams": "O then as I first sank on the pillow, as if Sleep had indeed a material realm, as if when I sank on my pillow, I was entering that region & realized Faery Land of Sleep—O then what visions have I had, what dreams—the Bark, the Sea, all the shapes & sounds & adventures made up of the Stuff of

Sleep and Dreams, & my Reason at the Rudder / O what visions <mastoid> as if my Cheek and Temple were lying on me gale o'mast on 00 Seele meines Lebens!—& I sink down the waters, thro' Seas and Seas—yet warm, yet a Spirit—/"[11] "Seele meines Lebens!"—the sea is the soul of Coleridge's life where all the repressed horrors dwell but also the sparks of new life.

Jung was similarly mesmerized by the intoxicating, mysterious, and autonomous nature of dreams. He also devoted some time to understanding the relationship between dream and visionary poetry. In a 1960 letter to the art critic Sir Herbert Read in which the two men discuss the psychology of modern art, particularly Picasso and James Joyce, Jung asks, "What is the great Dream?" He then answers his own question: the "great Dream" is the vision of a new world that "has always spoken through the artist as a mouthpiece."[12] The great Dream is a product, not of the personal but of the collective psyche where, as Jung says, "all men are caught in a common rhythm."[13] It is in this common rhythm that we will look for an answer to the riddle of this sphinx of modern literature.

The Big Read

Despite (or perhaps because of?) its mysterious imagery, *The Ancient Mariner* received a significant resurrection in the spring of 2020 with the creation and publication of *The Ancient Mariner Big Read*, a daily online reading of the poem broken up in forty sections and thus lasting forty days.[14] Curated by the English writer Philip Hoare and the artists Angela Cockayne and Sarah Chapman, and hosted by the University of Plymouth's Art Institute, the *Big Read* took three years to produce. Well-known actors and celebrities such as Jeremy Irons, Tilda Swinton, Willem Dafoe, Marianne Faithfull, and Iggy Pop, along with many impassioned Celtic voices, contribute to the poem's sublime retelling. Artwork commissioned especially for this project, coupled with an alluring original soundscape, amplifies the poem's already seductive vibe. *The Big Read* is broken down into forty chunks and thus allows us to travel slowly and pause on each image or stage in the poem, as if we were walking through a multimedia presentation in a museum. A suggestion: to get the most out of this book I recommend that you watch and listen to *The Big Read* (available for free on their website, YouTube, and Spotify) as an accompaniment. Let the voices in *The Big Read* speak to you, then dive in.

I must admit that this recent upload of *The Ancient Mariner* into popular culture is surprising to me! My hunch is that the *Big Read* is not reflective of any renewed contemporary passion for nineteenth-century literature per se but of a collectively felt necessity to reach out toward the enigmatic *meaning* of our times. The *Big Read* website effectively acknowledges this when it labels Coleridge's visionary night-sea journey "a founding fable of our modern age" and "an iconic literary tale for the 21st century." Other mainstream media sources insist that the poem reflects the dark side of Western history. One reason, as the *Guardian* headline for its review of *The Big Read* proclaims, "why Willem Dafoe, Iggy Pop and more are reading *The Rime of the Ancient Mariner* to us" is because its descriptions of "slavery, ecocide, plague" comprise "the warnings of Coleridge's poem [that] resound down the ages."[15] The *New Yorker* headline for its review of *The Big Read* tells us that *The Ancient Mariner* is "The Epic Poem You Need for Quarantine."[16] *The Ancient Mariner* is the epic poem we need today, but not because it resonates with our angst over the quarantine imposed by COVID-19. A vastly more general and foreboding sense of apocalypse—the destruction of the world *as we know it*—is the setting in which Coleridge's poetic vision speaks to us most vividly and clearly.

The Way of Salvation through Symbolic Death

Today, the exponential growth of technology, felt in part via the in-person vs. screen-split self created online, and the promise and peril of the exponential explosion of artificial intelligence loom large. Sadly, it is practically cliché to point out that global warming, overpopulation, the specter of an approaching civil war in the United States, rising gun violence and mass shootings, economic uncertainty, the increasing odds of another world war, and the decline of traditional political and religious structures are ever present in the cultural foreground or background.

In 1957, the year the Soviets successfully launched the world's first artificial satellite and tested the first intercontinental ballistic missile, at the height of the cold war, Jung wrote a letter to the Reverend David Cox offering his diagnosis and prognosis for Western civilization: "We are threatened with universal genocide unless we can work out the way of salvation by a symbolic death."[17] Some seventeen years later, Martin Luther King Jr. spoke in similar terms of death and rebirth when he addressed the fate of America at the Southern Christian Leadership Conference in retreat at Frogmore, South Carolina, just a few months before his assassination in Memphis on April 4, 1968. "For its very survival's sake," King declared, "America must re-examine old presuppositions and release itself from many things that for centuries have been held sacred. For the evils of racism, poverty, and militarism to die, a new set of values must be born."[18] When it comes to delivering a diagnosis and prognosis for our collective survival, Jung and King go to the heart of the matter, to the human heart. They both call for revolution, not in the form of literal political violence but in the form of a fundamental transformation of our ruling assumptions, perceptions, and beliefs—symbolic as distinct from literal death.

Having lived through two world wars, Jung was pessimistic about the possibility of deep societal transformation. However, he always believed that if enough individuals faced themselves, one person at a time, this could possibly lead to collective change eventually.[19] Jung called this process of facing ourselves individuation. Individuation, Jung writes, is "only experienced by those who have gone through the wearisome but indispensable business of coming to terms with the unconscious components of the personality."[20] Individuation is the process which allows the deeper levels of the Self—importantly including shadow sides of ourselves that we are loath to admit—to emerge into conscious awareness. Unfortunately, this process is so difficult and so radically disruptive that it is analogized in myth and dream to death. To individuate is to go through a process of dying to who we were, or thought we were, to who others expect us to be, to the values and beliefs that contain and support us. To individuate, in other words, is to symbolically die and be reborn.

Death, both literal and symbolic, is front and center in *The Rime of the Ancient Mariner*. As a specter ship sails out of the setting sun, the Mariner exclaims, "Is that a DEATH? and are there two? / Is DEATH that woman's mate?" DEATH takes all two hundred men aboard the ship while the Mariner, as a lonely individual, becomes the property of the daimonic female LIFE-IN-DEATH. As a result, he endures seven nights of symbolic death before being reborn on the eighth. Jung and King proclaim the need for the death and rebirth of values; Coleridge shows us *how* that happens and what the process looks and feels like from the perspective of a modern man, a Christian, and a product of the European Enlightenment.

Coleridge's epic night-sea journey is a Book of the Dead akin to the ancient Egyptian *Amduat* that purports to describe and map "what is in the underworld." But this poem is not a myth; it is the literary creation of a modern man in contact with an "ancient man," the "bright-eyed Mariner." I suggest that the juice of the poem lies in the intersection of ancient themes—such as symbolic death and rebirth—with Coleridge's personal psychology and, beyond this, how these ancient themes are playing out today, calling us to a dynamic transformation of consciousness.

Before we dive into the depths of this alchemical exploration, we will need an introduction to the genesis of *The Ancient Mariner* and a brief synopsis of the poem itself.

The Genesis of *The Rime of the Ancient Mariner*

In November of 1797, when the poet Samuel Taylor Coleridge was twenty-five years old and already well known, a neighbor of his, a Mr. Cruickshank, had an eerie dream about a ghost ship sailing out of the setting sun. This dream gripped Cruickshank, so much so that he felt compelled to run next door to tell his neighbor Coleridge about it. I suppose Cruickshank imagined that of all the men he knew, certainly Coleridge would be the one to appreciate and perhaps understand this strange dream. If so, Cruickshank was more on target than he could have known, for when Coleridge and Wordsworth started out on a long walk to the seashore that same November, Cruickshank's dream found its way into what was originally intended to be a short poem to defray the costs of their walking tour. Very soon, however, that short poem turned into the opus of Coleridge's life: *The Rime of the Ancient Mariner.*

Wordsworth suggested one motif, the shooting of the albatross, and dropped out. But Coleridge was gripped. He worked feverishly hard on this poem for nearly five months after returning from that walking tour and finished it on March 23, 1798. *The Ancient Mariner* was published that same year as *The Rime of the Ancyent Marinere* in a collection of poems, coauthored with Wordsworth, entitled

Lyrical Ballads (1798). *Lyrical Ballads* is generally considered to be the genesis of English Romanticism. *Lyrical Ballads*, however, was only the beginning. Coleridge voyaged with the Mariner throughout his life, taking his opus through two major revisions. There is an 1817 version, published in *Sibylline Leaves*, a collection of Coleridge's poetry, that changes much of the archaic English of the original version and adds a prose gloss. Coleridge's nephew, Henry Nelson Coleridge, published the final and most widely read version, the 1834 version (the year Coleridge died) in *The Poetical Works of S. T. Coleridge*. We use the 1834 version throughout this book.

A Synopsis of *The Rime of the Ancient Mariner*

The Rime of the Ancient Mariner begins as the Ancient Mariner stops three young Wedding Guests on their way to a wedding. The Mariner transfixes one of them, forcing him to listen to his "ghastly" tale of a spellbinding sea voyage.

The Mariner sets off from shore, "merrily" dropping below the hill, church, and lighthouse on land. Soon after, a violent northern "STORM-BLAST" blows his ship off course, chasing him down to the South Pole, where his ship becomes hopelessly stuck in the ice. Suddenly, an "ALBATROSS" appears. The crew hail the bird in God's name, and he circles the ship, splits the ice, and brings a "good south wind" that pushes the ship back home. Then, for no apparent reason (and no reason is given in the poem), the Mariner shoots the ALBATROSS with his crossbow. At first the crew is aghast, certain that the Mariner's "hellish" murder of this "pious bird of good omen" will "work 'em woe." When the sun rises at dawn, however, and burns away the fog and mist, the crew change their minds: "'Twas right said they, such birds to slay, / That bring the fog and mist." But when the dawning sun rises to its apex at noon the breeze drops down and the crew find themselves adrift in the doldrums of a solar Wasteland where there is, famously, "Water, water every where / Nor any drop to drink."

In this exclusively solar world, everything is seen clearly—there is no mist as in the lunar landscape of the Albatross—but it is also a death-scape in which the ocean rots and "slimy things did crawl with legs / Upon the slimy sea." The crew's lips are "baked black" by thirst, so much so that nobody can speak. As they lie close to death in this lifeless place, the crew now change their minds again and decide that the wretched Mariner "killed the bird / That made the breeze to blow"; they hang the dead Albatross around the Mariner's neck as an emblem of his guilt.

As the burning sun sets in the West, a specter ship sails between the Mariner's ship and the sun. This ship carries two passengers, a female, LIFE-IN-DEATH who "thicks man's blood with cold," and her mate DEATH. These two daimonic figures play a game of dice for the fate of the crew, and DEATH takes all the crew, every man on board, except the Ancient Mariner who becomes the property of LIFE-IN-DEATH.

Darkness falls, the moon rises, and instantly the two hundred men on board fall dead, cursing the Mariner with their dead eyes, and the Mariner is left "all, all, alone" at sea. He turns his eyes to the sky to pray to God above, but a "wicked whisper" turns his "heart to dust" and as he stares into the "rotting sea" he identifies with "a thousand, thousand slimy things [that] / Lived on; and so did I." He endures seven nights of agonizing alienation from God, nature, and humanity so great he wishes for death but cannot die. Finally, after enduring great suffering, on the eighth night, a revelation happens, a breakthrough, a redemptive transformation of self and world. Instead of cursing the repulsive creatures of the depths, a "stream of love" for the water-snakes "springs" from his heart while, in the moonlight beyond the "shadow of the ship," he sees water-snakes moving "in tracks of shining white." Within the "shadow of the ship" they "coiled and swam; and every track / Was a flash of golden fire." "O happy living things!" he cries out as he blesses them "unaware." As he blesses the snakes, the Albatross falls from the Mariner's neck and sinks "like lead / Into the sea."

Now there is water to drink everywhere, both in dream and reality.

> The silly buckets on the deck,
> That had so long remained,
> I dreamt that they were filled with dew;
> And when I awoke, it rained.

"To Mary Queen the praise be given," the Mariner tells the Wedding Guest. "She sent the gentle sleep from Heaven, / That slid into my soul."

The Mariner's ship then begins the journey home. On the way, the dead bodies of the crew are reanimated and sail the ship as it is driven onward from below by a nature spirit from "the land of mist and snow." Driving the ship in this way is so powerful that the Mariner falls down in a "swound," a "trance," in which he hears "two voices in the air" speaking to each other. They reveal that because this man has "with his cruel bow . . . laid full low / The harmless Albatross," that he "hath penance done, / And penance more will do."

The Mariner's ship finds its way back home to where it departed from. He sees the glorious sight of hill, kirk, and lighthouse top on land, and "with sobs did pray—/ O let me be awake, my God! / Or let me sleep alway." The "spell" of his visionary sea voyage is "snapt." But one vision remains: the Mariner sees "A man all light, a seraph-man" standing on every dead body, a "heavenly sight," a "lovely light" sending signals to the land. Attracted by "those lights so many and fair," three men from shore row out to investigate, a Pilot, the Pilot's Boy, and a Christian Hermit. But upon drawing closer to the Mariner's ship, they sense something ominous, something strange and uncanny. The Pilot declares "Dear Lord! It hath a fiendish look . . . / I am a-feared." As their boat comes closer to the Mariner's ship, a rumbling sound "split the bay" and the Mariner's ship goes down "like lead" in a whirlpool. The three men in the rowboat pull the Mariner's body—"like one that hath been seven days drowned"—up into their little boat "swift as dreams." The Mariner, as the fourth man added to the trinity of men in the boat, simply moves his lips to speak and the Pilot shrieks and falls "in a fit." The Mariner takes the oars as the Pilot's Boy "doth crazy go," declaring "full plain I see, / The devil knows how to row." The "Holy hermit" can only raise his eyes to Heaven and pray.

The Mariner's journey back to land from sea is thus intensely problematic. Once back on land, the Mariner asks the Christian Hermit to shrive his soul, but this holy Hermit can "scarcely stand" in the Mariner's presence and is unable or unwilling to grant him the holy rite of absolution. The Hermit can only ask, "What manner of man art thou?" Unable to answer, the Mariner is driven by a burning agony in his heart to recite *The Rime of the Ancient Mariner* on the spot, his tale the answer to the Hermit's question. From then on, the Mariner is compelled to tell his tale to men that he knows "must hear me." To these men, he tells the Wedding Guest (who is one of them), "my tale I teach."

At the end of the poem, both Mariner and Wedding Guest turn away from the wedding. Instead of attending the "marriage-feast," the Mariner chooses the community at church.

> O Wedding-Guest! this soul hath been
> Alone on a wide wide sea:

So lonely 'twas, that God himself
Scarce seemèd there to be.

O sweeter than the marriage-feast,
'Tis sweeter far to me,
To walk together to the kirk
With a goodly company!—

But church does not cure him of his burning agony or the compulsion to recite his tale. The Mariner continues to wander "like night," obsessively telling his tale to an uncomprehending world, the "everlasting Wandering Jew" as Coleridge would later refer to him. Coleridge's poem ends with the young Wedding Guest "stunned" by the Mariner's night-sea journey. He rises the following morning "a sadder and a wiser man."

In the next chapter we will turn to carefully consider Coleridge's personal life and its inherent, curious, and potent connections to, and expressions of, the psyche as we carry the resonance of the archetypal motifs from this synopsis in the background.

The great French illustrator Gustave Doré (1833–83) began a prolific career at the age of fifteen that led to an extraordinary portfolio of visionary, even mythic, engravings ranging from Milton, Dante, and the Bible to Shakespeare. The amazing cinematic elements that make Coleridge's masterpiece one of the most exciting and memorable poems in the English language are unforgettably memorialized in Doré's magnificent engravings to *The Rime of the Ancient Mariner.* The engravings reproduced throughout this book are taken from the 1878 American edition of *The Rime of the Ancient Mariner.*

PART 1

Samuel Taylor Coleridge

CHAPTER 1

"Alone on a Wide Wide Sea"

Coleridge's Biography

While my focus is on the collective and symbolic significance of Coleridge's *Rime of the Ancient Mariner*, the collective dimensions of Coleridge's poem are, of course, grounded in Coleridge's personal life. Here I turn to these personal dimensions and their possible relationship to Coleridge's poetry. The entire corpus of Coleridge's poetry is a rich well to draw from in this respect, as well as Coleridge's other writings, especially his autobiographical *Letters*. Coleridge's commentary on his life and art in the *Biographia Literaria* is another crucial resource, as is *Aids to Reflection*, the *Notebooks*, *Table Talk*, and *Marginalia*. The *Letters* and *Notebooks* are especially valuable as they reveal a very personal side of the man. In his *Notebooks*, Coleridge bares his soul; he was often concisely and brutally honest in his appraisal of himself and his psychological dilemmas. Perhaps most revealing are the autobiographical letters Coleridge wrote in his twenties to close friends. These lay out some of the memorable events of his childhood. Much of what follows is taken from those letters as well as the masterful two-volume biography by Richard Holmes, *Coleridge: Early Visions* (1990) and *Coleridge: Darker Reflections* (1999).[1]

The Youngest Child

Samuel Taylor Coleridge (born October 21, 1772, died July 25, 1834) was the youngest of his father's thirteen children, three from a first marriage and ten from a second, the son of a pastor and school master residing in Ottery St. Mary in Devon in the South of England. Coleridge's father was fifty-three when his youngest was born.

From early childhood onward Coleridge was an intellectual prodigy; at the age of three he could read a chapter of the Bible. By the age of twenty-five Coleridge reported that he had "read practically everything," a self-described "library cormorant." As a child, Coleridge seemed to be the favorite of both his mother and father and appeared to be generally happy and well cared for, although at times he could be lonely and not adapted to the typical world of boys—for example, being more fascinated with the imaginary world of fairy tales and dreams than with sports and games. As a child, he spent long hours alone with his books and imagination, so much so that he describes himself as "despised and hated by the boys." Already at the age of six Coleridge lived inside the ghostly hauntings of imagination which brought him into violent collision with social expectations. In a journal entry, Coleridge writes about an experience at the age of six in which his father became violently upset with his young son's proclivity to lose himself in a fairy-tale world of fantasy while neglecting reality.

> At six years old I remember to have read Belisarius, Robinson Crusoe, & Phillip Quarll—and then I found the Arabian Nights' entertainments—one tale of which (the tale of a man who was compelled to seek for a pure virgin) made so deep an impression on me (I had read it in the evening while my mother was mending stockings) that I was haunted by spectres, whenever

> I was in the dark—and I distinctly remember the anxious & fearful eagerness, with which I used to watch the window, in which the books lay—& whenever the Sun lay upon them, I would seize it, carry it by the wall, & bask, & read—. My Father found out the effect, which these books had produced—and burnt them.—So I became a *dreamer*—and acquired an indisposition to all bodily activity . . . and before I was eight years old, I was a *character*.[2]

Despite his father's opposition to his immersion in imagination against "all bodily activity," Coleridge was convinced that his fate of being a "*dreamer*" during childhood was not merely a morbid escape from reality but at the same time a window into "the Vast, the Great, and the Whole." Through his early reading of fairy tales, he developed a larger perspective on the human condition than he otherwise would have had. His capacity to "regulate all my creeds by my conceptions and not my sight" played a formative role in his intellectual development. "From my early reading of Faery Tales, & Genii &c &c—my mind had been habituated to the Vast—& I never regarded my senses in any way as the criteria of my belief. I regulated all my creeds by my conceptions not by my sight—even at that age. Should children be permitted to read Romances, & Relations of Giants & Magicians, & Genii?—I know all that has been said against it; but I have formed my faith in the affirmative.—I know no other way of giving the mind a love of 'the Great', & 'the Whole'.—"[3] And yet Coleridge was also aware that being a *dreamer* as a child alienated him from his friends and turned him into what appears to be a rather nasty little fellow, filled with resentment and contempt. "I became very vain," Coleridge says of himself, "and before I was eight years old, I was a *character*—sensibility, imagination, vanity, sloth, & feelings of deep & bitter contempt for almost all who traversed the orbit of my understanding, were even then prominent and manifest."[4] That qualifier "even then" proves that Coleridge was aware of these traits within himself as an adult.

Thus, the problematic as well as inspiring dimensions of Coleridge's artistic personality are apparent from a very early age; both the negative and positive aspects of being a *dreamer* are inextricably woven into each other. There is another world apart from the senses—the *Vast*—that is an immense storehouse of creativity and imagination that develops from childhood into the mature genius of his visionary poetry. At the same time, a preference for that dreamlike world over the everyday world contributed to alienation, schizoid defenses against the demands of real life, narcissism, and an inferiority-superiority complex.

The Orphan

From birth to the age of ten it appears that Coleridge lived an idyllic life in the Devon countryside, doted on by his mother and deeply connected to his father. But at the age of ten, he suffered significant trauma. Tragedy struck when Coleridge's father died suddenly and unexpectedly at the age of sixty-three. His father had returned home from sending another of his sons, Coleridge's older brother, off to join the navy. Rejecting an offer from friends to stay overnight, Coleridge's father gave as his reason that although he was not a "superstitious" man (he was a Christian minister after all), he had a dream the night before in which Death, as he is commonly portrayed, touched him with his scythe. The father returned straight home because of this dream, complaining of an upset stomach. His wife made him some peppermint tea, he told her he felt much better, and then he fell asleep and died. Samuel, ten years old, awakened in the night by his mother's screams, tells us in a letter written years later as an adult that he knew instantly, "Father is dead," although he did not know his father had returned home.

His father's death was devastating. It forever altered the course of Coleridge's development. Having no father meant, among other things, that Coleridge's idyllic childhood days in the countryside of Devon were over. Coleridge's mother could no longer support her youngest son and was forced to send him away to a charity boarding school in London founded in 1552 by Edward VI called Christ's Hospital.

While at Christ's Hospital, Coleridge continued to show a brilliant, prodigal aptitude for academics. He was a glittering personality there; his mesmerizing eloquence was legendary. But Coleridge was lonely. At the age of sixty, less than two years before his death, Coleridge still remembered his years at Christ's Hospital with trembling emotion, illustrating how indelibly traumatic this time was for him. "The discipline at Christ's Hospital in my time was ultra-Spartan—all domestic ties were to be put aside. 'Boy!' I remember Boyer [the Headmaster] saying to me once when I was crying the first day of my return after the holidays, 'Boy! the school is your father! Boy! the school is your mother! Boy! the school is your brother! the school is your sister! the school is your first cousin, and your second cousin, and all the rest of your relations! Let's have no more crying!'"[5] The headmaster's words were cruel but accurate. Coleridge's mother never once visited him in his years at Christ's Hospital. Moreover, Coleridge never, like the other boys, went home for the holidays. Instead, he was forced to wander the streets of London when the school would close, seeking refuge in the homes of his schoolmates.

The fact that Coleridge remembered the trauma he suffered at this boarding school with such emotion at the age of sixty shows the deep effect the school had on him. How was Coleridge instructed to deal with his loneliness and more generally his feeling side as distinct from his thinking side—we could say his need for Mother at all levels—in this ultra-Spartan environment? He was told to turn toward the archetypal Father, to become ultra-Spartan himself, to suppress and dissociate his emotions. For a sensitive soul such as Coleridge, that was never going to be a solution. To compensate for positive mother love being remote and unreal, Coleridge composed poems as a teenager to his nurses at Christ's Hospital and did his best to join the families of his friends, drawing close to *their* mothers. Later, as he got older, Coleridge developed a habit of falling in love with, eventually even marrying, the sisters of his close friends. For example, his wife Sarah Fricker was the sister of his friend Robert Southey's wife and his amanuensis and muse Dorothy Wordsworth was his friend William Wordsworth's sister. After he was married to Sarah Fricker, Coleridge suffered through a long, impossible, and most likely unconsummated love affair with another Sara (whom he referred to in his poetry as Asra) and another sister, this time the sister of Wordsworth's fiancée, Sara Hutchinson.

Another very important sense of alienation from Mother was alienation from Mother Nature. Coleridge's only connection to nature at Christ's Hospital, he says, were the times he could steal away to the roof and stare at the stars. One sees this in his poem "Frost at Midnight" (1798).

> But O! how oft,
> How oft, at school, with most believing mind,
> Presageful, have I gazed upon the bars,
> To watch that fluttering *stranger*! and as oft
> With unclosed lids, already had I dreamt
> Of my sweet birth-place, and the old church-tower,
> Whose bells, the poor man's only music, rang
> From morn to evening, all the hot Fair-day,
> So sweetly, that they stirred and haunted me
> With a wild pleasure, falling on mine ear

Most like articulate sounds of things to come!
So gazed I, till the soothing things, I dreamt,
Lulled me to sleep, and sleep prolonged my dreams!
And so I brooded all the following morn,
Awed by the stern preceptor's face, mine eye
Fixed with mock study on my swimming book:
Save if the door half opened, and I snatched
A hasty glance, and still my heart leaped up,
For still I hoped to see the *stranger's* face,
Townsman, or aunt, or sister more beloved,
My play-mate when we both were clothed alike!

. . . For I was reared
In the great city, pent 'mid cloisters dim,
And saw nought lovely but the sky and stars.

Around the same time he wrote "Frost at Midnight," Coleridge wrote the *Ancient Mariner*. It is no accident that *The Rime of the Ancient Mariner* centers itself emotionally on a feeling of aloneness.

Alone, alone, all, all alone,
Alone on a wide wide sea.
So lonely 'twas that God himself
Scarce seemèd there to be.

Coleridge also wrote the following letter to his brother around this time.

At times my soul is sad, that I have roamed through life, Still
most a stranger, most with naked heart
At mine own home and birth place.

It is not difficult to see Coleridge seeing himself as the Mariner, namely as

Some night-wandering man whose heart was pierced
With the remembrance of a grievous wrong[6]

Similarly, Coleridge analogizes himself as a tree that had been "too soon transplanted" and for this reason was left with "leaves of feeble stem," leaves too weak to withstand the rain and storms of life.[7]

The missing mother was a deep complex for Coleridge to contend with. It informed his life from the age of ten to his death at sixty-one, his poetry, his journals, his search for substitute mothers, and an unrelenting and unfulfilled desire for love. Jung writes, "The more remote and unreal the personal mother is, the more deeply will the son's yearning for her clutch at his soul, awakening that primordial and eternal image of the mother for whose sake everything that embraces, protects, nourishes, and helps assumes maternal form."[8] Those who are familiar with Coleridge will certainly recognize him mirrored in Jung's words about the lack of maternal relationship generating a deep yearning for "that primordial and eternal image of the mother." Coleridge's mother wound manifested all throughout his life as unfulfilled erotic longing. In her article "The Orphan Archetype," Rose-Emily Rothenberg describes the fundamental feelings and experiences associated with an orphan complex as unworthiness, primal guilt, deep unmet yearnings for the Mother, self-pity, dependency, playing the innocent child, a profound pull toward death, an inferiority-superiority pattern, and a search for substitute Mothers.[9] Again, those who are familiar with Coleridge's life would agree that this complex of attributes closely describes him, as we have seen Coleridge describe himself.

As a compensation for the love he felt was absent in his life, Coleridge had an astonishing capacity to seek for what was missing in his imagination. In his poem "Constancy to an Ideal Object" (1828), for example, Coleridge writes about the ideal objects of his mind as if they were Brocken spirits in the mist.

And art thou nothing? Such thou art, as when
The woodman winding westward up the glen
At wintry dawn, where o'er the sheep-track's maze
The viewless snow-mist weaves a glist'ning haze,
Sees full before him, gliding without tread,
An image with a glory round its head;
The enamoured rustic worships its fair hues,
Nor knows he makes the shadow, he pursues!

Mother was one of these ideal objects; her image appears to have symbolized the invisible world of the spirit: "yea, what the blue sky is to the mother, the mother's upraised eyes and brow are to the child, the type and symbol of an invisible Heaven!"[10] But there is also a horrifying vision of the negative mother in Coleridge's imagination. In *The Rime of the Ancient Mariner*, a horrific death mother, "the nightmare LIFE-IN-DEATH," accompanies her mate "DEATH" and "thicks man's blood with cold."

From these few examples we can feel the point: at Christ's Hospital, Coleridge was alienated from *Mother*, not only his personal mother but also from a feeling of communion with brothers, sisters, and extended family, anything resembling emotional warmth and nurturing, food, nature, and beauty. From the age of ten onward the pain of abandonment branded Coleridge's psyche, even affecting him physically, for Coleridge was often ill in childhood and as a young adult, at times coming close to death.

Coleridge's Mother complex is thus a gateway to the realm of the untrodden regions of psyche. Will those regions bring Life, Death, or Life-in-Death? Will the encounter with the repressed unconscious be regenerative (leading to the process of soul-making) or destructive (as, for example, addiction or mental illness)? This question lies at the bottom of all creative souls. And, of course, the answer with Coleridge as with all of us is both yes and no in powerful complements. Gifts emerge and develop *through* wounds, not despite them. Impossible longings have their cause in neglect but at the same time they seek a goal, a telos, a hidden need to explore the matrix, or "Mother," from which the ego emerges (i.e., a longing, in Jung's words, for "that primordial and eternal image of the mother for whose sake everything that embraces, protects, nourishes, and helps assumes maternal form"). That longing was true of Coleridge to a superlative degree, and his Mariner takes the journey.

His Fateful Dilemma

Coleridge was a wounded child, a motherless child. However, this fact does not fully explain his psychology. There are many fascinating aspects of Coleridge's personality, abiding aspects that manifest spontaneously before any demonstrable crises or unusual developmental breaks.

In Coleridge's autobiographical memoir, for example, he recollects a memory from the age of two, his first memory, that seems to him to demonstrate an innate character setting him in motion from within. In a letter written to a close friend in the same year Coleridge began to work on *The Ancient Mariner*, March 1797 (when he was in his mid-twenties), Coleridge conveys a sense of a psychic disposition that he can only call "*ominous*": "From October 20th, 1778 [actually 1773] to October 20th, 1774 [age two].—In this year I was carelessly left by my Nurse—ran to the Fire, and pulled out a live coal—burnt myself dreadfully—while my hand was being Drest by a Mr. Young, I spoke for the first time (so my Mother informs me) & said, 'Nasty Doctor Young!'—the snatching at fire, & the circumstance of my first words expressing hatred to professional men, are they at all *ominous*?"[11] At the age of two Coleridge was already an infant shaman, a Prometheus stealing fire and rebelling against paternal authority ("Nasty Doctor Young!"). As an adult, Coleridge held a high opinion of Prometheus, that Greek Titan who steals fire from the gods and gives it to humanity, which he saw as uniting the "rebellious Spirit" with "the Divine Friend of Mankind." "Prometheus—that truly wonderful Fable, in which the characters of the rebellious Spirit and of the Divine Friend of Mankind (*Theos Philanthropos*) are united in the same person: and thus in the most striking manner noting the forced amalgamation of the Patriarchal tradition with the incongruous scheme of Pantheism."[12] I suggest that the personal and mythic character of *Coleridge's* life, *his* fateful dilemma, is found in this early memory. Character is destiny and Coleridge's felt sense of this is *ominous*.

Idealistic Hopes

After graduating from Christ's Church, Coleridge attended college at Cambridge, where he won academic honors but also accrued huge debts; he spent the little money he had keeping up with the fashion and lifestyle choices of his wealthy classmates. Also, he put more energy into the radical politics of the French Revolution than his studies. Soon deep in debt and unable to pay his tutors, Coleridge's plan was to win the Irish lottery. When said plan failed, overwhelmed with guilt and shame, Coleridge ran away from the whole world at the age of twenty-two. He joined the army under a pseudonym, Silas Tomkyn Comberbache (STC), and swung from unbridled infantile freedom to strict containment in the saturnine structures of military discipline. Perhaps this *enantiodromia*, a swinging from one polarity to the other unconsciously, was a recapitulation of Coleridge leaving his idyllic childhood home in Devon and entering the strict disciplinary environment of Christ's Hospital. In any event, Silas Tomkyn Comberbache's career as a soldier was a complete and utter failure. Some have speculated that he may possibly have been the worst soldier in the history of the British army. Fortunately, Coleridge's brother was able to secure his release by finding another man who agreed to take his place as a soldier. Comberbache/Coleridge was officially discharged from the British army on the grounds of insanity.

Returning to Cambridge, Coleridge resumed his studies. More importantly, he fell in with a core group of poet-scholars and political friends, including the future poet laureate Southey, the poet Robert Lovell, and others as idealistic as he was. Together they hatched a plan to leave England behind and sail to America where they would start a community of farmer-philosophers on the banks of the Susquehanna River in the northeastern United States. They called this community Pantisocracy, which means "all rule equally," and based their ideals on the enlightened rationalism that inspired the French Revolution: "Liberty, Equality, Fraternity."

Women were necessary for this plan; wives were needed. Therefore, according to Southey, "each young man should take to himself a mild and lovely woman for his wife, it would be her part to prepare their innocent food, and tend their hardy and beautiful race."[13] Southey, following this plan, married Edith Fricker. Coleridge followed suit and married Edith Fricker's sister Sarah. Another Pantisocracy adventurer, Robert Lovell, married the third Fricker sister, Mary, while George Burnett proposed unsuccessfully to the fourth Fricker sister. However, when Southey came into an inheritance that allowed him to live in London, the plan began to unravel. Soon, Southey backed out and the other members followed, all except Coleridge. When Pantisocracy dissolved in 1795, Coleridge became despondent; he again quit Cambridge before earning a degree, this time never to return. But by then he was bound in marriage to Sarah Fricker, primarily out of solidarity to Pantisocracy.

The demise of Pantisocracy was a crushing blow to Coleridge's amazingly naive and idealistic sense of hope. Another crushing blow lay close ahead when the French Revolution went to the devil. Coleridge was one of many young political radicals of the late eighteenth century who genuinely believed that the French Revolution would usher in paradise on earth. When the revolution disintegrated into power, terror, and horrific violence, Coleridge fell deeper into disillusionment. When Napoleon's army invaded peaceful and neutral Switzerland on October 10, 1797, Coleridge's hope that political revolution would produce an ideal society gave a death rattle. Hope died, but then it soon was reborn, transformed into a vision of revolution coming from within, a psychological, spiritual, and imaginal revolution with the power to transform both self and world through contact with the eternal laws of nature, both inner and outer.

Coleridge wrote "The Recantation: An Ode" (later renamed and published as "France: An Ode") in February 1798 and published it in the *Morning Post* on April 16, 1798. This long poem details Coleridge's journey through his idealistic political phase, through the death of politics as a scheme of salvation, and into the rebirth of "the spirit of divinest Liberty" through the individual's psychological and spiritual relationship with the "eternal laws" of nature as distinct from the temporal laws of politics. This transformation only came about, however, because Coleridge drank to the dregs the crushing realization that the supposed liberators of France were as much tyrants as those they deposed; the rebels were not free but "Slaves by their own compulsion!"

> The Sensual and the Dark rebel in vain,
> Slaves by their own compulsion! In mad game
> They burst their manacles and wear the name
> Of Freedom, graven on a heavier chain!

Coleridge wrote "France: An Ode" about the time that he completed *The Ancient Mariner*. In other words, as Coleridge worked on his most famous poem, he was inspired by a vision of liberty as contact with the eternal laws of inner and outer nature. Again, from "France: An Ode":

> O Liberty! with profitless endeavour
> Have I pursued thee, many a weary hour;
> But thou nor swell'st the victor's strain, nor ever
> Didst breathe thy soul in forms of human power.
> Alike from all, howe'er they praise thee,
> (Nor prayer, nor boastful name delays thee)
> Alike from Priestcraft's harpy minions,
> And factious Blasphemy's obscener slaves,
> Thou speedest on thy subtle pinions,
> The guide of homeless winds, and playmate of the waves!
> And there I felt thee!—on that sea-cliff's verge,
> Whose pines, scarce travelled by the breeze above,
> Had made one murmur with the distant surge!
> Yes, while I stood and gazed, my temples bare,
> And shot my being through earth, sea, and air,
> Possessing all things with intensest love,
> O Liberty! my spirit felt thee there.

In a letter to his good friend John Thelwall (a fellow radical political activist considered at the time by some British officials to be the most dangerous man in Britain) written October 14, 1797, just four days after Napoleon invaded Switzerland and some six months before "France: An Ode," Coleridge gives us further insight into his frame of mind at the time. "I should much wish, like the Indian Vishna, to float about along an infinite ocean cradled in the flower of the Lotos, & wake once in a million years for a few minutes—just to know I was going to sleep a million years more . . . I can *at times* feel strong the beauties, you describe, in themselves, & for themselves—but more frequently *all things* appear little—all the knowledge, that can be acquired, child's play—the universe itself—what but an immense heap of *little* things? . . . My mind feels as if it ached to behold & know something *great*—something *one* & *indivisible*—and it is only in the faith of this that rocks or waterfalls, mountains or caverns give me the sense of sublimity or majesty! But in this faith *all things* counterfeit infinity!"[14] In his wish "to float along an infinite ocean," Coleridge is far from the Bastille. But he is close to the Ancient Mariner. To be clear, and this is an important point that is often misunderstood, Coleridge's "return to nature," if one could call it that, is not a regression, not a backward-looking event in which modern consciousness disappears—no. For Coleridge, nature is not sublime and majestic in itself; on the contrary, "the universe itself . . . [is] an immense heap of *little* things." Coleridge's desire to return to nature is permeated by an ache to go forward, to progress, "to behold & know something *great*—something *one & indivisible*." Coleridge's Ancient Mariner takes that journey.

Coleridge's Psychological Typology

Throughout his entire life, Coleridge was habituated to the *Vast*. He oriented through intuition and imagination, not by facts but by visions and possibilities. He was happiest dwelling in possibility. If he lost hope, he withered. His relationship to everyday reality, to money, home, and his body, was constantly troublesome. In the Jungian language, Coleridge was an introverted intuitive type with strong thinking as his auxiliary function. Extroverted sensation, the function of relationship to outer reality, was inferior.

What was Coleridge's relationship to feeling? This wavered throughout his life; sometimes he gave himself over to the flow of inner values, sometimes he repressed feeling and split it off. Coleridge's feeling judgments assisted and cooperated with his thinking in his poetry and prose, which he believed was both a strength and a disability as a writer. "I feel strongly, and I think strongly; but I seldom feel without thinking, or think without feeling. Hence tho' my poetry has in general a hue of tenderness, or Passion over it, yet it seldom exhibits unmixed & simple tenderness or Passion. My philosophical opinions are blended with, or deduced from, my feelings: & this, I think peculiarizes my style of Writing. And like every thing else, it is sometimes a beauty and sometimes a fault."[15] Coleridge used his intellect as much to distance himself from feeling as to complement it. For instance, in his personal relationships, if the subject of conversation turned toward his inner feeling, he tells us, he would often either throw up a wall of eloquence as a defense or silently sulk out of the room. He sometimes even wondered about the possibility that he had "a cowardice of all deep feeling" and was sure, in any event, that he often used his intellect as a writer and a man as a means of "running away and hiding" from his feelings: "My eloquence was most commonly excited by the desire of running away & hiding myself from my personal and inward feelings, and not for the expression of them, while doubtless this very effort gave a passion and glow to my thoughts."[16] In other words, Coleridge's feeling could easily introvert and sink down into the well of the unconscious to be lost to conscious awareness, whereas thinking more easily extroverted as both a defense against feeling as well as a complement to it.

Love and Laudanum in the Magical Years

During his twenties, while Coleridge was writing *The Ancient Mariner*, he found himself struggling in an unhappy and unfulfilling marriage. As mentioned earlier, he married the sister of the wife of his friend Southey from the Pantisocracy venture, Sarah Fricker, out of obligation to Pantisocracy rather than passion or love. Theirs was a domestic partnership that was conventional, kind but lacking fire, and challenging for that reason. Coleridge would often refer to his wife Sarah as "Mrs. Coleridge."

After quitting Cambridge, after the death of Pantisocracy, and after the failure of the French Revolution, while he was married to Sarah Fricker, Coleridge struck up a dynamic friendship with his fellow poet William Wordsworth and his sister Dorothy. His time with William and Dorothy was magical, a once-in-a-lifetime meeting that would prove to be the most creative and enjoyable of Coleridge's life. All of Coleridge's famous visionary poetry came during this period: "Kubla Khan," "Christabel," *The Rime of the Ancient Mariner*. Intoxicated by his relationship with kindred spirits, Coleridge would regularly leave his comparatively prosaic wife and their infant son and roam the hills of the Lake District with the Wordsworths for days and weeks. Long midnight walks evolved into extended poetic recitations and compositions while Mrs. Coleridge remained dutifully, but not happily, at home tending their infant child and the domestic duties. She sometimes asked to be included, but as the "missing fourth," so to speak, in this Holy Trinity, she was out of place.

Around this time Coleridge began to regularly use and abuse opium, specifically laudanum, a powerful opioid narcotic mixed with brandy taken in the eighteenth and nineteenth centuries, like Tylenol is taken today, for physical ailments such as toothache. Molly Lefebure reports in her book *Samuel Taylor Coleridge: A Bondage of Opium*, "At one time S.T.C., so he told [a benefactor], was taking four to five ounces of laudanum a day; once he, himself, said, he took nearly a pint (there are twenty fluid ounces in an English pint)."[17] If this report is accurate, then at this stage in his life Coleridge's regular use of four to five ounces of laudanum daily was about fifty times the current medically recommended dose.[18]

While there is much debate as to the extent to which opium opened the doors of perception and illuminated Coleridge's poetic visions, what is not in doubt is that the poisonous addiction he developed was the debilitating curse of his life. From his thirties to his death at the age of sixty-one, Coleridge was an addict living in a time that did not understand addiction, and he cursed his bondage to opium as his most horrific downfall.

Before he wrote *The Rime of the Ancient Mariner*, "Kubla Khan," and "Christabel," Coleridge was already a well-known poet. But his poetic fire reached a fever pitch during these magical years of his twenties. No doubt the influences of William and Dorothy, the natural beauty of the Lake District, and laudanum all contributed to these few miraculous years during which Coleridge became even more renowned for his charismatic and mesmerizing brilliance. "Wherever he went," writes Ted Hughes, "his overpowering eloquence, what he himself described as the 'velocity' and 'music' of his thought, the voluminous sweep of his torrential ideas, the sheer energy of his mind, became a legend."[19] Coleridge's inward and powerfully felt feelings and experiences of the daimonic nature of the imagination are nowhere more vividly expressed than in his poem "Kubla Khan; or, A Vision in a Dream: A Fragment" (written in 1797, first published 1816), which was, according to the poet himself, the result of an opium-induced reverie.

> But oh! that deep romantic chasm which slanted
> Down the green hill athwart a cedarn cover!
> A savage place! as holy and enchanted
> As e'er beneath a waning moon was haunted
> By woman wailing for her demon-lover!
> And from this chasm, with ceaseless turmoil seething,
> As if this earth in fast thick pants were breathing,
> A mighty fountain momently was forced:

Amid whose swift half-intermitted burst
Huge fragments vaulted like rebounding hail,
Or chaffy grain beneath the thresher's flail:
And mid these dancing rocks at once and ever
It flung up momently the sacred river.

. . . .

. . . And all should cry, Beware! Beware!
His flashing eyes, his floating hair!
Weave a circle round him thrice,
And close your eyes with holy dread
For he on honey-dew hath fed,
And drunk the milk of Paradise.

These lines give full confession to the secret way in which Coleridge experienced his vocation as a poet. Coleridge kept "Kubla Khan" almost completely to himself, carrying it around with him in his coat pocket for nineteen years and giving readings to close friends only, until he finally published it at the insistence of Lord Byron in 1816, nineteen years after writing it.

That fever-pitched visionary experience expressed in "Kubla Khan" proved too powerful to sustain. The feelings that burst upon Coleridge during the time he wrote *The Rime of the Ancient Mariner* were burning him alive, much like the coal that his two-year-old Promethean self snatched from the fire. At the age of twenty-eight, Coleridge turned away from his daimonically frenzied imagination in the name of sanity, declaring "the poet is dead in me" and bringing to mind the way his father burnt his "Faery Tale" books as a child. "Poetry is out of the question. The attempt would only hurry me into that sphere of acute feeling from which abstruse research, the mother of self-oblivion, presents an asylum."[20] Coleridge sought asylum from "the sphere of acute feeling" in intellectual defenses, "abstruse research." During his thirties and up to the end of his life, he looked more and more to the conventional Church as an "asylum" against his daimonic visions and turned his back on the sea. Yet, this was not a solution, neither for the poet nor the man. "The Pang More Sharp Than All," published in 1817, almost twenty years after *The Ancient Mariner*, is a poem of regret in which Coleridge confesses losing contact with "the wondrous 'World of Glass'" and "The magic image of the magic Child," thus confining himself to self-imposed alienation that caused him "To live and yearn and languish incomplete!"

> Ah! He is gone, and yet will not depart!—
> Is with me still, yet I from him exiled!
> For still there lives within my secret heart
> The magic image of the magic Child,
> Which there he made up-grow by his strong art,
> As in that crystal orb—wise Merlin's feat,—
> The wondrous "World of Glass," wherein is held
> All long'd for things their beings did repeat;—
> And there he left it, like a Sylph beguiled,
> To live and yearn and languish incomplete!

Coleridge's monumental *Biographia Literaria* (1817), composed the same year as "The Pang More Sharp Than All," is an effort to come to conscious terms with the poetic imagination that drove him to the brink of madness in his twenties.

Midlife and Beyond

With the poet within him dead, Coleridge left England and his wife and child to study philosophy in Germany. He then spent years in Italy working for the British government, sending home what little money he could scrape together periodically. At one point, he did not see his family for over seven years. When he did return home, he amicably separated from Mrs. Coleridge.

Throughout his life, but especially midlife and beyond, Coleridge suffered from ill health. His midlife became increasingly dark, wrecked by his opium addiction, which destroyed his hopes for a happy life through physical suffering, mental anguish (including periods of suicidal depression), and guilt. His friends and patrons helped him financially, but still Coleridge never seemed to have enough money. From 1816 to his death in 1834, Coleridge resided primarily in the home of the doctor James Gillman and his family in Highgate, a suburb of London. Gillman was able to moderate Coleridge's use of opiates through strict supervision. Welcoming Coleridge into his family (who accepted him as such), Gillman surely helped to assuage the poet's feelings of being a perpetual orphan. And Coleridge remained miraculously productive during this time. Yet, like his Mariner, the feeling of being "all, all alone / Alone on a wide wide sea" haunted him perpetually.

Despite his feelings of alienation, Coleridge had close and extremely devoted friends. He was greatly loved despite his many faults and failings, of which he had no harsher critic than himself. Upon his death, Wordsworth remarked, "He was the greatest man I ever knew." His lifelong friend Charles Lamb wrote, "Never saw I his likeness, nor probably can the world see it again."[21] Coleridge wrote his own epitaph, probably in 1833, a year before his death.

Epitaph

Stop, Christian Passer-by!—Stop, child of God,
    And read with gentle breast. Beneath this sod
        A poet lies, or that which once seem'd he.
            O, lift one thought in prayer for S. T. C.;
    That he who many a year with toil of breath
Found death in life, may here find life in death!
        Mercy for praise—to be forgiven for fame
He ask'd, and hoped, through Christ. Do thou the same.

CHAPTER 2

Psycho-analytical

Coleridge as a Proto-Depth Psychologist

When he accepted the Goethe Prize for literature, Freud graciously acknowledged that the poets and philosophers before him discovered the unconscious while he, Freud, merely discovered the scientific method whereby the unconscious could be studied. Henri Ellenberger takes Freud's acknowledgment of the influence of poetry on the development of depth psychology a step further; in his comprehensive survey entitled *The Discovery of the Unconscious*, Ellenberger portrays both Freud and Jung as less distinguished imitators of the Romantics. "There is hardly a single concept of Freud or Jung that had not been anticipated by the [Romantic] philosophy of nature . . . Freud and even more Jung are late epigones of romanticism."[1] Ellenberger's assertion that "Freud and even more Jung are late epigones of romanticism" is half correct.

It is true that the twentieth-century concept of the unconscious is essentially a Romantic concept. It is also true, as we shall see in more detail in this chapter, that there are remarkable parallels between Romanticism and depth psychology. The goal of depth psychology, however, is not merely to discover the unconscious, and not merely to express that discovery poetically and philosophically (the Romantics did a masterful job of that); psychology, however, is a practical discipline whose goal is to help the conscious ego *relate* to the unconscious in the name of sanity.

In actual practice, the goal of a depth analysis is to integrate the discovery of the unconscious into real, lived life. Coleridge's theory of the function of art seems to have aimed at this goal as well. "In every work of art, there is a reconcilement of the external with the internal. The conscious is so impressed on the unconscious as to appear in it. . . . He who combines the two is the man of genius; and for that reason he must partake of both."[2] And yet the reconciliation of conscious and unconscious, external and internal, proved to be, in practice, impossibly difficult for Coleridge and other great geniuses of British Romanticism, at times in dramatically different ways.[3] Shelley, for example, tended to connect to the internal and unconscious via an apocalyptically literalized form of suicidal ideation[4] and died by drowning at the age of thirty after his boat capsized during a storm. Before this, however, Shelley had already drowned on dry land. His wife Mary Shelley wrote immediately after her husband's death, "I was never the Eve of any Paradise, but a human creature blessed by an elemental spirit's company & love—an angel who imprisoned in flesh could not adapt himself to his clay shrine & so has flown and left it."[5]

Coleridge took a different course. Coleridge survived his encounter with the unconscious by seeking asylum in the collectively sanctioned lifeboat of conservative politics, abstract philosophy, and traditional religion. While Shelley rejected land in favor of the sea and died at the age of twenty-nine, Coleridge turned his back on the sea in search of solid footing on terra firma and lived to be sixty-one. But in each case, the successful integration of conscious and unconscious that Coleridge abstractly recognized to be the goal of a "man of genius" remained in practice unrealized.

The function of twentieth-century depth psychology is not an attempt to imitate the Romantics but to address the *crisis* of Romanticism, namely, an inability to unite land and sea, conscious and unconscious, outer and inner, in a stable and vital wedding.[6]

Jung and Coleridge

It is well known that Jung was deeply influenced by German romantics such as Goethe and C. G. Carus. It is reasonable, therefore, to wonder about Jung's relationship to Coleridge. Jung had certainly heard of Coleridge, but there is no indication that Jung had deeply read his poetry or prose or been significantly influenced by his ideas. To my knowledge, the only appearance Coleridge makes in Jung's writings is a lighthearted reference in Jung's ETH Lectures of 1939 that "it is obvious that two or three form a congregation, a Church; whereas one individual is not a Church in spite of Coleridge's saying that he was a member of the only true Church and at the moment its only member!"[7] This is a funny comment but there is no indication that Coleridge ever made it. Furthermore, when it comes to *The Ancient Mariner*, Coleridge's Mariner does not embrace being the one and only member of the true church; rather, he turns his back on his individual path and seeks to rejoin the collective congregation.

Despite an apparent lack of any significant historical connection between Coleridge and Jung (or perhaps especially because of that lack of connection), as I read through Coleridge's poetry, prose, letters, notebooks, *Table Talk*, and *Marginalia*, I was shocked to discover how closely Coleridge's ideas and language concerning the psychology of the unconscious parallel and anticipate Jung's. Again, these parallels are even more remarkable given the fact that, as far as I can tell, Jung was not directly influenced by Coleridge.

Coleridge consistently describes himself as a "psychologist." He uses words like "association," the "unconscious," and "self" in ways that recall Jung's use of those words over a century later. For example, Coleridge was passionately convinced of the existence of an unconscious mind. He thought that psychological laws governed the unconscious. He sought to discover those laws, pay heed to them, and heal himself through the practice of "analysis." "The most watchful analyst of his own mind," Coleridge writes, "must be guided by the known laws of psychology."[8] Speaking of his own psychological problems, Coleridge confided to his notebooks, "Surely this is well worth a serious analysis, that understanding I may attempt to heal."[9]

Coleridge invented the term "psycho-analytic." He also invented the term "psychosomatic," a neologism coined to describe the nature of dreams. Dreams fascinated Coleridge. He thought of dreams as expressions of the body belonging to a "somatosphere," as well as being "psychognometic" or indicative of the mind. Dreams were important to Coleridge not only as a poet, as we have seen, but also as a "watchful analyst" of his own mind. In his everyday life Coleridge recorded many dreams in his *Notebooks* and wondered what they meant, but he confessed that he was rarely able to decipher them. Nevertheless, Coleridge took dreams seriously as psychological metaphors, much as Jung would over a century later, so much so that he describes dreams as "the most difficult and at the same time the most interesting problem of psychology." Coleridge also recognized that dreams have an implicit order, a dramatic structure. In a *Notebook* entry, Coleridge entitles his dream figures "Dreamatis Personae" and reflects on how autonomous those dream persons are, how "detached," like characters in a play, with their own thoughts, intentions, and personalities. In the

Jungian language, we would say that Coleridge recognizes dream figures as personifications of autonomous complexes.[10]

Coleridge also anticipated Jung's theory of introversion and extroversion when he states that there are "two types of men," the Aristotelians and the Platonists, beyond which it is "next to impossible to conceive a third."[11] Coleridge conceived of himself as a born Platonist, or, in Jungian terms, an introvert. He acknowledges that even at the age of eight years old, "I regulated all my creeds by my conceptions not by my *sight*."[12] This introverted bias can be seen in remarks such as "true Freedom" is "the outward [as] determined by the inward as the alone self-determining Principle."[13] "The pith of my system," Coleridge informs us, "is to make the senses out of the mind—not the mind out of the senses, as Locke did."[14] As a watchful analyst of his own mind, Coleridge recognized that extroversion was his weak spot, both in perception and in judgment: "Now with me the peccant and the weak part has always been in the application of the sense and judgment to outward things."[15]

Perhaps the most striking and important parallel between Coleridge and Jung, however, is their shared instinctive as well as philosophical reaction against the doctrine of scientific and philosophical materialism. Coleridge pejoratively calls the deterministic or causal attitude that dominated the scientific view of the world in the nineteenth century the "mechanical philosophy." Jung would similarly denigrate the materialistic point of view of nature as "that damned clockwork fantasy." Coleridge places his own idea of the "primary Imagination," namely, "the living Power and prime Agent of all human perception . . . a repetition in the finite mind of the eternal act of creation in the infinite I AM," in direct contrast to the mechanical philosophy.[16] Coleridge's primary Imagination thus comes quite close to Jung's sense of consciousness as "a second world creator." Finally, in his later writings,

Jung recognizes that the archetype is not merely psychic but psychoid, that is, inhering in both matter and mind; Coleridge was convinced of this more than a century earlier. There is "a symbol established in the truth of things," he asserts; the symbol is "one of the great organs of the life of Nature."[17] We will revisit Coleridge's ideas concerning the essential unity of psyche and nature in our discussion of *The Rime of the Ancient Mariner*, especially with the Mariner's blessing of the water-snakes and the ascension of "Mary Queen."

Even More Parallels

Indeed, there are so many parallels between Coleridge's thinking and Jung's that for ease of reference, I have organized the following excerpts from Coleridge's writings under headings taken from Jungian concepts—analytical psychology, individuation, the collective unconscious, anima, symbols, dreams, alchemy, and the union of opposites—to highlight them. The quotation below are a selection of some of Coleridge's ideas that anticipate Jungian psychology strikingly and directly but are not explicable by conscious, historical transmission. Please bear with the abstract simplicity for now. The ramifications of each of these topics for the discovery of the unconscious in Romantic poetry and philosophy resonate forever, and we will have the opportunity to revisit them in the second part of this book.

Coleridgean Concepts Related to Analytical Psychology in General

"The language of the dream," "the unconscious," "association," "self"[18]

"Psycho-analytical"[19]

"The most watchful analyst of his own mind must be guided by the known laws of psychology."[20]

"Surely this is well worth a serious analysis, that understanding I may attempt to heal."[21]

"In the treatment of nervous cases, he is the best physician who is the most ingenious inspirer of hope."[22]

"The law of association . . . formed the basis of all true psychology . . . being that to the mind which gravitation is to matter."[23]

Individuation

"In every work of art there is a reconcilement of the external with the internal; the conscious is so impressed on the unconscious as to appear in it. . . . He who combines the two is the man of genius; and for that reason he must partake of both."[24]

"I define life as *the principle of individuation*, or the power which unites a given *all* into a *whole* that is presupposed by all its parts. The link that combines the two, and acts throughout both, will, of course, be defined by the *tendency* to *individuation*."[25]

The Collective Unconscious

"In all societies there exists an instinct of growth, a certain collective, unconscious good sense."[26]

"The greater and, perhaps, nobler, certainly all the subtler, parts of one's nature must be solitary. Man exists herein to himself and to God alone—yea! In how much only to god! How much lies below his own consciousness!"[27]

"If the intelligent faculty should be rendered more comprehensive, it would require only a different and apportioned organization—*the body celestial* instead of *the body terrestrial*—to bring before every human soul the collective experience of its whole past existence."[28]

Anima

"The same Providence that visited Jacob by Signs, Visions, and guiding Impulses, formed him with an original aptitude for & susceptibility of the same.—N.B. By *feminine* qualities I mean nothing detractory—no participation in the *Effeminate*. In the best and greatest of men, most eminently—and less so, yet still present in all but such [as] are below the average worth of Men, there is a feminine Ingredient.—There is a *Woman* in the Man—tho' not *perhaps* the Man in the Woman—Adam *therefore* loved *Eve*—and it is the Feminine in us even now, that makes every Adam love his Eve, and crave for an Eve—Why, I have inserted the dubious 'perhaps'—why, it should be less accordant with truth to say, that in every good Woman there is the Man as an Undersong, than to say that in every true and manly Man there is a translucent Under-tint of the Woman—would furnish matter for a very interesting little Essay on sexual Psychology."[29]

"The truth is, a great mind must be androgynous."[30]

Symbols

"The imagination . . . that reconciling and mediatory power, which incorporating the reason in images of the sense and organizing (as it were) the flux of the senses by the permanence and self-circling energies of the reason, gives birth to a system of symbols, harmonious in themselves, and consubstantial with the truths of which they are the conductors."[31]

"They and only they can acquire the philosophic imagination, the sacred power of self-intuition, who within themselves can interpret and understand the symbol, that the wings of the air sylph are forming within the skin of the caterpillar, those only who feel in their own spirits the same instinct which impels the chrysalis of the horned fly to leave room in the involucrum for antennae yet to come. They know and feel that the *potential* works *in* them, even as the *actual* works on them!"[32]

Dreams

"psychosomatic," "somatosphere," "psychognometic," (indicative of the mind),[33] neologisms Coleridge coined to describe the nature of dreams.

"[Dreams are] the most difficult & at the same time the most interesting Problem of Psychology . . . the solution of this Problem would, perhaps, throw great doubt on this present dogma, that the Forms & Feelings of Sleep are always the reflections & confused Echoes of our waking Thoughts, & Experiences."[34]

Alchemy

"I am persuaded that the chymical technology, as far as it was borrowed from Life & Intelligence, half-metaphorically, half-mystically, may be brought back again . . . to the use of psychology. . . . Thus innocence is distinguished from Virtue & vice versa—In both there is a positive, but in each opposite. A Decomposition must take place in the first instance, & then a new Composition, in order for Innocence to become Virtue. It loses a positive—& then the base attracts another different positive, by the higher affinity of the <same> Base under a different Temperature for the Latter."[35]

The Imagination, "is a synthetic and magical power" which "dissolves, diffuses, dissipates, in order to re-create."[36]

"The common end of all *narrative*, nay, of *all* Poems is to convert a *series* into a *Whole*: to make those events, which in real or imagined History move on in a *strait* Line, assume to our Understandings, a *circular* motion—the snake with its Tail in its Mouth."[37]

The Union of Opposites

"I cannot describe how much pleasure I have derived from 'Extremes meet' for instance; or, 'Treat everything according to its Nature,' and 'Be'! In the last I bring all inward Rectitude to its Test, in the former. All outward Morality to its Rule, and in the first all (problematic) Results to their Solution, and reduce apparent Contraries to correspondent Opposites. How many hostile Tenants has it enabled me to contemplate, as Fragments of the Truth—false only by negation, and mutual exclusion."[38]

"But in the Deity is an absolute Synthesis of opposites. Plato in Parmenide and Giordano Bruno passim have spoken many things well on this aweful Mystery/ the latter more clearly."[39]

"Esemplastic,"[40] neologism to describe the tendency of imagination to shape contraries into a oneness.

The poet, "diffuses a tone, and spirit of unity, that blends, and (as it were) *fuses*, each into each, . . . reveals itself in the balance or reconciliation of opposite or discordant qualities."[41]

Important Differences

Those with an understanding of Jungian psychology will no doubt find these similarities between Coleridge's and Jung's understanding of the psyche to be amazing, as I did.

Coleridge was truly a proto-depth psychologist. Given this, it makes sense that whoever chose the epigram to Jung's autobiography

Memories, Dreams, Reflections (perhaps the editor and coauthor Aniela Jaffé), the one sentence which sums up the essence of Jung's life, would select a quote from Coleridge's *Notebooks*: "Of a great metaphysician / He looked at (into?) *his own Soul* with a Telescope / what seemed all irregular he saw & *shewed* to be beautiful Constellations & he added to the Consciousness hidden worlds within worlds."[42] For all the parallels, however, there are also important differences.

To repeat, Jungian psychology is influenced by Romanticism, but at the same time is a response to the *crisis* of Romanticism, the incapacity to bridge conscious and unconscious. Unlike Jung, Coleridge, as a man not a thinker, did not have a strong ego capable of confronting, wrestling with, and integrating the visionary world of the unconscious that he peered into so deeply and wrote about so brilliantly. In addition, also unlike Jung, Coleridge did not have support from others that may have allowed him to achieve his theoretical goal of uniting conscious and unconscious. Most significantly, Coleridge could never integrate the dark message of the unconscious into his philosophical, ethical, and religious values; the visions we will explore with his Mariner were intensely threatening to both Coleridge's Christian beliefs and his identification with reason and intellect.

PART 2

Departure

CHAPTER 3

"It Is an Ancient Mariner"

Confrontation with Some Other Consciousness

"It is an ancient Mariner, / And he stoppeth one of three." Thus begins *The Rime of the Ancient Mariner.*

Three young Wedding Guests are on their way to a wedding when an ancient man appears out of nowhere, grabs one of them, and forces him to listen to a strange tale. The Wedding Guest is aghast and exclaims:

> "By thy long grey beard and glittering eye,
> Now wherefore stopp'st thou me?
>
> The Bridegroom's doors are opened wide,
> And I am next of kin;
> The guests are met, the feast is set:
> May'st hear the merry din."

The Wedding Guest is "next of kin" to the Bridegroom, he can hear the "merry din" of the wedding, the "doors are opened wide," and now he is waylaid by some freak? He wants nothing to do with the bizarre stranger who grips him with his skinny hand and separates him from his family and friends. "Hold off! unhand me, grey-beard loon!" the Wedding Guest cries out.

He holds him with his skinny hand,
"There was a ship," quoth he.
"Hold off! unhand me, grey-beard loon!"
Eftsoons his hand dropt he.

Releasing his grip, the bright-eyed Mariner mesmerizes the Wedding Guest with his "glittering eye."

He holds him with his glittering eye—
The Wedding-Guest stood still,
And listens like a three years' child:
The Mariner hath his will.

The Wedding-Guest sat on a stone:
He cannot choose but hear;
And thus spake on that ancient man,
The bright-eyed Mariner.

The Wedding Guest is transfixed, unable to tear himself away, a "three years' child" trapped in the gaze of an apparent lunatic. Thus begins our journey into the birth, death, and rebirth of the modern soul.

"This Body Dropt Not Down"

In the first part of this book, we emphasize Jung's insight that symbolic death is the alternative to literal genocide. "Die and be reborn"—we will revisit this theme many times throughout Coleridge's visionary poem. We later find it in the Wedding Guest's fear that the Mariner has died at sea.

"I fear thee, ancient Mariner!
I fear thy skinny hand!
And thou art long, and lank, and brown,
As is the ribbed sea-sand.

I fear thee and thy glittering eye,
And thy skinny hand, so brown."—
"Fear not, fear not, thou Wedding-Guest!
This body dropt not down.

The Wedding Guest believes he is face-to-face with a ghost, and the Mariner must reassure him that he did not literally die at sea. As we shall see, however, his entire world did, everything known and familiar: his crew, his God, his sense of self. Coleridge knew the power of imagination that "dissolves, diffuses, dissipates, in order to re-create."[1] Exposed to the full force of activated archetypal contents in the depths of the mind's oceans, the Mariner does, in fact, "die"; he is fundamentally and irrevocably transformed. The Wedding Guest's fear is thus not a fear of literal death but a fear of symbolic death. Another way to phrase this is to say that the Wedding Guest is afraid of going mad ("unhand me, grey-beard loon!"). He loses contact with consensual reality and feels dread, an eerie feeling of "obstinate questionings / Of sense and outward things, / Fallings from us, vanishings,"[2] in Wordsworth's language.

Marie-Louise von Franz was a young Wedding Guest when she met an Ancient Mariner in the form of C. G. Jung in 1933. Von Franz was eighteen at the time, a high school student, and the famous psychologist was fifty-eight, a "Methuselah" as she said. There was a feeling of being led onto the lunatic fringe at that meeting when Jung told her the tale of a female patient of his who lived on the moon. Surely, von Franz rationally responded, this woman *imagined* she lived on the moon, she did not *actually* live on the moon. But Jung insisted. Von Franz remembers that she "went away thinking that either he was crazy, or I was." Over time however, von Franz gradually came to understand that Jung had introduced her to "the reality of another realm of reality—the hidden inner world," a world most people do not know about and do not want to know about.[3] Most modern persons assume that their conscious, rational sense of "I" is the only psychic reality and thus become terrified when some other consciousness appears, perhaps in the form of a sudden burst of rage or a depression that one cannot get rid of, perhaps obsessive thoughts, addictions, striking dreams that come from who knows where, falling in love, inspiration.

The Mariner is taking the Wedding Guest with him on a voyage into that hidden inner world.

Ego diurnus and *ego nocturnus*

Insofar as *The Rime of the Ancient Mariner* begins with the image of an apparent madman forcibly alienating a young man from family, friends, and the celebration of life, it is easy to understand why some psychologically minded commentators interpret the character of the Ancient Mariner as a personification of Coleridge's family of origin traumas—in other words, as a reflection of repressed painful memories that hindered Coleridge's ability to thrive in society.[4] Coleridge did indeed experience a lot of early trauma, as we saw in his biography. Without in the least denying the severity of that trauma and the painful role it played in Coleridge's development, I suggest that the initial meeting of Wedding Guest and Mariner is reflective of a bipolarity of the self that is not idiosyncratic to Coleridge but belongs to all of us.

Just as there is both sea *and* land, night *and* day, moon *and* sun, a right brain *and* a left, there is an unconscious *and* a conscious personality. Jung knew from boyhood that he was a personality number one *and* a personality number two. In the *Red Book*, Jung generalizes these two personalities as the spirit of the times and the spirit of the depths. From boyhood on, Coleridge was another of the unusual ones who are aware of being two people. There was, he knew, another "*Self*," an "unleavened *Self*" that did not rise to Heaven but wrapped itself like a snake around his heart. Although Coleridge tried mightily to will that other self away, he never could. "Ah, but even in boyhood there was a cold hollow spot, an aching in the heart, when I said my prayers—that prevented my entire union with God—that I could not give up, or that would not give me up—as if a snake had wreathed around my heart, & at this one spot its mouth touched at & inbreathed a weak incapability of willing it away . . . that spot in my heart [is] even my remaining and unleavened *Self*—all else the Love of Christ in and thro' Christ's love of me."[5] "Who that thus lives with a continually divided Being can remain healthy!" Coleridge agonizes in an 1805 journal entry.[6] Coleridge's split self is, I suggest, mirrored in the bewildering and terrifying meeting of Mariner and Wedding Guest. I am *not* suggesting, however, that experiencing another consciousness in oneself besides the "I" is necessarily indicative of lunacy (i.e., schizophrenia or dissociative identity disorder). I am also not suggesting that this initial imagery in Coleridge's epic poem can be fully explained by reducing it to personal trauma.

Coleridge writes of "two Consciences, the earthly and the spiritual" that are present not only within himself in an idiosyncratic, pathological, or extraordinary way but in many people, if not everyone. There is an "I" of the day and an opposing "I" of the night, an "*ego diurnus*" and an "*ego nocturnus*."[7] The *ego nocturnus* is sublime as Edmund Burke defines the word in his classic 1756 work *The Sublime and the Beautiful*,[8] that is, vast, dark, uncertain, confused, outside the known rational order and carrying a frightening power to compel and destroy. The Ancient Mariner is sublime; he travels "like night," alienated from the daylight world of conventional collective society and "seven days drowned" in the depths. The Wedding Guest, by way of contrast, is the beautiful *ego diurnus*, the everyday or earthly conscience, a "gallant" as Coleridge writes in the prose gloss, coming from the old French *gale*, pleasure, rejoicing, and *galer*, to have fun, to be lighthearted, amiable, and related to society. When the Mariner's skinny hand and glittering eye make contact with the Wedding Guest, *ego nocturnus* touches *ego diurnus*, ancient (archetypal) meets young (personal), unknown meets known, sublime meets beautiful, night meets day, vast meets finite, unconscious meets conscious, the spirit of the depths meets the spirit of the times, internality meets externality. It all happens suddenly, unbidden. We learn later that the Ancient Mariner knows the man who "must" hear him; there is no choice in the matter. The Wedding Guest is *called* to an adventure into the unknown "with the force of a revelation," as Jung writes, "to make his life flow into that greater life—a moment of deadliest peril!"[9]

Many of the Romantics were aware of being "two Consciences," as Coleridge puts it, or "two consciousnesses"[10] in Wordsworth's language. Rather than pathologizing that awareness, they tended to regard it as intrinsic to their creative vocation. For example, as Wordsworth composed his epic autobiographical poem *The Prelude*, he was aware of being "conscious of myself / And of some other Being."[11] The only difference between Wordsworth and everyone else, however, is that Wordsworth *knows* there are two poles to psychic life, whereas "the trembling throng / Whose sails were never to the tempest given"[12]—like the Wedding Guest—are blissfully unaware of this fact. Awareness of the two consciousnesses transforms Coleridge's and Wordsworth's understanding of the composition of poetry from merely an aesthetic or literary exercise into an alchemical *mysterium coniunctionis*, an alchemical mixing vessel in which the two consciousnesses mix. "A man of genius," Coleridge writes, combines "conscious" and "unconscious" and thereby reconciles "the external with the internal."[13] For Wordsworth poetry is "a soul in the process of making itself," a "dark" and "inscrutable workmanship" by which the "discordant elements" operative between the "two consciousnesses" gradually begin to "cling together / In one society."[14] As we will see throughout our journey with the Mariner, the degree to which this alchemical operation is successful or not in *The Rime of the Ancient Mariner* is an open question.

Is the confrontation with some other consciousness within ourselves pathological or initiatory? According to the mathematics here, two-thirds of the population will never get gripped by an Ancient Mariner; God will let them go and remain identified with collective consciousness. The Wedding Guest is a sadder and a wiser man at the end of the poem for hearing the Mariner's tale. His pathology *is* the initiation. Who is blessed and who is cursed, the two Wedding Guests that got away or the one who could not?

The Glittering Eye of Lunar Imagination

Coleridge and William and Dorothy Wordsworth conceived *The Ancient Mariner* together on a long moonlit walk. That is auspicious in terms of the content of this poem, for the shimmering, silver illumination of moonlight dissolves clear boundaries and allows the play of imagination to interact with physical forms more directly than in the clear light of day. In the moonlight, a tree is more than a tree, shadows take on a life of their own, and every noise is portentous. Imagination comes alive in the moonlight. Things glitter with the inner light of imagination just like the Mariner's "bright," "glittering eye." The poetic eye is the eye that glitters in the moonlight.

In Coleridge's "Monody on the Death of Chatterton" (1790), the eyes of the legendary poetic prodigy Thomas Chatterton (1752–70) have "glorious meanings" that shine with "more than the light of outward day." Similarly, in Coleridge's "Apologia pro Vita Sua" (1800), "The Poet" has an eye that shines with a "magnifying power" that frees him from the confines of literal fact. This capacity is a "gifted ken" inspiring the poet with "phantoms of sublimity" that are invisible to others. He sees *more* than others do.

> The Poet in his lone yet genial hour
> Gives to his eyes a magnifying power:
> Or rather he emancipates his eyes
> From the black shapeless accidents of size—
> In unctuous cones of kindling coal,
> Or smoke upwreathing from the pipe's trim bole,
> His gifted ken can see
> Phantoms of sublimity.

Later in the poem we read that—like the Mariner—the ocean has a "bright eye" that "glimmers" on its surface, a reflection of the moon, as if the ocean were looking up to his "lord"; the moon is lord over the sea, just as the moon is lord over the Mariner. The eyes of the dead crew "glitter" in the moonlight. Similarly, In Coleridge's "Christabel" (1797), the daimonic female Geraldine's eye glitters in the moonlight just as the eyes of Coleridge's magical infant son Hartley in "Frost at Midnight" (1798) and "The Nightingale" (1798) do. Nowhere in Coleridge's oeuvre, however, does the glittering light of the Mariner's lunar eye shine brighter, more vividly, or more dramatically than in the outrageously fantastic "Kubla Khan, or, A Vision in a Dream: A Fragment" (1797; 1816). This poem above all others reads like a manifesto of Romanticism. In it, the inspired poet has "flashing eyes."

> Beware! Beware!
> His flashing eyes, his floating hair!
> Weave a circle round him thrice,
> And close your eyes with holy dread.

"Kubla Khan" is how Coleridge *really* experiences the effects of poetic imagination.[15] The Mariner is that inspired daimonic visionary in "Kubla Khan." Although the Wedding Guest is afraid of him for being a "grey-beard loon," surely Coleridge, being who he was, knew that the goddess Athena is "bright-eyed" when he chose to give his Mariner that name. Surely Coleridge knew that Plato interprets the bright-eyed goddess as divine intelligence.

Lunar light is feminine throughout *The Ancient Mariner*. In Jung's language, the spellbinding and entrancing power of the Mariner's lunar charisma comes from the feminine dimension of a man's unconscious, the anima, or, in Coleridge's language, the "*Woman* in the Man," the "feminine Ingredient," the "translucent Under-tint of the Woman" that is responsible for "Signs, Visions, and guiding Impulses."

> The same Providence that visited Jacob by Signs, Visions, and guiding Impulses, formed him with an original aptitude for & susceptibility of the same.—N.B. By *feminine* qualities I mean nothing detractory—no participation in the *Effeminate*. In the best and greatest of men, most eminently—and less so, yet still present in all but such [as] are below the average worth of Men, there is a feminine Ingredient.—There is a *Woman* in the Man—tho' not *perhaps* the Man in the Woman—Adam *therefore* loved *Eve*—and it is the Feminine in us even now, that makes every Adam love his Eve, and crave for an Eve—Why, I have inserted the dubious "perhaps"—why, it should be less accordant with truth to say, that in every good Woman there is the Man as an Under-song, than to say that in every true and manly Man there is a translucent Under-tint of the Woman—would furnish matter for a very interesting little Essay on sexual Psychology.[16]

Men usually project the anima onto women, but it is also possible to experience *her* directly as an inner energy, say as a fantasy, a mood, a dream, or an impulse to creativity, either positively as a muse or negatively as an addiction to delusion, or both.

As a feminine image in *The Ancient Mariner*, the lunar "more than the light of outward day" carries a paradoxical brightness just like the moon itself, which appears white then black, both white and black at the same time, a bright white disk one day, an abyss of darkness another. A close friend once noticed a "half-unearthly, half-morbid" glare in both Coleridge and his Mariner. "It is painful to observe in Coleridge, that, with all the kindness and glorious far-seeing intelligence of his eye, there is a glare in it, a light half-unearthly, half-morbid. It is the glittering eye of the Ancient Mariner."[17] This man evidently feels like a Wedding Guest entranced by the Ancient Mariner! As distinct from the Wedding Guest, however, he recognizes Coleridge's "glorious far-seeing intelligence" as well as the lunacy. Coleridge also felt the paradox of his capacity to see phantoms of sublimity. In his "Monody on the Death of Chatterton," Coleridge feels the pull of the dark side of the prodigal poet to such an extent he is compelled to take a step back from Chatterton's grave, "lest kindred woes pursue a kindred doom." What Coleridge is referring to here is the tragic fact that Chatterton committed suicide at the age of seventeen by drinking poison.

In his early to mid-twenties, Coleridge was deep in all sorts of out-of-the-way books, dreaming along with Hermetic literature, Obi witchcraft, Greenland shamanism, and native American medicine men.[18] "I have long wished," he states around the time he wrote *The Ancient Mariner*, "to devote an entire work to the Subject of Dreams, Visions, Ghosts, Witchcraft, &c,"[19] that is, just the type of "supernatural" images "from whatever source of delusion" that haunts his Mariner. Coleridge was well acquainted. For instance, he did not believe in the "existence of Ghosts &c.," but that was only because he had "seen too many of them."[20] Once Coleridge had the experience of touching his body and seeing silver light flash forth, to such an extent that he drew arcane symbols and words on himself in glowing silver light. Here is Coleridge the Ancient Mariner! But Coleridge was also a Wedding Guest, bewildered and overwhelmed by these glittering states of consciousness in which dream and reality blurred. Coleridge was inspired by enthusiasm and also terrified of it as a kind of addiction to delusion that threatened him with fanatical madness; he was the recipient of visions but also had to warn himself: "Beware! Beware! / His [own] flashing eyes, his [own] floating hair!"

The paradoxical experience of the erotic-psychotic imagination is mirrored throughout Romantic poetry. In John Keats's wonderful "La Belle Dame Sans Merci: A Ballad" (1819), to take just one example, a daimonic female, "a lady in the meads, / Full beautiful—a faery's child," seduces a young knight with her "wild, wild" eyes and "language strange," qualities that remind us of the anima-possessed Mariner. She tells this young knight, "I love thee true." But does she really? "La Belle Dame sans Merci / Hath thee in thrall!" a throng of death-pale warriors, kings, and princes warn the young knight in a dream, and he wakes from his erotic visions "alone," "haggard and so woe-begone" "on the cold hill's side," just another in a long line of patriarchal victims of the "*Woman* in the Man"—the visionary imagination.

A Strange Power of Speech

Coleridge had his Mariner's glittering eye. He also possessed—or was possessed by—the Mariner's "strange power of speech," a preternaturally enchanting voice resonating with the archetypal language of the soul. "The impact of an archetype," as Jung writes, "stirs us because it summons up a voice that is stronger than our own. . . . Whoever speaks in primordial images speaks with a thousand voices; he enthralls and overpowers."[21] Looking back on his first meeting with the famous poet Coleridge, William Hazlitt remembers the spellbinding effect of meeting this inspired poet. "That spell is broke; that time is gone for ever; that voice is heard no more: but still the recollection comes rushing by with thoughts of long-past years, and rings in my ears with never-dying sound."[22] "Have you ever heard me preach?" Coleridge once asked his friend and fellow poet Charles Lamb (1775–1834). "My dear Coleridge," Lamb replied, "I've never heard you do anything else."[23] Most likely, Lamb had in mind fond memories of his friend as a teenager at Christ's Hospital endlessly entrancing bystanders with tales of poetic and metaphysical mystery visions. "How have I seen the casual passer through the Cloisters stand still, entranced with admiration (while he weighed the disproportion between the speech and the garb of the young Mirandula), to hear thee unfold, in thy deep and sweet

intonations, the mysteries of Jamblichus, or Plotinus . . . , or reciting Homer in his Greek, or Pindar."[24] The teenage Coleridge is, for Lamb, a "young Mirandula," a reference to Giovanni Pico della Mirandola (1463–94), a Renaissance nobleman and philosopher who at the age of twenty-three wrote the *Oration on the Dignity of Man* that is sometimes referred to as the "Manifesto of the Renaissance." This treatise consists of nine hundred theses on philosophy, religion, science, and magic as well as holding the immortal honor of having been the first printed book to be banned by the Catholic Church.

Deconstructing Imagination: A Romantic Defense of Poetry

How do *we* feel about men who speak straight out of the dream-like revelations of the unconscious? Have you ever met such types? What would you do if a strange old haggard homeless man came up to you on the street, grabbed you by the arm, and started speaking the dream language? It would not be surprising if you were to react just like the Wedding Guest—"unhand me, grey-beard loon!"

History is filled with examples of ambivalence to the visionary imagination. For example, as if he had just read "Kubla Khan" or *The Rime of the Ancient Mariner*, Plato (424–348 BCE) declares in *The Republic* that all poets are divinely mad; they are possessed by gods and daimons and have no idea what they are talking about. For this reason, as well as the apparent fact that poetry does not serve any useful function, Plato banishes all the poets from his ideal society. He does not want any Ancient Mariners roaming about "like night," gripping people at random in his ideal world! Plato does offer one proviso however, one way for the poets to return. If either the poets or the lovers of poetry can offer a philosophical *defense of poetry* as something not only enchantingly beautiful but also true, useful, and real, then Plato will listen "in kindly spirit."[25]

The Romantics, living as they did so close to the fire of divine madness, all glittering with silver, lunar light, were highly motivated to take up Plato's challenge. Like many of the Romantics, Coleridge was a poet but also a philosopher and self-confessed psychologist; he not only saw visions and dreamt dreams but reflected on what his visions and dreams might mean; he did his best to use his capacity for reason to differentiate the objective from the subjective revelation. As we have seen earlier, Coleridge was among the first to interpret the mythopoetic imagination as an essentially inner psychological phenomenon and the first to suggest the need for a "psycho-analytical" understanding of mythology.

In his *Biographia Literaria* (1817), Coleridge offers a fascinating defense not only of poetry in general but of *The Rime of the Ancient Mariner* specifically; he tells us that he wrote *The Ancient Mariner* with "poetic faith" in the "shadows of imagination" that grant access to facts about "our inward nature" that would otherwise be opaque to consciousness.[26] But Coleridge does not stop there; he continues with a compelling and fascinating defense of imagination per se as not only true and real poetically in the narrow sense of that word but also as essential to our perception of the world. There are, Coleridge asserts, three dimensions to imagination: 1) the primary imagination, 2) the secondary imagination, and 3) fancy. The secondary imagination inspires creative art while the "primary Imagination," he writes, is the "living Power and prime Agent of all human perception." "The Imagination then I consider either as primary, or secondary. The primary Imagination I hold to be the living Power and prime Agent of all human Perception, and as a repetition in the finite mind of the eternal act of creation in the infinite I Am. The secondary I consider as an echo of the former, co-existing with the conscious will, yet still as identical with the primary in the kind of its agency, and differing only in degree, and in the mode of its operation. It dissolves, diffuses, dissipates, in order to re-create; or where this process is rendered impossible, yet still at all events it struggles to idealize and to unify. It is essentially vital, even as all objects (as objects) are essentially fixed and dead." Coleridge's primary Imagination is most definitely *not* our contemporary dictionary definition, namely "the faculty or action of forming new ideas, or images or concepts of external objects not present to our senses."[27] On the contrary, imagination is the faculty that, as perception, makes external objects *present* to our senses. As "a repetition in the finite mind of the eternal act of creation in the infinite I AM," imagination is comparable to God, the creator of the world. Many of the Romantics believed something like this. "The Imagination is not a State: It is the Human Existence itself," William Blake declares in plate 33 of his visionary opus *Milton* (1810). From this perspective, the Mariner's glittering eye *emits* light and imagination creates our experience of the world as true and real.

The most famous and most explicit Romantic response to Plato's challenge, however, must be Shelley's *A Defense of Poetry* (1821), a late essay written a year before Shelley's untimely death. This essay focuses on the social value of the poet. Knowing that "enthusiasm" is found "both in the fleshy seeing of the crowd and the highest flights of poetic imagination,"[28] Shelley argues that the difference between the two is that the "fleshy seeing of the crowd" does not create anything useful whereas the "poetic imagination" is "the unacknowledged legislator of the world." "Poetry" is much more than a literary activity; it is participation with, and admiration of, the true and the beautiful wherever we find it, in religious belief, scientific theory, technology, politics, ethics—everything. Everything humanity has ever created was first imagined. Even Plato's *Republic*, which banishes the poets, is, in Shelley's sense, poetry.

In "The Fall of Hyperion: A Dream" (abandoned before Keats's death in 1821), Keats recognizes, with Shelley, that both fanatic and poet deal with the same raw material; the primary source material of both is the dream. Keats opens "Hyperion" with the line, "Fanatics have their dreams." And yet, so do poets. What is the difference between them? It is their approach *to* the material. As Shelley notes, the fanatic sees and experiences the dream through a "fleshy seeing" (i.e., literal seeing or fundamentalist faith as distinct from poetic faith). For Keats the crucial difference between the fanatic and the poet is that the poet saves "Imagination" by *telling* the dream with "the fine spell of words," whereas the fanatic is mutely possessed by "dumb enchantment."[29]

> For Poesy alone can tell her dreams,
> With the fine spell of words alone can save
> Imagination from the sable charm
> And dumb enchantment

For Keats the poet is "a sage, / A humanist, physician to all men," while the fanatic is the knight in "La Belle Dame Sans Merci," mutely entranced and wandering alone on the "cold hill side," enthralled *by* the dream instead of actively speaking with and engaging with the dream *as dream*.

The distinction between poet and fanatic is easier to state in principle than to recognize or attain in experience. Is the Ancient Mariner an "unacknowledged legislator of the world" or a fanatic? Which camp does Keats belong to? It is not clear, not even to Keats himself: "Whether the dream, now purposed to rehearse / Be poet's or fanatics will be known / when this warm scribe my hand is in the grave."

The Ancient Mariner in Jungian Analysis

Can we trust imagination? Put into the context of the poem, is the Mariner's glittering eye real illumination or superstitious delusion? In his *Visions Seminars*, Jung ponders this question as the distinction between "subjective psychology" and "creative imagination," a question, Jung says, that is "the great philosophical problem" central to the everyday practice of psychotherapy. "You know there is still doubt in our mind whether this is the eye that receives light, or whether it is the eye that emits light. . . . Is that thing into which I am entering my own eye, or is it the creative womb of the world? That expresses itself next in the question which every patient will put to me: Is that merely my eye, or is it creative substance? Is it a psychological fantasy or is it substantial life? Is it true or not? If it is subjective psychology, it is not true; if it is creative imagination, we can credit it with something, then we are likely to create something. You see, this question is simply the great philosophical problem whether our psyche is merely a perceptive organ, nothing but a derivation or appendix to physical processes, or something akin to a cosmogonic factor."[30] The Mariner's tale is "real in this sense," Coleridge tells us, it conveys a "dramatic truth" that clothes the "shadows of imagination" that dwell in "our inward nature" in "a semblance" of literal fact.[31] Such conjectures may seem far from the practice of psychotherapy. But everyday psychoanalysis would be impossible without poetic faith in the symbolic truth of imagination. Can we learn to see our complexes, transferences, and projections not through the "fleshy seeing" of the crowd but through the symbolically tuned eye of poetic imagination? A capacity for symbolic thinking allows both patient and analyst to trust imagination as reliable, true, and real instead of fearing it as literal distortion or delusion.

One sees this if one analyzes dreams. The work of the French philosopher of poetics and science Gaston Bachelard (1884–1962), rooted in the poetics of German and English Romanticism, recognizes "the great function of poetry is to give us back the situations of our dreams."[32] The corollary is also true: dreams give us back the situations of poetry. "In certain sorts of dreams," Coleridge writes, "the dullest Wight becomes a Shakespeare,"[33] but even if our dreams are not reminiscent of Shakespearean dramas, at a bare minimum they allow us to realize 1) the unconscious is there, and 2) it knows things that consciousness does not. Like the Ancient Mariner with the Wedding Guest, the dream tells us something we do not know, do not want to know, but need to know. In this spirit, I offer four contemporary dreams in which an Ancient Mariner confronts a Wedding Guest. Just as the confrontation between Mariner and Wedding Guest takes place at the start of Coleridge's poem, all four of the following dreams were dreamt by persons in Jungian analysis either at, or very near, the beginning of their analysis.

Dream 1: The Skinny Old Man from India

The first dream is my own. Years before I began working on Coleridge's poem, I dreamt of my own Ancient Mariner. Remarkably, as in *The Ancient Mariner*, there is in this dream confrontation with a strange homeless ancient man, "a preparation for marriage and marriage themes." My dream went as follows:

> *There is an old misshapen man, like a beggar, but also looking like he's from India or an old wise man at the same time. He is totally skinny, with a big hump on his back, in very bad shape. I am passing by him in a parking lot at the beach. He is in the back of a pickup truck, in the tailgate part, where he has just spent the night in the cold, surviving only by deep meditation. I am struck with pity for him and also angry at myself, for upon*

seeing him I remember seeing him before and wanting to help him, but evidently I didn't do anything to help him.

I go get a couple of towels, beach towels, including my green one, and give them to him for warmth. He is grateful. I ask him if he would like a place to stay? He says, yes, he would. I offer for him to stay with me. Yet at the same time, I hesitate just a bit, recognizing his misshapenness and also being a little afraid.

Then I see him walking in the parking lot toward a booth at the beach, like a food booth, where he is talking with a man behind the counter about me. He is already looking so much better! As if my act has already started to transform him. The man behind the counter has favorable things to say about me, like a recommendation. There is said something to the effect that his development will be linked to mine—or, how much he will grow will depend on my size. So, the Indian man is concerned about me for that reason.

The rest of the dream involved preparation for marriage and marriage themes.

The old man's skinny body, his alienated, lonely appearance, his homeless wandering, my fear of him, replicate the Ancient Mariner–Wedding Guest dichotomy in significant detail. For me, the ancient man is from India, the other side of the world, a place I had never been and hence an appropriate metaphor for another consciousness. The fate of that other consciousness is mutually linked to the ego, "how much he will grow will depend on my size." In other words, the two sides need each other.

Dream 2: Happy Birthday

The second dream comes from a woman in her late twenties who was going through a severe depression with suicidal ideation brought on by an abrupt crisis. Near the start of her analytic process, she dreamt she was working as a maid in a bed and breakfast on the third or fourth floor (this was not her job in waking life). In this dream, a man climbs up the steps with a bag slung over his back. He sees her, she sees him, and she is terrified because she knows that this man is carrying a sack filled with women's dismembered body parts. As the dreamer runs in terror into the streets at night, trying to escape, he runs after her. And then she does something extraordinary; she stops, turns around, and faces this terrifying figure. As she does so, the fiend walks up to her and says something unexpected: "Happy birthday." It was not her birthday at the time.

The statement in the dream is a symbol. The carrier of dismemberment is a dark Messiah, a carrier of rebirth. As we worked with this dream together, I wrote out a line from an ancient initiation rite in the session and handed it to this woman: "I count the day of my initiation as the day of my birth." She kept that little piece of paper close to her in the months to come.

This young woman was on the brink of suicide. Instead of literal death however, she "worked out the way of salvation through a symbolic death," as Jung puts it, by turning around and facing her worst fears. Her self was dis-membered and then re-membered anew. About a year later, this woman started a new career and a new relationship with a man who would become her husband and the father of two beautiful children. While it is true that her terrifying encounter with her own personal version of the Ancient Mariner drove her—as with the Wedding Guest—out of a status quo identification with her too-small psychological role of being a caretaker (a "maid"), it also drove her into a more authentic and differentiated sense of self.

Dream 3: The Aboriginal Man

The third dream is taken from the beginning of a Jungian analysis of a thirty-year-old Caucasian American man. In the dream, this man retires from a party into a room to be by himself. He crawls into bed and goes to sleep. Then suddenly a man, large and looking like a tribal Maori from New Zealand, comes into the room, approaches the dreamer, and takes out a knife. The dreamer knows that this man needs his permission to perform some sort of ritual on him and he silently gives permission. As he does so, the aboriginal man cuts the dreamer's wrist. The dreamer can feel all the blood draining out of his body, up to the point where he is on the edge of death. Then, the tribal man takes out a white bandage and binds up the wound that he inflicted.

In waking life this man was in a process of consciously confronting the transformation of his identity in the form of a career change, the loss of familial relationships, and the breakup of his marriage. The dream does not whitewash the suffering he is going through; his life's blood is being drained from his body. But the dream also pictures that life-threatening event as initiatory. The same primal force that threatens to kill the dreamer also bandages him up. This dream reminded me of Herman Melville's *Moby-Dick* (1851), in which a depressed white man, Ishmael, encounters a tattooed Polynesian "cannibal" Queequeg. Ishmael is afraid of Queequeg at first, and Queequeg initially threatens to kill Ishmael, but they become friends and by the end of the novel this "Ancient Mariner" indirectly saves Ishmael's life.

Dream 4: Get Out of Your Mother's House

The fourth dream comes from a Caucasian American man in his early forties. This man dreamt that an older African American man was trying to break into his grandmother's house where he is living in the dream. In waking life this man did not live with his mother or grandmother or spend any time with them; they lived in different cities.

> *A black man is outside of my grandmother's house; I am looking at him, and he sees me through the large plate glass windows. I am terrified and call 911 for help, but the line is dead. The black man breaks into the house. I run outside in fear, trying to escape, but I run into the intruder on the stairs. He has changed into an old man with a white, close-cropped beard. I throw a stone at him, but it just glances off his shoulder.*

Like a Wedding Guest confronted by an Ancient Mariner, the dreamer tries to run away from the man who pursues him. Also like the Wedding Guest, he is unable to escape.

We worked with this dream using Jung's technique of active imagination. The dreamer brought the dream back to mind in the session and began with the ending which does not go well. In his inner imagination he stopped throwing rocks at the old man and instead asked him a question: "What do you want?" Surprisingly, the man answered: "You need to get the hell out of your mother's house." This response was a shock to both of us! I remember the numinous feeling in the room as this statement came out of the blue, entirely unexpected. "You need to get the hell out of your mother's house" was neither a product of this man's conscious mind nor mine but it was the perfect diagnosis. There are many societies in which older men literally drive the boys out of their mother's house as part of their initiation into manhood. My patient, like most contemporary Western men, never had any such initiation, so the unconscious took over in midlife and gripped him from within.

The surprising fact revealed by this dream is that the presenting symptom of the *ego diurnus*, namely anxiety, was not actually the problem. Rather the problem was "living in his mother's house," that is, his encapsulation within a positive mother complex, which in his case meant nurturing a secret and deeply held belief that he was a special child entitled by that inherent specialness to automatic success, fame, and happiness. His anxiety is a dark Messiah forcing him to become conscious of where he is in the mother's house so that he can get out of the mother's house. But getting out necessarily entails fear because "living in the mother's house" has worked so well up to this point as a fantasy bubble defending him from harsh reality.

As this man, as a Wedding Guest, listened to his Ancient Mariner, he became concomitantly less hostile to the compensatory dynamics of the unconscious, and his symptoms of anxiety gradually began to diminish.

When the *ego nocturnus* enters our lives, we usually do not welcome him. Rather, like the Wedding Guest, in some way, shape, or form we cry out, "unhand me, grey-beard loon!" But if we do not run, and if we have a bit of poetic faith, something positive can happen. These four Wedding Guests encountered four versions of their own personal Ancient Mariner and were positively transformed by that encounter. The takeaway is that there *might possibly* be something meaningful in the approach of the *ego nocturnus.* Simply holding that as a possibility can encourage us all to take the fearful step of turning around and facing ourselves. "We know that the mask of the unconscious is not rigid," Jung writes; "it reflects the face we turn towards it. Hostility lends it a threatening aspect, friendliness softens its features."

The Ancient Mariner Is a Messiah

How many people take seriously the proposition that, as a poet, Coleridge speaks to us of reality and truth as well as beauty and feeling? This book takes that proposition seriously. So, following that up, what is the meaning of the enigmatic Mariner? Who is he?

Jung's theory of complexes is a helpful lens to look through as we explore this question. Jung defines complexes as "a collection of imaginings, which, in consequence of their autonomy, are relatively independent of the central control of the consciousness and at any moment liable to bend or cross the intentions of the individual."[34] Complexes are usually created through difficult or traumatic personal memories that are incompatible with our conscious sense of self and carry emotional charges that are beyond our capacity to integrate. For example, a negative father complex is born from the negative experience of one's father. But complexes also have an archetypal core (the *Father*) that informs our personal capacity to experience not only our biological father as a father but also as a mentor, a guide, or a tyrant. Most of us are probably used to hearing that we have complexes, but, more to the point, the archetypal core of any complex can have *us* in the same gripping and transfixing way the Ancient Mariner has the Wedding Guest. The archetypal core of a complex is a dynamism, not an airy idea; it crosses our will, forces us off our intended path, fascinates us, renders us powerless to escape. The power of an archetypal constellation is thus both stunning and terrifying to behold.

The Ancient Mariner is an example of an archetypal complex active in Coleridge's psyche. What complex might that be? I suggest he personifies Coleridge's messianic complex. To be clear, I am not suggesting that the Mariner is a *Christ* figure; he is not an image of Jesus, for Coleridge's messianic imaginings take him beyond the traditional Christian mythos of his time and place. The Mariner personifies the internalization of a messianic pattern in Coleridge's psyche; this strange figure, this outcast from collective society, reveals to us what it looks and feels like for Coleridge to voyage beyond the conscious values and conceptions of his time and place, to be possessed by a crazy desire to go beyond collective norms in search of a new revelation of God. We will have ample opportunity in the chapters that follow to explore in detail how the Mariner, as a son of the Mother, not the Father as Jesus was, brings a lunar light from the sea that was never to be found in the "kirk" or "lighthouse" on land.

There are, however, many similarities between Coleridge's depictions of the Mariner and his descriptions of Christ. Just as Christ calls his disciples, the Ancient Mariner knows who he must speak to.

> At an uncertain hour,
> That agony returns:
> And till my ghastly tale is told,
> This heart within me burns.
>
> That moment that his face I see
> I know the man that must hear me:
> To him my tale I teach.

Consider Coleridge's poem "Religious Musings" as well. In this poem, completed in 1796, approximately two years before *The Ancient Mariner*, Coleridge describes Jesus in terms quite like the Mariner, as "Despised," a "Man of Woes," yet at the same time shining with a "peculiar and surpassing light." Coleridge draws here from references found in the book of Ezekiel that Christian tradition interprets as prophetic of the coming of Jesus.

> Thou, Man of Woes!
> Despised Galilean! For the great
> Invisible (by symbols only seen)
> With a peculiar and surpassing light
> Shines from the visage of the oppressed good man.[35]

The Mariner is also a despised individual whose eyes glow with "a peculiar and surpassing light." The Mariner reflects the Jesus theme, as we shall see later in the poem, when he bites his flesh and drinks his own blood as if celebrating a Last Supper with himself to benefit the entire crew; it is as if the crew "were drinking all." Finally, there is another subtle but fascinating hint of the connection between Mariner and Jesus near the end of the poem. When the Mariner returns to land after his adventure at sea he seeks absolution from a Christian Hermit. But that holy Hermit can barely stand in the Mariner's presence and can only ask, "what manner of man art thou?" Coleridge must have known these were the words the disciples exclaimed to themselves after Jesus calmed a storm that threatened to capsize their little fishing boat: "But the men marveled, saying, 'What manner of man is this, that even the winds and the sea obey him!'"[36] Taken in this context, the Mariner is to the Hermit as Jesus is to his disciples. He is bewildering, beyond the Hermit's comprehension.

But Coleridge explicitly tells us that his Mariner is an antithesis to Jesus. He is, Coleridge states, "the everlasting wandering Jew." "He was in my mind the everlasting wandering Jew—had told his story ten thousand times since the voyage, which was in his early youth and fifty years before."[37] The Wandering Jew is a thirteenth-century Christian legend in which a Jewish man, so the story goes, is said to mock Jesus as he carries his cross to Calvary. As a punishment for his blasphemy, Jesus curses Ahasuerus to wander the earth until the end of time. From the thirteenth century to the Middle Ages, there were many reported sightings of the everlasting Wandering Jew traveling his solitary path all over Christian Europe, like the Mariner, always there in the night, in the shadows, always carrying a strange sacred or heretical light. As we shall see, Wandering Jew–like, the Mariner rejects Christ when he kills the Albatross "as if it had been a Christian soul" and wanders the earth alone as penance. From the depth psychological perspective, the Wandering Jew is not a literal person and also not a story of how the Jews killed Jesus; he is a symbolic self-portrait of Christianity's *own shadow* projected *onto* the Jew as an all-too-familiar scapegoat.

Following this analysis, if the Mariner is the Wandering Jew as Coleridge says he is, then the Mariner is the Christian shadow. And this is exactly why, I suggest, the Mariner is a Messiah. I say this because when I use the term "Messiah" I do not refer to any historical person but to an archetypal personification of one who travels beyond tradition and brings new values, a new revelation, to society. Jesus fit that pattern in this time; he upset the social and religious order and was executed as a criminal and a heretic. But the pattern exists before and beyond Jesus. The Mariner is a Messiah because the Messiah brings new values, and new values are always *new*; by necessity this means that they are always found in the shadow side of collective consciousness. The shadow side is where the new light is born, for the new is always incomprehensible to the old and is thus judged as madness or evil by the status quo ante. The messianic figure of Jesus claims to not destroy the Mosaic law but fulfill it; two thousand years later, the Mariner carries a new revelation that does not deny Christianity but goes beyond it as well.

It belongs to the messianic pattern to be incomprehensible to others as the Mariner is; Jesus, for example, spoke in parables that even his disciples could not understand, and the Mariner's tale is similarly incomprehensible to the characters in the poem who hear him, just as *The Rime of the Ancient Mariner* was incomprehensible those who read it in Coleridge's own time, as it still is today. But it does not belong to the messianic pattern that the Messiah does not comprehend himself, does not know what manner of man he is, as is true for the Mariner!

The right place for the human being is between sea and land but the Mariner is drowning on dry land, obsessed with a sense of being under the influence of a supernatural agency yet without any understanding of the meaning of that experience. For the unifying panacea of a living symbol to be poured out to the world, which is the function of a Messiah, there must be a human being who sees, feels, and understands the symbol, who can perceive its meaning. Otherwise, there is no meaning, just enchantment. When we meet him at the beginning of the poem, the Ancient Mariner is a "hypnotized hypnotist" in the words of the Jungian analyst Eric Neumann, a spellbinding mouthpiece for the unconscious and, as such, close to madness himself and constellating his own sense of madness in others.

Who is the Ancient Mariner? Is he a Messiah or a fanatic? This is the unanswered question throughout the poem. Is Coleridge's messianic complex a revelation or merely a feeling of being under supernatural agency from whatever source of delusion? My suggestion is that the Ancient Mariner is potentially a post-Christian Messiah for the modern world—that is, if anyone can understand him. This book is an attempt to understand.

CHAPTER 4

"Below the Kirk, below the Hill, below the Light-House Top"

Setting Off from Shore

For most modern people, life on land consists of schedules to fulfill, the raising of children, love interests, work projects, relationships with friends, accomplishments, money, general survival, and adaptation. But there is also another world, the sea. "Though inland we be," Wordsworth writes, "our souls have sight of that immortal sea":[1] from the psychological perspective, the relatively timeless, archetypal dimension of the psyche, the unconscious matrix out of which ego consciousness is continuously born and is continuously dying. From the very beginning, *The Rime of the Ancient Mariner* declares itself to be a modern example of a mythic *nekyia* or *katabasis*, a night-sea journey, a descent "below" the cultural landmarks.

> "The ship was cheered, the harbour cleared,
> Merrily did we drop
> Below the kirk, below the hill,
> Below the light-house top.

The Mariner's voyage is a dropping down below the collective spirituality of the Christian church (the kirk), ordinary social reality (the hill), and the European Enlightenment (the lighthouse top) in search of what is missing in the collective consciousness. The Mariner is an avatar, a word derived from the Sanskrit *avatāra* meaning "descent." As if to make the point even more explicitly, Coleridge immediately introduces the most primal image of symbolic death and rebirth, the descent and ascent of the Sun.

> The Sun came up upon the left,
> Out of the sea came he!
> And he shone bright, and on the right
> Went down into the sea.

The circuitous journey of the Sun is an emblem of the Mariner's journey; like the Sun, the Mariner will descend into the sea (die) and come up again (be reborn).

The journey of the Sun—the light by which everyone sees, the source of all life—is *the* primordial image of the symbolic death and renewal of consciousness. The image goes back at least 3,500 years to the ancient Egyptian *Amduat* (ca. 1500 BCE) or the book of what is in the underworld, which tells the story of how the Sun god dies in the west and journeys on a ship through the waters below before being reborn in the east.[2] The Egyptians painted the journey of the Sun in the underworld on the walls of the tombs of pharaohs to help guide them on their journey through death. The pharaohs, and later many Egyptian people, hoped to accompany the Sun god on his journey after they died and thus attain the secret of eternal renewal. But the *Amduat* also states that it is good for the living to have knowledge of the underworld, "a true remedy [proven] millions of times." In other words, it seems that the ancient Egyptians had an inkling of symbolic as well as literal death.

From the modern psychological perspective the Romantics took toward their poetic journeys, going *below* symbolizes a journey into "some untrodden region of [the] mind" rather than a literal death or a metaphysical place.[3] In stanza 29 of his amazing poem "Adonais: An Elegy on the Death of John Keats" (1821), Shelley replaces the Egyptian Sun god with a "godlike mind," the poet's own mind, that like the Sun rises from and sinks into "the spirit's awful night."

> "The sun comes forth, and many reptiles spawn;
> He sets, and each ephemeral insect then
> Is gather'd into death without a dawn,
> And the immortal stars awake again;
> So is it in the world of living men:
> A godlike mind soars forth, in its delight
> Making earth bare and veiling heaven, and when
> It sinks, the swarms that dimm'd or shar'd its light
> Leave to its kindred lamps the spirit's awful night."[4]

As it is with the Sun, "so it is in the world of living men," Shelley states. And so it is in Jungian analysis as well where patients who embark on the analytical process often have dreams and fantasies of descent into "the spirit's awful night" we call the unconscious.

Into the Darkness

Taken within the context of Coleridge's poetry, the journey of the Mariner below the hill, kirk, and light-house top is a journey of depression. In "Lines Written at Shurton Bars, September 1795," Coleridge uses the image of "beneath the light-house tower" to describe a landscape of melancholia.

> Even there—beneath the light-house tower—
> In the tumultuous evil hour . . .
>
> And there in black soul-jaundic'd fit
> A sad gloom-pampered Man to sit.

The "sad gloom-pampered Man" "beneath the light-house tower" in "Shurton Bars" suffers from a "black soul-jaundic'd fit," a morbid condition. He is alone, alienated from the warmth of family and conjugal love. But the imagination also comes alive in this solitary landscape; lightning flashes reveal the presence of a "toiling tempest-shatter'd bark," a ghost ship that with the next lightning flash proves to have never been there at all!

When mountain surges bellowing deep
With an uncouth monster-leap
Plung'd foaming on the shore.

Then but the Lightning's blaze to mark
Some toiling tempest-shatter'd bark:
Her vain distress-guns hear:

And when a second sheet of light
Flash'd o'er the blackness of the night—
To see *no* Vessel there!

Is "Shurton Bars" a premonition of *The Rime of the Ancient Mariner* which would follow a few years later?

Leaving aside the question of whether depression is necessary to poetic creativity, as a psychoanalyst I can assert with moral certainty that depression belongs to the journey of psychological transformation. A depression is not an illness. Or rather, it is not only an illness. Without discounting the value of clinical diagnoses, it is significant to note that in all the myths in which life energy disappears from consciousness (the sun) and descends into the unconscious (the sea), the journey "below" in search of an enigmatic treasure not found "above"—such as in the ancient Egyptian *Amduat*, the Greek Orphic and Eleusinian mysteries, various shamanic and initiatory rituals worldwide, the Christian rite of baptism, the death and rebirth opus of alchemy—is horrifying but also meaningful and transformative. Romantic literature follows suit. Keats's "The Fall of Hyperion: A Dream," Shelley's *Prometheus Unbound*, Wordsworth's *The Prelude*, and Coleridge's *The Rime of the Ancient Mariner* are but a few examples.[5]

It is very common, however, in the modern West to think of depression only as something that needs to be immediately fixed. And understandably so. If a depression goes deep enough, one inevitably deals with emotions, as well as somatic symptoms, that can become life-threatening. Certainly, all psychotherapists and all those who have lived through a depression are aware of how depression can render us immobile, overwhelm us with despair, leave us fragmented or blown to bits, eroded from within and left for dead without energy for life. And yet, the feeling of being depressed can have causes other than illness; a stage of life may be coming to an end, or we may be confronting the loss of someone we love or feel overwhelmed by inner or outer realities we have sought to avoid. In addition, it is important to differentiate consciously suffered grief, that is, deep sadness usually caused by death of one sort or another, from clinical depression. Grief, like distress, loss, disappointment, and misfortune, is human and it can lead to wisdom, or knowledge born of experience. In fact, developing the strength and conscious capacity *to grieve* is in many cases the antidote to depression.

The typical sadness that life inevitably brings, even a severe and unusual state of darkness, can become a doorway to transformation *if* we confront and actively engage it. Things change by dying, which is why Jung believed that symbolic death is the antidote to literal genocide. This archetypal truth, however, is foreign to the modern mind. The modern mind resists death in all forms and fights against it, much as the Wedding Guest struggles to free himself from the Mariner.

Merrily Did We Drop

In his book *The Enchafèd Flood: or, The Romantic Iconography of the Sea* (1950), W. H. Auden points out an important and meaningful fact: in classical Western literature, the sea is always a place of purgatorial suffering. Only dire necessity suffices to venture into the sea. Any other motivation is hubris, excessive pride or defiance of the gods, ignorance, foolishness, even madness. In other words, if a sea voyage is taking place in ancient literature, you can be sure that something has gone drastically wrong on land. "The putting out to sea," Auden asserts, "the wandering, is never voluntarily entered upon as a pleasure . . . it is a pain which must be accepted as cure, the death that leads to rebirth, in order that the abiding city may be built."[6] Another way to put this, from the psychological point of view, is to say that if a regression into the unconscious is taking place—personally in psychotherapy or collectively as in a crisis in society—you can be sure something has gone drastically wrong with the conscious standpoint, and so there is a sinking down of energy into the unconscious in a search for what is missing; the descent of consciousness (the sun) into the unconscious (the sea) has a goal as well as a cause.

Why does the Mariner set out to sea? What is he seeking? The poem does not say. Looking back in time, however, we know that in the late eighteenth and early nineteenth centuries European cultural and religious values were starting to wear thin. The tremendous changes brought about by the industrial and scientific revolutions, as well as the erosion of fundamentalist faith in the traditional God of the Bible, were all starting to be felt. On the one hand, the Romantics fully embraced the Enlightenment project, but on the other hand they were canaries in the coal mine who sensed before others the unintended negative consequences of enlightened rationalism and the scientific and industrial revolutions that emerged from it. Feeling deeply that all was not right on land, the Romantics were compelled, in one way or another, to set sail and find what collective consciousness was missing. As a reward, the culture often mistook them for heretics or madmen.

When the Mariner sets off from shore, he "merrily" drops below the cultural icons, as if on a pleasure cruise.

> "The ship was cheered, the harbour cleared,
> Merrily did we drop
> Below the kirk, below the hill,
> Below the light-house top.

While it is easy to quickly pass over these lines, if we listen to them with psychological ears their innocence is astonishing. Merrily did we drop into the underworld? Merrily did we descend into the banished, repressed, unknown, and unexplored dimensions of the psyche? "Deliberately to seek the exile is still folly," as Auden notes. The Mariner is on a ship of fools, for he is the only one who will return from the voyage alive, and this only after going through a living death.

France: A Recantation

The Mariner's "merrily did we drop" attitude reflects a naivete noticeable in Coleridge as a young man. As mentioned in part 1, Coleridge had never set foot on a ship when he wrote *The Ancient Mariner* but he had metaphorically departed from shore; he threw the full weight of his enthusiastic imagination into the French Revolution and Pantisocracy, that over-the-top fantasy of creating a society of poet-farmers on the banks of the Susquehanna River in the United States where all were to "rule equally." Both adventures were inspired by the dream of the European Enlightenment—

liberty, equality, and the perfectibility of human nature through reason. Thomas Poole, one of Coleridge's closest friends who respected Pantisocracy but did not participate, wrote in a letter, "Could they realize [Pantisocracy] they would, indeed, realize the age of reason."[7] Realizing the age of reason was the dream not only of Pantisocracy but of the French Revolution as well; the revolutionaries famously renamed the cathedral at Notre Dame from "Our Lady" to the "Temple of Reason."

Being irredeemably idealistic and naive as he "merrily" dropped below collective consciousness, it is obvious in hindsight that Coleridge would inevitably be crushed by the unconscious shadow side of Pantisocracy and the French Revolution (i.e., by unrecognized power drives). As a young political and philosophical revolutionary, Coleridge was blind to the unreasonable dimensions of the human psyche that loom large, like saurian monsters, "Below the kirk, below the hill, / Below the lighthouse top." With Robespierre's executions by guillotine in 1793–94, a prolonged and almost impossible to believe sustained act of psychotic revenge that took the lives of over 17,000 perceived enemies, Coleridge's faith in realizing the age of reason was viscerally challenged. In 1795, when one of the original visionaries of Pantisocracy, the poet Southey, inherited some money and decided to stay in London, that naive idealism continued to be tempered. Then, in 1798, when Napoleon invaded peaceful Switzerland, Coleridge's intellectual defenses shattered and he fell hard into "Reality's dark dream!" ("Dejection: An Ode").

As it turns out, setting off from shore to apocalyptically transform the self and the world was, and is, much less rational and involves a lot more pathology than Coleridge imagined in his early twenties. Apparently sensing this in April of 1798, Coleridge confesses the death of his hope to create liberty on earth in "The Recantation: An Ode," later renamed "France: An Ode."

> The Sensual and the Dark rebel in vain,
> Slaves by their own compulsion! In mad game
> They burst their manacles and wear the name
> Of Freedom, graven on a heavier chain!
> O Liberty! with profitless endeavour
> Have I pursued thee, many a weary hour;
> But thou nor swell'st the victor's strain, nor ever
> Didst breathe thy soul in forms of human power.

"The Sensual and the Dark rebel in vain, / Slaves by their own compulsion!" That is a potent and piercing psychological condemnation of the revolutionaries born of bitter experience: political revolution is doomed to fail if it does not address the power problems within *every* human heart.

"In Reality, It Doesn't Go like That, but Quite Differently"

In 1915, the second year of World War I, Jung attended a sermon by the pastor Adolf Keller which brings to mind Coleridge's ship "merrily" descending below the cultural landmarks in search of renewal. Jung listened as Pastor Keller delineated what he believed to be the three stages of psycho-social transformation: 1) self-knowledge and self-reflection leading to, 2) a revision of attitude that brings about, 3) the brotherhood of mankind. Keller's sermon must have had a "merrily did we drop" feeling to it, for Jung wrote Keller a letter thanking him for the sermon and appreciating Keller's good intentions but also diplomatically suggesting that Keller's point of view is unrealistically idealistic: "In reality, it doesn't go like that, but quite differently."

In this important early letter, Jung offers Keller a preview of what would later become Jung's theory of individuation, a conceptual term that refers to a process of psychological development akin to mythic symbolic death. Jung's early map also has three stages, but they are much darker than Keller's. The first is "Introversion" or the individual's disengagement from society, that is, setting off from shore. This necessarily involves hate and misunderstanding as it brings one down into the "libido in the mother," or contact with energies in the unconscious that the rational mind experiences as a psychotic awakening of the archaic. The descent into the libido (the sun), into the mother (the sea), is horrific but also meaningful for it eventually leads to "hatching," or mystical union.

> Dear Friend!
>
> Thank you very much for your Day of Prayer and Repentance sermon, the beautiful word which I have taken into my heart. May I make a small remark about your psychological process? Of course, under the assumption, that I know, you couldn't have expressed it any differently in your sermon.
>
> You describe the process: Self-knowledge and Self-reflection—Revision of Attitude—Brotherhood of Mankind. With this logical insight, I agree. Why are human beings such fools as not to do this? They could, by means of insight and will—as we have been doing to this day. In reality, it doesn't go like that, but quite differently. Namely, this process must be lived (i.e. long and intensively): Then the following occurs:
>
> I. Stage: Introversion: The individual's disengagement from society. Due to the too strong common attitude, this does not work without misunderstanding, animosity and hate = war.
>
> II. Stage: Libido in the mother: Awakening of the archaic = psychosis. Unleashing of the highs and lows. An almost

anarchistic situation, in any case, dissolution of society to the highest degree (Dismemberment motive).

III. Stage: Hatching: Mystical development and union, about which I know too little, which I can sense rather than know. Because we have not come that far in our own experience. The dismemberment of the old is not yet completed. The isolation is awful. It has its start in national isolation.[8]

"The task in these times," Jung concludes, "is to preach to the first stage: Guiding the person to turn inwardly," which necessarily involves "the individual's disengagement from society." There is an obvious parallel here to the imagery of the Mariner dropping below the kirk, the hill, the lighthouse top on his way out to sea. Coleridge's Mariner similarly finds himself face to face with the "libido in the mother," a bizarre inner world where "slimy things . . . crawl with legs upon the slimy sea," where sexual drives and fantasies repressed as evil and unethical by the Christian status quo demand to be seen, where swamplands of archaic imagination banished as delusion in the age of reason are all too real, before he receives the transformative revelation of a "flash of golden fire" in the dark depths. By the time Coleridge writes the *Biographia Literaria* in 1817, he seems to be well aware that exploring the human soul includes exploring "the reptile's lot."

> The butterfly the ancient Grecians made
> The soul's fair emblem, and its only name—
> But of the soul, escaped the slavish trade
> Of mortal life! For in this earthly frame
> Ours is the reptile's lot, much toil, much blame
> Manifold motions making little speed
> And to deform and kill the things,
> Whereon we feed.[9]

As an older man, twenty years after the Bastille, Coleridge realized that humans have a reptilian limbic brain that is as brutal and cold-blooded as an alligator and geared toward prey-predator dynamics rather than high-flying ideals. Jung seems to have sensed from the start of his departure from shore that "the isolation is awful," that the "archaic = psychosis," and that when it comes to the hoped-for goal, "mystical development and union," he knows "too little."

A year later Jung was forced to practice what he preached. In 1916, Jung began his own journey inward, his own disengagement from society, as recounted in the *Red Book*. As in *The Ancient Mariner*, Jung's *Red Book* begins with the image of a ship sailing away from hill and kirk on land. What setting off from shore meant for Jung included renouncing his status as the de facto crown prince of Freud's psychoanalytic movement, resigning from his prestigious professorship at the ETH (the MIT of Switzerland), stopping all publication of papers and books, and engaging taboo sexual relationships and seemingly psychotic inner states. Jung experienced everything he wrote about in his letter to Pastor Keller and lived his disengagement from society long and intensively.

When Jung returned to shore, he told his tale publicly in the (relatively speaking) rational voice of a medical doctor in the *Collected Works*. There, Jung declares the spirit of the depths to be neither evil nor delusional but natural and meaningful. Although society at large did not comprehend Jung's tale, the collective did see him as an Ancient Mariner, to such an extent that *Time* magazine put Jung on the cover in 1955, at the ripe old age of eighty, under a banner reading, "Exploring the Soul."

When Coleridge's Mariner sails off from shore, he takes the first step on the journey into the secret depths of the mind's oceans. When a terrifying storm blasts his ship off course, the journey begins in earnest.

CHAPTER 5

"And Now the Storm-Blast Came"

The Great Wind Takes Control

Any feeling the Mariner might have briefly enjoyed that he is "merrily" setting out on a pleasure cruise is quickly blown to bits when a STORM-BLAST arises at sea. Wherever the ship's crew *think* they are heading, or wherever it is that they *want* to go, is irrelevant now: The great wind is in control. In Greek, the word for wind is also the word for spirit, *pneuma*. This is true in Hebrew as well, *ruach*. The wind is God. A "sound like the rush of a violent wind" accompanies the presence of the Holy Spirit on Pentecost. In dreams and myths, thunderstorms, like many natural phenomena such as earthquakes and fires, represent tremendous psychosomatic upheavals. One cannot consciously control powerful emotion any more than one can stop the wind. In a 1959 letter, Jung describes "God" as "an apt name given to all overpowering emotions in my own psychic system, subduing my conscious will and usurping control over myself."[1]

The Mariner's ship is not in the hands of a beneficent deity. It is pursued by a "foe" who is both "tyrannous and strong." In the biblical tradition, the North wind is the shadow side of the divine spirit. Descartes reports a dream in which a torrential North wind blows him around in a circle three or four times and then pushes him violently toward a church. In her commentary on this dream, von Franz points out that Descartes was in doubt whether that North wind was the spirit of God or Satan, for in the Bible "Satan," von Franz writes, "was thought to be a *ventus urens* [burning wind], coming out of the North."[2] Similarly, Isaiah 14:12 associates the North with Lucifer, and Jeremiah 1:14 states, "From the North shall an evil wind break forth upon all the inhabitants of the land."[3] Surely Coleridge, being who he was, must have been familiar with these biblical resonances as he wrote of the northern STORM-BLAST taking the ship under its control. Coleridge capitalizes STORM-BLAST in this passage, something he does only three other times in the poem, with the ALBATROSS, DEATH, and LIFE-IN-DEATH. The feeling effect of the capitalization is that it magnifies the importance of the image and draws us in. The French artist Gustave Doré (1832–83) appears to have been very much drawn in; his engraving of Coleridge's STORM-BLAST depicts a terrifying, almost unbelievable tempest that dwarfs the Mariner's ship with huge waves and cyclones.

Coleridge's lines here are particularly evocative.

> And now the STORM-BLAST came, and he
> Was tyrannous and strong:
> He struck with his o'ertaking wings,
> And chased us south along.
> With sloping masts and dipping prow,
> As who pursued with yell and blow
> Still treads the shadow of his foe,
> And forward bends his head,
> The ship drove fast, loud roared the blast,
> And southward aye we fled.

In fleeing, the crew demonstrate how much they are under the control of the storm. The word "catastrophe," in fact, comes from

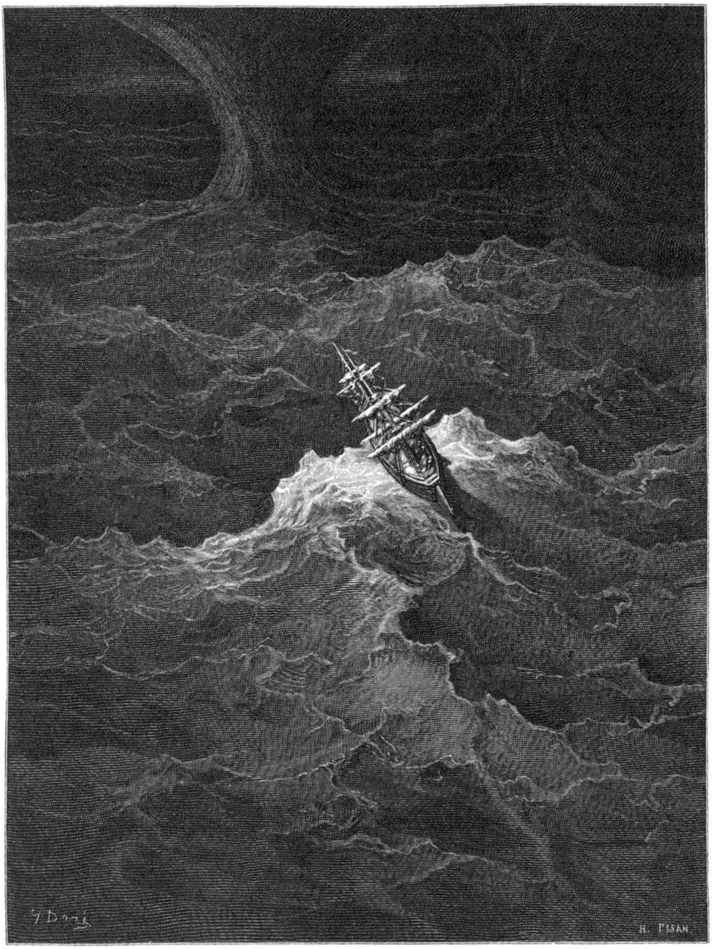

the Greek *kata* or going down, and *strophe* or turning, as in *strophos*, an ancient Hellenic whirling wheel that is related to the whirlwind. The Mariner's STORM-BLAST is a catastrophe in the classical sense of the word—a whirlwind forces him *down*. In Coleridge's "Monody on the Death of Chatterton" alluded to earlier, a "vexing Storm-blast" expresses the "bleak freezings of neglect" that blew Chatterton's life apart and drove him to suicide.

Thee, Chatterton! these unblest stones protect
From want, and the bleak freezings of neglect.
Too long before the vexing Storm-blast driven
Here hast thou found repose!

Coleridge could empathize with Chatterton for he was driven from within by similar emotional tempests.

While it is true that our own journey toward wholeness might start, as Joseph Campbell famously points out, with following our bliss, it is equally likely to begin with a terrifying and unwanted evacuation order from within that forces us out of previous adaptations, with an eruption of blocked-up rage, an obsession that appears seemingly out of nowhere, anxiety or some other type of ego dystonic emotion related to the bursting forth of repressed trauma. A midlife crisis, or the threat of losing a primary relationship, any number of catastrophic experiences can drive us against our will into the unknown.

Clinical psychology is devoted to understanding the causes of our catastrophes by tracking them back to events in our personal lives and helping us move beyond them, we hope, with the goal of returning to normal. But from the Jungian perspective, the STORM-BLAST has a hidden goal. The catastrophe can lead where we do not want to go but need to go.

Artists are especially susceptible to these storms. "A creative person," writes Jung, "has little power of his own life. He is not free. He is captive and drawn by his daimon and fated to follow his or her own yearnings far from the beaten path."[4] Very often in Romantic literature the poet's psychopathology, his or her genuine suffering, daimonically drives him or her away from the safety of the status quo on land and toward a new revelation out at sea. In Shelley's "Adonais: An Elegy on the Death of John Keats" (1821), for example, a tempest arises "darkly, fearfully," and drives the poet's "spirit's bark" far away from the "trembling throng" on land. The storm alienates the narrator in "Adonais" from society but ushers him toward the "Eternal."

> The breath whose might I have invok'd in song
> Descends on me; my spirit's bark is driven,
> Far from the shore, far from the trembling throng
> Whose sails were never to the tempest given;
> The massy earth and sphered skies are riven!
> I am borne darkly, fearfully, afar;
> Whilst, burning through the inmost veil of Heaven,
> The soul of Adonais, like a star,
> Beckons from the abode where the Eternal are.

Shelley's inner storm is dark and frightening, but it is also meaningful. Similarly, Nietzsche's Unknown God who "roams through my life like a storm" is essential to his creativity.

> Once more, before I move on
> and set my sights ahead,
> in loneliness I lift my hands up to you,
> you to whom I flee,
> to whom I, in the deepmost depth of my heart,
> solemnly consecrated altars
> so that ever
> your voice may summon me again.
> Deeply graved into those altars
> glows the phrase: To The Unknown God.
> I am his, although I have, until now,
> also lingered amid the unholy mob;
> I am his—and I feel the snares
> that pull me down in the struggle and,
> if I would flee,
> compel me yet into his service.

I want to know you, Unknown One,
Who reaches deep into my soul,
Who roams through my life like a storm—
You Unfathomable One, akin to me!
I want to know you, even serve you.[5]

Driven by the STORM-BLAST, our personal lives are chaotic, upsetting, and out of control. However, a wish to only sail in peaceful harbors can lead to a life that is stultifying, merely normal, routinely comfortable, cut off from inspiration and growth. In "Dejection: An Ode" (1802), a poem written to his unrequited love Asra, Coleridge finds himself uncomfortably caught in the latter situation. The remedy? Coleridge evokes a "deadly" storm—his feelings of passion for a woman not his wife projected into the storm—in the hope that it "might startle [his] dumb pain," "set [his] soul abroad," and break him out of numb dissociation.

And oh! that even now the gust were swelling,
    And the slant night-shower driving loud and fast!
Those sounds which oft have raised me, whilst they awed,
    And sent my soul abroad,
Might now perhaps their wonted impulse give,
Might startle this dull pain, and make it move and live!

"We possess *art*," Nietzsche writes, "lest we *perish of the truth*."[6] In "Dejection," it is "Reality's dark dream" that threatens to psychologically kill Coleridge. Lest he perish of the truth, Coleridge deliberately leans into the swerve of the morally ambiguous and borderline psychotic dimensions of his erotic imagination in which heretical, daimonic, sexual, and pagan qualities swirl around in passionate chaos. These are the qualities Coleridge's split-off soul needs, and, since his feelings toward Asra are relatively split off from conscious acceptance and are not lived, he projects them into the wind as a hoped-for savior. There is chaos in the storm, but also a "mighty poet." The storm is a "mad Lutanist" that "mak'st Devil's yule," exactly the medicine that might save Coleridge's too-realistic, too-conventional, too-repressed, too-domesticated, too-normal life.

In "Dejection," the storm tells a story of wounded men suffering on the battleground of life, shuddering with cold. There is another voice in the storm as well, the terrified moans and loud screams of a lost girl searching for mother.

> A tale of less affright,
> And tempered with delight,
>
> As Otway's self had framed the tender lay,—
> 'Tis of a little child
> Upon a lonesome wild,
> Nor far from home, but she hath lost her way:
> And now moans low in bitter grief and fear,
> And now screams loud, and hopes to make her mother hear.

Perhaps the lost girl is Coleridge's innocence lost on the masculine battlefield of life; perhaps she is his feeling of being an orphan; perhaps she simply personifies the feeling of losing contact with *Life*. The anima is the archetype of Eros and Life, the emotional experience of feeling alive. That is what Coleridge lacks as he sits down to write "Dejection."

There is also a mythic story to consider. In Greek mythology, the maiden Persephone screams for her mother Demeter as Hades drags her to the underworld. The Persephone myth was the basis of the ancient Greek Eleusinian mystery rites, celebrated continuously from the fifteenth century BCE all the way to the fourth century CE, in which the initiates participated in a ritualized *imitatio Demeter*, a search for the feminine spirit lost to the underworld. Similarly, Orpheus searches throughout Hades for his lover Eurydice. Orphic mystery rites came to Coleridge's mind as he listened to Wordsworth recite his autobiographical night-sea journey, "The Prelude," which was for Coleridge "that prophetic lay . . . an Orphic song indeed."[7] The same could be said of *The Ancient Mariner*. As we shall see in detail later, *The Rime of the Ancient Mariner* is *Coleridge*'s Orphic song, his prophetic lay, his search in the darkness of the underworld for a feminine spirit lost to conscious life.

CHAPTER 6

"The Land of Mist and Snow"

Trauma and Transcendence

The STORM-BLAST takes the keel and drives the Mariner's ship into a frozen wasteland at the bottom of the world, a land of ice and snow, an impersonal white world where the crew find themselves far from the hill, kirk, and lighthouse on land, a place devoid of people and even animals, a dramatic way station of magnetism and danger essential to the Mariner's unfolding journey.

And now there came both mist and snow,
And it grew wondrous cold:
And ice, mast-high, came floating by,
As green as emerald.

And through the drifts the snowy clifts
Did send a dismal sheen:
Nor shapes of men nor beasts we ken—
The ice was all between.

The ice was here, the ice was there,
The ice was all around:
It cracked and growled, and roared and howled,
Like noises in a swound!

As the Mariner's ship drifts aimlessly through the mist, the ice surrounds him on all sides: It makes uncanny, wild sounds, it "cracked and growled, and roared and howled, / Like noises in a swound!" reminding one of the famous lines from Shakespeare, "It [life] is a tale / Told by an idiot, full of sound and fury, / Signifying nothing."[1] "Swound," an old English word for fainting, also rings in the ear as a combination of "sound" and "wound." Thus, the "noises in a swound" evoke the sensation of losing consciousness, a failure of apperception, the mental process by which we assimilate new experiences by relating them to something known or familiar. Such is the psychological experience of being *lost*; it is a loss of orientation, a loss of meaning, a descent into chaos.

The South Pole in *The Ancient Mariner* is a lunar world: "All the night, through fog-smoke white, / Glimmered the white Moonshine." Coleridge had read books speculating that the moon is a frozen ocean. In the margins of one of these books he writes, "Moon has little or no atmosphere. Its ocean is frozen. It is not yet inhabited, but may be in time."[2] We remember Jung's psychotic patient who "lived on the moon." This woman was a victim of sexual abuse in early life, and the overwhelming force of that devastating experience caused her to retreat from reality. Reality, and contact with people, was too painful. And so, instead of living, she sought shelter in an impersonal icy solitude of a world of pure imagination. Psychosis, and schizoid defenses that are less intense forms of psychosis, freezes the conscious personality in figurative ice to protect it from reexperiencing the "bleak freezings" of early trauma.

All the various psychological defenses—repression, denial, projection, dissociation, intellectualization—seek to protect consciousness from reexperiencing trauma, but they each do so in different ways. The borderline personality, on the one hand, is caught in an eternal fire of passionately enacted suffering; schizoid types, on the other hand, turn toward the ice, dissociate from suffering, and thereby lose not only the fires of passion but even a feeling of warmth and connection to self and others. For example, a therapist I was supervising once told me that in working with a borderline patient filled with unpredictable rage, it felt to her "like the whole room was on fire." By way of contrast, a schizoid patient sitting in my office once described feeling icy cold as he reexperienced early abandonment memories, even though the room was at a normal temperature.

Trauma and Transcendence

Paradoxically, there is an archetypal radiance in the icy white world, as well as danger. Icy white world landscapes can evoke both trauma and transcendence. I remember being both mesmerized and terrified by the whiteness of the snowy peaks all lit up in the moonlight one night in Colorado. I felt both the magnificence and the inhumanity; this impersonal world was astonishing, mesmerizing, and beckoning with sublimity and awe, but I also knew that if I were left out in the snow overnight in forty-below-zero weather, I would die! My body would lose its human warmth and turn cold. D. H. Lawrence expresses this paradox clearly and beautifully: "The ice and the upper radiance of snow are brilliant with timeless immunity from the flux and warmth of life. Overhead they transcend all life, all the soft moist fire of the blood. So that a man must needs live under the radiance of his own negation."[3]

In Dante's fourteenth-century *Inferno*, the ninth circle of hell is all ice and reserved not for saints but for figures such as Cain and Lucifer who departed from the conventional pathways of the known, the good, and the sacred. From Nietzsche's perspective, it is his rebelliously expanded consciousness that lands him in the ice, and then the ice becomes a loneliness all its own: "Light am I . . . this is my loneliness to be begirt with light. . . . Alas, there is ice around me, my hand burneth touching iciness."[4] Similarly, Saint Teresa of Avila (1515–82), a mystic whose life was defined by intense psychological and physical suffering, testifies that her ecstatic spiritual visions were accompanied by a somatic sense of cold. She experienced that coldness as the presence of the divine. "In these raptures," as she calls them, "the soul no longer seems to animate the body; its natural heat therefore is felt to diminish and it gradually gets cold, though with a feeling of very great joy and sweetness." And Shelley speaks of a pure white world set apart from ordinary personal life as "the white radiance of Eternity." His "spirit's bark" is, like the Mariner's, blasted far from the shore of human community but is not lost; it sails to the Eternal.

> The One remains, the many change and pass;
> Heaven's light forever shines, Earth's shadows fly;
> Life, like a dome of many-coloured glass,
> Stains the white radiance of Eternity.[5]

Shelley's ecstatic desire to connect to the Eternal is so intense, so all encompassing, that he even yearns for death to touch it: "—Die, / If thou wouldst be with that which thou dost seek!"

"Frost at Midnight"

Coleridge's poem "Frost at Midnight" (1798), written the same year as *The Ancient Mariner*, is a beautiful meditation on the paradox of trauma and transcendence in the white world. It begins with this line: "The Frost performs its secret ministry / Unhelped by any wind." As the poem develops, Coleridge brings us into his little cottage as he looks out over a snowy landscape late at night. The moon is above, frost nips at the windows, his wife is in bed, and he is alone with his infant son sleeping peacefully by his side. All is calm and silent, "so calm, that it disturbs / And vexes meditation with its strange / And extreme silentness."

The silence leads Coleridge, and us, into a meditative reverie that takes him back through a string of associations to the years of freezing neglect he endured as a child and teenager at Christ's Hospital, the school and orphanage he attended after the death of his father at the age of ten. To fully appreciate "Frost at Midnight," we must know that Coleridge spent seven years at Christ's Hospital after his father died, years in which he dreamt of his "sweet birth-place" in the Devon countryside but never returned, years in which his mother never once visited him, years in which other boys would go home for holidays while Coleridge would wander alone through the streets of London. Coleridge survived by imagining. He imagined he was back at home in Devon. He imagined friends and family were visiting him at Christ's Hospital.

As the "gentle breathings" of his baby son Hartley slip into his thoughts, Coleridge's mind becomes permeable to these early painful memories. But he also opens to "abstruser musings." The "deep calm" evokes memories of being trapped "'mid cloisters dim," but the "secret ministry" of frost "quietly shining to the quiet Moon" also inspires imagination. Coleridge was a prisoner but his infant son Hartley will wander free.

> . . . For I was reared
> In the great city, pent 'mid cloisters dim,
> And saw nought lovely but the sky and stars.
> But *thou*, my babe! shalt wander like a breeze
> By lakes and sandy shores

"But *thou*, my babe!" The secret ministry of frost is imagination at work, secretly ministering to Coleridge's trauma with its own autonomous life just as snowflakes form themselves into beautiful mandalas, healing and transforming frozen memories of abandonment into patterns of hope.

The Albatross Splits the Ice

Turning our attention back to the Mariner's ship, we find it stuck in the ice seemingly without hope of rescue or escape. All seems doomed. But suddenly an Albatross appears. He sails out of the fog, circles the ship, and splits the ice.

> And round and round it flew.
> The ice did split with a thunder-fit;
> The helmsman steered us through!

The Iconology of Cesare Ripa (1624)—a highly influential seventeenth-century guide to the symbolic meaning of emblems found in Egyptian, Greek, Roman, and other sources—states, "When the sea men meet a swan with their ship, that is a good sign; for then the ship is not swallowed up by the waves."[6] So it is in *The Rime of the Ancient Mariner*. The Albatross is the secret ministry of frost taken wing, an angel of imagination, healing the trauma of being "on the Moon," stuck in a frozen, schizoid world.

CHAPTER 7

"At Length Did Cross an Albatross"

Spirit from Above

Stuck in the ice, apparently without hope, a white bird suddenly appears out of the mist and fog—Coleridge's Albatross. The crew welcomes the Albatross "in God's name," "as if it had been a Christian soul." The "pious bird of good omen" circles "round and round" the ship and miraculously splits the ice, freeing the ship and bringing a "good south wind" (the antidote to the northern STORM-BLAST) that sends the ship back home.

> And round and round it flew.
> The ice did split with a thunder-fit;
> The helmsman steered us through!

Like the Shekinah (God's presence in the Hebrew tradition based on a Semitic root meaning "to settle, inhabit, or dwell," often used to refer to birds nesting), the Albatross perches on the mast of the ship like God's presence on the Ark of the Covenant for nine evenings, presiding over vespers, the evening prayer: O God, come to our aid. *O Lord, make haste to help us.* "Whiles all the night, through fog-smoke white, / Glimmered the white Moon-shine," at night, deep in the sea, in the moonlight and white mists, the

Albatross brings a sacred experience of hope to the lost crew of two hundred men.

Vespers is a Catholic prayer, but the sacred presence of a godlike bird as saving grace is common to many religious traditions. Joy Harjo, who served three terms as the twenty-third poet laureate of the United States from 2019 to 2022, beautifully captures the sacred spirit of Coleridge's Albatross from the perspective of a woman originally from the Muscogee Nation in Oklahoma in her "Eagle Poem" (1990).

> To pray you open your whole self
> To sky, to earth, to sun, to moon
> To one whole voice that is you.
> And know there is more
> That you can't see, can't hear;
> Can't know except in moments
> Steadily growing, and in languages
> That aren't always sound but other
> Circles of motion.
> Like eagle that Sunday morning
> Over Salt River. Circled in blue sky
> In wind, swept our hearts clean
> With sacred wings.
> We see you, see ourselves and know
> That we must take the utmost care
> And kindness in all things.
> Breathe in, knowing we are made of
> All this, and breathe, knowing
> We are truly blessed because we
> Were born, and die soon within a
> True circle of motion,
> Like eagle rounding out the morning
> Inside us.
> We pray that it will be done
> In beauty.
> In beauty.

As a contrast to the Albatross in *The Rime of the Ancient Mariner* who appears to a crew of two hundred men and whose natural habitat is the night, the mist, and the moon, in "Eagle Poem," a magnificent eagle, in daylight, on Sunday morning, brings a living prayer to one woman. Rather than welcome the bird in God's name in a traditional Judeo-Christian sense, the narrator says, "We see you, see ourselves." She knows that she prays to "[our] whole self / To sky, to earth, to sun, to moon / To one whole voice that is [us]." I will return to the depth, complexity, and unity of Harjo's vision in the discussion of Coleridge's understanding and experience of imagination later in this chapter.

The Wandering Albatross

One can feel the symbolic resonance of Coleridge's Albatross in parallels taken from poetry, like Harjo's eagle. But one can also intimately connect with these animals of imagination by knowing something about the biological animal.

The name "albatross" dates to the fifteenth century, when Portuguese sailors first ventured down the coast of Africa and came across large black-and-white birds with powerful bodies. They called these birds "alcatraz," meaning large seabird. Later, English sailors corrupted the name to "albatross." The wandering albatross of the Antarctic, which Coleridge's Mariner encounters, is the largest and most impressive of all the twenty-three species of albatross. It is an incredible, majestic animal, an eagle of the sea. With a strong, large hooked beak and a wingspan of eleven to thirteen feet, the wandering albatross is one of the largest flying birds in the world. These birds often follow ships at sea, circling "round and round." Not only this, albatrosses regularly circle "round and round" the globe! They set off in a straight line and keep going until they return home.

Scientists know that migratory songbirds have two compasses, one celestial and one magnetic, and they believe the same is probably true for seabirds. One contemporary theory, yet to be proven, is that migratory seabirds see the magnetic field of the earth. However they manage it, in a single flight, wandering albatrosses can cover distances of an incredible 1,800 to 9,300 miles, greater than the diameter of the earth. Coupled with their long lifespan of up to eighty-five years, albatrosses travel farther during their lifetimes than any other animal. One scientist calculated a conservative estimate that by age fifty the average albatross has probably traveled 3,747,600 miles.[1] It is possible for albatrosses to cover these vast distances because they lock their wings in place and soar, thus gliding effortlessly on the compressed air above the waves. In this way, the birds reach speeds of fifty miles per hour, and one has even been clocked in a swooping burst of seventy miles per hour. Utterly magnificent in the air, the albatross is relatively ungainly on land. The wandering albatross rarely comes in for a landing except to feed and breed and then waddles around uncomfortably, attributes that remind me of Coleridge's intuitive genius and the limitations of his high-flying bird when it came to living on the ground.

The magnificent Albatross may thus invoke feelings of a deep instinctual pattern within us, one that knows how to survive stormy seas, that knows the way home, an instinctual pattern of orientation, a deep knowing beneath the rational mind.

The Secret of the White Bird in Psychotherapy

In folklore and myth, the hero, or the one in need, typically turns to the guidance of animals only when all has failed, when willpower and rationality come up against an "impossible problem." So it is in *The Rime of the Ancient Mariner*: the Albatross appears only when all is lost, when the crew cannot find their way out of the ice themselves. So it is in Jungian analysis as well.

In 1996 I was lost at sea. In the afterword to this book, I go into some detail about my personal story, but for now I will just say that the conventional paths toward career, love, family, and God had disappeared. It was as if an earthquake had reduced the goals and values of my conventional, normal, suburban life to rubble. Without a foundation on land, I was lost at sea, disoriented, and precariously placed in a dangerous state of alienation and depression. Like the ship's crew in *The Ancient Mariner*, all felt meaningless, chaotic, stuck, dark. I could not stop being depressed, and the consequences were becoming dire.

Not knowing what else to do, I reached out for psychological help. The night before my first session with a Jungian analyst, I had a dream. As is widely known in Jungian psychology, the initial dream is a clear indicator of both the problem and the solution to the problem, if there is one. In this initial dream the secret to my depression was to find a white winged bird—in my case, to "find the Dove."

> *I am having my first meeting with a woman psychologist. I arrive at her office, she greets me, and we begin the session. I feel sad and low and begin to talk about my depression. At one point, she looks in my eyes very intently and says, "What we must do is find the Dove, find where the Dove is, that is the secret." As the session ends, we get up and I hug this woman. She is large, solid; hugging her feels like wrapping my arms around a big oak tree.*

A wise woman appears in the semblance of a psychologist, acknowledges my suffering, and delivers the healing message. She points to the animal. She, not I, knows the secret. Of course, I projected that dream woman onto my analyst, and she became in my eyes that wise woman. But the secret belongs to the feminine principle.[2]

Coleridge, the proto-depth psychologist, says, "In the treatment of nervous disorders, he is the best doctor who is the most ingenious inspirer of hope." The dream was my best doctor. In a rare burst of enthusiasm, I went out and bought art supplies and painted

Thomas Elsner, *Find the Dove* (1996), used with permission of the author.

the dream on a large canvas, 4' × 2'. In this painting, a white bird descends from above in mist over a black background and the words of the female psychologist frame the image. I vividly remember putting this painting up on a wall and staring at it; it seemed so other, so utterly unlike anything I would ever say, or ever think. Under no circumstances would I have ever let anyone other than my analyst see this painting. I knew the feeling of the black, but the white bird shining through the darkness like Coleridge's Albatross crossing "thorough the fog" was strange, ego dystonic. The painting was *my* secret, as was the fact that I was in psychotherapy at all.

Years later I discovered that Jung had to "find the Dove." In Jung's *Red Book*, his autobiographical account of a psychological crisis so severe it bordered on psychosis, the first chapter is entitled "Refinding the Soul," and inside the first beautifully embellished letter of that chapter there is a white dove with outstretched wings. "I found you where I least expected you," Jung writes to his soul as a white winged bird in the *Red Book*; "you climbed out of a dark shaft." The genesis of Jungian psychology thus mirrors the situation in Coleridge's *Ancient Mariner* and my own psychological landscape: a modern man searches in disorientation, despair, and depression for a white winged bird. Not being a religious believer, I eventually came to welcome the white bird, not in God's name (as the ship's crew do in *The Ancient Mariner*) but rather in the name of the living symbolic dimensions of the unconscious mind.

Remembering that the Albatross circles "round and round" the ship, I was drawn, in this respect, to Coleridge's descriptions of the symbolic in *The Statesman's Manual* (1816). There, Coleridge uses the image of "self-circling" to describe the "living educts of imagination" that organize an otherwise chaotic flux of sense impressions—the "noises in a swound"—into a "system of symbols." In this passage, Coleridge beautifully expresses the truth, reality, and supreme value of the symbolic as "a translucence of the Eternal through and in the Temporal": "A Symbol . . . is characterized by a translucence of the Eternal through and in the Temporal. It always partakes of the Reality which it renders intelligible; and while it enunciates the whole, abides itself as a living part in that Unity, of which it is the representative."[3] The symbolic shines with a meaning that is *really there* in inner and outer nature. The Albatross personifies the symbolic in Coleridge's sense of that word.

The White Bird and Christianity

Christianity was the mythic context of the Mariner's time and place, and it was also Coleridge's religion. Coleridge was the son of a clergyman, born, raised, and buried a devout member of the Church of England. Three years before he published *The Ancient Mariner*, in 1795 at the age of twenty-three, Coleridge had already published the first of his many theological works, *Lectures on Revealed Religion*. It is no surprise then that the crew welcome the Albatross "with joy and hospitality" through the lens of Christian faith—"As if it had been a Christian soul, / We hailed it in God's name." The sea

This image derives from Genesis 8:6–12, "And again [Noah] sent forth the dove out of the ark; and the dove came to him in the evening; and, lo, in her mouth was an olive leaf plucked off: so Noah knew the waters were abated from off the earth."

bird hovers above the Mariner's ship "like Jesus in the sky," to borrow a phrase from Jackson Browne's "Rock Me on the Water" (1972).

> Rock me on the water
> Sister, will you soothe my fevered brow?
> Rock me on the water

The baptism of Jesus by John the Baptist. Ceiling mosaic at the Arian Baptistery in Ravenna, Italy.

> I'll get down to the sea somehow
> Oh, people, look among you
> It's there your hope must lie
> There's a seabird above you
> Gliding in one place like Jesus in the sky

Throughout the Bible, the white winged bird is a divine messenger who brings hope when all is lost. One famous example is the story of Noah's ark in which the dove brings back an olive branch as proof that God's flood is at an end. The white bird also descends from Heaven during Jesus's baptism. "And Jesus, when he was baptized, went up straightway out of the water: and, lo, the heavens were opened unto him, and he saw the Spirit of God descending like a dove, and lighting upon him."[4] The presence of the white bird is what marks the difference between baptism as a ritual of symbolic death and rebirth and simply taking a swim, or drowning.

Poetic Faith in the Truth and Reality of Imagination

Confessed Christians make up about a third of the world's population today, over two billion people. There are billions more believers from other faiths. Many modern souls, however, do not welcome anything in God's name. An estimated two billion people identify as atheists and agnostics. Practically the entire modern world, therefore, can be divided into three categories: Religious believers, atheists, and agnostics. For those who no longer believe in God, any idea of a "holy spirit" is delusion, or fantasy; for them, the Albatross is just a bird. But there have always been persons guided by poetic faith in the truth and reality of imagination per se, as distinct from either fundamentalist faith or materialistic rationalism. These are the solitary individuals who see things differently from others and are therefore as likely to be burned at the stake as heretics as to be canonized as saints, sometimes both. Jung was one of these types. Disparaged as a mystic by the atheistic rationalists, Jung was at the same time banished by many theists as a heretic for psychologizing away God.

One of the most beautiful examples of poetic faith is a passage from Melville's *Moby-Dick*. It comes to us through Ishmael's eyes, through his description of a numinous encounter with an albatross in the Antarctic. Ishmael is strikingly reminded of Coleridge's Albatross as he recounts his own vision of "secrets which took hold of God."[5]

> I remember the first albatross I ever saw. It was during a prolonged gale, in waters hard upon the Antarctic seas. From my forenoon watch below, I ascended to the overclouded deck; and there, dashed upon the main hatches, I saw a regal, feathery thing of unspotted whiteness, and with a hooked, Roman bill sublime. At intervals, it arched forth its vast archangel wings,

> as if to embrace some holy ark. Wondrous flutterings and throbbing shook it. Though bodily unharmed, it uttered cries, as some king's ghost in supernatural distress. Through its inexpressible, strange eyes, methought I peeped to secrets which took hold of God. As Abraham before the angels, I bowed myself, the white thing was so white, its wings so wide, and in those for ever exiled waters, I had lost the miserable warping memories of traditions and towns. Long I gazed at that prodigy of plumage. I cannot tell, can only hint, the things that darted through me then, but at last I awoke; and turning, asked a sailor what bird was this. A goney he replied. Goney! I never had heard that name before; is it conceivable that this glorious thing is utterly unknown to men ashore! Never! But some time after, I learned that goney was some seamans' name for albatross. So that by no possibility could Coleridge's wild Rhyme have had aught to do with those mystical impressions which were mine, when I saw that bird upon the deck. For neither had I then read the Rhyme, nor knew the bird to be an albatross. Yet, in saying this I do but indirectly burnish a little brighter the noble merit of the poem and poet.

Ishmael is transfixed. He has never seen an albatross and does not even know its name but as he comes up from the decks below is immediately astonished and mesmerized by this bird's wild majesty. As with the ship's crew in *The Ancient Mariner*, Ishmael's thoughts turn to God. Like Coleridge, he emphasizes the whiteness of the bird: "As Abraham before the angels, I bowed myself, the white thing was so white, its wings so wide."

The Ancient Mariner was published some thirty or forty years prior to the date in which *Moby-Dick* is set, the 1830s or 1840s. Thus, Ishmael takes pains to convince us that his experience has nothing to do with Coleridge's famous poem, for, as he says, "neither had I then read the Rhyme, nor knew the bird to be an albatross."

The "mystical impressions" flooding Ishmael in the presence of the Albatross, he insists, are his alone; imagination creates the perception of "vast archangel wings." It is nature inside and out—not Coleridge's personal imagination—that is the source of the bird's "spiritual wonderment." "Bethink thee of the albatross, whence come those clouds of spiritual wonderment and pale dread, in which that white phantom sails in all imaginations? Not Coleridge first threw that spell; but God's great, unflattering laureate, Nature." Melville's Albatross is "the white phantom [that] sails"—not only in *The Ancient Mariner* and not only in Ishmael's personal fantasy—but "in all imaginations."

So why is it then that the crew of the *Pequod* do not see "this glorious thing" as Ishmael does with a power of supernatural speech and "inexpressible, strange eyes" that mirror the secrets of God? The crew in *Moby-Dick* are typical modern men for whom the albatross is nothing-but a bird, a "goney," a mere object. They are released from the spell of traditional fundamentalist faith, but are left with only the "fleshy seeing of the crowd," as Shelley puts it; they lack poetic faith in the truth and reality of imagination. That is also the case on land where, it seems, everything is a gooney bird, nothing an archangel. That is why Ishmael is depressed and why, instead of committing suicide or murder, his feelings turn toward the sea. "Whenever I find myself growing grim about the mouth; whenever it is a damp, drizzly November in my soul; whenever I find myself involuntarily pausing before coffin warehouses, and bringing up the rear of every funeral I meet; and especially whenever my hypos get such an upper hand of me, that it requires a strong moral principle to prevent me from deliberately stepping into the street, and methodically knocking people's hats off—then, I account it high time to get to sea as soon as I can. This is my substitute for pistol and ball. With a philosophical flourish Cato throws himself upon his sword; I quietly take to the ship. There is nothing surprising in this. If they but knew it, almost all men in their degree, some time or other, cherish very nearly the same feelings towards the ocean with me."[6] Instead of succumbing to the depression and despair he experiences on land, Ishmael sets off to sea to hunt for the "white thing [that] was so white." He touches that whiteness in the semblance of the mystic albatross. Later, of course, the big catch is the white whale Moby Dick. Moby Dick is not, as Coleridge's Albatross appears to be, an emblem of pure, one-sided innocence, purity, beauty, and love but is also filled with the *terror tremendum*, the "transcendent horrors" of both spirit and nature, "a certain nameless terror" of the divine.

The Fate of Imagination in the Modern World

Ishmael's albatross appears to him cloaked in "clouds of spiritual wonderment and pale dread." Similarly, the Albatross in *The Ancient Mariner* dwells in white mist, fog-smoke, and Moon-shine.

> In mist or cloud, on mast or shroud,
> It perched for vespers nine;
> Whiles all the night, through fog-smoke white,
> Glimmered the white Moon-shine.

For the rational spirit of the European Enlightenment, the "mist" and "Moon-shine" that circle around the Albatross are emblematic of ignorance, delusion, and superstition. You cannot see clearly in the fog and can easily get lost. Similarly, moonshine means foolish talk, illusion. For Coleridge, however, "Moon-shine" is a luminous revelation direct from the unconscious mind itself—like a dream. In Coleridge's notes written on an unsealed leaf of Jakob Böhme's *Works 1764–81*, he compares the mind of the inspired eighteenth-century German mystic Böhme, whom he admires, to a "*luminous mist*": "But being a poor and unlearned man he contemplated Truth and the forms of Nature thro' a *luminous Mist*, the vaporous darkness rising from his *Ignorance* and accidental peculiarities of fancy and sensation, *but the Light streaming into it from his inmost Soul.* And even when he wanders in the shades, ast tenet umbra Deum [yet the shadow contains a God]."[7] For Coleridge, the luminosity that streams from Böhme's "*inmost Soul*" and shines through the "vaporous darkness" of his scientific ignorance is not delusion, nor madness; it is God.

Similarly, in Coleridge's "Dejection: An Ode," there is a "light, a glory" which issues forth from the "soul itself" as "a fair luminous cloud / Enveloping the Earth" and uplifts the mind with all that "we aught behold, of higher worth."

> O Lady! We receive but what we give,
> And in our life alone does Nature live:
> Ours is her wedding garment, ours her shroud!
>   And would we aught behold, of higher worth,
> Than that inanimate cold world allowed
> To the poor loveless ever-anxious crowd,
>   Ah! From the soul itself must issue forth
> A light, a glory, a fair luminous cloud
>   Enveloping the Earth—
> And from the soul itself must there be sent
>   A sweet and potent voice, of its own birth,
> Of all sweet sounds the life and element!

Imagination is Nature's "wedding garment" and her "shroud," the human voice hidden in "all sweet sounds." In "Constancy to an Ideal Object" (1828), Coleridge takes pains to remind us that all our ideal objects, all our gods, laws, art, philosophy, religion, science, mathematics—everything—are reflections of the human form.

And art thou nothing? Such thou art, as when
The woodman winding westward up the glen
At wintry dawn, where o'er the sheep track's maze
The viewless snow-mist weaves a glist'ning haze,
Sees full below him, gliding without tread,
An image with a glory round his head;
The enamoured rustic worships its fair hues,
Nor knows he makes the shadow he pursues!

For Coleridge, and the Romantics in general, we are not *Homo sapiens*, wise humans, but *Homo imaginatus*, imagining humans. Even *Homo faber*, man defined as the maker of tools, depends on *Homo imaginatus*, for everything we have ever made was first imagined. The narrator in "Eagle Poem" knows this; she says of the eagle, "We see you, see ourselves." But the ship's crew are unaware that "we receive but what we give, / And in our life alone does Nature live."[8]

It is difficult, and thus rare, for our species to recognize the presence of imagination per se. One the one hand, imagination is traditionally interpreted through the eyes of fundamentalist faith as God, the gods, or reified metaphysics. On the other hand, enlightened modernity equates imagination with a distortion of fact, or fantasy, as in "you're imagining things," or "that's just a myth"—something unreal, something we are better off without, something that others might be trapped in but not us. Very seldom do we stop to reflect whether *our* most cherished values might be products of imagination. "I'm a good person," "social justice," "we can change the world into a better place," "the rational is the good," "continued economic growth," "fairness," "save the planet," "technology will save us," "I'm going to be famous," "American exceptionalism," "be true to yourself"—even these generalized platitudes carry the de facto power of religious icons if we worship them without recognizing we create the shadows we pursue.[9] Today, "politics" is very often the word we give to the churning cauldron of archetypal imagination that religions used to specialize in. When religious containers are shattered, however, as they are for the most part today, then political figures and ideologies become unrecognized containers for deep and powerful archetypal energies. In the late 1950s, at the very height of the Cold War, Jung pointed this out. "You can take away a man's gods," he observes, "but only to give him others in return": "The dictator State has one great advantage over bourgeois reason: along with the individual it swallows up his religious forces. The State takes the place of God; that is why, seen from this angle, the socialist dictatorships are religions and State slavery is a form of worship. . . . The policy of the State is exalted to a creed, the leader or party boss becomes a demigod beyond good and evil, and his votaries are honoured as heroes, martyrs, apostles, missionaries. There is only one truth and beside it no other. It is sacrosanct and above criticism. Anyone who thinks differently is a heretic."[10] These insights of Jung's are chillingly accurate, and more relevant today than ever. A 2017 *Forbes* article entitled *Is Ideology Becoming America's Official Religion?* makes much the same point.[11]

There are many who are "experts at" recognizing the fundamentalism of others, but few, it seems, who have the capacity to reflect on their own. Those who believe in the Second Amendment, just to pick one example among many, as something not only worth dying but killing for, are as devoted to a sacred ideology as the most devout believer in any metaphysical deity. I have talked with people on both sides of the political aisle who, completely straight-faced and in all sincerity, have told me how the world would be better off if they could only kill "the Republicans" or "the woke leftists." Sometimes, I ask them how many people they would be willing to kill in pursuit of their ideal society? "The Republicans," for instance, comprise about forty million people in the United States. While most of us are not likely to kill or die for our political convictions—the immense power of social conditioning, cowardice of pain and death, and fear of punishment hold us back from acting out these murderous impulses—none of us are immune to feeling a pull toward power and revenge, especially where we feel wronged, invalidated, or devalued.[12]

This is all to say that imagination is a powerful force with the utmost practical consequences. Imagination can destroy us, and it also makes life worth living. Even granting our collective tendency toward one-sidedness, literalization, and fundamentalism, where would we be without imagination? We would be lost in the chaos, like the Mariner's ship is lost.

> And through the drifts the snowy clifts
> Did send a dismal sheen:
> Nor shapes of men nor beasts we ken—
> The ice was all between
>
> The ice was here, the ice was there,
> The ice was all around:
> It cracked and growled, and roared and howled,
> Like noises in a swound!

Devoid of imagination (*anima*, animal, *anima mundi*), we do not see the world as it is but as an "inanimate, cold" world, the Mariner's land of ice and snow before the Albatross appears.

I suggest, therefore, that developing the capacity to welcome *our sacred values with hospitality in whatever form they take and wherever they might appear* with poetic rather than fundamentalist faith is a step forward in the evolution of human consciousness. There is "a grandeur in the beatings of the heart," as Wordsworth writes.[13] This does not mean, however, that we must elevate that grandeur to the level of a metaphysical dogma to appreciate its value, nor devalue it as an illusion to recognize its humanity. In between the dichotomy of fact and delusion, a dichotomy that almost defines the modern mind, there is a third alternative, the symbolic, that unites them both. Coleridge's Albatross personifies the symbolic. The fate of the Albatross is the fate of the symbolic; this is the central dynamic in *The Ancient Mariner.*

The White Dove Hidden in the Lead

A tenth-century Islamic alchemist living in Egypt, Muhammad Ibn Umail, wrote that "the white winged bird" is "the operator of the work from its beginning till its end. And without it the work cannot exist."[14] The alchemists of old knew there was a "white dove hidden in the lead" and they searched for the shining revelation in the abject darkness of mind and nature. As a Jungian analyst, I can affirm the value of their search. A psychoanalysis without imagination is a psychoanalysis of causation but no purpose, of facts without meaning, of loss but no sacrifice, willpower but no inspiration, knowledge but no wisdom. The symbolic expresses the unconscious, and that is why Jungian analysis, at its finest, seeks to constellate an atmosphere that is conducive to the unfolding of the symbolic expressions of the autonomous, indwelling spirit—the Dove, the Albatross.

The white bird brings hope; when all is lost, we *must* find it. And then, sometimes, we must also sacrifice our ideals and sacred truths in the name of further development. "You should be a vessel of life, so kill your idols," Jung writes in the *Red Book.*[15] In *The Ancient Mariner*, that means that the Albatross, the one-sidedly good, innocent, high-in-the-sky spiritual ideal, must die.

PART 3

Initiation

CHAPTER 8

"I Shot the Albatross"

The Birth of the Modern Soul

Part 1 of *The Rime of the Ancient Mariner* ends with this stark line: "—With my cross-bow / I shot the ALBATROSS."

> "God save thee, ancient Mariner!
> From the fiends, that plague thee thus!—
> Why look'st thou so?"—With my cross-bow
> I shot the ALBATROSS.

The poem never reveals why the Mariner shoots the sacred bird, but what we do know is that, many years later when he confronts the Wedding Guest, the Mariner is still possessed by demons of guilt and regret. "I had done a hellish thing," the Mariner cries out.

Killing the Albatross is the central crisis in *The Rime of the Ancient Mariner*. "I shot the ALBATROSS" is the ending of part 1. The following five parts, six out of seven in total, all end with a reference to the Mariner's "hellish" crime.

> *Part Two*
> Ah! well a-day! what evil looks
> Had I from old and young!

Instead of the cross, the Albatross
About my neck was hung.

. . .

Part Three
And every soul, it passed me by,
Like the whizz of my cross-bow!

. . .

Part Four
The self-same moment I could pray;
And from my neck so free
The Albatross fell off, and sank
Like lead into the sea.

. . .

Part Five
"Is it he?" quoth one, "Is this the man?
By him who died on cross,
With his cruel bow he laid full low
The harmless Albatross.

The spirit who bideth by himself
the land of mist and snow,
He loved the bird that loved the man
Who shot him with his bow."

. . .

Part Six
I saw a third—I heard his voice:
It is the Hermit good!
He singeth loud his godly hymns
That he makes in the wood.
He'll shrieve my soul, he'll wash away
The Albatross's blood.

Sacrilege

The shooting of the Albatross in *The Rime of the Ancient Mariner* is defined by the Mariner as a sacrilege. At the same time, it is also a sacrifice creating space for new developments, something that is not explicitly acknowledged in the poem.

The sacrilegious dimension of the Mariner shooting the Albatross reflects the modern world's degenerating relationship between humans, animals, and God. For instance, as if he were describing the Ancient Mariner himself, the nineteenth-century German philosopher Arthur Schopenhauer (1788–1860) writes that "men are the devils of the earth, and the animals are its tormented souls."[1] Most likely, Schopenhauer was not thinking of Coleridge when he wrote that line; perhaps he had European sailors in mind, "sportsmen" as they called themselves, who routinely "fished" albatrosses by line and hook or shot them out of the sky. The sailors would then haul the birds onboard and break their wings before tossing them back into the sea. Or perhaps Schopenhauer was thinking of the British merchant sealers who were hard at work on Albatross Island near Tasmania exterminating the seal population for profit while Coleridge wrote the *Ancient Mariner.* While they were at it, these men also killed vast numbers of albatrosses for their feathers as the birds nested peacefully on land. The sailors called them "gooney birds."[2] Why? Because these birds were, the sailors thought, so stupid that they did not immediately flee in terror when human beings came around. What a staggering, yet unintentional, confession of the devilish nature of modern consciousness.

The horrific reduction of nonhuman animals to objects in the modern West extends to the foundations of science. In the seventeenth century, the intelligentsia in Europe wondered, "Do animals have souls?" People like René Descartes (1596–1650) answered that question with a resounding "No." Descartes did not welcome nonhuman animals as if they were "Christian soul[s]." Instead, he saw animals as objects and treated them accordingly. A particularly gruesome example can be found in Descartes's experiments, where he reportedly spread-eagled dogs to boards and dissected them alive without anesthetic at public demonstrations, marveling at how their still-beating heart valves opened and closed on his fingers, all the while dismissing the animals' howls of pain as nothing but the noises of biological machines.[3] Descartes's vivisection of dogs, as well as other animals such as cows and rabbits, holds a special place among the most hellish crimes that human beings have ever committed. Descartes's scalpel is a real-life example of the Mariner's crossbow and arrow.

It may sound strange to say that animals do not have souls if one knows that the word "animal" is based on the Latin *animalis* from *anima*, breath or soul. But that conclusion is easier to comprehend once one realizes that many philosophers during the seventeenth and eighteenth centuries in Europe identified soul, their own as well as that of animals, with rationality and self-awareness. Emotion, somatic reactions, and instinctual responses had nothing to do with soul, or as we would say today, consciousness; these were perceived as nothing but mechanical responses to stimuli. Thus, the screams of tortured dogs are not language but biological noise.

We human beings become devils of the earth when we disconnect intellect from feeling. Then we experience ourselves as separate from the world. Thus, one can reverse Schopenhauer's statement and it remains equally true: "Men are the devils of the earth, and their souls are tormented animals." Certain materialistic scientists and philosophers of the time treated their own souls as they treated those of nonhuman animals. This attitude filtered down into the general groundwater of modern consciousness, affecting many of us centuries later.

In dreams, tormented animals belong to our worst nightmares. Near the start of my work in Jungian analysis, I had such a dream, a horrific dream, in which all the animals in the jungle had been murdered and their bodies piled up in a gruesome mass.

> *I am in a jungle, standing there, an observer, looking around. In the center of my field of vision is a horrific nightmare image: a very large pile of dead animal bodies. They look like a mass grave, as if somebody had killed them all and thrown them all together, a mass, just a dead mass of animals. I have no sense of connection to this sight, or the story of what happened. A woman emerges from the jungle; she is wild, clearly the ruler of this place, the "Lady of the Beasts." When she sees the grave of animals, evidently for the first time, just learning they had all been killed, she becomes furious. Her eyes lock on me. She draws a stone knife and advances toward me, uncontrollable with rage. She believes I have done this and she is about to kill me. Just as she raises her knife a voice says "No!" and she stops, but not before cutting me slightly with the knife.*

The death of all the animals in this dream is an intimately personal and, at the same time, collective problem. It points to a peculiarly modern enmity between humanity and nature—within and without—that is symbolically mirrored in the sacrilegious trajectory of the Mariner's arrow. The killing of the Albatross is, in Coleridge's own words, an image of "nature in antithesis to the mind, as object to subject, thing to thought, death to life!"

Sacrifice

The Ancient Mariner is set in a Christian cosmos and is replete with the archetypal imagery of traditional folklore and myth. The

Albatross is not just a bird. He is a "pious bird of good omen." Therefore, when the Mariner raises his crossbow to shoot the Albatross, he takes aim at God. In his famous engraving of the Mariner shooting the Albatross, Gustave Doré pictures the bird with outstretched wings like Christ's arms on the cross. He also matches the angle of the Mariner's arrow to exactly that of the lance thrust into Jesus' side. Clearly, the idea is that when the Mariner kills the Albatross, he kills Christ.

Worldwide, traditional wisdom states that murder of the sacred object entails destruction. When Christ dies in the biblical story, darkness covers the land from noon until three, the curtain of the sanctuary is torn in two from top to bottom, the earth quakes, rocks are split, and tombs are opened.[4] In folklore, the protagonist who kills or fundamentally disregards the advice of the helpful guiding animal—what could a stupid fox teach me?—always goes down the tubes. One can also observe the dark consequences of killing the sacred animal in dreams. For example, when a man kills a white bird in an American woman's dream, as recounted in Jung's *Visions Seminars*, and darkness falls, Jung comments that it is "exactly what one would expect."[5]

At this point in the poem, the crew are contained within traditional Christian wisdom. Therefore, they expect that some hellish thing will "work 'em woe" after the Mariner shoots the sacred animal that "made the breeze to blow!"

> And I had done a hellish thing,
> And it would work 'em woe:
> For all averr'd, I had killed the bird
> That made the breeze to blow.
> Ah wretch! said they, the bird to slay,
> That made the breeze to blow!

But when the Holy Ghost dies in *The Ancient Mariner*, something happens that is exactly what they did *not* expect!

> Nor dim nor red, like God's own head,
> The glorious Sun uprist:
> Then all averred, I had killed the bird
> That brought the fog and mist.

Christ on the cross with lance in his side. Fra Angelico (ca. 1440) Fresco at the Dominican monastery at San Marco, Florence.

'Twas right, said they, such birds to slay,
That bring the fog and mist.

God dies, but darkness does not fall, the breeze does not stop to blow. On the contrary, the Sun rises and the ship sails on triumphantly with the breeze at its back as if it were winning a race, the "first" to sail into uncharted seas.

The fair breeze blew, the white foam flew,
The furrow followed free;
We were the first that ever burst
Into that silent sea.

Freed from unconscious dependence on some miraculous spirit, the crew rejoice in their active will; they "burst" into virgin territory, a description oozing with masculine-yang *virtue*—action, vitality, movement, speed, freedom. The Sun rises "like God's own head," the birth of the modern soul as it takes the place of God.

Coleridge's poem is not just a recapitulation of traditional wisdom; it is a founding fable of the modern age. While mythic wisdom regards the killing of a sacred animal as the Mariner himself regards it, as a "hellish thing," in the modern age, killing the Albatross, so to speak, is a good thing, a Promethean advance that ushers in progress, liberation from superstition, and the emergence of the *I* from its identification with tradition and the *We*—in other words, a sacrifice necessary for further development. Killing the Albatross ushers in a new dawn that promises so much: awakening from dogmatic slumbers, freedom from superstition, clear vision, the discovery of a new world.

No longer spellbound by the "Moon-shine," the crew seem to wake up from a dream. In the clear light of day, they see how things really are: the Albatross is just a bird. He did not *really* save their ship, they only *imagined* he did. Therefore, the crew change their minds about the Mariner killing the Albatross. No longer are they afraid of divine retribution; now they boldly affirm, "'Twas right . . . such birds to slay, / That bring the fog and mist." When the Mariner shoots the Albatross, he does so as an *I* against the collective *We* ("I shot the ALBATROSS"). But now the Mariner's *I* is the new *we*, the new collective truth ("We were the first that ever burst / Into that silent sea"). Killing the Albatross transforms the Mariner and crew into modern men.

I therefore suggest a rewrite of Coleridge's prose gloss at this point, one that accurately locates the meaning of killing the Albatross within the transformational context of the poem itself. Instead of the moral at the end which reads "and to teach, by his own example, love and reverence to all things that God made and loveth!" we should substitute the following: "And to teach, by his own example, that the death of the Albatross is a necessary sacrifice to make the Sun rise." When the sacred white bird dies, the Mariner's ship is no longer a vessel of the Christian Middle Ages but of the age of European Enlightenment.

Enlightenment

The Enlightenment is a complex political, social, psychological, religious, and scientific phenomenon. It is closely allied with the technological and scientific revolutions, the French and American revolutions, the death of traditional religious belief, and the liberation of thought and speech from the metaphorical and literal shackles of king and pope. Nevertheless, in his 1784 essay *Answering the Question: What Is Enlightenment?*, Immanuel Kant, one of the most influential eighteenth-century philosophers, sums up the whole movement in one beautifully simple phrase: *sapere aude*. Dare to know. This, Kant affirms, is "the motto of the enlightenment."[6] Over a century earlier, in 1660, the British Royal Society, the oldest scientific organization in the world and still active today, had already chose as its motto something very similar: *Nullus in verba*—take nobody's word for it.

According to Kant, every person—not only the king or the pope—has the potential to use their own understanding. Few, however, realize that potential. This is not due to a lack of intelligence but of courage. Thinking for yourself is hard enough, but Kant's point here is that even if you should somehow accomplish it, your reward might be, more often than not, to be sanctioned or even sentenced to death, or at the very least ostracized and canceled, as we say today, by the collective judgments of your neighbors. Few can bear the loneliness of daring to know, for it requires a kind of audacity that puts one at odds with the status quo.

For example, in 1663, the pope prohibited Descartes's books because of the central place Descartes gave to the *I* and to reason. But in the sixteenth to the eighteenth centuries, being a freethinker could not only get you canceled, it could also get you killed. Sixty-three years before the pope canceled Descartes, in 1600, the Roman Catholic Church burned Giordano Bruno (1548–1600) at the stake for daring to assert that the earth revolves around the sun, for daring to wonder if other stars might be distant suns, for daring to speculate that those suns might have their own planets, for daring to entertain the possibility that those planets could be teeming with extraterrestrial life. Thirty years later, in 1632, the Roman Inquisition would have handed Galileo Galilei (1564–1642) an immediate death sentence after finding Galileo "vehemently suspect of heresy" if Galileo had not recanted his position that, based on observation and reason, heliocentrism is the correct view of earth's place in the cosmos. Descartes shot the Albatross, as did Bruno and Galileo, and they all paid a price for their audacity.

Thomas Paine (1737–1809), one of the British-born Founding Fathers who fought for the independence of the United States, was a political revolutionary but he also, very Ancient Mariner–like, rejected "the three frauds, *mystery*, *miracle*, and *prophecy*," famously declaring, "my own mind is my own Church." [7] He made this audacious declaration in *Age of Reason*, a popular bestseller at the time that demonstrated the tension between reason and religion in the modern era, published in 1794. It is not difficult to imagine Paine reading *The Ancient Mariner* in 1798 a few years after publishing the first two parts of *The Age of Reason* and finding the Mariner a kindred spirit, for the Mariner also dares to know, affirms his own mind as his own church, and thus liberates himself and the crew from the fog and mist of superstitious ignorance. Paine was another Ancient Mariner who shot the Albatross but, living almost two centuries after Bruno, thankfully was never in danger of execution for thinking for himself.

In the opening sentences of Paine's *Age of Reason*, one finds the words "I" and "my" no less than five times, and "we" zero times. "It has been my intention, for several years past, to publish my thoughts upon religion. I am well aware of the difficulties that attend the subject, and from that consideration, had reserved it to a more advanced period of life. I intended it to be the last offering I should make."[8] Significantly, the first use of the word *I* in *The Rime of the Ancient Mariner* occurs when the Mariner declares "I shot the ALBATROSS." Before that, there are only references to a "ship," a "crew," a *we* who all think and act alike. Robert G. Ingersoll (1833–99), a famous nineteenth-century American freethinker, another Ancient Mariner, gives us a vivid picture of what it looks like in everyday life when an individual affirms "'Twas right . . . such birds to slay, / That bring the fog and mist." The use of the word *I* appears six times in Ingersoll's passage below, with no mention of a *we*.

> When I became convinced that the universe is natural, that all the ghosts and gods are myths, there entered into my brain, into my soul, into every drop of my blood the sense, the feeling, the joy of freedom. The walls of my prison crumbled and fell. The dungeon was flooded with light and all the bolts and bars and manacles became dust. I was no longer a servant, a serf, or a slave. There was for me no master in all the wide world, not even in infinite space. I was free—free to think, to express my thoughts—free to live my own ideal, free to live for myself and those I loved, free to use all my faculties, all my senses, free to spread imagination's wings, free to investigate, to guess and

> dream and hope, free to judge and determine for myself . . . I was free! I stood erect and fearlessly, joyously faced all worlds.[9]

When he realized that the universe is merely natural and that "all the ghosts and gods" are "myths," Ingersoll felt no sacrilegious guilt, no disorienting loss of meaning. Quite the contrary, like the ship's crew in *The Ancient Mariner*, Ingersoll experienced the death of God as a glorious liberation made possible by dispelling the fog and mist of superstition through the dawn of the glorious sun of enlightened reason. "I shot the ALBTROSS" and "the furrow followed free," the Mariner declares. "I was free!" Ingersoll exclaims. For Ingersoll, the death of God is not a sacrilege but a sacrifice; killing the white wings of religious dogma leaves him "free to spread imagination's wings" into worlds beyond traditional religious belief.

The Albatross and the Scientific Revolution

Francis Bacon (1561–1626), an older contemporary of Descartes's and a progenitor of modern science, fully justifies the trajectory of the Mariner's arrow in his *New Organon or True Directions concerning the Interpretation of Nature* (1620).

On the title page to the first edition of Bacon's *New Organon* we find an engraving of a ship sailing into uncharted seas past the pillars of Hercules, the dividing line between known and unknown in the ancient world, a sign of *go no further*. It is the ship of the Ancient Mariner, "the first" that ever burst into "silent seas." The epigram sums up the meaning of this voyage: "Many will travel and knowledge [*scientia*] will be increased." But there is a price to be paid for sailing the ship of knowledge into uncharted waters, a price of admission. One must kill the Albatross. In Bacon's words, one must sacrifice "a dream of our own imagination" if one is ever to see the facts of nature "simply as they are": "And all depends on

Frontispiece to Bacon's *The New Organon: or, True Directions Concerning the Interpretation of Nature* (England, 1620).

keeping the eye steadily fixed upon the facts of nature and so receiving their images simply as they are. For God forbid that we should give out of a dream of our own imagination a pattern of the world; rather may he graciously grant to us to write an apocalypse or true vision of the footsteps of the Creator imprinted on his creatures. . . . Wherefore if we labor in thy works with the sweat of our brows, thou wilt make us partakers of thy vision and thy Sabbath."[10] Killing the "dream of our own imagination"—the Albatross—gives birth to the scientific revolution. In Bacon's vision, science replaces traditional religion as the "true vision of the footsteps of the Creator."

Another motto, therefore, of the spirit of modernity, along with *sapere aude*, might be "sacrifice subjective imagination to discover objective fact." We find this motto informing Joseph Wright of

An Experiment on a Bird in the Air Pump, Joseph Wright of Derby (1768). National Gallery, London.

Derby's iconic eighteenth-century masterpiece of British art *An Experiment on a Bird in the Air-Pump* (1768), in which the birth of modern science is pictured as coinciding with the death of a white bird. Wright published this painting thirty years before the first printing of *The Ancient Mariner*.

Here we find yet another Ancient Mariner in the guise of a natural scientist holding an air pump instead of a crossbow: perhaps Joseph Priestley (1733–1804), a member of the Lunar Society in Birmingham who influenced the formation of a similar scientific society in Wright's town of Derby. Whoever the scientist in Wright's painting may be, he is demonstrating how the double-barreled air pump, a technological marvel of the seventeenth and eighteenth centuries, can suck the air out of a glass vessel and thereby create a vacuum. The proof of this is that the bird placed inside the vessel cannot fly and cannot breathe.[11] Not only birds but mice and frogs regularly died in these experiments as astounded audiences witnessed the mechanics of respiration first hand. The experiment clearly reveals that animals live by the biological mechanics of respiration alone and not by any vital spirit, mysterious ether, or *anima mundi*. Proof of the physical vacuum thus creates a concomitant religious void, and the science of pneumatics replaces the religious *pneuma*. Perhaps this is why the poet William Blake declared empirical science based on reductive reasoning to be "the Religion of the Pharisees who murdered Jesus."[12]

The proto-scientist in Wright's painting is focused entirely, almost eerily, straight ahead on his audience—us—as he conducts his experiment. He seems almost possessed; in any event, he is totally unconcerned about the fate of the bird, for its death is a necessary sacrifice of the old God made in the name of the new—knowledge. The oldest of the two girls is full of feeling and cannot bear to watch. But the man standing next to her seems to be saying, "'Twas right . . .

such birds to slay," for, as the white bird dies in the vessel above, illumination shines from below from within or behind a flask containing a strange object sometimes interpreted as the human brain. That light is the light of reason, the light of modern consciousness, of the modern *I*, and it shines "like God's own head."

Killing the Albatross thus inspires physics, chemistry, astronomy, and biology. But it also inspires Romantic literature as well. Romanticism radiates with the light of human consciousness freed of metaphysical projections. There is no such thing as Romantic literature without the death of the Albatross. In his "Ode to Psyche" (1819), for example, Keats recognizes that traditional religious imagery is dead and gone, the burnt embers of a fire lit in a past eon. After God is dead, however, Psyche remains as the "brightest" deity of all.

> O brightest! though too late for antique vows,
> Too, too late for the fond believing lyre,
> . . .
> I see, and sing, by my own eyes inspir'd.
> . . .
> Yes, I will be thy priest, and build a fane
> In some untrodden region of my mind

Paine rationally recognizes that his own mind is his own church, and Keats does as well, but in distinction to Paine, for Keats there are "untrodden region[s]" of the mind, regions of truth and reality accessible by the poetic imagination that merely rational philosophers, natural scientists, and Deists have limited access to.[13] Those are the regions of the mind that a century later Freud and Jung explored not as metaphysics and religion but as the poetry and *science* of the unconscious.

Prometheus and the Fall of Man

After the Mariner kills God and makes the Sun rise, the crew treat him as if he were Prometheus, a Luciferian figure who steals fire from the gods and gives it to humanity. Prometheus is often evoked as a kind of patron saint of the Enlightenment and of the scientific revolution. Mary Shelley, for example, entitles her prophetic novel of the dawn of science *Frankenstein; or, The Modern Prometheus* (1818) and alludes to Coleridge's *Ancient Mariner* many times throughout this wonderful book.

Coleridge appreciated the paradoxical figure of Prometheus; he is, Coleridge says, "the rebellious Spirit and the Divine Friend of Mankind." "Prometheus—that truly wonderful Fable, in which the characters of the rebellious Spirit and of the Divine Friend of Mankind (*Theos Philanthropos*) are united in the same person: and thus in the most striking manner noting the forced amalgamation of the Patriarchal tradition with the incongruous scheme of Pantheism."[14] However, when it came to finding a mythic image to express the cultural knowledge Coleridge saw rising to prominence around him in the late eighteenth and early nineteenth centuries, the biblical Fall of Man seemed a far more accurate analogy than the Greek Titan.

For Coleridge, the Mariner's crossbow, or the scientist's air pump, that places "nature in antithesis to the mind, as object to subject, thing to thought, death to life" was no Promethean liberation.[15] No, for Coleridge, the philosophy of mechanism (i.e., deterministic materialism that splits the world into dead objectivity and delusional subjectivity) was the "Antichrist." The Mariner's crossbow and arrow is "the product of an unenlivened generalizing understanding" spreading like a "contagion" throughout the educated population of Europe.[16]

In other words, the birth of the modern soul was, for Coleridge, the Fall of Man. In an 1815 letter to Wordsworth, Coleridge takes pains to remind his best friend and collaborator that, as far as Coleridge is concerned, the meaning of their joint philosophical and poetic work revolves around the recognition of "*a Fall* in some sense, as a fact," and the working out of "a manifest scheme of Redemption." One can read the following passage from Coleridge's letter, therefore, as reflective of Coleridge's intentions in writing *The Rime of the Ancient Mariner*: "To have affirmed *a Fall* in some sense, as a fact . . . to point out however a manifest scheme of Redemption from this slavery, of reconciliation from this enmity with Nature—what are the obstacles, the Antichrist that must be and already is . . . by the substitution of Life . . . for the philosophy of mechanism which in everything that is most worthy of the human Intellect strikes Death, and cheats itself by mistaking clear Images for distinct conceptions, and which idly demands conceptions where Intuitions alone are possible or adequate to the majesty of the Truth."[17] "With my crossbow / I shot the ALBATROSS," says Coleridge the poet. "The philosophy of mechanism which in everything that is most worthy of the human Intellect strikes Death," responds Coleridge the philosopher.

Satanic Self-Idolatry

Modern consciousness is proud to see itself as "God's own head." For Coleridge, however, the birth of the modern soul was a "hellish thing," more specifically, an egocentric, even megalomaniacal, power drive by which the ego replaces the I AM. From the standpoint of biblical tradition, within which both Coleridge and his Mariner are consciously (but not unconsciously) contained, the assertion that identity is subjectively defined is not an act of Promethean enlightenment but Satanic darkness. In Christian tradition it is said that the bright angel Lucifer falls into hell and becomes Satan when he refuses to recognize any authority outside his own will. Coleridge reminds us of this in his psychological interpretation of Milton's *Paradise Lost* (1667) when he states, "the character of Satan is pride and sensual indulgence, finding in self the sole motive of action."[18] Elsewhere, Coleridge identifies the Satanic with the quality of "rebellious self-idolatry." "But in its utmost abstraction and consequent state of reprobation, the will becomes Satanic pride and rebellious self-idolatry in the relations of the spirit to itself and remorseless despotism relatively to others."[19] We can practically feel the Mariner squeezing the trigger of his crossbow as we read these lines.

For the eighteenth-century French poet Jacques Clinchamps de Malfilâtre, the modern belief that "the Sun rises only for me" does not rise to the mythopoetic level of the Satanic. Nevertheless, it is illusory and precarious.

> Man said: the sky is about me . . . ,
> The Sun rises only for me . . .
> Proud mortal, dispel these illusions . . .
> What are we, . . . to let our pride reach such extremes?[20]

Malfilâtre's use of the word "pride" here is an allusion to the ancient Greek idea of hubris, that is, mortal disregard of the gods which inevitably awakens Nemesis, the goddess of retribution. In Sophocles' *Oedipus Rex* (429 BCE), Oedipus displays immense hubris when he rejects the dream of ornithomancy—the ancient divination practice of looking for signs in the flight of birds—and, very Ancient Mariner–like, asserts the centrality of the *I*. "I solved the riddle [of the Sphinx] by my wit alone," Oedipus arrogantly declares; "mine was no knowledge got from birds."[21] Despite Oedipus's confidence in his rational autonomy however, he inexorably falls prey to the oracle that he will kill his father and marry his mother. In the end, after his fate unfolds regardless of what he consciously wants or intends, Oedipus gouges out his eyes with his dead mother/wife's brooches as if to admit the blindness of his rational and ego-centric way of seeing things.

Narcissistic Defenses against the Self

Satanic self-idolatry and hubris are two examples of religious and ancient parallels to the image of the Ancient Mariner shooting the Albatross. Clinical psychologists today, however, do not use these terms when describing people who act as if their ego is "God's own head," or as if the Sun rises only for them; the correct diagnosis is narcissistic personality disorder. And it can be said that the Mariner—not as a person but as a personification of modern consciousness—displays narcissistic traits, both when he shoots the Albatross and throughout the poem, namely, a lack of empathy and disregard of the perspectives of others (both bird and crew), fear of abandonment, troubled relationships, deep depression, and pathological guilt.

We know from clinical experience how narcissistic machinations ("the world is supposed to be this way, I'll just make it be this way") employ fantasies of power and control as an attempt to defend the ego against uncomfortable feelings of insecurity, vulnerability, and ignorance. Seen through the lens of clinical narcissism, therefore, the Mariner's arrow appears as a narcissistic defense against relatedness with nature, with God, with the *we* of human community, against all that the ego cannot understand and control, against anything that runs counter to its will, that is not compatible, comprehensible, or controllable by the *I*. There is a dangerously unrecognized—even if sacrilegiously necessary—narcissism at the foundation of modern consciousness.

Morals and Meaning

The Mariner is identified with the sacrilegious, rather than sacrificial, experience of killing the sacred bird. He kills the Albatross, descends into hell, and returns to shore a repentant traveler compelled to teach, as the prose gloss explains, "by his own example, love and reverence to all things that God made and loveth!" Coleridge speaks to his audience here.

Years later, however, Coleridge publicly disowned this moralistic dimension of the poem. In a selection from his *Table Talk* dated May 31, 1830, in response to an appraisal of *The Ancient Mariner* by the prominent literary critic Anna Laetitia Barbauld (1743–1825), Coleridge says that he regrets the unfortunate "obtrusion of the moral sentiment so openly on the reader."

> Mrs. Barbauld once told me that she admired the *Ancient Mariner* very much, but that there were two faults in it—it was improbable and had no moral. As for the probability, I owned that that might admit some question; but as to the want of a moral, I told her that in my judgment the poem had too much; and that the only, or chief fault, if I might say so, was the obtrusion of the moral sentiment so openly on the reader as a principle or cause of action in a work of such pure imagination. It ought to have had no more moral than the *Arabian Nights'* tale of the merchant's sitting down to eat dates by the side of a well, and throwing the shells aside, and lo! a genie starts up, and says he *must* kill the aforesaid merchant, *because* one of the date shells had, it seems, put out the eye of the genie's son.

Speaking as a critic of his own poetry, Coleridge's opinion is that the "only, or chief fault" of *The Ancient Mariner* is that it has "too much" of a moral. Presumably what he has in mind are the closing stanzas of the poem that seem to wrap everything up with a tidy bow.

Farewell, farewell! but this I tell
To thee, thou Wedding-Guest!
He prayeth well, who loveth well
Both man and bird and beast.

He prayeth best, who loveth best
All things both great and small;
For the dear God who loveth us,
He made and loveth all.

These are moralistic lines indeed, and they are incongruous with the depth, mystery, and paradox of the Mariner's journey.

Moralism is not the same thing as meaning. The two differ in the same way that imagination and fantasy differ. Fantasy, or as Coleridge calls it, "fancy," is a faculty of "CHOICE" and "no other than a mode of Memory emancipated from the order of time and space." Imagination, by way of contrast, is a doorway to truth and reality that belongs to the highest province of poetry; at his or her best, the poet "blends and fuses by that synthetic and magical power Imagination." Imagination is not identical to consciousness but "co-exists with the conscious will" and is therefore a "mysterious power" that seeks to "create a new sense" as it "dissolves, diffuses, dissipates, in order to re-create."[22] Imagination is a revolutionary; fancy tends to affirm the status quo. Thus, the "moral sentiment" in *The Ancient Mariner* affirms the traditional Christian piety that, as will become evident later, the poem's "pure imagination" meaningfully challenges. Although Coleridge's consciously constructed moralism near the end of *The Ancient Mariner* explains very clearly that shooting the Albatross is a hellish crime understandable only in terms of guilt and regret, the *meaning* of shooting the Albatross in the poem itself suggests something else entirely. The Mariner's continuing journey, and our own journey in following him, is symbolically (rather than moralistically) concerned with the meaning of this "hellish" act.

Opus contra naturam

To sum up, when the Ancient Mariner kills the Albatross, he dares to know and declares "my own mind is my own Church." Because of his audacity, the Sun rises and the Mariner leads the ship of Western civilization out of the Christian Middle Ages into the age of European Enlightenment. The death of the Albatross is thus a sacrilege but also a sacrifice necessary for a shift from collective to individual, from reliance on religious dogma to empirical science and rational philosophy, from the Middle Ages to modernity. Shooting the Albatross is the crime against God that makes the Mariner a modern man and his tale a founding fable of the modern age.

In the Bible, I AM is the name of God. When he declares, "I shot the ALBATROSS," the Mariner places the *I* at the center of everything—not God, not nature, not human community, not the self—but the *I*. When the Mariner shoots the Albatross, human consciousness takes the place of God as if it were "God's own head," and this experience is felt as enlightening and liberating. The challenge for us, therefore, in understanding the meaning of shooting the Albatross in *The Rime of the Ancient Mariner*—and the birth of the modern soul—is the idea that evil plays a necessary role in evolution. However one understands the nature of evil, whether as murder, objectification, atheism, materialism, sin, pride, hubris, unresolved trauma, or narcissism, the Mariner's "hellish" crime is an *opus contra naturam* and *contra deus*, a work of nature against nature, a work of God against God. If the poem's moralism is an attempt to escape this paradox, one can only sympathize, for to the (like it or not) Christian sensibilities that have shaped the moral compass of the West for everyone, not only believers, the idea that evil is meant, that it belongs to the process of transformation, that it is part of God, so to speak, is incomprehensible and intolerable.

Soon, the Mariner's Sun that rises at dawn with the glorious promise of illumination will turn dark and destructive. We must keep in mind that *The Rime of the Ancient Mariner* does not end with the Enlightenment. We are only at the end of part 1 of the poem! There are seven parts to *The Ancient Mariner*, six more to come. As the Mariner faces the horror and grief of shooting the white bird, he unexpectedly finds himself en route toward the death of the Sun, an encounter with the unintended negative consequences of the Enlightenment, and the return of the repressed feminine before he finally breaks out into a renewed experience of beauty and love for the miracle of life on earth. His sacrilegious-sacrificial voyage thus leads him—and us—not only back into the historical past but forward into a prophetic future based on Christianity and the Enlightenment but going beyond them both, a way forward defined by symbolic death.

CHAPTER 9

"Water, Water Every where, nor Any Drop to Drink"

From Enlightenment to Wasteland

When the Mariner declares "I shot the ALBATROSS," the Sun (i.e., modern consciousness) rises "like God's own head" and dissipates the mist concealing objective reality and impeding conscious intention. This is a purely positive event at first, "glorious" and liberating. But in almost no time at all, the solar Enlightenment becomes dangerously antithetical to life.

The promise of the Sun rising at dawn newborn and "glorious" fails to live up to its promise when it reaches its "bloody" apex at noon. At its zenith, there are no shadows, no fog and mist, no moonshine, no Albatross, no dream of imagination. Everyone sees in the clear and bright light of day how things really are. And what is the result? The wind dies down. The ship stops. Drifting in the doldrums, the crew finds itself in a two-dimensional world, "As idle as a painted ship / Upon a painted ocean."

> All in a hot and copper sky,
> The bloody Sun, at noon,
> Right up above the mast did stand,
> No bigger than the Moon.

Baking in extreme, unrelenting heat, the crew quickly become "weary." Their eyes are "glazed," their "lips baked black." Especially deadly is the lack of water: "Every tongue, through utter drought / Was withered at the root." It is here that we find the famous lines: "Water, water, every where / Nor any drop to drink."

> Day after day, day after day,
> We stuck, nor breath nor motion;
> As idle as a painted ship
> Upon a painted ocean.
>
> Water, water, every where,
> And all the boards did shrink;
> Water, water, every where,
> Nor any drop to drink.
>
> And every tongue, through utter drought,
> Was wither'd at the root;
> We could not speak, no more than if
> We had been choked with soot

At first, the promise of day is entirely positive. Now the word "day" echoes eerily and forebodingly, "Day after day, day after day."

An interesting detail in the poem, which gives us some insight into the dynamics of the Sun at noon throughout, is that throughout *The Ancient Mariner*, the Mariner's ship always stops moving whenever the Sun is overhead. When the Sun stands "right above the mast" at noon, the ship stops moving, the Sun "had fixed her to the ocean." Later in the poem, we read the following:

> The sails at noon left off their tune,
> And the ship stood still also.

Furthermore, whenever the Sun is overhead, not only does the ship stop moving but the Mariner stops telling his story.

The Sun came up upon the left,
Out of the sea came he!
And he shone bright, and on the right
Went down into the sea.

Higher and higher every day,
Till over the mast at noon—
The Wedding Guest here beat his breast,
For he heard the loud bassoon.

As noted previously, Coleridge wrote *The Ancient Mariner* to express the "shadows of imagination." When the sun is straight above the mast there are no shadows, and the ship of imagination stops dead in its tracks. In "Religious Musings," Coleridge calls the image of a waning Sun at noon "ghastly" (a word he also uses to describe the Mariner's tale).

> For who of woman born may paint the hour,
> When seized in his mid course, the Sun shall wane
> Making noon ghastly!

In other words, the bright Sun at noon is a negative image in *The Ancient Mariner*, or one that runs counter to the thrust of the tale itself as "a poem of pure imagination."

Depression, the Noonday Demon, and Various Mythic Wastelands

We usually associate depression with darkness, but in *The Ancient Mariner*, depression comes when the light is brightest. With the Sun straight above the mast, the crew is "sad as sad could be" and nature falls silent, filled only by the echo of the crew's own voices.

> Down dropt the breeze, the sails dropt down,
> 'Twas sad as sad could be;
> And we did speak only to break
> The silence of the sea!

In the exclusively conscious, masculine world of the solar Enlightenment, the inner life dries out and the outer world stops speaking.

Coleridge's insight here is not idiosyncratic; Andrew Solomon wrote a book about depression, his own and that of others, entitled *The Noonday Demon: An Atlas of Depression* (2001) that won the 2001 National Book Award, was a finalist for the 2002 Pulitzer Prize, and made *The Times* list of one hundred best books of the decade.[1]

Solomon's titular description of depression, "the Noonday Demon," comes from the ninety-first psalm where God is analogized as a protective bird whose wings shelter David from "the destruction that wasteth at noonday."

> He that dwelleth in the secret place of the most High shall abide under the shadow of the Almighty . . .
>
> He shall cover thee with his feathers, and under his wings shalt thou trust.

Coleridge, being who he was, must have been aware of the ninety-first psalm when he wrote of the Mariner's ship burning up at noon-day without the protective wings of the Albatross overhead. Once happy to be rid of the bird "that brought the fog and mist," the crew now miss those wings. Drifting in the doldrums, the ship's crew are rationally Enlightened, but they are also marooned in an exclusively masculine wasteland. The crew are all men, the Sun is a "he," and there are no women anywhere. All is yang and no yin, all sun no moon, all day no night, all fire no water, all reality no imagination—all death no life! Even impersonal feminine symbols such as water, mist, cold, night, and moon are missing. One finds parallels to the Mariner's predicament not only in the Bible but also in Egyptian, Greek, and Chinese mythology as well as twentieth-century poetry. As his ship drifts in the doldrums without wind or water to drink, the Mariner is in the Seventh Hour of the ancient Egyptian *Amduat* (ca. 1500 BCE), the book of what is in the underworld, where dark forces swallow up all the water so that the ship of the pharaoh cannot continue its journey. He is the deceased soul in the Orphic burial rites, originating around the fourth century BCE, "parched with thirst," having lost the memory of his or her divine origin.[2] In the Chinese *Tao Te Ching*, the water of life belongs to a "Mysterious Female" who is "there within us all the while" as an inner spring of life that "never runs dry."[3] We do, however, need to be able to "draw upon" her. The brightness of the enlightened modern mind has lost that capacity to draw upon that mystery; there is "water, water, every where" but it is all inaccessible, "nor any drop to drink." The ship and its crew are alienated from "the passion and the life, whose fountains are within" as Coleridge puts it in "Dejection: An Ode." The lesson of *The Ancient Mariner* at this point is clear: humanity cannot live by the Sun alone. Taken to an extreme and missing its lunar complement, solar consciousness does not reveal the world as it is; it creates a fallen world.[4] At this point in the poem, we may begin to feel that imagination is not an airy illusion, a fog obscuring objective reality we can easily live without; rather, imagination is vital to *human* life.

"The Romantic poetry," Coleridge explains, "appeals to the imagination rather than to the senses and to the reason as contemplating our inward nature."[5] Coleridge's poetry is living water from the inner fountains that seeks to heal the modern wasteland. In 1798, Coleridge's vision was a prophetic anticipation of the unanticipated negative consequences of modern consciousness leading to a desiccated self and world in which we know "only / A heap of broken images," as brilliantly expressed by T. S. Eliot in *The Waste Land* (1922) over a century later.

> What are the roots that clutch, what branches grow
> You cannot say, or guess, for you know only
> A heap of broken images, where the sun beats,
> And the dead tree gives no shelter, the cricket no relief,
> And the dry stone no sound of water.[6]

Eliot's wasteland is poetic metaphor, of course, descriptive of a felt sense of modernity in crisis. Today, with the looming reality of climate change, many people are gripped by the image of solar heating literally turning the earth into a wasteland.

CHAPTER 10

"The Water, like a Witch's Oils, Burnt Green, and Blue and White"

Soul from Below

Conscious engagement with the mystery of transformation is rare. For one, it is hard for most of us to realize, even as an idea, that darkness—figurative death, depression, regression—is necessary for change. I recall a patient of mine, for instance, a man in his thirties, who was living through a horrific depression and suffering it to his bones. As he used the therapeutic space to allow dissociated trauma from early life to come into consciously felt awareness, he had a dream in which symbols appeared that pointed to new life coming out of death. Being a new analyst, I too quickly and overly excitedly blurted out, "You are in a transformation process!" I'll never forget how he responded: his head bowed down, his arms clasped together, forearms on his thighs, he said in a low, slow voice, "It doesn't feel like transformation . . ." What if I were to say to you, "You are in a transformation process," what might you think? Perhaps you would imagine yourself glowing with light or becoming stronger or wiser or younger or more beautiful—better in some way. You might not think of the caterpillar curled up in the chrysalis dissolving and turning to goo. If you did, you might not want to be transformed. Typically, we do not change unless we *must*. Deep changes to the personality and worldview are most often imposed on us through suffering, not consciously sought after. The "extenders of our consciousness," says Coleridge, are "sorrow, sickness, poetry, and religion." He continues, "The truth is, we stop in the sense of life just when we are not forced to go on, and then adopt a permission of our feelings for a precept of our reason."[1]

The Mariner is not consciously seeking transformation; he is laboring under dire necessity, and unless the Mariner changes—unless something changes!—he will die in the desiccating heat of the solar wasteland.

An Anti-Narcissus

As the Mariner drifts at sea, strung out and desperate, he stares into the mirror of the waters below. Narcissus-like, he glimpses his own reflection; unlike Narcissus, he is disgusted by what he sees. The Mariner sees things that should not be, slimy things, the antithesis of the idealized Christian or spiritual bird of the air.

> The very deep did rot: O Christ!
> That ever this should be!
> Slimy things did crawl with legs
> Upon the slimy sea.

When the Albatross dies, the reptiles come to life. The Mariner is repulsed—*of course* he is. These slimy things personify psychological contents that his Western patriarchal mind and Christian spirit repress. Peering down into the waters below instead of up at the Albatross in the sky above is a U-turn leading the Mariner into the opposite of what he expects and knows, the reverse of what he hopes for, away from everything known and familiar. The waters below are, therefore, inevitably disgusting and terrifying to the conscious mind. "O Christ! / That ever this should be!"

As he stares into the mirror of the waters, the Mariner is like an alchemist peering into a flask and witnessing the alchemical *nigredo* and *putrifactio*, the darkening, the rotting. Reptiles are the first creatures to appear in the imaginal visions of the alchemical opus, not as a sign of something that should not be but as an indication that the initial union of conscious and unconscious—the opus of transformation—is beginning.[2] As a symbol, the reptile represents the future as well as the past because it is what is unevolved within us, an image of the saurian tail in the survival centers of the limbic system.[3] For a person who, like Coleridge, identifies with the intellect and high-flying spiritual idealism, these "slimy things" are a catastrophe; they feel extremely dangerous to the stability and sanity of the conscious personality. But as compensatory dimensions of the unconscious mind, they are the *prima materia* of transformation and evolution if adequately contained and engaged.[4]

Alchemical Projections in the Slimy Seas

Since I am introducing parallels between alchemy and Coleridge's *Ancient Mariner*, it might be worthwhile to offer a brief explanation of the history and meaning of alchemy from the depth psychological point of view. Most educated Westerners have been taught that alchemists were strange people impossibly struggling in the Middle Ages to literally turn lead into gold. But the actual practice of alchemy was more complex than that. Historians of science view alchemy simply as an ignorant attempt at chemistry. But from the depth psychological point of view, alchemy is an imaginal phenomenology descriptive of a conscious encounter with the archetypal-symbolic dimensions of the unconscious mind.[5] Invalid as chemistry, but valid as projected psychology, the bizarre imagery of alchemy is not merely delusion, superstition, or proto-science; rather, it makes visible those "shadows of imagination" that Coleridge sought to make visible in writing *The Rime of the Ancient Mariner*.

Alchemy flourished in the West and Middle East for almost two thousand years. The tradition began in ancient Greece and Hellenistic Egypt. The Islamic world adopted alchemy when the Muslims conquered Egypt between 649 and 646 CE. From there, alchemy entered Jewish and Christian Europe, where it flourished, mostly in secret, before its generally agreed-upon death around the time of Robert Boyle's book *The Skeptical Chemist* in 1661. The dynamics and imagery of the alchemical imagination, however, found a surprising resurrection in the poetics of eighteenth- and nineteenth-century Romanticism.[6] Jung, in fact, was convinced that Goethe (1749–1832) and his friend C. G. Carus (1789–1869) were unconsciously building a bridge between the alchemical fantasies of the past and the empirical depth psychology of the future, a bridge founded in a common realization between the two disciplines that the transformation of consciousness required metaphorical filth. "The aspirations of the alchemists had found their highest poetic expression in Goethe's *Faust*. At the time Carus wrote, he certainly could not have guessed that he was building the philosophical bridge to an empirical psychology of the future, which would take quite literally the old alchemical dictum: *in stercore invenitur*—'it is found in filth.'"[7] Although in Jung's opinion Carus "certainly could not have guessed" that his work was a link in a golden chain between medieval and Renaissance alchemy and twentieth-century depth psychology, Coleridge, a contemporary of Carus and Goethe, certainly did guess something like that and said so. "I am persuaded that the chymical technology, as far as it was borrowed from life and intelligence, half-metaphorically, half-mystically, may be brought back again . . . to the use of psychology."[8] Coleridge drew on the "half-metaphorical, half-mystical" language of alchemy throughout his poetry and "psycho-analytic" prose. For instance, when Coleridge writes in his *Biographia Literaria* that the imagination "dissolves, diffuses, dissipates, in order to re-create," that is pure alchemical metaphor. As with Coleridge's sense of imagination, alchemy is true and real as a projected symbolic self-portrait of a dynamic process of development—specifically initiatory death and rebirth—active in our inward nature.

It is true that many alchemists foolishly wasted their money and lives on an impossible attempt to literally turn lead into gold. But others knew that the true material of their opus was to be approached through poetic rather than literal or fundamentalist faith. "Our gold is not the common gold," states the *Rosarium Philosophorum* (1550); alchemy must be transmitted mystically and that "only he who knows how to make the Philosopher's Stone understands the words which relate to it."[9] Zosimos (ca. 300 CE) speaks of "this Stone which is not a stone, a precious thing which has no value, a thing of many shapes which has no shapes, this unknown which is known of all."[10] And the preeminent Islamic alchemist Muhammad Ibn Umail (900–960 CE), known as the sheik or senior in European alchemy, even entitles his best-known alchemical text *The Book of the Explanation of the Symbols*.[11] From this perspective, turning lead to gold symbolizes the creation of consciousness.

Alchemy is thus linked to Romanticism and depth psychology through the common thread of imagination, especially dark imaginings. What is collectively banished as dark, repulsive, disgusting, taboo, and evil becomes, in alchemy, Romanticism, and depth psychology the *prima materia*, that is, the compensatory dynamics, drives, and images in the unconscious that when actively worked with are the source of change.

The Slimy Seas of Psychological Regression

The Mariner's "slimy things [that] did crawl with legs / Upon the slimy sea" would undoubtedly have been familiar to alchemists of the Middle Ages and Renaissance as the *putrificatio* by which old forms die so that new forms can be born. In psychological or conceptual terms, Jung would see this imagery as suggestive of the process of regression—not regression in the sense of an illness or a retreat into infantilism but in the sense of a symbolic death seeking rebirth.

In the following passage, Jung describes the nature and purpose of regression and uses the same term as Coleridge, "slime from the depths," to describe the contents that "regression brings to the surface." I suggest we listen to this quote as if Jung were commenting directly on *The Rime of the Ancient Mariner*. "What regression brings to the surface certainly seems at first sight to be slime from the depths, but if one does not stop short at a superficial evaluation and refrains from passing judgment on the basis of a preconceived dogma, it will be found that this 'slime' contains not merely incompatible and rejected remnants of everyday life, or inconvenient and objectionable animal tendencies, but also germs of new life and vital possibilities for the future. . . . When these functions are activated by regression and so reach consciousness, they appear in a somewhat incompatible form, disguised and covered up with the slime from the deep."[12] Does it sound strange that Jung places such a positive value on regression? In the popular mind, the phrase "you're regressing" can sound like an insult, something like "you're bad," or "stop that." Freud initially defines regression as the frightening prospect of being possessed by primal, uncivilized drives belonging to our evolutionary biology, which is, indeed, how Coleridge tended to view such contents. For instance, madness is a "perversion of the senses" and "a recession of the spirit." In a particularly telling confession, one that will no doubt seem exorbitant to contemporary ears, Coleridge writes that if the conscious will and rational faculties are lowered "even for a single moment," then the "lower or bestial states of life rise up into action and prominence" and "the man" might be "mad forever."[13]

Today, most psychoanalysts view regression as a process that takes one backward and downward, so to speak, into a prior state of development or into the reexperiencing of traumatic experiences split off from consciousness through defense systems such as repression, suppression, dissociation, denial, compartmentalization, and addiction. Literary critics with a psychological point of view tend toward this point of view. Why is Coleridge tormented by hideous nightmares in "The Pains of Sleep" (1803)? It is because of Coleridge's repressed emotions relating to unrequited love for a woman not his wife (Asra), his withdrawal symptoms from opium addiction, and too much claret. These types of reductive interpretations focus on *causes*. They are not wrong, but they are one-sided because they overlook the teleological, or future-oriented, nature of contents brought to light by a "descent into the underworld," which is what the journey might be aiming at. For Jung, regression cooks up "germs of new life and vital possibilities for the future"—not germs as carriers of disease but living substances capable of becoming a new organism or part of a new organism.

One does not always attain the new life, of course. People can stay stuck in a regression and get nowhere, or even be destroyed by it. But Jung suggests that this type of stagnation happens when we are unconscious of the *meaning* of what is happening and therefore resist the process. Therefore, instead of seeking to escape a regression or defend against it, Jungian psychology encourages an active leaning into the downward movement, an intentional going backward and downward, so that the process might find its goal. That requires an ego that is independent and strong enough to engage the nightmare and not be destroyed by it. The Mariner is the only *I* onboard the ship, and, as such, the only one who undergoes symbolic death and eventually finds the gold. As we shall see, the other two hundred members of the crew just die. To them, the regression is nothing but destruction.

Regression is a shocking catastrophe. But how *much* shock we feel varies in accordance with our conscious attitude. The further away the unconscious contents are from conscious awareness, the more abhorrent they appear. The *nature* of the repressed contents or, more specifically, how they appear to us varies in relationship with our conscious attitude. For example, if our conscious goal is to be reasonable, then our slimy seas are the irrational. If we are identified with patriarchal values, then the feminine is our rejected otherness. Concomitantly, if we are feminists, then the disgusting contents approaching from within and without are patriarchal. If we identify with the physical-sexual, then the slime is the mental-spiritual, and vice versa. If we value the conventional, the unconventional is something to avoid. Those who identify with independence fear vulnerability. Those who have suffered overwhelming betrayal at the hands of parents and caretakers may even experience love itself as terrifyingly threatening. In any event, the principle is always the same: The missing, split-off dimensions of the self we need for wholeness are always at first covered up with slime from the deep; it is always *in stercore invenitur.*

Into the Witch's Cauldron

From the patriarchal perspective that informs alchemy, Romanticism, and depth psychology, the "slime," as Coleridge sees it in *The Ancient Mariner*, can be formalized in one word—the Feminine.

Wherever the sparks of new life may be for the Mariner, they are certainly not to be found in the solar wasteland where there is water everywhere but not a drop to drink, where everything is masculine, where the Sun shines bright above the mast illuminating the world as a *He*, where God is a Father, and there are no women around. Even impersonal images of the feminine such as water, cold, night, fog, mist, and moon are missing from the wasteland. It would not be surprising, therefore, if the Mariner's regression were to bring about a compensatory conformation with the missing feminine principle. And this is exactly what we find. There is a witch's cauldron down there.

> About, about, in reel and rout,
> The death-fires danced at night;
> The water, like a witch's oils,
> Burnt green, and blue and white

"About, about, in reel and rout" is an allusion to a chant by three witches in Shakespeare's *Macbeth* (1605) in which the witches weave a curse for a mariner.[14] They do not kill him, but they do deprive him of sleep and condemn him to seven nights of torture, exactly what lies in store for our Mariner as well.

Coleridge was a visionary in the Romantic tradition, but he consciously identified with the rational intellect and with Christian spirituality. Therefore, the compensation from below comes in the form of "Nature" as a "wary, wiley, long-breathed old witch" opposed to "Lady MIND": "But Alas! Alas! That Nature is a wary, wiley, long-breathed old witch, rough-lived as a turtle and divisible as the Polyp, repullulative in a thousand Snips and Cuttings, integra et in toto [whole and entire]! She is sure to get the better of Lady MIND in the long run, and to take her revenge too."[15] Even as a child Coleridge experienced himself as torn between the contraries of Christ and an "unleavened *Self*," like a snake "wreathed around my heart." "Ah, but even in boyhood there was a cold hollow spot, an aching in the heart, when I said my prayers—that prevented my entire union with God—that I could not give up, or that would not give me up—as if a snake had wreathed around my heart, & at this one spot its mouth touched at & inbreathed a weak incapability of willing it away . . . that spot in my heart [is] even my remaining and unleavened *Self*—all else the Love of Christ in and `thro' Christ's love of me."[16] We shall find the tension between Christ and the Serpent later in *The Ancient Mariner*. It runs throughout Coleridge's poetry. For instance, in "Christabel," composed during the same period as *The Ancient Mariner*, the innocent maiden Christabel is safe at home in her father's castle. She leaves the patriarchal daylight world of "custom and law" only to unexpectedly, in the middle of the night, confront the daimonic Female Geraldine in the woods. Geraldine shines bright in the moonlight like the Mariner, her gems glitter wildly in her hair, and she implores Christabel for help, telling her that she has been abducted by five men. But this seemingly lost and innocent Woman harbors a dark secret. In a dream, Christabel sees it: a bright green snake coils around a dove's wings and neck.[17] Christabel is the bird, Geraldine the snake.

Coleridge tells us of a strong personal reaction against the figure of Geraldine; the thought of her, he says, fills him with "a *deep* unutterable Disgust."[18] Coleridge's experience of disgust is always set off by dimensions of the psyche that lie outside the well-traveled pathways of the patriarchal, Christian, intellectual spirit. In his

Notebooks, Coleridge writes that he has "always been preyed on by some Dread," and he associates his sense of perpetual underlying dread with the body, with physical facts that seem disgusting, chaotic, and psychotic, even evil.[19] The body—Nature—is a witch's cauldron filled with reptiles. "O Christ! / That ever this should be!" the Mariner exclaims.

The Albatross around the Mariner's Neck

When the Mariner kills the Albatross, his shipmates, contained in the traditional Judeo-Christian myth, are at first sure he is a "wretch" who will "work 'em woe." Then, when the Sun rises, the crew make a sudden conversion to the age of reason and, as if they were all a group of French philosophes, declare, "'Twas right, said they, such birds to slay / That bring the fog and mist." Now the crew change their minds again. Finding themselves stuck in the doldrums and dying of thirst, stuck in a churning cauldron of horror emerging from the "slimy seas" with "evil looks," the crew hang the dead Albatross around the Mariner's neck as an emblem of his crime. He made the Sun rise, but in this devil's bargain killed their symbolic life and landed them in an unlivable world.

CHAPTER 11

"Instead of the Cross, the Albatross about My Neck Was Hung"

The Transitus of Modern Man

The Albatross around the Mariner's neck is one of the most famous and unforgettable images in *The Rime of the Ancient Mariner*. Indeed, the image is so powerful and unforgettable, so compelling, that it has bridged the vast divide between eighteenth- and nineteenth-century literature and contemporary popular culture. "I have an albatross around my neck" colloquially means, as we all know, that I am carrying around an unwanted and unnecessary, usually annoying, burden, as in, "that broken-down old car is an albatross around my neck." Yet, the Mariner carrying the Albatross around his neck "instead of the cross" has mythic resonances that go much deeper than this colloquial understanding. It is one of the juiciest images in this poem of pure imagination. The image resonates with mythic associations of the *transitus dei* (i.e., the carrying of the death of God on the way to God's renewal).

In a 1933 seminar led by Jung and published as *The Visions Seminars*, a Miss Howells asked Jung the following question: "Will you please discuss further the psychological experience of the *transitus*

A statue of the Ancient Mariner by Alan Herriot, erected in 2003 near the harbor at Watchet, Somerset, UK. Samuel Taylor Coleridge lived for a time at nearby Nether Stowey and was inspired by the harbor at Watchet to write *The Rime of the Ancient Mariner.*

"Ah, well a day! what evil looks." From *The Rime of the Ancient Mariner*, illustrated by Herbert Cole, 1900.

of modern man? How does he take into his new psychological experience the carrying of the religious symbol of sacrifice?"[1] When the Mariner carries the dead Albatross around his neck, he answers Miss Howells's question. The transitus of the Mariner is the transitus of modern man.

"Instead of the Cross, the Albatross / About My Neck Was Hung"

Over three thousand years ago, in ancient Egypt, there lived a pharaoh named Akhenaten, aka Amenhotep IV (18th Dynasty, died in 1335 BCE), a proto-Enlightenment figure whose idea of progress was to worship the Sun alone. In the name of Atum, the solar deity, he forbade worship of all the other traditional Egyptian deities and rejected the *Amduat* (1426 BCE), the ancient Egyptian book of the underworld. Akhenaten's idea was to turn ancient Egyptians into Sun worshipers while rejecting all the other gods, something that went completely counter to the collective and traditional religious beliefs of the time. From the psychological perspective, Akhenaten's desire to worship the Sun alone is a metaphorical expression of a wish to live in a purely conscious world where respect for the unconscious (the underworld or night world) is irrelevant. Akhenaten's solar fundamentalism caused immense destruction, not only literally in the sense that he tore down temples, but also psychologically in that he did violence to the spirits and minds of his people by destroying their symbolic life. Akhenaten ruled for seventeen years, and during his reign the people obeyed his commands. But when he died, his monuments were destroyed, his statues dismantled, and his name removed from the list of Kings. Some twelve years after his death, archival records refer to Akhenaten as "the enemy" and "the criminal."

Some three thousand years later, Coleridge's Mariner is in a similar position to Akhenaten vis-à-vis the ship's crew: he kills the Albatross, dispels the fog and mist, makes the sun rise, and for this becomes, for them, the "enemy" and the "criminal." With "evil looks" the crew hang the dead Albatross around his neck as an emblem of guilt for destroying their symbolic life.

Ah! well-a-day! what evil looks
Had I from old and young!
Instead of the cross, the Albatross
About my neck was hung.

We remember, however, that the crew once praised the Mariner for killing the Albatross. In doing so, they become accomplices in this crime. Therefore, when the crew hang the Albatross around the Mariner's neck "with evil looks," they inauthentically disown their own complicity. "The shipmates," Coleridge writes in the prose gloss, "in their sore distress, would fain throw the whole guilt on the ancient Mariner: in sign whereof they hang the dead sea-bird round his neck." The subtext is that the ostensibly Christian crew self-righteously brands him a "Christ killer" for killing the bird the crew welcomed "as if it had been a Christian soul." With the Albatross around his neck, the Mariner is officially the "everlasting Wandering Jew," as Coleridge once called him in conversation; he carries the collective shadow projected onto him as a scapegoat—guilt, heresy, evil, and sacrilege. Carrying collective shadow projections is the psychology behind antisemitism. The "wandering Jew," as we noted in chapter 3, is thus the Christian shadow.

Carrying collective shadow projections is an unavoidable consequence for anyone who creates beyond collective norms. The image of the "holy criminal" (from Antigone to Jesus to Jean Genet's 1949 novel *The Thief's Journal*) is a metaphorical pattern that expresses the essence of all artistic originality in the narrow and the broadest sense, from actual artistic geniuses to those who seek to become individuals. Thomas Mann, for example, in his essay *Dostoevsky in Moderation* (1945), writes that "certain conquests made by the soul and mind are impossible without disease, madness, crime of the spirit." Speaking of Nietzsche, Mann repeats himself: "His personal feelings initiate him into those of

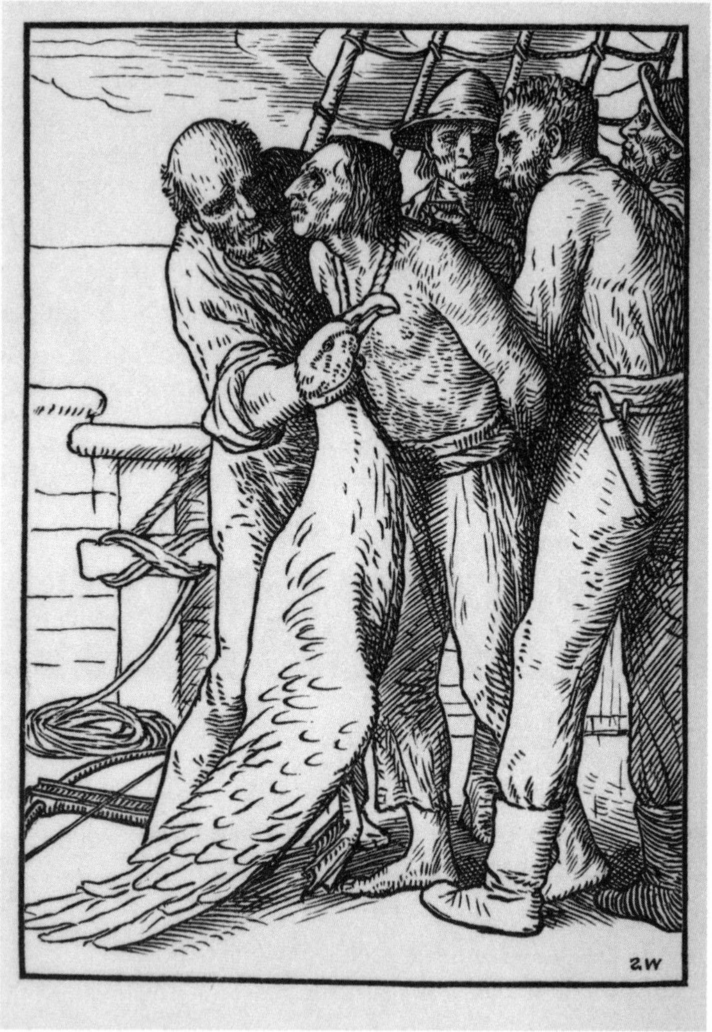

William Strang, the Albatross around the Mariner's neck, from Essex House Press, *The Rime of the Ancient Mariner*, 1903.

the criminal. . . . In general all creative originality, all artist nature in the broadest sense of the word, does the same. It was the French painter and sculptor Degas who said that an artist must approach his work in the spirit of a criminal about to commit a crime."[2]

Jung experienced the intrinsic relationship between creativity and guilt in 1913 when, in an important early dream, he shot and killed the Germanic warrior hero Siegfried, not with a crossbow but with a rifle, as Siegfried gloriously drove his chariot out of the rising sun.[3] At that time in his life, Siegfried represented Jung's highest values, that is, willpower, success, vitality, and ego strength. Compelled from within to shoot Siegfried (as Coleridge's Mariner seems compelled to shoot the Albatross), Jung, also like the Mariner, experiences "unbearable . . . guilt" as well as "disgust and remorse for having destroyed something so great and beautiful." Translating his dream into conceptual language however, Jung later affirmed the necessity of both his crime and his guilt: "The first step in individuation is tragic guilt."[4]

The *transitus dei*

The relationship between individuation and tragic guilt is akin to that between individuation and symbolic death. One sees this expressed not only in dreams (as in Jung's dream of shooting Siegfried) and literature (the Mariner shooting the Albatross) but also in mythic ritual. For example, in the cult of Mithraism, popular with Roman soldiers from the first to the fourth centuries CE, the god Mithra, a solar deity, kills the "bull of his mother" (the *tauroctony*), and carries the dead bull (the *transitus*) on his back. Mithra's slaying and carrying of the bull is a sacrilegious murder, but also a ritual sacrifice of brute natural instinct and impulse made in the name of willpower, ego strength, and discipline—all solar-masculine qualities developing at that time.

Relief of Mithra, the Persian sun god, sacrificing a bull. Dating from around 100–200 CE. On display in the Louvre Lens Museum, France.

In keeping with the mythic pattern, during the reign of the Roman emperor Tiberius (14–37 CE), while Jesus was alive or shortly after, the historian Plutarch reports that a Greek sailor named Thamus heard a divine voice cry out over the sea, "Thamus, are you there? When you reach Palodes, take care to proclaim that the great god Pan is dead." Soon after, the entire crew onboard Thamus's ship heard several mysterious voices groaning and lamenting the death of the great, beautiful, and wild god Pan. From the standpoint of paganism, the death of Pan is a horrible sacrilege. But from the standpoint of Christianity, it is a necessary sacrifice

Mithra Carrying the Bull, c. 389, discovered at the Sidon Mithraeum in Lebanon in the nineteenth century and displayed at the Louvre Museum, Paris.

of natural impulse made in the name of ethical and spiritual development. In keeping with the theme of the transitus, Jesus carries the cross, a cut-down tree emblematic of the pagan nature religions that Christianity would supplant. Two-thousand years later, as Christianity is dying with the birth of the modern soul, the Mariner carries the dead image of Christ (as the Albatross) on his journey toward the revelation of a new God image. The Mariner is a sacred criminal. In this he is like Jesus, who was killed as a heretic and a criminal. The pattern is the same, but the content is different. Now the Mariner carries the Albatross "instead of the cross," the dead Christian God image instead of the dead pagan nature religion, on his way to the birth of a new, post-Christian image of the divine.

In Mithraism and Christianity, as in *The Ancient Mariner*, the *transitus dei* involves carrying the dead God of the past. Sometimes, however, the *transitus dei* involves carrying a new, living God image. When Christianity was newborn and growing like a child, legend has it that St. Christopher (whose name means Christ-bearer), a Christian martyr from the third century, carried an unknown child on his back across a river. With every step, the child grew heavier and heavier until, when he finally reached the other side, Christopher said to this unknown child: "You have put me in the greatest danger. I do not think the whole world could have been as heavy on my shoulders as you were." The child replied: "You had on your shoulders not only the whole world but Him who made it. I am Christ your king, whom you are serving by this work." Then the child vanished.[5]

It is a heavy burden to carry a living God. Many modern people, however, do not live with the feeling of carrying any spiritual burden at all. The conventional way today is to live a risk-managed existence based on purely conscious and practical considerations,

Albrecht Dürer, *The Bearing of the Cross*, from *The Engraved Passion*, 1512. On display at the Art Institute of Chicago, Clarence Buckingham Collection.

and, in this way of life, it is impossible to know what the *transitus dei* is. Paradoxically, however, it can be a nightmare to carry no burden, to be weightless, meaningless, to live a purely egocentric life. Many people want to feel they are carrying something meaningful that is heavy, but cannot reason out what that might be, and cannot simply make up something to assuage the lightness of their being. Values are not brainchildren; we cannot invent them.

In Nietzsche's *The Gay Science* (1882–1887), published almost a hundred years after *The Rime of the Ancient Mariner*, he famously

Albrecht Dürer, *Saint Christopher Carrying Christ*, 1521. British Museum, London, UK.

declares that God is dead, we murdered him like the Mariner murders the Albatross.[6] And what happens next? After God is dead, Zarathustra carries his heaviest burden as himself.

> *someone who knows!*
> *someone who knows himself!*
> The wise Zarathustra! . . .
>
> You sought the heaviest burden:
> there you found *yourself*—
> you cannot cast your self aside . . . [7]

By the end of *The Ancient Mariner*, we shall see that Nietzsche's "heaviest burden"—self-knowledge—is the Mariner's as well, that is, after he blesses the water-snakes and the dead Albatross falls from his neck "like lead" and sinks into the sea.

Turning Toward Midnight

For Jung, the expiation of tragic guilt incurred by killing God comes through creativity. In compensation for the psychological and spiritual *horror vacui* Jung opened by sacrificing the patriarchal values that were, for him at that time, "so great and beautiful," Jung discovered new values on his night-sea journey and offered these back to the collective through his *Collected Works*, many public seminars and lectures, and decades of work with individuals.

The Mariner tells his story—*The Rime of the Ancient Mariner*—as his offering of new values to replace those he killed when he killed the Albatross. But he does so through unconscious compulsion. He is split between sea and land. At sea, as we shall discover, the Mariner comes to bless the water-snakes at night, in the moonlight, in the shadow of the ship, and experiences a new revelation of the sacred. By way of contrast, when he comes back to shore he turns away from that experience and seeks to expiate the guilt of his "hellish" crime not through a sacrificial conscious participation with the creation of new values but by repenting and doing penance for his sacrilege. As mentioned earlier, the Mariner attempts, on the conscious level, to replace the dark but prophetic meaning of his sea voyage with the moralism of life on land. In the latter chapters of this book, we shall see how the Mariner tries to go back to church, and how ineffectual this regressive restoration of the persona is.

Putting the central image of *The Ancient Mariner*—the murder of the Albatross—in the mythic context of sacrifice, symbolic death, and the *transitus dei* allows us to more clearly understand how carrying the Albatross "instead of the cross" is not a mistake, an accident, or an evil sin requiring penance but a transformation of sacrilege into sacrifice and, ultimately, a stage on the way to the discovery of a new God image. When the Mariner carries the Albatross instead of the cross, he personifies the transitus not of the past but of modern man, as Miss Howells put it in a seminar with Jung, of the birth, death, and rebirth of the modern soul, as this book is entitled.

Killing the Albatross makes the Sun rise. But there are many more developments to come. The Mariner is not only an avatar of the Enlightenment; he carries the potential birth of spirituality that is not anti-Christian but post-Christian, that does not deny the Enlightenment but goes beyond its materialistic, egocentric, and mechanistic one-sidedness. As we follow the Mariner deeper into the underworld, we will witness a rare and stunning process: namely, how a new image of God is born as the ego turns toward the darkness and eventually, after a lot of suffering, finds a relationship with it.[8]

Everything that has happened so far in the poem—setting off from shore, getting blown off course, drifting through the ice, being freed from the ice, seeing an Albatross circle above the ship, shooting the Albatross, getting stuck in the doldrums, dying of thirst, seeing slimy things in the sea, carrying the dead Albatross—all this could actually have happened on any one of the many European sea voyages that Coleridge had read of and was fascinated with. But now, with the water burning "like a witch's oils" and the first emergence of the darkly repressed Feminine principle of Nature and the body—the psychosomatic unconscious—there is a shift into realms of pure imagination. That shift begins when the Mariner celebrates a Last Supper with himself, when he bites his own flesh and drinks his own blood.

CHAPTER 12

"The Night-mare LIFE-IN-DEATH Was She"

The Return of the Feminine and the Death of the Modern Soul

For know there are two worlds of life and death:
One that which thou beholdest; but the other
Is underneath the grave, where do inhabit
The shadows of all forms that think and live
Till death unite them and they part no more;
Dreams and the light imaginings of men,
And all that faith creates or love desires,
Terrible, strange, sublime and beauteous shapes.
There thou art, and dost hang, a writhing shade.

—Shelley, *Prometheus Unbound*

As the Mariner drifts in the Wasteland, the Sun, once radiant "like God's own head," sets into the sea. Tracking the course of the Sun, the Mariner looks west, the mythic direction of the land of the dead, a forbidden but longed-for locus of destruction and renewal that, according to Wordsworth, portends a "wildish destiny."[1] Out of the west, something appears in the sky, a strange something that only the Mariner can see.

> There passed a weary time. Each throat
> Was parched, and glazed each eye.
> A weary time! a weary time!
> How glazed each weary eye,
>
> When looking westward, I beheld
> A something in the sky.

The Mariner wants to cry out to the crew and tell them that something is approaching, but his lips are so withered black, so sealed shut "through utter drought" by the heat of the "bloody Sun," that the only water left to drink is the fountain within. Out of sheer desperation he bites his arm and sucks his blood.

> With throats unslaked, with black lips baked,
> We could nor laugh nor wail;
> Through utter drought all dumb we stood!
> I bit my arm, I sucked the blood,
> And cried, A sail! a sail!

He drinks his blood and can speak. But not only that, when the Mariner drinks his "life blood," this ceremonial drink grants him access to another world. He no longer sees a "something in the sky" but a ghost ship sailing out of the setting sun.[2] That approaching ship is a "she," the first feminine pronoun to appear in the Mariner's voyage, and she carries two passengers: LIFE-IN-DEATH, a "Night-mare" Female who "thicks man's blood with cold," and her mate DEATH.

According to Coleridge, *The Rime of the Ancient Mariner* is a tale of the emotional and psychological effects that "every human being" experiences when they believe themselves to be under "supernatural agency" from "whatever source of delusion." Now we see the source:

the Mariner's supernatural delusions are nothing more nor less than the dreams and nightmares of his body and blood. And he must fully encounter them.

A Something in the Sky

We remember that when the ship is stuck in the freezing ice, the Albatross flies in through the fog and mist to save it. Now that the ship is burning up in a fiery wasteland, something else flies in.

> When looking westward, I beheld
> A something in the sky.
>
> At first it seemed a little speck,
> And then it seemed a mist;
> It moved and moved, and took at last
> A certain shape, I wist.
>
> A speck, a mist, a shape, I wist!
> And still it neared and neared:
> As if it dodged a water-sprite,
> It plunged and tacked and veered.

"A speck, a mist, a shape, I wist!" the Mariner cries out. This strange shape tracks a chaotic, unpredictable course as it "plunged and tacked and veered," a UFO, or as they are now called, a UAP.

Coleridge's psyche tended to plunge and veer; his poet's pen for instance, especially during the visionary years of his mid-twenties, was autonomously possessed by a mysterious power that even seems to have unconsciously influenced Coleridge's way of walking. William Hazlitt describes this in his famous essay, "My First Acquaintance with Poets." "I observed that he [Coleridge] continually crossed me on the way by shifting from one side of the footpath to the other. This struck me as an odd movement; but I did not at that time connect it with an instability of purpose or involuntary change of principle, as I have done since. He seemed unable to keep on in a straight line."[3] Hazlitt is disturbed by Coleridge swerving off course. For Hazlitt, the nonlinear (the Feminine!) is involuntary, inferior, odd, and connotes "instability of purpose." His rational mind prefers straight lines, Cartesian grids, mathematical abstractions, the Mariner's crossbow. Straight lines are known, predictable. They also connote civilization as distinct from wild nature. When we fly in an airplane and look down from above, for instance, the appearance of straight lines—tilled fields or city streets—is a sure sign we are over a human community. Nature, however, within and without, tends to move in serpentine paths of curves and oscillations. Spirals and circles are the patterns and rhythms of our DNA, of the galaxies. Jung noticed, "if one lives with the blood," as the Mariner is beginning to do once he drinks his own blood, then straight lines are an offense. "If one lives close to the earth, if one lives with the blood, there are some things which one simply cannot do or imagine. For instance, to make a straight line through nature, like a railway that disfigures a whole countryside, is an offense to nature—not to the forest or the mountain, they do not lament, but to our own nature. It violates the blood, because our blood knows no straight line."[4]

As the crew rots in the solar Wasteland and the specter sails out of the setting sun, the Mariner thinks this ship will be their salvation, coming "hither to work us weal." However, as the ship draws closer, the Mariner's confidence is shaken. At first, he sees only a Woman on board, "the Night-mare LIFE-IN-DEATH." Then he recognizes a male figure as well, her mate DEATH.

The western wave was all a-flame.
The day was well nigh done!
Almost upon the western wave

Rested the broad bright Sun;
When that strange shape drove suddenly
Betwixt us and the Sun.

And straight the Sun was flecked with bars,
(Heaven's Mother send us grace!)
As if through a dungeon-grate he peered
With broad and burning face.

Alas! (thought I, and my heart beat loud)
How fast she nears and nears!
Are those *her* sails that glance in the Sun,
Like restless gossameres?

Are those her *ribs* through which the Sun
Did peer, as through a grate?
And is that Woman all her crew?
Is that a DEATH? and are there two?
Is DEATH that woman's mate?

Her lips were red, *her* looks were free,
Her locks were yellow as gold:
Her skin was as white as leprosy,
The Night-mare LIFE-IN-DEATH was she,
Who thicks man's blood with cold.

Coleridge repeats the feminine pronouns *she/her* eight times in the passage above and even italicizes *her* three times, so it is difficult to miss the point: here comes the feminine principle missing from the rational, solar Wasteland, that is, the repressed, tabooed, and dreaded dreams of the Mariner's body and blood coming up from the underworld to compensate for the Enlightenment Sun shining like "God's own head."

Coleridge relies heavily on the use of gendered pronouns to describe the approach of LIFE-IN-DEATH. In my opinion, however, it is important to remember that LIFE-IN-DEATH is the personifica-

tion of an archetypal image lurking deep in a man's unconscious being. Her appearance conjures up an experience of autonomous otherness that men sometimes project onto and identify with actual women but that is essentially symbolic. In *The Ancient Mariner*, "she" is a nightmare for the masculine principle when it is identified with solar reason and high-in-the-sky spiritual values. *The Rime of the Ancient Mariner* is not a political statement of the twenty-first century. I say this because I want us to enjoy, stay with, and respect the symbolic power of the opposites in Coleridge's vision and not allow that vision to be dissipated by gender identity issues that belong to the spirit of our times.

In alchemy, the transformation process can be tracked through colors: black is first (*nigredo*), then white (*albedo*), followed by yellow (*citrinitas*) and red (*rubedo*). In the 1798 version of *The Ancient Mariner*, DEATH is a jet-black skeleton, and in our 1834 version, LIFE-IN-DEATH is colored with the other three colors in the alchemical process—white, yellow, and red. Her skin is "white as leprosy," her hair is yellow, her lips red. "In the heat of the nigredo," Jung writes, "the 'anima media natura holds dominion.'" [5] In this chapter, carefully and with compassion, we will pick up some of the particulars of Coleridge's life and psychology that illuminate both the power and the suffering involved with the archetypal image of LIFE-IN-DEATH and its relevance for us today. It is breathtaking to feel the Mariner touch the darkness of the soul, the shock of unworked wounds, the terror of an unknown otherness lurking deep down in the masculine psyche.

LIFE-IN-DEATH in Christian Tradition

As always, a dose of poetic faith and a bit of mythic context will help us orient to the symbolic meaning of Coleridge's poetry. In naming the woman on the ghost ship LIFE-IN-DEATH, Coleridge draws from a deep well of Christian tradition. The first woman in the Bible, Eve, is said to be "the mother of all living, [who] became the fount of death to all living."[6] It is typical in the Christian, Gnostic, and Manichean philosophies for the feminine to be associated with the body and the material world (Mother Nature), which seem, like the moon, to be in constant flux between life and death. This is distinct from the pure, unchanging, eternal perfection of the celestial and spiritual heavens where the Christian God is supposed to dwell.[7] The *anima mundi* (the soul of the world), the *anima media natura* (the central soul, nature), and the *anima corporum* (the soul of the bodies) are said to be "divine in the beginning, but being made effeminate by sensual desire, came here below to generation and destruction."[8] In the book of Romans, St. Paul contrasts the *living* spirit of God with the *deathly* aspect of the body: "To be carnally minded," Paul says, "*is* death . . . for those who live according to the flesh set their minds on the things of the flesh, but those who live according to the Spirit, the things of the Spirit. For to be carnally minded *is* death, but to be spiritually minded is life and peace. Because the carnal mind *is* enmity against God: for it is not subject to the law of God nor indeed can be."[9]

In *The Thunder: Perfect Mind*, however a Gnostic poetic fragment from the Nag Hammadi Library, Wisdom is a feminine being who is both Life and Death, both carnal and spiritual. Wisdom says of herself:

> I am the first and the last . . .
> I am the whore and the holy one . . .
> I am the mother of my father . . .
> I am the wisdom of the Greeks
> And the knowledge of the barbarians . . .
> I am the one who has been hated everywhere
> And who has been loved everywhere.
> I am the one whom they call Life,
> And you have called Death . . .
> The angels, who have been sent at my word,
> And of gods in their seasons by my counsel.

For the Christian author of the alchemical *Aurora Consurgens* (written in the fifteenth century, attributed to Thomas Aquinas), Sophia, the feminine personification of divine wisdom, initially appears to the adept clothed in a garment of "living death." "But first you must tear off this garment which you wear—this cloak of darkness, this web of unconsciousness, this [prop] of evil, this bond of corruption, this living death, this visible corpse, this tomb you carry about with you, this inner robber."[10] "Wisdom and the 'corrupting humour,' or the death-dealing woman," von Franz writes, seeming a bit shocked, "represent one and the same thing."[11]

By knowing and appreciating these historical and mythic amplifications, we may see more clearly the archetypal dimension of LIFE-IN-DEATH: the death-dealing Woman in *The Rime of the Ancient Mariner* is a "Night-mare" for both the Mariner's Christian mindset and Enlightenment consciousness because she represents values, drives, images, and ideals that are considered evil in his spiritual worldview and irrational or even psychotic in his intellectual worldview. The Mariner's fear of the Feminine is like a garment thrown over her, obscuring the wisdom of his own body and blood.

Cadentia

Onboard their specter ship, DEATH and LIFE-IN-DEATH play a game of dice for the fate of the crew. DEATH wins everyone except for the Mariner, who becomes the property of LIFE-IN-DEATH.

> The naked hulk alongside came,
> And the twain were casting dice;
> "The game is done! I've won! I've won!"
> Quoth she, and whistles thrice.

With the game of dice, we find ourselves in a cosmos operating by very different rules than those prescribed by the "philosophy of mechanism," as Coleridge calls it (i.e., the Mariner's crossbow and arrow), for the throwing of dice was originally an oracle, a divination technique, like the throwing of coins or yarrow stalks in the

I Ching, performed to gain insight into the hidden meaning of events in time. The word "chance," in fact, comes from the late Latin *cadentia* or falling, as in dice falling. All oracles operated under the common assumption that apparent chance is the manifestation of a secret underlying order opaque to conscious apprehension.

The "glorious Sun" of the Enlightenment, of course, rejects all divination as the superstitious remnants of a pre-scientific age. From the perspective of deterministic materialism, what we call chance hides no secret divine meaning; it is not even truly *chance* but rather a projection of our ignorance of causal events, for reality is the motion of matter driven by cause and effect, motion that is in principle one hundred percent rationally predictable. From this perspective, divination practices cannot possibly be anything but systems of confabulation—fog, mist, and moonshine. "'Twas right said they, such birds to slay, / That bring the fog and mist."

Nevertheless, a troubling question arose in the seventeenth and eighteenth centuries: Is it possible to predict what will happen with any individual roll of the dice? It turns out the answer is no, a disturbing fact for people who find security in predictability. However, by carefully and rationally analyzing games of chance like dice, Pascal, Fermat, Huygens, and Bernoulli solved this conundrum through the calculus of probabilities. Given a long enough series of seemingly random events to work with, deterministic certainty was mathematically confirmed.

With the discoveries of quantum physics in the early to mid-twentieth century, however, doubt returned as to the universal validity of causal determinism at the microphysical level. Einstein famously pushed back against those who hypothesized that chance might play a role in the quantum cosmos when he reportedly said, "God does not play dice!" What Einstein actually wrote to Max Born in 1926 was: "Quantum mechanics . . . delivers much, but does not really bring us any closer to the secret of the Old One. I, at any rate, am convinced that *He* does not play dice."[12] But in the *Ancient Mariner*, *She* does. With the return of the Feminine principle, apparent chance returns to the world as a game of dice expressing a secret meaning hidden in the nexus of events. Over a century later, Jung would call this "dice game" synchronicity, an acausal connecting principle based on the shared meaning of inner and outer experience.

The Cold Death Mother

The "Night-mare LIFE-IN-DEATH . . . thick's man's blood with cold," as Coleridge writes. Cold is an archetypally feminine, or yin, quality; the cold Moon is contrary to the hot Sun. In Coleridge's "Christabel," the innocent maiden Christabel leaves her father's house and "kneels before the huge oak tree" alone at night. There she meets a daimonic Female, Geraldine, on "the other side" of the oak within the "Moonshine cold." "That bosom old / That bosom cold," Christabel exclaims. In Goethe's *Faust*, the "lofty mystery" of the "Goddesses" or "Mothers" makes even the fires of the devil's blood run cold.

> Mephistopheles: This lofty mystery I must now unfold.
> Goddesses throned in solitude, sublime,
> Set in no place, still less in any time,
> At the mere thought of them my blood runs cold.
> They are the Mothers![13]

Clinical experience shows that psychosomatic sensations, as well as psychic images of icy cold, often accompany traumatic experiences of maternal neglect and abandonment and are triggered in the remembering of them. From the psychological point of view, a safe and warm maternal experience is a safeguard against the cold "land of the dead," that is, the archetypal world of the collective unconscious. Integrated attachment experiences of maternal presence and protection wire the nervous system through attunement to create healthy modes of self-regulation between psyche and soma that enable us to embrace life with the same passion, love, and sense of safety that embraced us as infants and children. However, if the maternal experience is disturbed, neglected, abused, or somehow broken, there is a corresponding lack of attunement in the psyche or body to oneself and others, and this can result in a feeling of being cold and lifeless. In "Christabel," for instance, Christabel's mother died in childbirth, leaving a lacuna in her soul through which the death Mother gains access. We learn in the poem that the spirit of Christabel's dead mother is Geraldine's enemy.

Images of children separated from their mothers appear throughout Coleridge's poetry. For example, in "The Wanderings of Cain" (1797):

> It was a climate where, they say,
> The night is more beloved than the day.
> But who that beauteous Boy beguiled,
> That beauteous Boy no longer here?
> Alone, by night, a little child,
> In a place so silent and so wild—
> Has he no friend, no loving mother near?

In *The Destiny of Nations* (1797), there are associations between abandoned children and icy-cold landscapes.

> And first a landscape rose
> More wild and waste and desolate than where
> The white bear, drifting on a field of ice,
> Howls to her sundered cubs with piteous rage
> And savage agony

And,

> The crisp milk frozen on its innocent lips,
> Lay on the woman's arm, its little hand
> Stretched on her bosom

Polar bear cubs separated from their howling mother, freezing, dead children in their dead mother's arms—these are images borrowed from the storehouse of Coleridge's own "bleak freezings of neglect" (as he writes in his "Monody on the Death of Chatterton"), his own chilling emotional experiences of perceived neglect and abandonment that exposed him to the dark Mother, the archetypal dimension of the unconscious that, when unmediated by human experience, "thicks man's blood with cold."

Coleridge once stated that he never knew the love of a mother. Although Coleridge's mother did not die in childbirth as Christabel's did, she did send Coleridge away to a boarding school in London after his father's sudden death at the age of ten. As mentioned earlier, in all his years at Christ's Hospital, Coleridge's mother never once visited her youngest son, and, unlike the other boys, Coleridge never once went home during the holidays. In our discussion of his famous poem "Frost at Midnight," we have seen how Coleridge reminisces about the chilly isolation of those years. But even before the age of ten, while he was still living at home in Devon, Coleridge ran away from his mother in an emotional fit and almost froze to death at night "all, all, alone" on the banks of the River Otter.

Coleridge's Sexuality and LIFE-IN-DEATH

In the alchemical imagination, the feminine personification of divine wisdom, Sophia, or the *Sapientia Dei*, is a prostitute who arouses *concupiscentia* in the adept. One of her appellations is *Sophia prunikos*, Sophia the whore. Many artistic representations of "the Night-mare LIFE-IN- DEATH" portray her as a hideous skeletal figure, but some picture her as a beautiful naked woman; perhaps the latter were inspired by Coleridge's sexualized description, "*Her* lips were red, *her* looks were free, / Her locks were yellow as gold." Moreover, the specter ship is "naked" ("The naked hulk alongside came . . ."); "like vessel like crew!" Coleridge writes in the prose gloss.

"And the twain were casting dice," from *The Rime of the Ancient Mariner* illustrated by Herbert Cole, 1900.

Thus, the figure of LIFE-IN-DEATH has sexual overtones. In French, orgasm is called "la petite mort," the little death, a symbolic expression that conveys the experience of letting go of consciousness and dying in the arms of a lover, into the Dionysian oneness of everything. A heterosexual man's experience of Woman, however, as one who "thicks man's blood with cold" is a very different experience from the woman who makes a man's blood run hot. Sadly, Coleridge paints a picture of frigidity when he and his wife are naked in bed together: "All [is] as cold & calm as a deep Frost." He believes this is because Sarah is "uncommonly cold in her feelings of animal Love."[14] This experience of Sarah may be accurate, a heartbreaking account of Sarah's frigidity, but it may also be a projection onto Sarah of Coleridge's frozen Eros.

Picasso is famously reported to have remarked to his lover Francoise Gilot, "For me, there are only two types of women—goddesses and doormats." Coleridge's erotic nature was like that; he was a man in a man's world for whom women were either domestic auxiliaries or, as Goethe writes in *Faust*, "Goddesses throned in solitude, sublime, / Set in no place, still less in any time." This is the famous Madonna-whore dichotomy, noticed by Freud in 1905, that characterizes the erotic imagination of many men who lack a positive maternal bond and are thus especially susceptible to an endless experience of the split feminine image.[15]

Coleridge was a spirit-mind-imagination creature who, sadly, at least as far as it is possible to tell from the written record, never chose a woman by the power of his blood or the power of the actual woman. As mentioned earlier, Coleridge married Sarah Fricker more out of an ideological commitment to the Pantisocracy venture than from any sort of real, passionate attraction, a chilly foundation for any marriage. "Mrs. Coleridge," as Coleridge was fond of calling his wife Sarah (who changed her name from Sarah to Sara because her husband preferred that spelling), found herself not among the goddesses but the doormats. One of the most vivid examples of this fact comes from Coleridge's account of returning home from a ten-month trip to Germany in 1798 with the Wordsworths, a trip that included a four-month stay at the University of

Göttingen to study German philosophy. Sarah was planning to go with her husband but had to stay behind due to the birth of their second son Berkeley. Berkeley tragically died in February 1799, however, and Coleridge was by all accounts heartbroken. Nevertheless, he chose not to return home until July. When he finally came back, Coleridge found the domestic situation to be less than ideal. Hartley, their firstborn son, got scabies in September, and the cottage had to be fumigated with sulfur. Then, in the heavy rains, the whole place flooded. Coleridge wrote the following in a letter to his friend Southey: "Our little Hovel is almost afloat—poor Sara tired off her legs with servanting—the house stinks of Sulphur . . . I however, sunk in Spinoza, remain as undisturbed as a Toad in a Rock."[16] The split between the earthy, domestic reality of "servanting" that Sarah carried and the world of mental and spiritual ideas that Coleridge employed to distance and shield himself from painful reality on the ground is on full display here. Sarah landed in Coleridge's everyday life, only to find herself alienated from her husband's erotic imagination, trapped in one side of his mother complex, the icy side, for which kindness is no cure.

By way of contrast, Coleridge's fantasies of Sara Hutchinson, aka Asra as Coleridge refers to her in his poetry and *Notebooks*, are warm, filled with images of "firelight, warm climates, exoticism."[17] Coleridge fell deeply in love with Asra, Wordsworth's sister-in-law, in 1799 while he was married to his wife Sarah. Coleridge desired her intensely but, paralyzed by his continually divided being, played out his desire exclusively on the level of a beautiful dream. "You stood before me like a thought, / A dream remembered in a dream," Coleridge writes in "Recollections of Love" (1807), almost certainly addressed to Asra, who was no domestic doormat but an idealized goddess. Coleridge's relationship with his very first love, Mary Evans, "whom for five years I loved even to madness," Coleridge confesses, from about 1788–1794, or from the ages of sixteen to twenty-two, was the sister of Tom Evans, a schoolboy whom he befriended at Christ's Hospital. Coleridge met Mary while visiting Tom at his home and fell in love with her, but in the years to follow kept his feelings to himself. As with Asra, his love for Mary was never consummated or realized. Finally, in October 1795, Mary married another man, and Coleridge married his wife Sarah Fricker that same month.

Coleridge's Nightmare Women

Coleridge's relationships with women are bound up with his mother complex. The "Night-mare LIFE-IN-DEATH" personifies the dark archetypal dimension of that complex.

As with many rational and spiritual men of his time, Coleridge's erotic imagination was terrifying to his conscious sense of self as well as fascinating and compelling. It was surprising to me, however, to discover the extent to which Coleridge, the great visionary poet, suffered so tremendously from a horror of the "Woman." Frightening female figures in Coleridge's dreams expressed a fear of natural cycles of life and death—of the body, of Nature personified as a witch—as well as emotions and fantasies that seemed crazy and dangerous and thus threatened his feeling of integrity and identity.

LIFE-IN-DEATH, Coleridge writes, is a "Night-mare." *The Oxford English Dictionary* gives one definition of nightmare as "a female spirit or monster supposed to beset people and animals by night." Coleridge had numerous nightmares of frightening females; they tormented him incessantly in his dreams. In 1803, for instance, Coleridge records a dream of a "frightful pale woman" (reminiscent of LIFE-IN-DEATH, who is pale as "leprosy") who gives a "shameful disease": "I was followed up and down by a frightful pale woman who, I thought, wanted to kiss me, & had the property of giving a shameful disease by breathing in the face."[18] Ted Hughes found and commented on another one, "a most frightful dream of a Woman," Coleridge wrote in his notebooks on November 28, 1800. "A most frightful dream of a Woman whose features were blended with darkness catching hold of my right eye & attempting to pull it out—I caught hold of her arm fast—a horrid feel—Wordsworth cried aloud to me hearing [my] scream—heard his cry [&] thought it cruel he did not come / but did not wake till the cry was repeated a third time—the Woman's name Ebn Ebn Thalud—When I awoke, my right eyelid swelled."[19] As Hughes notes in his discussion, the woman's name, Ebn Ebn Thalud, conjures up imagery of black night—ebony—an attribute of the goddess Isis in Apuleius's *Metamorphoses*, as well as the waters of death; *thalassa* in Greek means the sea and *thanatos* means death. Coleridge's dream of Ebn Ebn Thalud is thus significantly related to the figure of LIFE-IN-DEATH in *The Ancient Mariner*.

The nightmare Woman threatens to take out Coleridge's right eye, which sends him into a paroxysm of fear. When he awakes, his right eye swells. In a 1919 essay, *The Uncanny*, Freud notes that repressed ambivalence about sex can manifest as "anxiety about one's eyes, the fear of going blind."[20] Freud's reasoning here is that if men are at odds with their sexual impulses, then the unconscious creates a defense against those impulses that manifests as a fantasy of castration to rid oneself of the sexual conflict. But since castration is also frightening to the masculine ego, the unconscious disguises the castration fantasy by reimagining it as a fear of losing one's eyes. As proof, Freud offers the tragic story of Oedipus who, when he learns that he has slept with his mother, in disgust and despair, unable to accept what he has done, physically blinds himself with long gold pins from his dead wife's brooches.

The right eye is the eye of reason, so to speak, said to be connected to the left hemisphere of the brain that handles reading, writing, and calculations, while the right hemisphere of the brain processes information in terms of image and intuition. Therefore, one could say that Coleridge's nightmare Woman is a personification of the right hemisphere of his brain in all-out war against the left hemisphere. Another way to put this is to say that she is a personification of Coleridge's muse. Or, in Coleridge's philosophical language, a personification of the secondary or poetic imagination, namely "a superior voluntary control . . . co-existing with the conscious will" that "dissolves, diffuses, dissipates, in order to recreate."[21] But Ebn Ebn Thalud does not *coexist* with the conscious will; she dramatically *opposes* it. Moreover, Coleridge can feel her, touch her, a "horrid feel" he says. For Coleridge, the nightmare is a dream that has become sensuously real and, as such, is tantamount to madness.

Wotan, Attis, and the Great Mother

In his mid-twenties, Coleridge was Wotan, a godlike STORM-BLAST of poetic-prophetic imagination who brought magical runes out of deep waters and laid them out for all to see in the pages of his "Kubla Khan," "Christabel," and *The Rime of the Ancient Mariner*. Wotan, the Germanic god of storms and poets, is an especially clear archetypal parallel to Coleridge's relationship to ecstatic states of inspiration. For example, in the latter half of *The Ancient Mariner*, as the Mariner returns home after blessing the water-snakes in a redemptive revelation of the God in nature, storms begin, lightning falls, and the sky comes to life in a fiery burst of energy. Wotan is a god who—in distinction to Coleridge the man—*intentionally gouges out his right eye* and throws it as a sacrifice into the well of Mimisbrunnr located in the roots of the world tree Yggdrasil. He does this in exchange for the gift of inner sight, of prophecy and poetry given by the Earth Mother.[22] The Jungian analyst Eric Neumann argues that the Wotan myth is an example of "upper castration," that is, an intentional sacrifice of "the clear eye of higher knowledge" as the mythic price to be paid for visionary or prophetic inspiration.[23]

Did Coleridge refuse the sacrifice? Keats thought so. In a famous 1817 letter describing "Negative Capability," Keats criticizes Coleridge as incapable of "being in uncertainties, mysteries, doubts, without any irritable reaching after fact or reason": "Coleridge, for instance, would let go by a fine isolated verisimilitude caught from the Penetralium of mystery, from being incapable of remaining content with half-knowledge."[24] And it is true that, just as in the dream Coleridge recoils in horror at the prospect of losing his right eye, in his thirties Coleridge held fast to his intellect ("like God's own head") as a defense against the nightmare visions of his body and blood.

Whereas Wotan sacrifices his right eye as upper castration to *gain* poetic vision from the Earth Mother, in the Greek myth, Attis, the son of Cybele, the Mother of gods and humanity, sacrifices his genitals in a lower castration to *escape* the power of the Great Mother.[25] Cybele, the story goes, becomes entranced with her son's long-haired beauty and falls in love with him. But when Attis falls in love with the nymph Sangaritas, Cybele becomes enraged and kills the nymph. Attis then goes mad and castrates himself in a crazed attempt to rid himself of his sexual and erotic longings. "Ah, death to them! he said, and cropped his groin's weight. Suddenly, no signs of manhood remained. His madness became a model: soft-skinned acolytes toss their hair and cut their worthless organs."[26] For Attis, the power of the erotic imagination leads to madness, which leads to castration as an attempt to escape both.

At the time he wrote *The Ancient Mariner*, Coleridge was the Germanic Wotan. A few years later, he was the Greek Attis. Just three years after publishing *The Ancient Mariner* in 1798, Coleridge wrote "The poet is dead in me" in a hysterical, tragically despondent letter to William Godwin.[27] A year later, in his poem "Dejection: An Ode," Coleridge continues the castration theme: "And haply by abstruse research to steal / From my own nature all the natural man—/ This was my sole resource, my only plan." And the Attis theme continues even sixteen years after "Dejection," in an 1818 letter to an artist friend, W. Collins, where Coleridge admits that "poetry is out of the question. The attempt would only hurry me into that sphere of acute feelings from which abstruse research, the mother of self-oblivion, presents an asylum."[28] What Coleridge means by "abstruse research" is rational philosophy of the sort he studied at the University of Göttingen in 1799 in an attempt to escape the compelling pull of what began as poetic, erotic ecstasy but seemed more and more to turn into an addiction to delusion. Much as that nightmare woman Ebn Ebn Thalud threatened to tear out Coleridge's right eye, much as the "Night-mare LIFE-IN-DEATH" made the Mariner's "blood run cold," the fear Coleridge felt toward the feminine personification of his own soul at this time was not unlike the fear of being under the power of a "supernatural agency" "from whatever source of delusion," the very theme that, as Coleridge tells us, the Ancient Mariner is based on.

In midlife, not only abstruse philosophy but also conservative politics and Trinitarian Christianity were asylums from divine madness. For example, by the age of thirty-seven, when Coleridge founded and published "a literary, moral, and political weekly paper" called *The Friend* (1809–1810), his political leanings were far from the French Revolution; he was a conservative and traditional Tory. This was also around the time that Coleridge became the Church of England's de facto intellectual spokesman. Coleridge's most significant religious writings from this period are *Lay Sermons* (1817), *Aids to Reflection* (1825), and *The Constitution of Church and State* (1830), works which bear little similarity to *The Rime of the Ancient Mariner* (1798), "Christabel" (1797–1800), and "Kubla Khan" (1797).

Coleridge was not a god. Neither was he *only* the daimonic poet in "Kubla Khan." He was a gifted and terrified "Archangel a little damaged," and, truth be told, much more than a little.[29] Given Coleridge's devout allegiance to the Christian rational mind and spirit coupled with an autoerotic narcissistic wound amplified by opium addiction, his relationship with the Great Mother of the erotic unconscious was too overwhelming to contain, and, like Attis, he could neither unite with nor separate from the fires of passion. The cost of castrating his erotic imagination was high but it allowed him to survive. The cost of allowing the muse to fully have her way with him might have led Coleridge to either psychological death—madness—or physical death. There is no sign that Coleridge had any relationship during his lifetime that could have acted as a support or container to understand this dilemma and help him metabolize it.

The Jungian analyst Nathan Schwartz-Salant interprets the Attis-Cybele dilemma as "mankind's greatest dilemma. . . . It is still our *prima materia*, and it still contains a spirit of union that has not been extracted."[30] What can be said with certainty in the context of this book is that the Attis-Cybele mythologem contains a spirit of union that has not been extracted from *The Rime of the Ancient Mariner*. We will revisit this myth further when we discuss the Mariner's return to shore.

CHAPTER 13

Celebrating a Last Supper with Oneself

A Dream

We left off with our Mariner as he bites his own flesh and drinks his own blood, thus opening his consciousness to a bizarre, dream-like specter ship sailing out of the setting sun carrying both DEATH and LIFE-IN-DEATH, possibly a reverberation in Coleridge's memory of the dream his neighbor Mr. Cruickshank told him of a specter ship sailing out of the sun the same month he began to write *The Ancient Mariner.*

In a poetic fragment, Coleridge raises the question: "What if the dreaming psyche were *really real*?"

What if you slept
And what if
In your sleep
You dreamed
And what if
In your dream
You went to heaven
And there plucked a strange and beautiful flower
And what if
When you awoke

You had that flower in your hand
Ah, what then?[1]

Shortly after 9/11, I had a terrifying and unforgettable dream in which the solution to the problem of war was vividly expressed as a necessity to drink my own blood. It was certainly not beautiful, but it was one of the most powerful and unforgettable dreams of my life.

In this chapter we will discuss the psychological reality of my dream. By doing so, I hope to shed some light on the meaning of the imagery of drinking one's own blood as it appears in *The Ancient Mariner*, as well as explore the relevance of that image for our personal and collective lives today.

What Can One Person Do about the Problem of War?

On September 11, 2001, Al-Qaeda hijacked AA flight 11 and UA flight 175 and crashed these two airliners into the North and South Towers of the World Trade Center in New York City. An hour and a half later, both towers collapsed, killing 2,996 people, injuring 6,000 others, and causing at least $19 billion in property damage. I was far away from New York that day, in Switzerland, where I was engaged in training as a Jungian analyst. I vividly recall walking up the steps of the retreat center in the Alps where our seminars were held as one of my teachers passed me on the way down. Knowing that I was an American, with a shocked and shaken look on her face, she said, "Terrorists have attacked the United States!" Her announcement could not have been more incongruous with the tranquil surroundings I was in and my peaceful state of mind. All of us there in Switzerland, regardless of nationality, regardless of politics, were shaken and stunned, reeling with the massive effect of this event. We were soon glued to the television, trying to learn more but also wondering how much of the news we could take.

What could I, one little person, possibly do? This was the question that haunted me on 9/11, and for days to follow. Ten days later, I had a long dream which gave the answer: drink your own blood.

> *It is night and I am at a gathering of men, like some kind of secret society, outdoors in a parking lot. We have all driven there. I am going to give a lecture to this group. At one point two men are talking about the situation in the Middle East with Afghanistan. They are having an argument about it. One is my friend. I realize that my friend knows half the story from the United States side, and the other man knows the other half of the story from the Afghan side; they each have half the truth. As I realize that, I consider that it is my job to somehow unite them. They need to come together.*

At the start of the dream, the dream ego (i.e., me) is preparing to give a lecture to a gathering of men and then seeking to mediate the war between the United States man and the Afghanistan man. I realize that each side has half the truth. As the dream progresses, I am told what to do if I want the two warring sides to come together. I must cut my right hand and drink my own blood from a chalice. The whole scene is dark, intense, bizarre.

> *I say, "OK I will do it, go through with the ritual." Arrangements are made. My blood is taken with that dark knife, from the palm of my right hand, and poured into the chalice. Then a priest figure comes out, a dark figure in a trance state wearing a hood over his head. He is not talking. He walks around me. This is a very tense moment. He is whispering a trance prayer to Satan behind me, whispering into my ear, "Satan, Satan . . ." I can feel archetypal energies enter my body. They threaten to overwhelm me, as if I am losing consciousness. At that point I stop the sequence*

> *before I drink my blood. I say, "No—no more, that's it." They all protest. I say, "This is having a bad effect on my psyche, end of story, that's it." This is accepted reluctantly; everyone is agitated and angry. The spokesman disbands the group. I feel like in some years I will know more about what is going on here.*

A ritual ceremony, complete with invocations to Satan, an iron blade, and a chalice? This was beyond bizarre; it seemed psychotic, even evil. Hesitatingly, however, I agreed to go through with the ritual. I cut my right hand with the blade and put my blood in the chalice, but could not bear to drink my own blood. I woke up terrified.

The next day, shaken and deeply disturbed, I did my best to tell one of the Swiss analysts about the dream, but could barely talk. For the remainder of my time in Switzerland, over a week, I was unable to shake off a feeling of creepy anxiety, of disorientation akin to the intense fear I felt in the dream itself, akin to the fear others feel in the presence of the Ancient Mariner.

> I moved my lips—the Pilot shrieked
> And fell down in a fit;
> The holy Hermit raised his eyes,
> And prayed where he did sit.
>
> I took the oars: the Pilot's boy,
> Who now doth crazy go,
> Laughed loud and long, and all the while
> His eyes went to and fro.
> "Ha! ha!" quoth he, "full plain I see,
> The Devil knows how to row."

Yet, as the dream itself states, in time I would become more capable of understanding its nightmare message. In this respect I was immensely helped by the containing vessel, so to speak, of Jung's alchemical writings.

Taking Back Projections as Symbolic Death

The theme that runs like a red thread throughout this book is Jung's insight that "we are threatened with universal genocide if we cannot work out the way of salvation through a symbolic death."[2] As previously mentioned, Jung wrote this during the height of the Cold War. But already at the start of WWI, decades earlier, Jung had recognized that the problem of war will continue forever until "man puts the bloody knife into himself" instead of his perceived enemies.[3]

In her book *Encounters with the Soul* (1981), Barbara Hannah recounts a discussion in which someone asked Jung if he thought there would be a World War III. Jung answered that our only hope for survival is if enough people can stand the suffering involved with taking back projections from enemies outside. "I remember vividly that when Jung was asked in a discussion if he thought there would be atomic war, he answered: 'I think it depends on how many people can stand the tension of opposites in themselves. If enough can, I think we shall just escape the worst. But if not, and there is atomic war, our civilization will perish, as so many civilizations have perished before, but on a much larger scale.'" Hannah continues, "This shows the tremendous value which Jung set on standing the tension between the opposites, and, if possible, uniting them in ourselves. For if we project the dark opposite beyond the Iron Curtain or onto the terrorists, for example, we are failing to contribute the grain that we might place on the positive side of the world scale of peace or war."[4]

Shadowy contents boil in the bodies and blood of all of us. When we are unconscious of these contents, we inevitably project them. Drinking our blood, therefore, means introjecting, rather than projecting, the shadow. Integrating the shadow is incredibly challenging. We feel as if we are dying when we experience the changes the unconscious brings—changes in perception, changes in attitude, changes in embodied well-being, changes in emotional constitution, changes in states of consciousness—and we are dying to the person we were, or thought we were. As we become more whole, however, a grain of sand is taken off the negative side of the scales of sociopolitical conflict.

Celebrating a Last Supper with Ourselves

Jung's ventures into alchemy are difficult and strange, but they are also immensely helpful for understanding and appreciating the value of the archetypal symbolism of our dreams as well as visionary poetry. This is especially true for the bizarre image of eating and drinking oneself.

The two-thousand-year-old tradition of Western alchemy has an almost endless capacity to create variations on the theme of turning oneself into a circulatory process. While some of these images are disturbing—Zosimos, a Greek alchemist living in Egypt at the turn of the fourth century, dreamt of a priest who gruesomely consumes himself at the beginning of a transformation process—they are all central to the alchemical opus. The philosopher's stone is said to "consume a great quantity of its own spirit," which means, according to Jung, "self-impregnation by one's own soul." The pelican flask, a common symbol in medieval and Renaissance alchemy derived from a myth that the pelican bites her flesh and feeds her blood to her young, is shaped in a way that allows spirits to be distilled or extracted from the material at the bottom, rise, and then descend again to the matter below.[5] Perhaps the best-known alchemical image of eating and drinking oneself is the uroboros, the snake that eats its own tail.

Many years after my 9/11 dream, I came across a chapter in Jung's *Mysterium Coniunctionis* (1955) titled *The Regeneration of the King* in which Jung addresses the problem of war, the problem that occupied me at the time of my dream. War, Jung writes, is "sociopolitical insanity" caused by an unconscious enactment of inner psychic conflicts taking place "on the plane of projection in the form of political tension and murderous violence."[6] Effectively asking the same question that preoccupied me after 9/11—what can one person do?—Jung says that to contribute to peace we must take back those projections. In the symbolic language of the dream, of alchemy, of Romantic poetry, we must eat our own flesh and drink our own blood, not as an evil or psychotic practice but as a meaningful ritual.

Drawing from the imagery of the Catholic mass in a way that mirrors my dream exactly, Jung's prescription is to "celebrate a Last Supper with ourselves": "If the projected conflict is to be healed, it must return into the psyche of the individual, where it had its unconscious beginnings. He must celebrate a Last Supper with himself, and eat his own flesh and drink his own blood; which means that he must recognize and accept the other in himself. But if he persists in his one-sidedness, the two lions will tear each other to pieces. Is this perhaps the meaning of Christ's teaching, that each must bear his own cross?"[7] You can perhaps imagine the effect that reading this passage had on me many years after my dream.

I was comforted both by Jung's acknowledgment of the meaning of eating and drinking oneself as well as his acknowledgment of how difficult this is. "There is no meal worse than one's own flesh," Jung writes elsewhere.[8] Indeed. In his *Visions Seminars* (1930–34), some twenty years prior to the *Mysterium Coniunctionis*, Jung discusses the Satanic quality permeating my dream of putting my blood in the Holy Chalice. From the Christian perspective, the symbolism of drinking one's own blood is "almost a sort of Black Mass . . . an anti-Christian meal, the Christian communion but reversed": "Drinking the blood meant a reidentification with nature, as in the Dionysian cult it was a reconciliation of man estranged from nature through civilization. . . . But to reach the primitive level it is the reverse sacrifice, almost a sort of Black Mass, for it is necessary to give up certain accomplishments. . . . This is an anti-Christian meal, the Christian communion but reversed. It is not what is ahead or above that is to be assimilated—the thing that is greater, more differentiated, higher—but the thing that is lower, less differentiated, more ancient. This is to be reintegrated and thus brought back to life again, for the purpose of destroying the highly differentiated historical condition which we call the Christian age."[9]

From the depth psychological perspective, which is an interpretation of the dream symbolism, drinking one's own blood is a highly ethical expression of a desire to bring to life again "the thing that is lower." This desire runs throughout *The Ancient Mariner* and, when it comes to the impact of the image on us personally, represents a lifelong symbolic prescription to become more and more physically, emotionally, and experientially related to our complexes and their affective core, even—or especially—negative manifestations such as rage, jealousy, hate, and envy. That is the prescription for peace and an antidote to racism, sexism, homophobia—all the "-isms" and all the phobias.

For the Mariner, eating and drinking himself opens a doorway to the land of the dead through which the *terror tremendum* of the repressed Feminine spirit of the moon and of the night pours forth. Whereas my dream says, "drink your own blood from a vessel," the

Mariner drinks his blood straight from the vein. "Writing one hundred years before Freud's *The Interpretation of Dreams* (1900)," Ross Woodman notes, "Coleridge did not possess a science of the unconscious,"[10] in other words, a vessel to contain the fiery contents of his body and blood and thus help him relate to and metabolize the raw material of the spirit of the depths into his conscious life. As previously noted, this dynamic is the crisis of Romanticism that depth psychology evolved to address.

CHAPTER 14

"And Straight the Sun Was Flecked with Bars"

The Eclipse of the Sun

As the Mariner watches the specter ship, she drives between his ship and the setting Sun, like the moon eclipsing the Sun, and we witness the first conjunction of opposites in *The Ancient Mariner*. Masculine and feminine meet, fire and water combine, and sun and moon touch. It is not a pretty sight.

> The western wave was all a-flame.
> The day was well nigh done!
> Almost upon the western wave
> Rested the broad bright Sun;
> When that strange shape drove suddenly
> Betwixt us and the Sun.
> And straight the Sun was flecked with bars,
> (Heaven's Mother send us grace!)
> As if through a dungeon-grate he peered
> With broad and burning face.

As feminine draws close, she devours the Sun ("like God's own head") in her body. The Sun's "broad and burning face" gruesomely peers through the ship's ribs "as if through a dungeon-grate," suggestive of the ancient Platonic and Orphic doctrine of *soma sema*, "the body a tomb," the body as a prison house of finitude for the spirit.

Most of us probably do not feel any especially intense fear when witnessing an eclipse; we know it is just the moon passing between the earth and the sun. But the human species has not always known this. If one willingly suspends one's belief in astronomy, it is possible to feel what an eclipse might have felt like in an older age. Look up! The dragon is devouring the sun. Will the darkness last forever? From the psychological perspective, the terror of an eclipse is a projection into the sky of the human fear of both symbolic and literal death—both LIFE-IN-DEATH and DEATH. Such is the nature of LIFE-IN-DEATH imagined as an eclipse of the Sun, a mysterious power that kills to re-create. As an archetypal symbol in our dreams, the eclipse of the sun corresponds with a very scary experience, a feeling that the light has gone out. "What is the use of anything I have ever done or aspired to?" we might ask when an inner eclipse is happening in our lives.

I had a dream of an eclipsed sun almost thirty years ago. In this dream, I am with an unknown woman sitting on the floor of a beautiful and spacious art gallery. Many paintings line the walls, but the unknown woman wants to show me this painting, as it is the most important painting. When I woke, I thought to paint the dream because in the dream the image is a painting. In the afterword to this book, I go into more of the details of my personal story, but to stay with the painting for now, I remember at the time gazing at this image and seeing the jagged lines as if they were a shattered window. Looking back now, I see the shattering of my psychic window to the world, my conscious perspective, my values, beliefs, and goals all broken to pieces, a "heap of broken images" as in Eliot's

Thomas Elsner, *Eclipse of the Sun* (1996).

The Waste Land.[1] Clinically speaking, I was in a major depressive episode, checking all the boxes—depressed mood, loss of interest or pleasure in almost all activities, sleep disturbance, tiredness, fatigue, low energy, a sense of worthlessness, impaired ability to make decisions, recurrent thoughts of death, and suicidal ideation. As I painted the heart in the middle of the dark sun, however, I remember thinking that it looked like a fetus. This touched off an intuition that perhaps there is, or could be, a meaningful process of development hidden within what felt like *only* a catastrophe.

Many years after my eclipse of the sun dream, I came across the symbolism of the eclipse in my studies of Jung, particularly in Jung's alchemical writings, where I was stunned to find my own dream mirrored in the images of alchemy. Alchemists know that gold is produced *ex sol et umbra*, out of the sun and its shadow. The Jungian analyst Monika Wikman entitles her book about the transformation of consciousness *Pregnant Darkness*, a title taken from alchemy in which the black sun represents, as Jung notes, "a state of incubation or pregnancy."[2] The Jungian analyst Theodor Abt points this out as well in his book on Arabic alchemy: "This first union of sun and moon at the time of the eclipse is the moment of impregnation, 'before which there is no operation.'"[3]

In the dream, two hands clasp from opposite sides. Because I did not have the skill to draw those two hands, I substituted a geometric design creating the impression of a vessel or container for the black sun. My sun, my consciousness, was eventually reborn through the holding environment of analysis; *two* hands held my ego death, the therapist's hand and mine, one authentic step at a time. Without a working analytic vessel, there would have been no meaningful imaginal space for the transformation process to unfold *as a symbolic process*. In that case, DEATH, either psychologically as depression and madness or physically, would have been the ending as well as the starting point of the work.

In analysis, we work to create an atmosphere in which sun and moon, day and night, masculine and feminine, conscious and unconscious, are neither alienated nor fused but married through love and understanding. Even in the best of circumstances, however, we can never avoid the darkness; knowing the territory does not take away the suffering that comes from walking it as a vulnerable little human. "Rejoice when your matter turns black," the alchemists repeat over and over, but they also were realistic enough to repeatedly affirm that many have perished in their work.

For people (such as Coleridge) who are identified with the solar-masculine, the encounter with the lunar-feminine as an eclipse of the Sun is always the first step toward that hoped-for sacred wedding of contraries. And yet, the first contact of opposites—as in *The Ancient Mariner* where sun and moon, fire and water, day and night first touch—is always a psycho-physical-spiritual emergency, always a symbolic LIFE-IN-DEATH as the alternative to literal DEATH. The alchemical *nigredo* always dissolves old forms of consciousness before giving birth to the new.

CHAPTER 15

"The Hornèd Moon with One Bright Star"

Into the Belly of the Goddess

Then said the veiled shadow "Thou hast felt
What 'tis to die and live again before
Thy fated hour. That thou hadst power to do so
Is thy own safety; thou hadst dated on thy doom."

—Keats, "The Fall of Hyperion: A Dream"

As the Sun sets in the West, the feminine-lunar world ascends in the East, and Sun and Moon move like contrapuntal melodies in a musical composition. The Mariner and the crew are immersed in dark night. Some water returns as dew drips from the sails. LIFE-IN-DEATH "whistles thrice" and the "hornèd moon" rises with "one bright star" in her "nether tip."

The stars were dim, and thick the night,
The steersman's face by his lamp gleamed white;
From the sails the dew did drip—
Till clomb above the eastern bar
The hornèd Moon, with one bright star
Within the nether tip.

No star, of course, can ever appear *within* the moon, for the moon is roughly 250,000 miles away from the earth while the nearest star, Proxima Centauri, is 24,984,092,897,478.723 miles away, or 4.25 light-years. The star-dogged moon is the stuff of legend, not non-sense or "proto-science" but a symbol projected into the heavens that expresses the meaning of the drama taking place below.

"The true man is the star in us," writes Paracelsus (ca. 1493–1541); "the star desires to drive mankind toward greater wisdom."[1] The star symbolizes guidance from the eternal celestial world—in psychological language, the archetypal psyche as distinct from the personal which appears to us in the form of symbolic imagination rather than rational knowledge. Martin Ruland (1569–1611), a German physician and alchemist, asserts that "imagination is the star in man, the celestial or supercelestial body."[2] In the Bible, the collective hope for a Messiah is projected onto a star that rises in the East and guides the wise men to the birth of Jesus. The Mariner's star also rises in the East, guiding him to a new revelation of the sacred; his star leads not to Christ but straight into the belly of the *Taurokeros Mene*, the horned Moon, an epiphany of the goddess: "Hear, Goddess queen, diffusing silver light, / Bull-horn'd and wand'ring thro' the gloom of Night" sings an Orphic hymn to Selene, the Moon goddess (ca. third or second century BCE).[3]

The emblem of the crescent moon with one star inside her found in Muslim mosques and flags has its origin in goddess symbolism. Hekate, the holy protectress of Byzantium, an ancient Greek city that is today's Istanbul, was associated with a star and crescent. When Constantine (the emperor of Rome from 306 to 337 CE and the first Roman emperor to convert to Christianity) conquered Byzantium in 330, he declared the city to be the new capital of the Roman Empire, renamed it Constantinople, and the star and crescent became incorporated into the symbolism of the Christian

National flag of Turkey.

Mary, the *stella maris*. When the Ottoman empire conquered Constantinople in 1453, the star and crescent was adopted as a symbol of Islam. And, in 1798, the image reappears as one of the major symbols for the Romantics as they are guided by dark Eros into the shadow side of the Western mind. One finds the crescent moon in Keats's poem *Endymion* (1818), where she brings the shepherd boy Endymion dreams and visions that inspire his descent into the underworld. In "The Favors of the Moon," Charles Baudelaire (1821–67) imagines the moon as an "image of the fearful goddess, the fateful godmother, the poisonous nurse of all the moonstruck of the world." The crescent moon is also present in the twentieth-century art of Picasso, Joyce, and Pollock.

When the horned moon rises with one bright star in *The Ancient Mariner*, the Mariner is drawn into the mediatrix energy of the anima that belongs to a man's creative inner activity. The Mariner *is* that bright star in the belly of the Moon, the only member of the ship's crew pulled into her, the only one fated to undergo

LIFE-IN-DEATH instead of literal DEATH. For the patriarchal spirit, however, all death, symbolic or literal, is appalling. Therefore, for both Mariner and the ship's crew, the star-dogged moon is a *dis-aster*, a bad omen, an *astrum sinistrum*.

Coleridge had read of sailors' reports that the sight of a star within the moon foretells an evil event. The ship's crew all feel this way. They do not welcome the horned Moon "in God's name" as they did both the Albatross and the rising Sun! And with good reason. For them, the lunar initiation is pure poison; it means the sacrificial death of conventional consciousness. When the Moon rises, the crew fall dead.

> One after one, by the star-dogged Moon,
> Too quick for groan or sigh,
> Each turned his face with a ghastly pang,
> And cursed me with his eye.
>
> Four times fifty living men,
> (And I heard nor sigh nor groan)
> With heavy thump, a lifeless lump,
> They dropped down one by one.
>
> The souls did from their bodies fly,—
> They fled to bliss or woe!
> And every soul, it passed me by,
> Like the whizz of my cross-bow!

Coleridge divides the number of men onboard the ship into a quaternity—four times fifty living men—a symbolic totality of collective masculine consciousness. As mentioned previously in our discussion of the Mariner shooting the Albatross ("*I* shot the Albatross" [emphasis added]), the Mariner is the one among the many, the 201st man on board, the only individual. The philosopher's stone in alchemy is called the "solitaire" and the "orphan stone" because the experience of individuation, becoming oneself, carries with it a necessary and terrible feeling of aloneness. The Mariner bemoans the fact that he is "all, all alone" in his living death and identifies himself with all the "slimy things" in the sea below as the "beautiful" men all lie dead around him. Loneliness is a function of the Mariner's "soul in agony."

> Alone, alone, all, all alone,
> Alone on a wide wide sea!

And never a saint took pity on
My soul in agony.

The many men, so beautiful!
And they all dead did lie:
And a thousand thousand slimy things
Lived on; and so did I.

There is amazing, although unwelcome, psychological wisdom in these lines. When we encounter the shadow side of our personality we become, as Schwartz-Salant puts it, "ultimately abject to ourselves. We feel unlovable, without value, even disgusting." The word agony comes from *agon* in ancient Greek, meaning a struggle or conflict between opposing forces—in this case, the "many men" vs. the "*I*," the "beautiful" vs. the "slimy." These are among the opposites the Mariner now holds as an *agon* in his own soul. In addition, without the Albatross to mediate between "the sky and the sea, and the sea and the sky," these opposites also now weigh heavily on the Mariner's "weary eye."

I closed my lids, and kept them close,
And the balls like pulses beat;
For the sky and the sea, and the sea and the sky
Lay like a load on my weary eye,
And the dead were at my feet.

In these few lines, we witness a turning point in the evolution of human consciousness: when God (the Albatross) is dead, the human being becomes the locus of the symbolic.[4] It is a terrible suffering, a suffering so intense that the Mariner wishes for actual death but cannot die.

Seven days, seven nights, I saw that curse,
And yet I could not die.

The experience of symbolic death as the doorway to deep transformation is what the Wedding Guest fears as the Mariner hypnotizes him with his gaze, drawing him into the *agon*.

LIFE-IN-DEATH and the Obliteration of Ego Consciousness

Perhaps it is worthwhile here to take a step back and recall what brought the ship and crew to this point. It all goes back to the Mariner shooting the Albatross. As the crew fall over dead, their souls fly past the Mariner, "like the whizz of my cross-bow!" As we have seen, when the Mariner shoots the Albatross, he differentiates himself as an *I* from the *we*. As the voyage continues, that separation becomes more and more extreme. When the crew hang the dead Albatross around the Mariner's neck, they further separate from him as an enemy, heretic, and criminal. Now, when the Moon rises and all the men fall dead, the Mariner, the *I*, is totally alone, identified not with humanity any longer but with the "slimy things" of the depths.

This imagery is familiar to Jungian analysts working with patients in the initial stages of the individuation process. The first-generation Jungian Esther Harding describes her experience with a male patient as if she is familiar with the imagery in *The Ancient Mariner* and translating it into psychological prose. "Death, in the sense of ending, would be welcome, but this was a *living death*, without beginning and without end. It represents, in fact, the obliteration of ego consciousness . . . for an adult who has developed ego-consciousness and a sense of responsibility, to fall into such a condition spells the death of the ego, or insanity, unless out of this experience a new light might dawn."[5] Harding's patient welcomes death but cannot die. He is trapped in a *living death*.

A male patient of mine near the beginning of his process reported the following dream in which he also wishes for death but cannot die.

> *I had a vivid and powerful dream that I was held hostage. I submitted to death. I was shot four times in the head. The reality of death was palpable, the finality. I did not end up dying. I heard them saying, "His skull is shattered!" and I wished for death.*

As Harding recognizes, for any adult with a developed ego, *living death*—regression, the eclipse of the sun—means insanity "unless out of this experience a new light might dawn." The Mariner looks up to Heaven in hopes of finding that light, "But or ever a prayer had gusht," "a wicked whisper" turns his "heart to dust."

> I looked upon the rotting sea,
> And drew my eyes away;
> I looked upon the rotting deck,
> And there the dead men lay.
>
> I looked to heaven, and tried to pray;
> But or ever a prayer had gusht,
> A wicked whisper came, and made
> My heart as dry as dust.

What is that "wicked whisper" saying? The poem does not tell us.

A middle-aged patient of mine heard a "wicked whisper" recently in an analytic session that reminded me of the Mariner's. About midway through the hour, he fell into a reverie, forgot himself for a moment, and launched into a vivid confession of the beauty and spiritual meaning of his life. Then suddenly the reverie broke and his whole countenance changed. Becoming silent, pausing for a moment, he suddenly announced, "I'm fucked." When I asked him what he meant, he replied that all he had just expressed meant nothing in the face of the picture of the cosmos given by science, which was, he said, empty space devoid of meaning and purpose. That is the true picture of how things *really* are; the rest is just subjective delusion, fantasy. In that moment, a wicked whisper turned his heart to dust. Similarly, when Blaise Pascal (1623–62), a mathematician, philosopher, and natural scientist educated during the Enlightenment, looked up into the sky, he felt a terrifying *horror vacui*. "When I consider the short duration of my life, swallowed up in an eternity before and after, the little space I fill engulfed in the infinite immensity of spaces whereof I know nothing, and which know nothing of me, I am terrified. The eternal silence of these infinite spaces frightens me."[6] Pascal's experience is a typical experience for the Enlightened modern mind, an unintended negative consequence of relying solely on the Sun, consciousness alone, as if it were "God's own head."

Coleridge describes his personal experience of alienation from God in strikingly similar language to his Mariner: "[I] have rolled my dreary eye from earth to Heaven, and found no comfort," Coleridge writes as he, like his Mariner, looks in vain for God. But then Coleridge realizes "the hour of anguish" *is* God's presence making his "heart more tender in regard of religious feelings": "Till it pleased the Unimaginable High & Lofty One to make my Heart more tender in regard of religious feelings. My philosophical refinements, & metaphysical Theories lay by me in the hour of anguish, as toys by the bedside of a Child deadly-sick. May God continue his visitations to my soul, bowing it down, till the pride & Laodicean self-confidence of human Reason be utterly done away; and I cry with deeper & yet deeper feelings."[7] Coleridge wrote the above in a letter to Benjamin Taylor in 1796, about two years before *The*

Ancient Mariner. His personal confession is a beautiful mirror of the poetic vision unfolding before us in this section of *The Ancient Mariner*.

Will God Come Back?

The Mariner experiences the agony of seven days and nights of initiatory suffering. The number seven is the number of lunar-feminine initiation. It is the number of the days in the lunar month (four times seven) as distinct from the number twelve that characterizes the solar year. In the Roman author Apuleius's (ca. second century CE) *The Golden Ass* or *The Metamorphosis*, Lucius immerses his head seven times in the sea before he prays to the goddess Isis under the full moon. Later, when the Mariner returns to shore, he does so as one "seven days drowned."

At this point in the poem everything masculine, save for the Mariner as the property of the daimonic Female, is gone. The Albatross is dead, the Sun is dead, the crew are dead, and the Father in Heaven is absent. "The game is done! I've won! I've won!" the daimonic Female LIFE-IN-DEATH cries out in triumph. This "nightmare" is the Mariner's salvation. As we shall soon see, on the eighth night a new revelation will be born, a revelation that unites the sacred and the slime, beauty and sublimity, that brings water back to the solar wasteland and heals the Mariner's alienation from God and Nature if not other human beings.

God is gone. Will God come back? The answer is yes, but not in the form of the Albatross. The Albatross is dead, forever killed by the Mariner's crossbow and arrow, namely, the "pride & Laodicean self-confidence of human Reason." He will not fly again in the poem. Many of the Romantics felt that epochal burden. It is "too late for antique vows," Keats confesses in his "Ode to Psyche" (1819). But a new religious vision awaits discovery, no longer in the realm of a metaphysical beyond but within "some untrodden region of my mind."

> O brightest! though too late for antique vows,
> Too, too late for the fond believing lyre . . .
>
> I see, and sing, by my own eyes inspired . . .
>
> Yes, I will be thy priest [Psyche] and build a fane,
> In some untrodden region of my mind.

In "Ode: Intimations of Immortality from Recollections of Early Childhood" (1804), Wordsworth laments the loss of "the visionary gleam" he had in childhood.

> —But there's a tree, of many, one,
> A single field which I have look'd upon,
> Both of them speak of something that is gone:
> The pansy at my feet
> Doth the same tale repeat:
> Whither is fled the visionary gleam?
> Where is it now, the glory and the dream?

Similar to Keats—and all the Romantics—Wordsworth seeks for the lost divinity in the chaotic and hellish depths of the "Mind of Man" in *The Prelude*, an unfinished autobiographical opus he started in 1798 at the age of twenty-eight and never finished (the "poem to Coleridge" he called it):

> Not Chaos, not
> The darkest pit of lowest Erebus,
> Nor aught of blinder vacancy, scooped out
> By help of dreams, can breed such fear and awe
> As fall upon us often when we look
> Into our Minds, into the Mind of Man,—
> My haunt, and the main region of my song.

What Wordsworth calls "our Minds" is a collective psychological underworld comparable to what Jung would later call the collective unconscious. It is in "the darkest pit of lowest Erebus" that the Mariner will find his flash of golden fire. "Open thine eye of fire from some uncertain cloud!" Coleridge writes in "Ode to the Departing Year" (1796): "O dart the flash! O rise and deal the blow! . . . Rise, God of Nature! rise." After the Mariner's seven days and nights of initiatory suffering in the belly of the Moon, the God of Nature will rise.

CHAPTER 16

"A Spring of Love Gushed from My Heart, and I Blessed Them Unaware"

Blessing the Water-Snakes: The Rebirth of the Modern Soul

To recap: LIFE-IN-DEATH sails out of the western gate, eclipses the Sun, and leads the Mariner through seven days and nights of initiatory suffering so intense he wishes for death but cannot die. And now, on the eighth night, something new happens: the Mariner blesses the water-snakes in God's name. Everything changes. The Mariner changes; the world changes.

There is a spellbinding quality to Coleridge's writing here that is especially vivid if read out loud. As we listen, we can feel the Mariner's soul return, transformed from below, as the "slimy things" he identifies with in his agonizing isolation transform into "happy living things" in parallel with the transformation of his consciousness.

> The moving Moon went up the sky,
> And nowhere did abide:
> Softly she was going up,
> And a star or two beside—
>
> Her beams bemocked the sultry main,
> Like April hoar-frost spread;

But where the ship's huge shadow lay,
The charmed water burnt always
A still and awful red.

Beyond the shadow of the ship,
I watched the water-snakes:
They moved in tracks of shining white
And when they reared, the elfish light
Fell off in hoary flakes.

Within the shadow of the ship
I watched their rich attire:
Blue, glossy green and velvet black,
They coiled and swam; and every track
Was a flash of golden fire.

O happy living things! no tongue
Their beauty might declare:
A stream of love gushed from my heart,
And I blessed them unaware:
Sure my kind saint took pity on me,
And I blessed them unaware.

The self-same moment I could pray;
And from my neck so free
The Albatross fell off, and sank
Like lead into the sea.

As we have seen in our reflections on the eclipse of the sun, when the sun, the source of all life and an emblem of collective consciousness (i.e., the light by which everyone sees in the clear light of day what is true and real), dies this is a sacred catastrophe, a time for deep introversion and reflection on the fact that we must make new commitments as to how we live our lives. We all will follow the path of the Sun; we all die, we are all reborn. The Mariner finds redemption from the Fall through a transformation of self and world that happens on its own, "unaware," autonomously, that has nothing to do with his head but everything to do with "the stream of love" gushing from his heart.

Previously, in the solar wasteland, the Mariner lifted his eye to Heaven and a "wicked whisper" turned his "heart to dust." Now, as he looks down into the moonlit sea, a sacred river flows out from his heart—"the passion and the life, whose fountains are within" and the "shaping spirit of Imagination" in "Dejection: An Ode," the sacred river Alph in "Kubla Khan"—into all of nature. Seven days and nights of initiatory suffering have released streams of feeling, of the "deeper and yet deeper feelings," as Coleridge said of himself, that the Mariner kept at bay through the "pride and Laodicean self-confidence of human Reason" (i.e., his crossbow and arrow), thus expressing Coleridge's personal faith that "deep thinking is attainable only by a man of deep feeling, and all truth is a species of revelation."[1]

"O happy living things! no tongue / Their beauty might declare," the Mariner exclaims. In an intimately confessional passage from the *Notebooks*, Coleridge gives us some insight as to why the Mariner's blessing of the water-snakes is so sacred: beauty mediates and thus redeems the split between "Truth and Feeling, the Head and the Heart" that, for Coleridge, constitutes the Fall of Man in the modern world. This revelation comes upon the Mariner as it came to Coleridge, namely, "flashlike, in the word, BEAUTY!"[2] Beauty is "the rhythm of the Soul's movements," alive both inside and outside in the perception of the world. "To a spiritual Woman," that is, to Coleridge's anima, beauty "is Music—the intelligible Language of Memory, Hope, Desiderium" flowing into the entire world, a subtle body present in everything around him, nothing subjective merely but rising to the level of the true and the real in the form of "implicit knowledge—a silent communion of the Spirit with the Spirit in Nature not without consciousness, tho' with the consciousness not successively unfolded!"

The Mariner sees flashes of golden fire in the darkness of the sea. These flashes of golden fire are sparks of the reborn sun still in the unconscious and not yet gathered into a unity, but appearing here as a promise or intuitive premonition that there may be a new collective consciousness hidden in the Mariner's horrific process of symbolic death that could give light and warmth and life to all. We have seen the "glorious Sun" rise after the Mariner shoots the bird "that brought the fog and mist," thus ushering in the age of European Enlightenment; the flash of golden fire that appears like a spark of a new dawn as the Mariner blesses the water-snakes is a new Enlightenment that includes the soul below, not only the intellect above. In his many masterful engravings, Doré pictures

this redemptive transformation as the Mariner staring down into the sea as death-fires dance at night, with the witch's oils burning amid devilish naked women.[3] In another engraving, these women in the sea transform into beautiful, sensual beings erotically reaching up to the Mariner with stars or flames of fire above their heads—flashes of golden fire reminiscent of those sparked by the water-snakes.

A flame is a vivid desire. A golden fire is not the devilish hellfire of obsessive emotional and physical energy but an image of the highest transpersonal value.[4] A thirty-year-old man in analysis reported the following.

> *I also had this vision before I went to sleep—every person with some truth in them had a flame over their heads. The most important thing in life was to keep this flame—one's soul, life essence—burning brightly. If all these flames were to go out, the world would be in darkness. The flame was one's love for God, an objective fact; angels can see it. The flame draws them down and attracts them.*

In this dream, one's "love for God" links the *I* with God. One famously finds this image at the dawn of the Christian eon, at Pentecost, where flames of fire appear above the heads of the apostles as they look up to God in the form of a white bird in the sky. The Mariner, however, having shot that white bird, having eaten his own flesh and drunk his own blood as a celebration of the Last Supper with his psychosomatic being, looks down into the fallen world of interior and exterior nature and finds the fulfillment of this Holy Communion in a sacred bond with all living creatures, even the lowest.[5] As the Mariner blesses the creatures of the depths below, we witness a post-Christian Pentecost. As a personification of modern consciousness, the Mariner is a *salvator macrocosmi* as Christ was a *salvator microcosmi* in the first century CE.[6]

The Mariner blesses the snakes in the "huge shadow" of the ship. The Christian Church is sometimes analogized as a ship, as the barque of St. Peter for example, and the nave of the church, the central approach to the high altar, comes from the Latin word *navis*, meaning ship. Is the Mariner's redemption coming from the shadow of the ship thus a Black Mass, an anti-Christian or Satanic ritual? Other characters in the poem call the Mariner "the devil" and, as we have seen, the Mariner himself says that he has done a "hellish thing" in killing the Albatross, the collective, traditional image of Christ. And yet the Mariner identifies as a Christian both when he blesses the snakes and throughout the poem. For him, the water-snakes swimming in the shadow of Christianity are "God's creatures of the great calm," as the prose gloss states. "Surely my kind saint took pity on me," the Mariner says as he blesses the snakes, affirming—"unaware"—that the Night, the Moon, and the slimy things in the sea are *also* sacred, *also* part of God, and thus extending the Christian spirit of love into the lowest unredeemed dimensions of psyche and nature. He adds the feminine, the sacred in nature, and the necessary role of evil to the Trinitarian and patriarchal image of God.

According to Jung, blessing the snake is "the psychological, or if you like to call it so, the spiritual or religious problem of today."

> But it proves to be a hell of shock when one becomes acquainted with oneself. A new book by Graf Keyserling will appear very soon, in which he will show you how he, as a Christian spirit, met the impact of the earth and how it got him. Nietzsche avoided it, he didn't dare look at the thing. That acceptance of man as he is, is the psychological, or if you like to call it so, the spiritual or religious problem of today; that is exactly what we are up against now. But the vision goes on and says that when that happens, the serpent will take the place of the Redeemer on the cross. That means the antichrist. What would seem to us the principle of evil, will be the redeeming symbol. Then again a cycle will be completed, and we shall be as if back at the first century A.D. when they discovered the serpent was really the Redeemer. You see, then something new may begin.[7]

Blessing the snake means blessing what seems to us to be evil but really is a process of "becom[ing] acquainted" with ourselves. This, Jung knew, "proves to be a hell of a shock" as it is for the Mariner in the poem. Getting the Mariner to the point where he finally accepts the slimy things in the sea as alive and beautiful requires him to bless as sacred what is antithetical to both his traditional Christian spirituality ("O Christ! That ever this should be") and the rationality of the age of European Enlightenment. Christian tradition famously identifies the snake with Satan; St. Patrick famously drove all the snakes from Ireland in the fifth century CE, following in the footsteps of the Christian Roman emperor Theodosius (who adopted the creed of Nicaea as the orthodox doctrine of Christianity), who, in 392 CE, forbade the offering of blood sacrifice and condemned nature-based worship as evil.[8] From the perspective the Enlightenment, the Mariner's visions are psychotic delusions.

In the *Visions Seminars*, Jung comments on a painting by Christiana Morgan, a young American woman, of a snake wrapped around a Christian cross as if the snake were a redeemer, and recounts a dream of Morgan's in which, like the Mariner, she accepts with love "the element," Jung comments, "which threatened her before with complete destruction." She embraces a snake and says, "You are beautiful to me."[9] As in *The Ancient Mariner*, Morgan's embrace of the snake in this dream signals a positive turning point in her psychological process. In reading Jung's extended commentary on this dream, it is easy to feel as if he is commenting on the blessing of the water-snakes in *The Ancient Mariner*, because he is. What it means psychologically to bless the snake is not limited to Morgan, or Coleridge; this imagery may not be alive and meaningful for everyone, but it was definitely alive and meaningful for the Romantic poets in general.

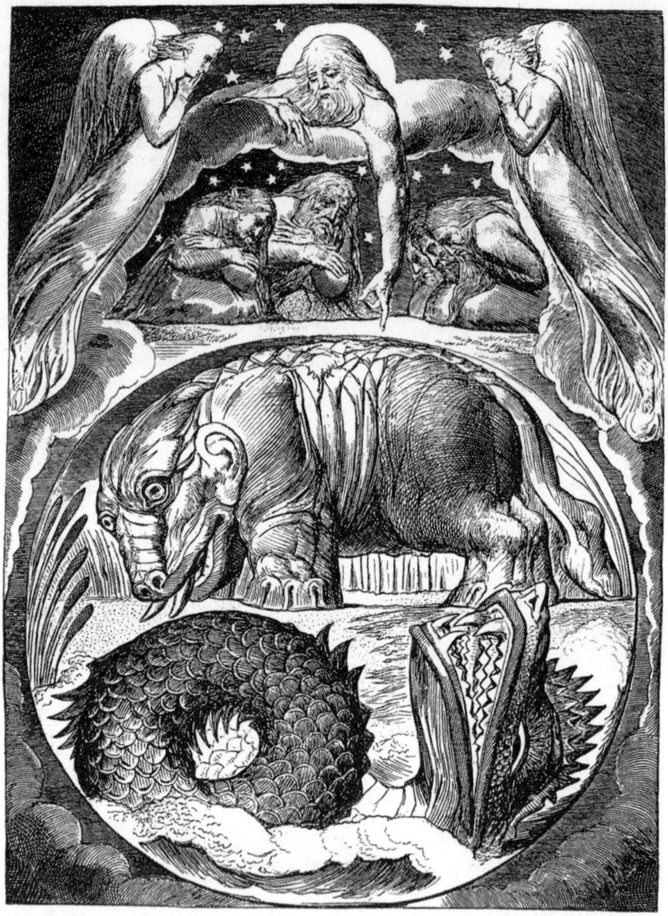

William Blake, *Behemoth and Leviathan*, 1825, reprinted 1874. Illustration from *The Book of Job*, Tate Gallery, London.

Shooting the Albatross and Blessing the Water-Snakes in Romantic Poetry

Shooting the Albatross and then ritually blessing water-snakes is a perfect and typical description of Romantic spirituality as a "natural supernaturalism," as the famous book on Romantic literature by

M. H. Abrams is entitled. Not only Coleridge but also Wordsworth, Shelley, Blake, Byron, and Keats all sacrificed the Albatross of medieval Christianity, passed through the void of atheism, and found a new confession of faith in the experience of cosmic religious feeling for inner and outer nature.[10]

Shelley, for example, was in his own time derided as an infamous atheist. For example, when Shelley capsized his boat the *Don Juan* during a summer storm off the Gulf of Spezia and drowned a month before his thirtieth birthday on July 8, 1822, the *Courier*, a prominent London newspaper, remembered him in a terse and unflattering obituary as "the writer of some infidel poetry [who] has been drowned: now he knows whether there is a God or no." Shelley earned this reputation. At the age of nineteen during his freshman year at Oxford in 1811, he anonymously penned a tract entitled *The Necessity of Atheism*. This essay, which Shelley printed and mailed to all the bishops and heads of colleges at Oxford, is an application of Enlightenment principles of rational proof set against traditional arguments for the existence of God. Shelley signed it, "Thro' deficiency of proof, AN ATHEIST." That was the arrow that shot the Albatross! And Shelley paid the price when the collective "crew" at Oxford University called him up, demanded to know if he wrote this, and, when he refused to say, expelled him after his freshman year.

Shelley was intellectually incapable of finding sufficient evidence for his culture's traditional notion of God. But he was not godless. Two years after *The Necessity of Atheism*, in note 13 of canto 7 of his long philosophical poem *Queen Mab* (1813), Shelley clarifies what he means when he says, "There is no God." "There Is No God. This negation must be understood solely to affect a creative Deity. The hypothesis of a pervading Spirit co-eternal with the universe remains unshaken." Given this note in *Queen Mab*, Shelley's *Necessity of Atheism* might have been more accurately entitled *Against*

Fundamentalism or *Against Metaphysics*; what Shelley meant when he called himself "AN ATHEIST" was not a wholesale rejection of the sacred but a rejection of the Bible as a literal, historical text, as well as the rejection of the idea of a transcendent metaphysical deity who creates the world from outside the world. For Shelley, atheism was necessary because there was insufficient proof for the existence of a metaphysical deity with the traditional qualities of the biblical God image. But there was also another necessity of atheism, a *secret* necessity of atheism besides its intellectual necessity: atheism is not a final resting place, not the final chapter in the unfolding story of the development of consciousness, but a necessary stage one must pass through on the way from the old image of God to a new image of God which unites the contraries sundered in traditional Christianity—God and humanity, spirit and nature, good and evil, inner and outer—and this uniting of what has been split in the Western religious consciousness both elevates the human being and brings the divine down to earth.

In Shelley's case (and this was true also for Coleridge, Blake, and many other Romantics), the human mind, not the *I* alone but the faculty of imagination, takes on a role previously ascribed to God, the creator of the world. Five years after *The Necessity of Atheism*, Shelley wrote "Mont Blanc: Lines Written in the Vale of Chamouni" (1816). In this amazing poem, the poet wonders aloud about the relationship between the mountain and "the human mind's imaginings."

> The secret Strength of things
> Which governs thought, and to the infinite dome
> Of Heaven is as a law, inhabits thee!
> And what were thou, and earth, and stars, and sea,
> If to the human mind's imaginings
> Silence and solitude were vacancy?

Mont Blanc is a *thou*—not an object but a subject, not dead but alive, sacred as every mountain is sacred, as the "earth, and stars, and sea" are sacred—because Mont Blanc participates in an intimate and mysterious relationship with "the human mind's imaginings."

Shelley, raised as a Christian, thus goes beyond the traditional fundamentalist faith of his times. He also, as a product of the Enlightenment and the scientific revolution, goes beyond materialistic philosophy. Three years after "Mont Blanc," in a short philosophical essay entitled *On Life*, Shelley turns the Enlightenment metaphor of imagination as a subjective mist obscuring the world of facts and reality on its head. For Shelley, it is not the fog and mist of subjective imaginings that obscure truth and reality; rather, the "mist of familiarity" obscures a truth so awesome that the frailty of the human mind needs to defend against it, a truth that might easily "absorb and overawe the function of that which is its object." What is that great truth? That "the solid universe of external things is 'such stuff as dreams are made of.'"[11] For Shelley, the external world is identical to "that which we are & feel," one and the same with "the wonder of our being."[12] Shelley would absolutely agree with Coleridge's vision in *The Ancient Mariner* that the adoration and awe the Mariner feels as he blesses the water-snakes are not signs that he is falling into subjective or psychotic delusion but that he is connected to reality as it is.

In "Tintern Abbey" (1798), it is Wordsworth's loss of innocence and his concomitant descent into "the still, sad music of humanity" that opens the poet to "a sense sublime / Of something far more deeply interfused" in both nature outside and "the mind of man."

> For I have learned
> To look on nature, not as in the hour
> Of thoughtless youth; but hearing oftentimes
> The still sad music of humanity,

Nor harsh nor grating, though of ample power
To chasten and subdue.—And I have felt
A presence that disturbs me with the joy
Of elevated thoughts; a sense sublime
Of something far more deeply interfused,
Whose dwelling is the light of setting suns,
And the round ocean and the living air,
And the blue sky, and in the mind of man:
A motion and a spirit, that impels
All thinking things, all objects of all thought,
And rolls through all things.[13]

Similarly, Wordsworth's *Recluse*, a self-proclaimed prothalamion, announces a coming *hierosgamos*, a sacred wedding or "great consummation," awakening "the sensual [the materialists] from their sleep / Of Death." It is not the poet who is asleep in a dream but the scientific and materialistic philosophers, and Wordsworth's poetry seeks to redeem them from a collectively held consciousness that, for both Wordsworth and Coleridge, constitutes the Fall of Man in the modern world. Again, the goal here is not to renounce Christianity but go beyond its traditional limits and thus fulfill it, not to renounce the rational intellect but push the human capacity for reason further and further into the weird margins of psyche and nature and thus fulfill it as well, the head of the Enlightenment snake eating its own tail, integrating what it had left behind as superstitious delusion. That great consummation demands that "the discerning intellect of Man" be married to "this goodly universe" in an act of "creation" through "love and holy passion," thus uniting science and mysticism on a new level. "This," Wordsworth concludes, "is our high argument."

For the discerning intellect of Man,
When wedded to this goodly universe

In love and holy passion, shall find these
A simple produce of the common day.
—I, long before the blissful hour arrives,
Would chant, in lonely peace, the spousal verse
Of this great consummation—and, by words
Which speak of nothing more than what we are,
Would I arouse the sensual from their sleep
Of Death, and win the vacant and the vain
To noble raptures; while my voice proclaims
How exquisitely the individual Mind
(And the progressive powers perhaps no less
Of the whole species) to the external World
Is fitted—and how exquisitely, too—
Theme this but little heard of among men—
The external World is fitted to the Mind;
And the creation (by no lower name
Can it be called) which they with blended might
Accomplish—this is our high argument.[14]

When the Mariner blesses the water-snakes, we see and feel that high argument in action.

The Mariner, all, all alone at sea, chants, with Wordsworth, "in lonely peace, the spousal verse / Of this great consummation" that The "Mind" is "exquisitely" fitted "to the external World," and "the external World is fitted to the Mind":

O happy living things! no tongue
Their beauty might declare:
A stream of love gushed from my heart,
And I blessed them unaware:
Sure my kind saint took pity on me,
And I blessed them unaware.

The self-same moment I could pray;
And from my neck so free

The Albatross fell off, and sank
Like lead into the sea.

That consummation is the Mariner's new prayer. In a state of ecstatic beauty and love for the water-snakes as they spark with flashes of golden fire, the Albatross falls from his neck and sinks "like lead" into the sea.

The sacred union of imagination and nature coming out of what the traditional religious imagination views as atheism is endlessly repeated throughout Romantic literature with a musician's sense of variation. Lord Byron (1788–1824), "mad, bad, and dangerous to know" according to his lover Lady Caroline Lamb, killed the Albatross of medieval Christian faith and carried its dead body around his neck. But in the third canto of his epic, five-hundred-page *Don Juan* (1819–24), Byron shakes that dead bird off his neck when he offers up a new credo: "My altars are the mountains and the ocean, Earth, air, stars."[15] Similarly, Blake's religious vision in *The Four Zoas* (1797) is that an "Eternal Man" lies scattered throughout the universe in the form of "tree & herb & fish & bird & beast," present "wherever a grass grows, Or a leaf buds."[16] Blake's Eternal Man is "Jesus the Imagination," Jesus as nothing more nor less than the human being raised to a full imaginal perception of itself. "To the eyes of a man of imagination," Blake writes in a letter to a critic, "nature is imagination itself. As a man is, so he sees."[17] Nature as imagination? Nothing could possibly be more contra to the prevailing scientific consensus of Coleridge's time, and ours as well, in which imagination was subjective and nature objective. And yet, this is the Mariner's credo at this point in the poem; when he blesses the water-snakes he has changed from a coldly calculating avatar of the mechanical philosophy with his crossbow to a man who sees and feels with the eyes and heart of imagination.

The result is a living, rather than a dead, relationship to Nature and the sacred.

The Romantics (as Christians) went beyond traditional Christianity to find God; they also (as children of the Enlightenment) went beyond the dogmas of the scientific revolution to find a new vision of nature. Keats, the only Romantic poet with scientific training (he studied to become a doctor at a hospital in London before leaving the medical profession to become a full-time poet), in his "Ode to a Nightingale" (1819), immerses the reader in a vision of nature utterly different than nature as seen through the lens of the scientific method.

> My sense, as though of hemlock I had drunk,
> Or emptied some dull opiate to the drains
>   One minute past, and Lethe-wards had sunk: . . .
>
> . . . Away! away! for I will fly to thee,
> Not charioted by Bacchus and his pards,
>   But on the viewless wings of Poesy,
>   Though the dull brain perplexes and retards:
>
> Already with thee! tender is the night,
>   And haply the Queen-Moon is on her throne,
>   Cluster'd around by all her starry Fays;
>   But here there is no light,
>   Save what from heaven is with the breezes blown
>   Through verdurous glooms and winding mossy ways.
>
> I cannot see what flowers are at my feet,
>   Nor what soft incense hangs upon the boughs,
> But, in embalmed darkness, guess each sweet
>   Wherewith the seasonable month endows
> The grass, the thicket, and the fruit-tree wild;
>   White hawthorn, and the pastoral eglantine;
>   Fast fading violets cover'd up in leaves;

And mid-May's eldest child,
The coming musk-rose, full of dewy wine,
The murmurous haunt of flies on summer eves.

Nothing could be further from the materialistic gaze than "Ode to a Nightingale." "I cannot see," the poet states, "darkling I listen." Enlightenment comes not in the clear light of day but at night, not by the bright light of the Sun burning away the mists of delusion but in the moonshine. Intuition ("I guess each sweet") guides the way. The poet does not analyze or classify the song of the nightingale; rather, he feels the song as an imaginal doorway to something "immortal" in which the boundaries between dream and reality blur: "Was it a vision, or a waking dream? / Fled is that music:—Do I wake or sleep?"

Perhaps these few examples will suffice to give us a feel for how the Romantic poets killed the Albatross and blessed the water-snakes. They were all Mariners of the mind's oceans who set sail from the hill, kirk, and lighthouse on land, not as a fantastical escape from dismal reality but as a search for an experience of mind and nature that was so ahead of their time that those "whose sails were never to the Tempest given"[18] could only understand it as heresy, atheism, and madness, or as a nostalgic attempt to return to a bygone era.

The Blessing of the Water-Snakes as Proto-depth Psychology

As we have seen throughout this book, the Romantic tradition leads seamlessly into the depth psychological. There are many points of similarity, many threads of continuity. Thomas Mann, born in Germany in 1875 (the same years as Jung) and the winner of the Nobel Prize for literature, points out one of these connections when he asserts that the "mysterious unity" of inner and outer that Wordsworth calls the "great consummation" and his "high argument" is "the alpha and omega of all psychoanalytic knowledge."[19] From the beginning with Freud, and still today, the psychoanalytic project is founded on a presumed relationship between inner character and outer destiny. The working hypothesis is that if one transforms one's psychological constitution, one transforms one's experience of the world. As we change, different things "happen to us," as we say.

The school of psychology that most nearly reflects the vision of "our inner nature" as the Romantics see it is the psychology of the unconscious founded by Freud and expanded on by Jung. According to Jung, "That we speak of an unconscious at all is due to the Romantic spirit."[20] In describing this development, Jung waxes poetic and comes close to Coleridge's revelation of the evolution of consciousness in *The Rime of the Ancient Mariner.*

> Since the stars have fallen from heaven and our highest symbols have paled, a secret life holds sway in the unconscious. That is why we have a psychology today, and why we speak of the unconscious. All this would be quite superfluous in an age or culture that possessed symbols. Symbols are spirit from above, and under those conditions the spirit is above too. Therefore it would be a foolish and senseless undertaking for such people to wish to experience or investigate an unconscious that contains nothing but the silent, undisturbed sway of nature. Our unconscious, on the other hand, hides living water, spirit that has become nature, and that is why it is disturbed. Heaven has become for us the cosmic space of the physicists, and the divine empyrean a fair memory of things that once were. But "the heart glows," and a secret unrest gnaws at the roots of our being.[21]

As Jung describes how religion becomes psychology, he unintentionally translates the poetics of Coleridge's *Ancient Mariner* into his unique brand of symbolic prose. Why do we have a psychology today? Because we have shot the Albatross, or, in Jung's words, "the stars have fallen from heaven." When Jung observes that, "Heaven has become for us the cosmic space of the physicists, and the divine empyrean a fair memory of things that once were," we recall the Mariner all, all alone at sea, praying to Heaven only to have a wicked whisper turn his heart to dust. When Jung speaks of the "secret life [that] holds sway in the unconscious," we remember the slimy things, death-fires, witch's oils, all the unlived life, unmetabolized trauma, repressed feeling, as well as psychological drives and contents that are incompatible with Christian spirituality and Enlightenment rationality that Coleridge's Mariner sees in the sea below. But "a secret unrest gnaws at the roots of [the Mariner's] being," and his "heart glows"; when the Mariner finally blesses the water-snakes as a stream of love gushes from his heart, he discovers what Jung would also discover a century after Coleridge's poem: namely, that "our unconscious hides living water, spirit that has become nature."

Blessing the Snake in Jungian Analysis

The following clinical example illustrates the point with material from a dream that draws explicitly, although unconsciously, from imagery in *The Ancient Mariner*.

A client of mine, a woman in her early thirties whom I will call Jane, initially came to see me because her fiancé had been tragically killed by a drunk driver. Her family and friends were so worried for her that a friend made the initial phone call to me; Jane was unable to make the call herself. In our initial meeting, her whole body was shaking, her hands would shake, and she was viscerally overcome by anxiety. Death permeated the psychic field in Jane's analysis, including her dreams. Jane's love for her deceased fiancé was pulling her to "join him in the other world," as she said—in other words, to commit suicide. There was death all around, and the determinative question from the start was: Will death express itself literally as suicide or symbolically as transformation?

After working with Jane for months, just as I was beginning to write on *The Rime of the Ancient Mariner* for my diploma thesis, she told me the following dream.

> *I walk into a room in a house. There on the wall in front of me is a huge, ten-foot-long snake. I am terrified to see it and immediately bolt from the room. As I'm running away a voice says, "The snake is an albatross."*

As you might imagine, when Jane told me this dream, I almost fell out of my chair! At the time, Jane was unaware both of my interest in the poem and of the poem itself. Not only had Jane never heard of *The Rime of the Ancient Mariner* but she also did not even know what an albatross was. When I asked her what she made of this dream, she replied, "Is an albatross a type of fish?" The dream made no conscious sense to her. It was, however, highly meaningful to me. Jane's dream and my work with *The Ancient Mariner* are a meaningful coincidence, an example of what Jung calls synchronicity.[22]

Jane's suicidal ideation centered on the sudden trauma of losing her fiancé. His death meant, among other things, the loss of hope. Jane was in real danger of committing suicide when the snake was *not* an albatross, that is, when her sense of reality was severed from hope. If the snake *was* an albatross, however, this meant that her experience of trauma was a meaningful event. This suggestion, however, is beyond challenging; it is almost impossibly difficult to accept, a fact that was reflected in Jane's dream as she ran out of the room when she saw the terrifying ten-foot-long snake, an instinctive reaction to overwhelming fear.[23] With the support of analysis, however, Jane stopped running, turned around, and faced her worst fears consciously and actively. She had many dreams and worked with them. As she did so, her suicidal ideation slowly diminished and finally disappeared. But not only this; Jane not only escaped suicide, she also experienced an inner transformation. It is true that her naive and youthful illusions about life shattered as the dark realities of life and death shot her Albatross out of the sky and an upwelling of terror and hopelessness threatened her—like a snake—from within. But as she confronted her slimy seas, a new sense of self emerged, one that was less innocent and that took account of life's dark side. After her analysis she was not the same person as before; there was more maturity and more depth to her character, less role-playing, less defensiveness, more realness, more authenticity. She started a new career, and after a few years, found a new relationship that evolved into marriage and children. After a lot of work and much suffering, Jane could affirm the message of her dream (for which the synchronistic reality of the dream is itself evidence): the numinous reality of the psychosomatic unconscious is both a terrifying danger and a source of hope.

The Transitus of Modern Man Fulfilled?

At this point in the poem, the Mariner has shot the Albatross, the Moon has eclipsed the Sun, and all the crew are dead. He has been forced by necessity to press forward as a lonely individual and sail into the depths of the mind's oceans as a Christian who does not deny Christianity but expands it into a loving acceptance of what was previously seen as evil, and as a child of the Enlightenment who seeks a future beyond solar rationalism and materialistic scientism. The dead Albatross falls from the Mariner's neck "like lead" when he blesses the living snakes and half discovers and half creates a new God image from the depths of an agonizing process of symbolic death. The discovery of a flash of golden fire in the sea appears to be the goal of the *transitus dei* of modern man for whom the Mariner is a representative, a flash of a new consciousness, and for this reason an intuitive promise of a new world. As the Romantics knew, and as the depth psychological tradition affirms, attaining that future does not require the intervention of a transcendent God, but it does require a massive expansion of the human *being*.[24]

The Mariner blesses the water-snakes in a visionary experience far out to sea. Jung's patient Christiana Morgan accepts the snake as beautiful in a dream. Jane accepts the snake as an albatross in her work with me in analysis. These are all examples that point the way to a possible future where conflicts between the head and the heart, good and evil—most generally between conscious and unconscious—are resolved. The symbols that point the way in poetry and dreams to the resolution of such conflicts are healing symbols. But there is so much work to do, so much dying, before one realizes them in life. Important to emphasize here is that Jane, the client of mine who dreamt that "the snake is an albatross," like the Mariner who blesses the water-snakes "unaware," had not the slightest idea what her dream might mean at first, or that it meant anything at all. Understanding came later, and slow, gradual attempts at integration after that. For the Mariner, on the other hand, understanding and integrating the message of his great Dream out at sea never happens. As a result, we shall see in detail later when the Mariner returns to shore, he remains agonizingly split between sea and land, the crisis of nineteenth-century Romanticism that twentieth-century depth psychology sought to address and that I seek to address throughout this book.

CHAPTER 17

Turning Lead to Gold

Alchemy, Romanticism, Depth Psychology, and the Contemporary Enigma of Consciousness

Looking forward in time from the Romantic period, we find significant parallels with depth psychology. Looking backward in time, we observe many similarities between Romanticism and the alchemical imagination. We have already mentioned some of these parallels—the rotting sea, the eclipse of the Sun—but perhaps the most explicit and obvious alchemical reference in the poem is the "flash of golden fire" that sparks in the sea as the Albatross falls from the Mariner's neck "like lead." Coleridge's juxtaposition of lead and gold at this crucial moment in the poem is quite patently an allusion to medieval and Renaissance alchemy.

Most of us know that the alchemists sought to turn lead to gold. What most of us do not know, however, is that alchemical gold is not the common gold. The English alchemist George von Welling (1655–1727) explains this in his *Opus Mago-Cabbalisticum*. "Our intention is not directed towards teaching anyone how to make gold but towards something much higher, namely how Nature may be seen and recognized as coming from God and God in Nature."[1]

Alchemical gold is God in Nature. And so it is in *The Ancient Mariner*: the flash of golden fire the Mariner finds in the sea is the *lumen naturae*, the *anima mundi*, the *deus terranus* as the formalized transformation of the dead, leaden body of the spirit from above into soul from below—"the universal and scintillating fire in the light of nature which carries the heavenly spirit within it," as Jung writes. Seeing Nature through these eyes is the medium of rebirth for the modern soul.

Gnosticism, Mysticism, and Seventeenth-Century Science

The image of a golden flash of fire in the sea in *The Rime of the Ancient Mariner* can be traced back to Gnosticism, a Christian and Jewish religious movement in the late first century CE. The Gnostics valued individual mystical experience over doctrinaire teaching and dogma. Hippolytus, a Christian theologian at the turn of the third century, reports that a Gnostic sect called the Sethians believed the *Nous* or Divine Mind, the "perfect God," takes form in this fallen world as sparks of light "overpowered in the dark and terribly bitter polluted water."[2] These scintillae, as the Gnostics call them, are the immortal soul of the universe, both spiritual and material at once, manifesting as "Light and Fire" when "moved or agitated."[3]

Gnosticism often pictures Sophia—a feminine personification of divine wisdom—as infusing, or herself being, a spiritual spark fallen into the darkness of the material world. In the twelfth century, the German Christian mystic Hildegard of Bingen (1098–1179) tapped into this Gnostic symbolism when she wrote of the *anima mundi*, or soul of the world, as a divine woman who "glow[s] in the water" as the "fiery life of divine substance," which has kindled "every living spark" inside nature.

Sed et ego ignea vita substantie divinitatis	And I am also the fiery life of divine substance:
Super pulcritudinem agrorum flammo	I flame above the beautiful fields
Et in aquis luceo	and I glow in the water
atque in sole, luna et stellis ardeo	and I burn in the sun, the moon and the stars[4]

Some five hundred years after Hildegard, in the sixteenth century, the "fiery life of divine substance" revealed itself to the German physician and alchemist Henry Khunrath (1560–1605)—an acquaintance of John Dee's and Paracelsus's disciple—as "fiery sparks of the soul of the world," and "seeds of light broadcast in the chaos" that are "identical to the Spirit of God," the "*Ruach Elohim*," dispersed "throughout the structure of the great world."[5] And then, at the height of the scientific revolution in the seventeenth century, the Gnostic-alchemical light in nature made itself visible as the discovery of phosphorus.

In Joseph Wright of Derby's painting entitled *The Alchymist, in Search of the Philosopher's Stone, Discovers Phosphorus, and Prays for the Successful Conclusion of His Operation, as Was the Custom of the Ancient Chymical Astrologers* (1771, reworked in 1795), Wright depicts the discovery of phosphorus as an awe-inspiring, religious revelation; an "alchymist" kneels in awe before a phosphorescent flask like Moses before the burning bush.[6] Wright identifies his "alchymist" with the "Ancient Chymical Astrologers." Yet the men who discovered phosphorus were by no means ancient—they were products of the seventeenth century. Still, most of us are not aware that for the first modern scientists, phosphorus was not *just* phosphorus; it was divinity imminent within the natural world.

A German merchant named Hennig Brand (1630–1710) discovered phosphorus in 1669. Brand was not searching for a new

The Alchymist, in Search of the Philosopher's Stone, Discovers Phosphorus, and Prays for the Successful Conclusion of His Operation, as Was the Custom of the Ancient Chymical Astrologers, Joseph Wright of Derby (1771, reworked 1795), 127 × 101.6 cm (50 × 40 inches). Derby Museum and Art Gallery, Derby, UK.

element; he was looking for a way to make gold. Following his intuition that the human body contained a secret treasure, and no doubt guided by the alchemical dictum *in stercore invenitur*, this merchant and alchemist collected fifty buckets of urine and allowed them to stand in the sun until they "bred worms." He then boiled the urine down to a paste in the hopes that it would contain gold.[7] Brand must have been disappointed when he did not find any gold in all that urine, but he did discover something else, something unexpected and fascinating. He distilled out a white, waxy material that glowed in the dark. He named this enigmatic material *phosphoros*, "the light-bringing" in Greek, and unintentionally became the first person to discover an element. In 1680, Robert Boyle (1627–91), well known as one of the progenitors of the modern scientific method and generally regarded as the first modern chemist, independently replicated Brand's discovery. Less well known is that Boyle practiced alchemy until the end of his life, testified that he had witnessed the transmutation of base metals to gold, and even successfully lobbied Parliament to repeal England's ban on alchemical transmutation.[8]

A few years after Brand's discovery, sometime before 1675, Christian Adolph Balduin (1632–82) created a phosphorescent form of calcium nitrate called "Balduin's phosphorus" that, when dried and heated in a vessel, became luminous. Balduin was sure that this mysterious luminous water distilled from his solution was not mere phosphorus but *hermetic* phosphorus, a *Spiritus Mundi*. A chapter in Balduin's 1675 book *Aurum Superius et Inferius* (Gold above and below) is entitled "Phosphorus Hermeticus sive Magnus Luminaris" (The hermetic phosphorus or the great light). While Balduin's mystical proclivities would not pass muster with the Royal Society today, they posed no barrier at all to his induction into that august scientific company in 1676, just eleven years prior to Newton's publication of the *Principia Mathematica*. Newton was thirty-two years old at the time Balduin became a member of the Royal Society and had been a member of the Royal Society since 1672.

Today, we recognize the flash of golden fire in the Mariner's luminous sea as naturally occurring bioluminescence. Before 1885, however, nobody knew what bioluminescence was. As the development of biochemistry unlocked nature's secrets during the eighteenth and nineteenth centuries, the alchemical vision of a *lumen naturae* was more and more dismissed as a superstitious remnant of a pre-scientific past. Even before then, when Coleridge published *The Ancient Mariner* in 1798 (only a century after Brand and Balduin), the mechanical, quantitative, and materialistic philosophy of nature was already explaining away the mix of mysticism and science commonplace in the seventeenth century as nothing but an unfortunate and embarrassing, if perhaps inevitable, consequence of science slowly emerging out of the slime of superstitious ignorance. At the time Coleridge published *The Ancient Mariner*, it was practically self-evident in scientific circles that religious feeling for nature (such as the Mariner feels) had no place in the scientific picture of the world. We saw this cold, detached, objective attitude toward nature in Wright's eighteenth-century *An Experiment on a Bird in the Air Pump* (1768) (published just thirty years before *The Ancient Mariner*), where a modern scientist gazes with intellectual detachment straight at us, the viewers, devoid of all emotion. There is no feeling in this man's face as he conducts his experiment, no revelation in his vacuum chamber, only a dying bird. This lack of feeling was thought to be a good thing; detached, abstract observation was considered to be a crucial way to gain knowledge of nature.

When the Mariner shoots the Albatross, he is Wright's scientist coldly conducting an experiment on a bird in the air pump. When he blesses the water-snakes, he is Wright's alchemist overawed with adoration for light in nature. Knowingly or not, Coleridge plagiarizes the alchemical recipe for phosphorus when he describes the flash of golden fire in the Mariner's sea. Just as Brand's urine "bred worms," the Mariner's rotting sea is filled with "slimy things." Just as it takes seven weeks for "flakes like Lightning, somewhat like the flame of Brimstone, and somewhat of a purplish color" to appear in the rotting urine, the Mariner stews in his rotting seas for seven days and nights before "flash[es] of golden fire" and "hoary flakes" of "elfish light" appear in the "charmed water [that] burnt alway / A still and awful red." Finally, just as alchemical phosphorus is the "Astrum Lunare Micro-cosmicum,"[9] a "hornèd moon with one bright star" presides over the Mariner's revelation of flashes of golden fire.

Coleridge contra Materialism

Whereas *scientists* in the sixteenth and seventeenth centuries were in danger of being dragged before the Inquisition, thrown in the dungeon, or burnt at the stake by the church for heresy against the religious view of self and world, by the early nineteenth century the feeling that detached observation was crucial to attaining an objective view of reality was so powerful that it displaced the religious point of view, and the accusation that one was *not following the science* became the damning indictment. Scientific societies never burned anyone at the stake for disagreeing with them, but the threat of being "canceled" (i.e., ridiculed and banished from the public forum) if one questioned the truth of deterministic materialism was, as it still is, very real.[10] Coleridge, of course, was in a bad position in this respect as he was in an all-out war against the materialistic trend of his times, an avowed enemy of the "philosophy of mechanism" or, as Jung once called it, "that damned clockwork fantasy."

It is very important to emphasize, however, that Coleridge was in no way anti-science—quite the opposite. In a letter to Thomas Poole dated March 23, 1801, written when Coleridge was twenty-eight, Coleridge states that by the age of thirty he hoped to "thoroughly understand the whole of Newton's Works." Yet Coleridge believed that he already understood Newton's foundational assumptions well enough to recognize Newton as "a mere materialist" and, consequently, the mechanical philosophy *imposed* on the scientific method as not only incomplete but also superficial and false. "I need not observe, My dear Friend, how unutterably silly & contemptible these Opinions would be, if written to any but to another Self. I assure you, solemnly assure you, that you & Wordsworth are the only men on Earth to whom I would have uttered a word on this subject. . . . My opinion is this: that deep thinking is attainable only by a man of deep feeling, and all truth is a species of revelation. . . . It is a rule, by which I hope to direct my literary efforts, to let my Opinions & my Proofs go together. It is *insolent* to *differ* from the public *opinion* in *opinion*, if it be only *opinion*. It is sticking up a little *i by itself i* against the whole alphabet."[11] Coleridge, as "a little *i by itself i*," knew that the *WE* of the scientific orthodoxy lay willing, ready, and able to throw him into the metaphorical equivalent of a medieval dungeon for his anathema opinion that feeling as well as thinking belongs to the search for truth and revelation as well as knowledge. The danger of being labeled "unutterably silly & contemptible" for believing this was so palpable in fact, that Coleridge dared not share his opinion with anyone but his two most trusted friends, the tanner Thomas Poole and the poet William Wordsworth.

I will emphasize this point again: Coleridge's quarrel was not with science per se. Coleridge had no problem with the empirical search for truth through observation and experiment; in fact, he was fascinated and delighted by this effort as well as intensely drawn into the beauty and ingenuity of Newton's experiments. Coleridge's only problem arose when the scientific method raised the materialistic-mechanical *philosophy* of nature to the status of an unquestionable ontological dogma. Then, and only then, did it become the Fall of Man.

In the early nineteenth century, Coleridge's point of view was a lonely one. That is not because Coleridge was regressing to a pre-scientific consciousness but because he went *beyond* the dogmatic spirit of his times. In this, he proves himself a true child of the Enlightenment—*sapere aude, nullas in verba*—Coleridge dared to think for himself and took no one's word for it, not even the word of the conventional scientific authorities. Coleridge was lonely because he belonged to the future. "Where . . . the nurture and evolution of humanity is the final aim," Coleridge writes, "there will soon be seen a general tendency toward, and earnest seeking after, some ground common to the world and to man."[12] All Coleridge had to do if he wanted to bring his little "*i by itself i*" into harmony with the rest of the alphabet was to wait a century or so. In his book *Relativity: The Special and General Theory—A Clear Explanation That Anyone Can Understand*, Einstein repeats Coleridge's critique of materialism almost exactly.

> All these space-like concepts [e.g., geometrical shapes, number, and motion] already belong to pre-scientific thought, along with concepts like pain, goal, purpose, etc. from the field of psychology. Now it is characteristic of thought in physics, as of thought in natural science generally, that it endeavors in principle to make do with "space-like" concepts alone, and strives to express with their aid all relations having the form of laws. The physicist seeks to reduce colors and tones to vibrations, the physiologist thought and pain to nerve processes, in such a way that the psy-

> chical element as such is eliminated from the causal nexus of existence, and thus nowhere occurs as an independent link in the causal associations. It is no doubt this attitude, which considers the comprehension of all relations by the exclusive use of only "space-like" concepts as being possible in principle, that is at the present time understood by the term "materialism" (since matter has lost its role as a fundamental concept).[13]

When Einstein asserts that "matter has lost its role as a fundamental concept" and describes materialism as an "attitude" in which "the psychical element as such is eliminated from the causal nexus of existence," he essentially summarizes and restates the main points of Coleridge's argument against the philosophy of mechanism. The only substantive difference between Einstein's opinion and Coleridge's is that Einstein has the backing of twentieth-century physics, while Coleridge does not.[14]

A Fire That Lights Itself: The Contemporary Enigma of Consciousness

In Wright's *Alchymist*, an "ancient chymical astrologer" stares straight into a numinous light in his flask, rapt in adoration, like Moses before the burning bush. Is this image truly reflective of an ancient attitude, or is there anything like a *phosphorus mirabilis* that causes scientists to bow down in astonishment as if before God today?

If there is anything like a contemporary equivalent of a *phosphorus mirabilis* it is the mystery of consciousness.[15] Consciousness is not explicable, or at least not yet explicable, by natural laws, and the fact that the causal origins of conscious are still unexplained can evoke a feeling response akin to Wright's alchemist in even the most hard-core materialists. For example, as if stating something so obviously correct that it could never be doubted by any sane person,

Ray Kurzweil, an inventor, a best-selling author on the evolution of technology, and the director of engineering for machine learning at Google (as materialistic a scientist as one can be), notes that there is "nothing mystical about a neuron." Yet Kurzweil recognizes that somehow neurons give rise to conscious agents. "I do believe in miracles," he admits; "I think that's a spiritual property, and the fact that consciousness came into being is a deeply mysterious spiritual kind of revelation." Kurzweil comes close here to Wright's "alchymist" bowing in awe before a light in nature when he goes on to affirm that "consciousness is the ultimate spiritual value."[16]

Coleridge was similarly deeply struck by the spiritual value of consciousness. Unlike Kurzweil, however, Coleridge did not, strictly speaking, see consciousness as a miracle. For Coleridge, the miraculous depended on the assumption that matter is "dead" and that something nonmaterial intercedes in the mechanical or causal laws of nature. Coleridge did not assent to that assumption because he did not start from the materialist position that the physical world is separate from consciousness. Rather, consciousness and the world are "a perpetual self-duplication of one and the same power into object and subject." "[The I AM] is a subject which becomes a subject by the act of constructing itself objectively to itself; but which never is an object except for itself, and only so far as by the very same act it becomes a subject. It may be described therefore as a perpetual self-duplication of one and the same power into object and subject, which presupposes the other, and can exist only as antitheses."[17] In chapter 8 of the *Biographia Literaria*, Coleridge expands on this idea. "Body and spirit," he writes, "are therefore no longer absolutely heterogeneous but *may*, without any *absurdity*, be supposed to be different modes or degrees in perfection of a common substratum."[18] Therefore, Cartesian dualism—upon which Kurzweil's sense of consciousness as a miracle is founded—is an "exploded" system. "If we were wholly uninfluenced by custom, and saw things as they are," Coleridge speculates in his essay on miracles, then the "heterogeneity of spirit and matter" which is the "very ground of all miracles" would "probably vanish." "It is not strictly accurate to affirm, that every thing would appear a miracle, if we were wholly uninfluenced by custom, and saw things as they are:—for then the very ground of all miracles would probably vanish, namely, the heterogeneity of spirit and matter. For the *quid ulterius*? of wonder, we should have the *ne plus ultra* of adoration."[19] Whereas Kurzweil feels the "*quid ulterius*? of wonder" as he reflects on the apparently miraculous emergence of consciousness from dead matter, Coleridge, like his Mariner when he blesses the water-snakes and sees that flash of golden fire in nature, feels the "*ne plus ultra* of adoration."

Another way to put this difference between Kurzweil and Coleridge is to say that, for Coleridge, there *really is* something mystical about a neuron. To be more precise, for Coleridge, there is something symbolic about a neuron, as there is with all the material world. "All minds think by some *symbols*—the strongest minds possess the most vivid symbols in the Imagination—yet this ingenerates a want, *pothon*, desiderium, for vividness of symbol: which something that is without, that has the property of outness (a word which Berkeley preferred to as 'Externality') can alone fully gratify & even that indeed not fully—for the utmost is only an approximation to that absolute union, which the soul sensible of its imperfection in itself, of its halfness, yearns after, wherever it exists free from meaner passions."[20] For Coleridge, the symbolic life is "more than a mere simile, the work of my own fancy"; it is "one of the great organs of the life of nature."[21] The symbol is really and truly *out there* in the world manifesting as "the property of *outness*." There is "a symbol established in the truth of things"; the symbolic is the "one Life within us and abroad" that haunts Coleridge's poetry and appears as the "primary Imagination" in his philosophical prose. "The Imagination, then, I consider either as primary, or secondary. The primary Imagination I hold to be the living Power and prime Agent of all human Perception, and as a repetition in the finite mind of the eternal act of creation in the infinite I AM." While Coleridge is careful to assert here that the primary Imagination is not God, it is nevertheless a godlike, second-world creator that generates ("unaware") our human experience of the world. We are typically not aware of how the psyche, inexorably and necessarily, creates our experience of the world every second of every day, and most of us do not experience perception as an imaginative act of world creation. But it is precisely that experience, I suggest, of consciousness as a second-world creator that evokes the *ne plus ultra* of adoration that redeems the Mariner from the spiritual Wasteland of a dead materialistic world.

Coleridge and the Scientific Critique of Materialism in the Twentieth and Twenty-First Centuries

Coleridge was on track with his intuition that the goal of future developments would be to find a common ground between psyche and nature. Scientific advances in the twentieth and twenty-first centuries are helping to heal the split between inner and outer, meaning and truth, and psyche and nature—the modern Fall of Man—that the philosophy of mechanism created in the preceding three centuries.

I recently came across an interesting example of how that reconciliation might be working itself out today while listening to the Lex Fridman podcast. Fridman is a young artificial intelligence researcher working on autonomous vehicles, human-robot interaction, and machine learning at MIT and beyond who hosts a fascinating, wide-ranging, and multidisciplinary podcast that dives into extended conversations with people on the cutting edge of contemporary cultural, psychological, spiritual, and political issues. On March 31, 2020, Fridman interviewed the mathematician and cosmologist Roger Penrose (b. 1931), a Nobel laureate in physics who is generally regarded as one of our greatest living scientists.

Near the end of the interview, Fridman asks Penrose "the most ridiculous, maybe the most important question. What is the meaning of life?" After some nervous, embarrassed laughter on both sides, and a low "oh God," Penrose composes himself and responds, "All I will say, I think it is not a stupid question. . . . You see, I tend to think that the mystery of consciousness is tied up with the mystery of quantum mechanics." From his face and body language, as well as his words, I imagine it must have taken Penrose decades to be able to push past the collective prejudices and judgments both within himself and from his scientific colleagues to publicly affirm that the question of meaning is not meaningless. Furthermore, Penrose says that he likes to call himself a scientist but not a materialist. That is because, as he says, "we do not know what the *material* is."

In linking the mystery of psyche with the mystery of nature, Penrose is closer to Coleridge than Bacon.

And yet Penrose is the exception today. When the Mariner shoots the Albatross, he does so as an *I* against the *we*. Today, that *I* has become *us*. We shoot the Albatross out of the sky every day when, in Coleridge's words, "we mistake clear Images for distinct conceptions, and . . . idly demand conceptions where Intuitions alone are possible or adequate to the majesty of the Truth,"[22] or, when, Oedipus-like, we believe we can solve the riddles of life by wit alone and need no knowledge got from birds. The collective consciousness of the modern educated West very much mirrors the image of the Mariner shooting down the Albatross and rejoicing in the dawning sun burning away the fog and mist of superstition. *Of course*, we say as a modern culture, we follow reason and fact in making decisions and setting priorities; what else would we do, listen to dreams? Throw the *I Ching*? All that sort of thing, we believe, went the way of the Albatross when consciousness emerged from the mist and fog of superstition and sailed into the clear light of day. Thus, the modern Western collective contempt for all "knowledge got from birds" is so characteristic, so commonplace, and so obviously correct that it is almost impossible to recognize as anything but normal. Today we "follow the science," and science is still identical, for the most part, as in Coleridge's time, with rational objectivity and deterministic materialism.

There are also many people today, however, who are at the same time haunted by a disturbing feeling that there is something incomplete, if not fundamentally off, sick, or perhaps even evil about the Mariner's crossbow. If we are one of these people, what should we do? Abandon the ship of reason and swim back to shore? Another option would be to do what the Mariner does—stay onboard the ship of knowledge and sail farther out. Let the Mariner's arrow fly farther. We need more science, not less, more psychology, not less, if we hope to reconcile our sense of meaning with our sense of truth and thus transform—with Coleridge's Mariner—the leaden dead spirit from above to gold from below.

CHAPTER 18

"To Mary Queen the Praise Be Given"

The Union of Spirit from Above with Soul from Below

Two thousand years ago, the Hellenistic Jewish philosopher Philo of Alexandria (25 BCE–50 CE) wrote that "progress is nothing else than the giving up of the female gender by changing into the male, since the female gender is material, passive, corporeal and sense-perceptible, while the male is active, rational, incorporeal and more akin to mind and thought."[1] For Philo, the goal is to change the female into the male; in *The Rime of the Ancient Mariner*, almost two millennia after Philo, the goal is to change the male gender into the female.

After the Mariner shoots the Albatross as a *he* and drinks his own blood, the Sun as a *he* sinks down, all two hundred men onboard drop dead, and God as the Heavenly Father goes missing. The ocean as a *she* becomes the locus of the demonic and the sacred, the Moon as a *she* rises, and the Witch, specter ship, and LIFE-IN-DEATH, all female, become vivid experiences and take control. Most importantly, as the Mariner blesses the water-snakes, the feminine image itself transforms from a nightmare into the Queen of Heaven and Earth.

Oh sleep! it is a gentle thing,
Beloved from pole to pole!
To Mary Queen the praise be given!
She sent the gentle sleep from Heaven,
That slid into my soul.

This is progress! "Mary Queen" responds to the Mariner's plight when the Father above is silent and heals the solar-masculine Wasteland by sending down the healing rain and sleep it so desperately lacks. The giving up of the male gender by changing into the female at the redemptive apex of *The Ancient Mariner* is a dramatic U-turn in the evolution of the Western mind.

The Mariner's redemption from the Fall is not a heroic act. He extends his consciousness beyond both traditional Christianity and the rationalistic materialism of the Enlightenment (in which the masculine sun as "God's own head" illuminates the world) not through more sun or more arrows, not through conscious intention and will, but through "sorrow, sickness, poetry, religion," as Coleridge himself experienced.[2] After suffering the feminine-lunar initiation for seven days and nights, the floodgates that blocked the waters of feeling and imagination in his heart open, allowing a hidden, mediumistic capacity for "Signs, Visions, and guiding Impulses" to *relate* to the spirit of nature instead of killing it, as when he shot the Albatross with his crossbow. The Mariner's "feminine qualities," again, to use Coleridge's own words, "a translucent Undertint of the Woman" having nothing to do with the "Effeminate" and present in the "greatest of men, most eminently," are responsible for the streams of imagination, feeling, and love radiating from his heart.

When it comes to understanding Coleridge's prophetic vision of the rebirth of the modern soul, there is good news and bad news to contend with. The good news is that rebirth is possible; the bad news is that this rebirth requires symbolic death. Symbolic death is the potent medicine that calls forth the rain, a unifying redemptive energy. For those of us raised within traditional religious forms or educated within the rational and materialistic assumptions of the Enlightenment, the possibility of opening our whole selves to the *ne plus ultra* of adoration and becoming, as Coleridge puts it, "all permeable to a holier power"[3] requires a conscious confrontation with abject states of consciousness. Humiliation, a word that means to make low, from the Latin *humus* meaning earth or ground, is the way to attune to the abject dimensions of the self, the snake, *so that* Mary Queen might ascend. The buckets on the ship are "filled with dew" only after the Mariner bends low, for grace is like rain or dew; there is tension in the clouds and then it all releases, like the gift of tears that come when authentic feeling finally arrives. It is only after seven nights of agonizing initiatory suffering that the "nightmare" Female transforms into a Queen.[4]

The Assumption of Mary in Catholic Dogma

In the Eastern Orthodox Church, Mary Queen is more than the mother who gives birth to Jesus; during the Easter Eve service she is *tekousa selene*, the moon that gives birth to the reborn sun. In the Catholic Church, Mary is also the Virgin of the Apocalypse found in the book of Revelation, a woman clothed with the sun, standing on the moon, crowned with twelve stars, and pregnant with a child.

Coleridge's reference to "Mary Queen" alludes to the Catholic tradition of the Assumption of Mary, a popular belief that the mother of Jesus ascended body and soul into Heaven. Although the Assumption is not found in the Bible, it is found in ancient liturgies honoring Mary's passing, as well as a fifth-century document known as the *Transitus Mariae*.[5] During the Middle Ages and

Giovanni Battista Tiepolo, *The Immaculate Conception* (ca.1767–69).

This image derives from the Apocalypse of Saint John, a passage that reads, "And a great sign appeared in heaven: A woman clothed with the sun, and the moon under her feet, and on her head a crown of twelve stars" (Revelation 12:1).

beyond, the Assumption was commonly recognized and steadily increased in popularity in conjunction with the various Marian miracles at Lourdes, where, during a series of appearances in 1858, Mary instructed the young Bernadette to dig in the nearby dirt, revealing a spring of water from which the church has declared seventy miracles. The tradition became official church dogma on November 1, 1950, when Pope Pius XII declared it so *ex cathedra* in the Apostolic Constitution of Pope Pius XII entitled *Munificentissimus Deus Defining the Dogma of the Assumption*. This means that today, if you are Catholic, you *must* believe that "the Immaculate Mother of God, the ever-Virgin Mary, having completed the course of her earthly life, was assumed body and soul into heavenly glory . . . where, as Queen, she sits in splendor at the right hand of her Son, the immortal King of the Ages."

The appearance of "Mary Queen" at the redemptive apex of *The Rime of the Ancient Mariner* is thus a Catholic image. Yet Coleridge was a member of the Church of England from birth, a Protestant denomination which has not had a feast day celebrating the Assumption since 1549. In 1794, Coleridge left that church to become a Unitarian, and in 1798, the year *The Ancient Mariner* was published, he briefly accepted a position as a Unitarian minister. Shortly thereafter, Coleridge experienced a religious crisis and did not return to any formal religion until he rejoined the Church of England in 1814 when he was forty-two years old. But Coleridge was never a Catholic. How is it, then, that the Queen of Heaven is *the* redemptive symbol of the Mariner's night-sea journey?

Let us allow ourselves the freedom here to ask the essentially Coleridgean question, not "Is it true?" but "What is the meaning of it?" As is often the case, the question of the symbolic meaning of the Mariner's voyage can be illuminated by dreams.

Mary Queen as Symbol and Dream

I am neither a professing Protestant nor Catholic and was not raised in any religious tradition. Nevertheless, as I was beginning to write on Coleridge's *Ancient Mariner* as my thesis in analytic training about twenty years ago, I had a dream that placed great importance on the Assumption of Mary in relationship to Coleridge's vocation as an artist.

> *Coleridge is an art student at a prestigious art school. Coleridge is getting into conflict with the school because he is always doing his projects in different ways than the traditions and rules prescribe. His inspiration to go his own way as an artist is fueled by the hope that the Assumption of Mary will happen in reality.*

The hope the Assumption would "happen in reality," the dream says, is what inspires Coleridge to "go his own way" outside the rules and norms of tradition.

At the time, this dream seemed to come out of nowhere. It was enigmatic. As I said, I was not familiar with the Assumption of Mary from any religious upbringing of my own. I had heard that the Assumption was important to Jung but could not have told you why. And as to how the hope that a Catholic dogma would happen "in reality" might possibly relate to Coleridge's capacity to "go his own way as an artist," well, I had no clue at all. Of course, I wondered what this dream might have to do with *me*, but I also recognized that the Assumption of Mary is related to Coleridge's reference to "Mary Queen" in *The Ancient Mariner*. And so, I wondered: Might the Assumption of Mary *really* have something to do with the meaning of Coleridge's art?

Feeling a bit the sacred fool, I investigated Coleridge's 1818 essay *On Poesy or Art* to find out. There, I was surprised to discover that

Coleridge defines art in a way strikingly akin to the religious imagery of the divine Mother as mediatrix between human and divine. "Art," Coleridge affirms, "is the mediatress between, and reconciler of nature and man."[6] Coleridge's definition of art resonates with traditional iconography of the Assumption in which Mary Queen is often depicted as a "mediatress" between Heaven and Earth; a white bird hovers over her head and a snake lies under her feet, the very image of an *axis mundi*. That imagery brought back to my mind the sundering of white bird and snake in *The Ancient Mariner* and the union of spirit from above and soul from below that Mary Queen personifies. While some orthodox interpretations interpret Mary as not standing on but crushing the serpent beneath her feet, in my humble opinion the image speaks for itself: Mary is a "mediatress" between above and below, light and dark, or, in the imagery of *The Ancient Mariner*, Albatross and water-snakes.[7]

Finding this hint, and others, I felt inspired to follow the trail further. I dove into Jung's writings, particularly his alchemical writings, in search of the psychological-symbolic meaning of the Assumption from Jung's perspective, where I discovered that Jung wrote extensively on the Assumption, especially in *Answer to Job*, *Mysterium Coniunctionis*, *Psychology and Alchemy*, and his correspondence with Wolfgang Pauli (1900–1958), a pioneer of quantum mechanics and a Nobel laureate in physics (the interested reader will find some of these references in the notes to this chapter).

Jung believed the dogma of the Assumption to be the most important Western religious development in four hundred years—since the Protestant Reformation.[8] One example of the Assumption in Jung's writings that particularly caught my attention is found in Jung's *Psychology and Alchemy* (1944), where Jung dis-

Johann Michael Faust, "*Speculum Trinitatis*," from *Compendium alchymist, novum, sive Pandora explicate*, Frankfurt, 1706.

cusses a woodcut of the Assumption and Coronation of Mary from Reusner's *Pandora* (1582), the fourteenth in a series of alchemical emblems describing the opus of transformation. Jung reprints an engraving from the 1706 version in which there is a high and a low dimension to the Assumption. The upper half is traditional: a Christ figure places a crown on the head of a woman, Mary, high above the world where nothing unclean or ugly enters in and the white bird of the Holy Spirit hovers over her head. The lower image is untraditional: a human figure pulls out a bird-fish-snake-human monstrosity from a lump of matter. This lower image is "the mirror image of the Holy Family," as the text says; in other words, an image of the Assumption and Coronation of Mary reversely arranged, as if seen in a mirror, revealing the underground or secret meaning of this traditional image.[9] The appearance of Mary Queen in *The Ancient Mariner* is like that in the alchemical *Pandora* image; the Mariner blesses snakes below as Mary appears as Queen above. Jung's *Psychology and Alchemy* entitles the *Pandora* image of the Assumption "The Glorification of the Body," and Jung interprets the lower image as the extraction of the *anima mundi* from matter.

Synchronicity and the Spiritualization of the Body

The title of the image of the Assumption in the *Pandora* text itself is "Imbibition of the Body." This title requires some explanation, as it is not immediately obvious what the Assumption has to do with imbibition.[10] Technically speaking, imbibition is a special type of diffusion in which one substance is absorbed by another, but more generally imbibition simply means a body is drinking in water, as when a seed takes in water, expands, and starts to germinate.

Ignotum per aeque ignotum, as the alchemists say, we explain the unknown by the equally unknown. In the alchemical imagination, water is spirit. Therefore, the alchemical imbibition of the body refers to the spiritualization of the body. The spiritualization of the body is itself a "mirror image," so to speak, of the incarnation of Christ in which the divine spirit is materialized. As a compensatory dynamic to that of Christ in which the Heavenly spirit above materializes below, with the Assumption of Mary, a human woman ascends into Heaven, body and soul, and is spiritualized. The alchemical imagination thus uses both a natural fact (imbibition) and a religious doctrine (the Assumption) as metaphors for the spiritualization of matter.

In the alchemical imagination, dew, or rain, another image found in *The Ancient Mariner* in association with "Mary Queen," symbolizes the reservoir of the universal spirit of nature that brings life to dead bodies. In an image from the *Rosarium Philosophorum* (1551) entitled *Ablutio vel Mundificatio* (washing or mundification; to cleanse, purge, or purify, as in the cleaning out a wound), the German text at the bottom of the page reads, "The dew fell down from heaven / And washed the black body in the grave." There is another interesting parallel between *Pandora* and *The Ancient Mariner* here: when Mary Queen ascends to heaven, the Mariner's dry-as-dust body drinks in water.

> The silly buckets on the deck,
> That had so long remained,
> I dreamt that they were filled with dew;
> And when I awoke, it rained.
>
> My lips were wet, my throat was cold,
> My garments were all dank;
> Sure I had drunken in my dreams,
> And still my body drank.

Again, *ignotum per ignotius*! It is obvious that the phrase "the spiritualization of matter" is as enigmatic as what it seeks to explain and thus, as an interpretation, requires interpretation. In the context of depth psychology our attempt to interpret this symbolism amounts to nothing more nor less than translating it into the language and mythos of psychology.

Synchronicity and the Imbibition of the Body

The Mariner dreams it rains, and it rains. As Mary Queen ascends, he drinks in his dreams and his body drinks. Inner and outer, above and below, spirit and matter, come together. Many of us have had, at some time or another in our lives, the experience of inner and outer events meaningfully coinciding. Perhaps we dream of a person or an event and that person or event appears in waking life.

Jung, for example, tells the story of walking through the woods with a woman as she tells him a deeply significant dream of a spectral fox walking toward her down the stairs of her family home. Suddenly, a real fox steps out of the woods and onto the path, walking in front of them both for a time. Dream and reality meaningfully touch here in a way that is not causally explicable. Jung named this phenomenon synchronicity. Synchronistic events convey the impression of a spiritualization of matter in which these two seemingly different substances are not divorced but meaningfully connected. Another way to put this is, using the natural metaphors of alchemy, to say that the dry body drinks in water. And indeed this is exactly what Coleridge does say in *The Ancient Mariner*.

Interestingly, the best-known story of synchronicity in the Jungian tradition, the story of the Rainmaker, parallels the imagery of both *Pandora* and *The Ancient Mariner*. This story has to do with the redemptive falling of rain during a dangerous drought. It is a true story that Jung heard from his friend Richard Wilhelm (1873–1930), a German sinologist, theologian, and missionary to China for twenty-five years whose greatest achievement as a missionary, he said, was that he failed to convert one single Chinese and was instead converted to a deep love, respect, and knowledge of Chinese culture. Wilhelm was also the first person to translate the *I Ching*, one of the most important books of world literature, into a European language, a translation that is still widely used today.

This is the Rainmaker story as Jung heard it from Wilhelm.

> There was a great drought where Wilhelm lived; for months there had not been a drop of rain and the situation became catastrophic. The Catholics made processions, the Protestants made prayers, and the Chinese burned joss-sticks and shot off guns to frighten away the demons of the drought, but with no result.

> Finally the Chinese said, "We will fetch the rain-maker." And from another province a dried up old man appeared. The only thing he asked for was a quiet little house somewhere, and there he locked himself in for three days.
>
> On the fourth day the clouds gathered and there was a great snow-storm at the time of the year when no snow was expected, an unusual amount, and the town was so full of rumours about the wonderful rain-maker that Wilhelm went to ask the man how he did it.
>
> In true European fashion he said: "They call you the rain-maker; will you tell me how you made the snow?"
>
> And the little Chinese said: 'I did not make the snow; I am not responsible."
>
> "But what have you done these three days?"
>
> "Oh, I can explain that. I come from another country where things are in order. Here they are out of order; they are not as they should be by the ordinance of heaven. Therefore the whole country is not in Tao, and I also am not in the natural order of things because I am in a disordered country.
>
> So I had to wait three days until I was back in Tao and then naturally the rain came."[11]

The Mariner gives Mary Queen the praise when the rain falls ("To Mary Queen the praise be given!"), and the Rainmaker also affirms that he did not make the rain ("I did not make the snow; I am not responsible.") In both *The Ancient Mariner* and the Taoist legend, conscious effort and willpower do not do the trick; rather, a secret order acausally present in psyche and nature heals a self and world out of balance once the individual comes into balance. According to Jung, the Assumption of Mary is "the Western equivalent of the union of yang and yin in tao."[12] Thus Coleridge perfectly channels the archetypal symbolism: naturally the rain falls when Mary Queen ascends, for then masculine and feminine, heaven and earth, the eternal and the temporal, sky and sea are in balance.

Something is real *for us* only if it is conscious and known. From the perspective of physics, matter is what is real, and science is our means of knowing about matter and thus knowing about reality. Therefore, for the so-called spiritualization of matter to be convincing to the modern mind, it must be not only poetically meaningful and psychologically comprehensible but also scientifically describable. Important to note in this respect is that Jung developed his synchronicity idea through a twenty-six-year-long collaboration with Pauli in which both the psychologist and the physicist came to conjecture that synchronicity takes its place, along with the psyche, as a fourth principle in nature in addition to the three principles of space and time, matter, and causality. Jung only dared to publish his essay "Synchronicity: An Acausal Connecting Principle" in *The Interpretation of Nature and the Psyche* (1952) alongside Pauli's essay "The Influence of Archetypal Ideas on the Scientific Ideas of Kepler."[13] As a modern image of the spiritualization of matter, synchronicity implies that the psyche experienced as meaning is not merely a poetic compensation for dismal reality but is *really there*, out there in the material world. There is a "symbol in the truth of things" as Coleridge puts it.

The Assumption of Mary, the Ancient Mariner, and the Quaternity

When Mary Queen ascends to Heaven, a queen takes her place with the king. This event effectively transforms the Christian Trinity into a Quaternity.

Over two thousand years ago in the West, as we saw in the quotation from Philo, there was a push in the collective psyche toward the development of archetypally masculine qualities: the ethical ideal, spirituality, willpower, and discipline. Therefore, throughout the Western world for millennia, the Trinitarian image of God in which God is exclusively good, spiritual, and masculine seemed true and real. Today, there is a push in the collective psyche toward wholeness and for the union of what has been sundered in the Western soul. Therefore, the Trinitarian image of God no longer seems or feels true or *real* to the modern mind, for it no longer mirrors our unconscious constitution. For those who belong to modern consciousness, the Trinity is an incomplete Quaternity. The Trinitarian image of God in Christianity is incomplete in part because it lacks the feminine, the human being, and the reality of evil.

The fourfold is an image of wholeness. The conscious mind is structured by four psychological functions, thinking, feeling, sensation, and intuition, an underlying structure made visible, for instance, in the universal symbolism of mandalas, or quadrated circles, as images of God. When we want to organize reality into a structural wholeness, we create fourfold Cartesian grids to map it. We also project the fourfold structure of the mind onto the material world when we say that there are four winds, or four directions. Everything we know about, everything we see, all we ever experience or are conscious of in the world, we know in the three dimensions of space, length, width, and height, and a fourth dimension of time. That is because the psyche, as a fourfold structure, frames our perception of the material cosmos. There may be other dimensions beyond the quaternity of space and time as many mathematical and physical theorists assert, but we do not directly perceive these in ordinary states of consciousness. Furthermore, all modern biology and physics is 4D. The information coding in DNA, as well as the mathematics that underlie nature's laws, is organized in quaternian (often 3 + 1) structures. The DNA code uses four nucleotide bases or "letters," adenine (A), cytosine (C), guanine (G), and thymine (T). Each of these fourfold nucleotide structures consists of three components such as ATG or CCC. There are three fundamental forces in the standard model in physics—the strong, weak, and electromagnetic—plus a fourth which is described separately from the others, gravity. While the strong, weak, and electromagnetic forces are mediated by photons and subatomic particles and involve electric and magnetic fields, gravity is the geometry of space and time and, as the fourth, is difficult to join to the three other forces. The search for a "theory of everything," or a theory of quantum gravity, is still ongoing.

The dogma of the Assumption—Mary Queen in *The Ancient Mariner*—is thus a symbolic starting point toward the realization of the Self as a fourfold structure. I say that the dogma is a starting point because although Mary is a human woman, she is also special; she is *perfectly* human, immaculately conceived without sin. Both *Pandora* and *The Ancient Mariner* hint that something darker, more earthy, is involved with the Assumption than the purified feminine.[14] Something like a water-snake is involved, something chthonic like the nightmare LIFE-IN-DEATH, the night, the shadow of the ship: the human body as it *really* is, the *anima mundi*, the reality of evil, something difficult to join with the members of the Trinity.[15]

The Mariner suffers mightily until the feminine image ascends to Heaven as the missing fourth. And then the Mariner himself becomes that fourth; he *is* the full force of the Quaternity, dark and light.[16] He is the missing fourth confronting a trinity of men, not once but twice in the poem. We witnessed the first example of this when the Mariner "stoppeth one of three" Wedding Guests and enters as the tabooed, dreaded, and lunatic fourth with the moonlight in his glittering eye. The second example we shall see later upon the Mariner's return to shore when three men pull the Mariner as the fourth into their little rowboat. Both times, the Mariner is terrifying to the two groups of three men he encounters; the

Wedding Guest calls him a "grey-beard loon" and desperately though unsuccessfully tries to escape his hypnotizing gaze, and two of the three men in the rowboat call the Mariner "the devil" and go "crazy" when he moves his lips to speak. In his confrontation with collective Christianity and the Enlightenment (the kirk and light-house on land), the Mariner as the missing fourth is felt as both evil and psychotic. Quoting Socrates in Plato's *Timeus*

(ca. 360 BCE) in which the fourth of Socrates' guests has been taken ill and is missing, Jung interprets the problem of 3 + 1 as the tension between reality and imagination. "Hence the opening words of the Timaeus 'One, two, three—But where, my dear Timeus, is the fourth . . . ?'—fall familiarly upon the ears of the psychologist and alchemist, and for him as for Goethe there can be no doubt that Plato is alluding to something of mysterious import. We can see now that it was nothing less than the dilemma as to whether something we think about is a mere thought or a reality, or at least capable of becoming a reality."[17] We will return to the agonizing conflict between imagination and reality in *The Ancient Mariner* when we discuss the Mariner's return to shore.

The Quaternity and the Imagination of Evil

The Ancient Mariner confronts us with the problem of the Quaternity: namely, a whole image of God *must* contain the feminine principle, but it also *must* contain evil. And by evil, I mean not only the painful recognition that evil exists but something even more dangerous and challenging to accept: evil is necessary for the evolution of consciousness.

In the alchemically inspired language of Jungian psychology, the transformation of consciousness is, Jung writes, "a *process* that begins with evil and ends with good."[18] In the language of *The Ancient Mariner*, the Mariner must kill the Albatross—a truly evil act in every sense—to bless the water-snakes and transform the feminine from a nightmare to the Queen of Heaven, a supremely good act. We have seen how the Mariner, as "the devil" who commits a "hellish" sacrilege in murdering the Albatross, becomes the only *I* onboard the ship. In his forward to R. J. Zwi Werblowsky's *Lucifer and Prometheus* (1952), Jung explains that "Milton's devil" is the "*principium individuationis*."[19]

From the perspective of Christian moralism that informs *The Ancient Mariner*, the Mariner's path to redemption is to repent his sins and seek absolution for shooting the sacred white bird. From the depth psychological and alchemical perspective, however, that runs as the meaningful symbolic phenomenology of the poem itself, although unacknowledged *in* the poem itself by the Mariner, the Mariner is the Merlin of the Holy Grail legend, the son of both a

Christian mother and the devil; he is the alchemical Mercurius, not the anti-Christ but a compensatory image to Christ, the *principium individuationis* who brings forth new light from the sea, new values, new consciousness, new ways of seeing through the moonlit illumination of the repressed feminine. As Jung says, Mercurius barely avoids identity with the devil only because he eventually leads to the union of contraries.[20] "To the Christian mentality, the dark antagonist is always the devil. As I have shown, Mercurius escapes this prejudice by only a hair's breadth. But he escapes it, thanks to the fact that he scorns to carry on opposition at all costs. The magic of his name enables him, in spite of his ambiguity and duplicity, to keep outside the split, for as an ancient pagan god he possesses a natural undividedness which is impervious to logical and moral contradictions. This gives him invulnerability and incorruptibility, the very qualities we so urgently need to heal the split in ourselves."[21] Similarly, the Mariner is not the spirit of pure evil but a spirit of redemption from a peculiarly Christian split between light and dark, and he redeems himself by creatively healing that split. It is true that, as the fourth missing from the Trinity, the Mariner's bright, glittering, lunar eye has no place in the status quo structures of the "kirk" and "lighthouse top" on land—traditional Christianity and the European Enlightenment—but it is always the case that all Messiahs and all rebel angels have no place in the status quo ante.[22] As the *principium individuationis*, the Mariner represents a process of psychological development that is not only historical but also prophetic and, as such, was too much, too strange, too incomprehensible, too soon for collective realization in Coleridge's time, as it still is for us today.

For example, in the West, ethics means striving for the good. This is a noble ideal, symbolically mirrored in the Trinitarian image of God in which nothing impure enters in. It is also impossible to live up to. If we aim for perfection, we fall short. The downside of all our efforts to strive to be "good" is an inevitable accumulation of shame and guilt, emotions that are so toxic that we almost always either drown in them or disown them (and thereby project them onto others) so as to not become overwhelmed. Antisemitism, racism, sexism, all "-isms," as well as many forms of hate and bigotry, to say nothing of ever-continuing crusades against a perceived axis of evil in the enemies outside of us, can be understood as the inevitable and sadly predictable result of repressing and then projecting evil.

But who can carry the burden of the shadow, the heaviest burden of self-knowledge?[23] Sooner or later, if we are to survive, we will have to become our own redeemers by carrying our own Cross, celebrating a Last Supper with ourselves—as the Mariner does—by confronting and accepting the reality that the problem of darkness lies in all human hearts, not just perceived enemies, wrongdoers, or scapegoats. There are no "good and bad people," as we say, only people capable of both good and evil with varying degrees of consciousness about these polarities within themselves.

Having an imagination for evil does not mean that we become evil; it means that we have our eyes on it. As Jung famously said, "One does not become enlightened by imagining figures of light, but by making the darkness conscious,"[24] an insight vividly expressed in the following dream and the painting that follows from it. The dreamer is a middle-aged woman working in Jungian analysis on the problem of evil where it confronts her personally, at home in her primary relationship.

> *I dreamt that there was a little being between us who was evil, and we could see him, and we could see his dark body, and the evil inside his body from which he acts, from which he moves and is propelled. We were looking at him, taking him in, really*

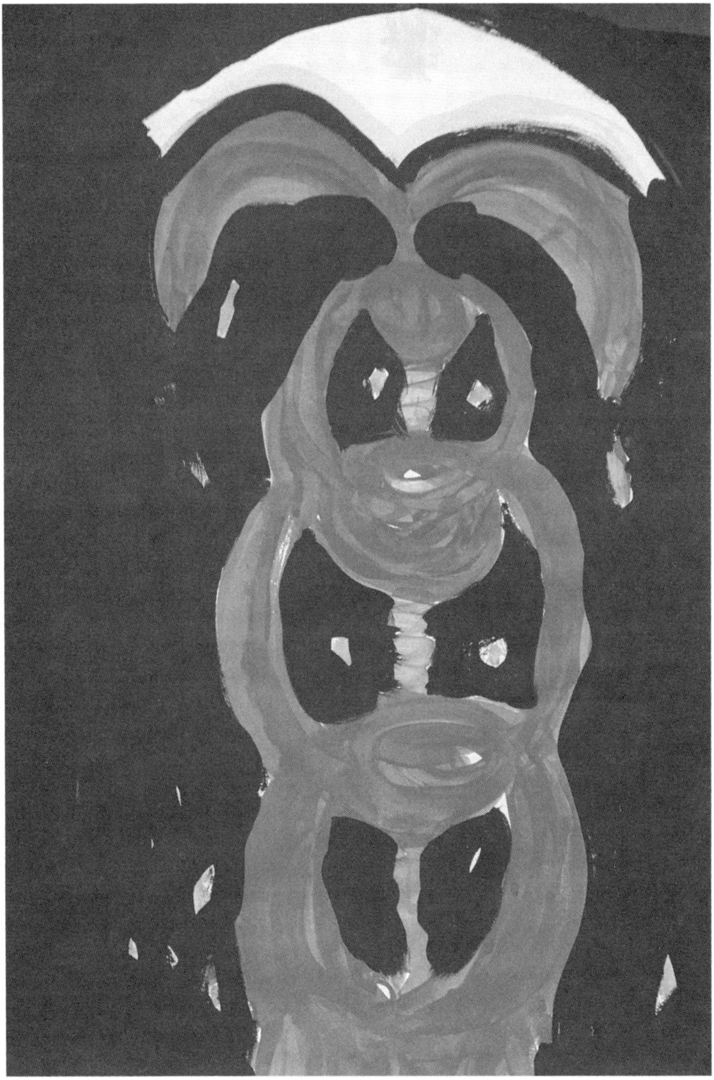

Anonymous, original painting, *The Evil Child with Light over Its Head* (used with author's permission).

grokking the tangible felt sense of his embodied evil. And in the dream, we were instructed to keep an eye on him together, continually.

Then after I painted him in his darkness, a voice said, "You are allowed to paint a little light above his head as long as you keep an eye on him." Meaning, only when you keep an eye on him is there a little light above his head. And the eye is a sophisticated eye that sees into the nature of the evil that he is embodying and the actions that are propelled out of that evil. That is what it means to keep an eye on him.

Mary Queen as the Fully Human Form of Consciousness

According to Catholic tradition, Mary Queen is the woman in the book of Revelation, clothed with the Sun and standing on the Moon. According to Jung, Mary Queen is "the Heavenly bride united with the Bridegroom,"[25] a symbol "intended to compensate the truly apocalyptic world situation today."[26] According to the Romanticism scholar Woodman, the *Assumptio* represents "the fully human form of consciousness . . . raising the unconscious operations of the physical body to the imaginal perception of it."[27] The Assumption of Mary thus symbolizes a desire in the collective psyche, a massive need, actually, to unite the physical facts of nature—including the dark reality of human nature—with spiritual imagination.[28] In the Catholic dogma of the Assumption, Mary is a human being in every way, not a goddess. Thus, the Assumption symbolizes what God intends for all human beings. We all have the capacity to become, in Coleridge's words, "all permeable to a holier power," to give birth to a perception of the subtle body through the Sun-Moon conjunction of conscious and unconscious.[29]

If you blur your vision a bit, you might see the unconscious operations of the physical body raised to an imaginal perception of it

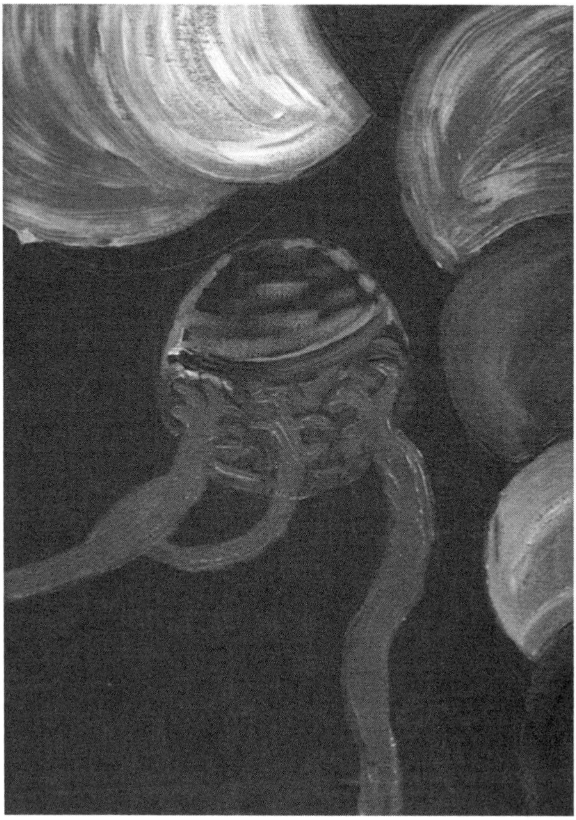

Thomas Elsner, *The Eighth Planet* (2005).

in the painting *The Eighth Planet*. This is a painting taken from a dream I had long ago as I was first working on *The Ancient Mariner*.[30] In my dream, an eighth planet—half-material and half-spiritual—is in the center, surrounded by seven planets. A 7 + 1 system is evident, as well as a 3 + 1; three arteries pump blood from below into the planet as the fourth. Like the Quaternity (the 3 + 1), the 7 + 1 symbolizes a process of development leading to a new stage, as with the seven notes of the Western musical scale that begin again with the octave, or the seven days of the week that lead to a new week on the eighth.[31] We see the 3 + 1 symbolism in *The Ancient Mariner* when the Mariner confronts those two trinities of men from shore, as well as the 7 + 1 symbolism when the Mariner undergoes seven days and nights of initiatory suffering before the Assumption takes place on the eighth. In addition, when the three men from shore pull the Mariner up into their rowboat as the fourth, they pull him up as a man "seven days drowned."

My dream of Coleridge and the Assumption of Mary emphasizes that the inspiration behind all Coleridge's art is that the Assumption will happen in reality. The 3 + 1 symbolism implies this question: Can the imaginal perceptions of the unconscious become part of our conscious picture of reality? Coleridge's own sense of art is that it seeks to do just that. "In every work of art," Coleridge argues, "there is a reconcilement of the external with the internal; the conscious is so impressed on the unconscious as to appear in it. . . . He who combines the two is the man of genius; and for that reason he must partake of both."[32] Jung's sense of the individuation process is, practically speaking, identical to both Coleridge's sense of the psychological function of art and the metaphysical dogma of the Assumption.[33]

CHAPTER 19

"The Upper Air Burst into Life!"

Nature and Supernature Come Alive

After the buckets on the deck are filled with dew, in both dream and reality, the Mariner's immersion in the lunar-feminine initiation continues to reverberate in the world. Once again, the theme of symbolic death comes into play.

> I moved, and could not feel my limbs:
> I was so light—almost
> I thought that I had died in sleep,
> And was a blessed ghost.

As the Mariner straddles the realms of life and death, both nature and supernature come alive in a tremendous burst of released energy. Now the *sky* as well as the *sea* bursts into a flash of golden fire in the moonlight. In the fury of a "roaring wind," the "upper air burst into life! / And a hundred fire-flags sheen" as the wind "did roar more loud," and "rain poured down from one black cloud" with "the Moon . . . at its edge." The streams of love that previously gushed from the Mariner's heart when he blessed the water-snakes in the sea now transform the sky above into rivers of water and lightning, again, with all of this happening at night, in the moonlight.

The stanzas describing the transformation of the upper air are powerful, spellbinding, quintessentially Romantic. Here, the Mariner is truly Wotanic; a massive blast of poetic storms takes over everything.

> The thick black cloud was cleft, and still
> The Moon was at its side:
> Like waters shot from some high crag,
> The lightning fell with never a jag,
> A river steep and wide.

The storm, the black cloud, the rivers of rain and lightning are blessed events—just as the water-snakes are blessed. When Nature is spiritualized, the natural world and the supernatural world touch, and everything comes alive!

> Beneath the lightning and the Moon
> The dead men gave a groan.
>
> They groaned, they stirred, they all uprose,
> Nor spake, nor moved their eyes;
> It had been strange, even in a dream,
> To have seen those dead men rise.

Perhaps Mary Shelley—who knew *The Ancient Mariner* well—had these stanzas in mind when she wrote *Frankenstein*, for in that amazing gothic novel as well it is the lightning from above that reanimates the dead bodies below.

Here again the theme of living death returns, the theme that makes the Wedding Guest afraid. Again, the Mariner must reassure him.

> "I fear thee, ancient Mariner!"
> "Be calm, thou Wedding-Guest!
> 'Twas not those souls that fled in pain,

Which to their corses came again,
But a troop of spirits blest

But is it really the case that blest spirits inhabit the bodies of the dead crew? One doubts it when the Mariner reveals that the dead men are still there, still cursing him with their eyes glittering in the moonlight, and reminding us of the Mariner's own half-morbid "glittering eye."

All stood together on the deck,
For a charnel-dungeon fitter:
All fixed on me their stony eyes,
That in the Moon did glitter.

The pang, the curse, with which they died,
Had never passed away

It is *because* living death is all around, it is *because* the collective masculine consciousness is still cursing the Mariner, that blessed events are happening. Music fills the air, now the music of birds and bubbling springs, now the music of angels, as the Mariner's sensual experience of the world changes from primarily seeing to hearing and thus to *feeling*. As we have seen earlier, Coleridge was very familiar with these "flashlike" revelations of "BEAUTY" in the half-created and half-perceived world of spiritualized Nature.[1] "To a spiritual Woman," the "silent communion of the Spirit with the Spirit in Nature" is "Music," Coleridge writes, not noise as with the cracking and growling, the roaring and howling, of "noises in a swound" the Mariner hears in the land of mist and snow early on in his voyage before the Albatross appears.

The Mariner's ship sails on toward home, now "moved onward from beneath" by a mysterious natural supernatural power. At noon, however, when "the Sun, right above the mast" did stand, the Sun "had fixed her to the ocean." We have mentioned this theme before; when the Sun is overhead the Mariner's ship stops and the Mariner stops telling his tale. But now the energy generated from the *agon*, or conflict, between Sun and Moon is so tremendous that, in the midst of this tension between the forward movement of the Mariner's ship and the regressive power of the sun, the ship bursts forward "like a pawing horse let go" with such velocity that the Mariner "fell down in a swound." The Moon creates all this movement.

> "What makes that ship drive on so fast?
> What is the ocean doing?"
>
> *Second Voice*
> "Still as a slave before his lord,
> The ocean hath no blast;
> His great bright eye most silently
> Up to the Moon is cast—
>
> If he may know which way to go;
> For she guides him smooth or grim."

The ocean has a "bright eye" that is the reflection of the Moon, just as the Mariner has a "bright eye." Both the ocean and the Mariner's soul are under the power of the lunar-feminine.

In a trance state, a seemingly ever-continuing experience of symbolic death "before my living life returned," the Mariner hears and discerns in his soul "two voices in the air."

> "Is it he?" quoth one, "Is this the man?
> By him who died on cross,
> With his cruel bow he laid full low
> The harmless Albatross.
>
> The spirit who bideth by himself
> In the land of mist and snow,

He loved the bird that loved the man
Who shot him with his bow."

The other was a softer voice,
As soft as honey-dew:
Quoth he, "The man hath penance done,
And penance more will do."

These two voices that travel in the air and the Mariner's soul are his inner response to what is happening all around him, and specifically zero in on the shooting of the Albatross: the Mariner deeply feels himself to be guilty, deserving the penance he has already suffered for his sacrilege, deserving of even more penance. Despite the fact that the Albatross fell from his neck "like lead" when he blessed the water-snakes in a revelation of the flash of golden fire in the sea, the Mariner still has that Albatross around his neck internally; he still feels that his redemption must come, if at all, through repenting his sins rather than through the creative revelation of a new image of God for which the death of the Albatross was a necessary sacrifice.

As he returns home, the Mariner's conscience reveals itself to be split between the unresolvable—for him—contraries of innocent love and cruelty.

The burden of sacrilege is very different from consciously carrying the blood on one's hands as a sacrifice. Sacrilege means taking away the sacred; sacrifice means making sacred. And it is always the most beautiful, the most valued, the most helpful guiding star that must be sacrificed for something new to develop. For the Mariner (and Coleridge), that sacrificial victim is the pure white bird of love and innocence; for Jung, it was the Germanic hero Siegfried. Jung grieved killing this inner "beautiful" figure but accepted his guilt as tragic but necessary for individuation. The Mariner cannot do this, as we shall see in more detail when we discuss the Mariner's return to church once he touches down on land.

For now, we gain some insight into the agony burning in the Mariner's heart as he returns home, an *agon* between sea and land so great it threatens to turn the entire night-sea journey into an evil fiend.

PART 4

Return

CHAPTER 20

"A Frightful Fiend Doth Close behind Him Tread"

The Challenge of Consciously Facing the Unconscious

He did it! Under the light of the moon, in the "huge shadow" of the ship, the Mariner blesses the abject and thereby redeems his enmity with God and nature. He finally blesses the snake and the feminine through a descent into the unity of all living things in which he participates in the archetypal round of creation through death and rebirth, thus helping the divine feminine come into the manifest world in a positive and life-giving way. At the end of his voyage both nature and supernature are vividly and powerfully alive.

As we follow the Mariner back home, we find ourselves inside another archetypal image that, like the Assumption of Mary, is central to Coleridge's concept of art. That is the uroboros, the snake that eats its own tail.

The goal of poetry, Coleridge tells us, is to make a straight line circular, to "convert a *series* into a *Whole*." "The common end of all *narrative*, nay, of *all* Poems is to convert a *series* into a *Whole*: to make those events, which in real or imagined History move on in a *strait* Line, assume to our Understandings, a *circular* motion—

the snake with its Tail in its Mouth."[1] As the Mariner sails home, guided by spirits and propelled by a mysterious supernatural power, he uroborically returns to where he started.

Oh! dream of joy! is this indeed
The light-house top I see?
Is this the hill? is this the kirk?
Is this mine own countree?

We drifted o'er the harbour-bar,
And I with sobs did pray—
O let me be awake, my God!
Or let me sleep alway.

Whereas it was kirk, hill, and light-house on the departure, now it is light-house, hill, kirk on the return. At the start of his voyage, the Mariner "merrily" drops below these cultural landmarks; coming back home he is overjoyed to find them again. Please God, let the sight of home be real and not another dream! Returning to shore, the "spell" of his visionary sea voyage is "snapt"; the Mariner looks back out onto the ocean and sees—just ocean.

And now this spell was snapt; once more
I viewed the ocean green,
And looked far forth, yet little saw
Of what had else been seen—

As the Mariner sails back inside collective consciousness, the sea becomes once again just the sea. Perhaps the whole voyage has been a hallucination and the Mariner's emotional experience of being under supernatural agency the product of "whatever source of delusion" (as Coleridge put it in his description of what he was getting at in writing *The Ancient Mariner*) imposes itself upon all those who feel that way.

Consciously Turning Around and Facing the Fiend

The Mariner's return to shore thus brings up the archetypal problem of the return, the final stage in the initiatory sequence—departure, initiation, return. The challenge of the return is the challenge of understanding, accepting, and integrating the heretical, phantasmagoric, and seemingly evil or psychotic dimensions of the unconscious mind with collective and personal consciousness.

When the Mariner reenters the sphere of collective consciousness, the spell of the sea is "snapt." But now that spell takes form as a "frightful fiend" pursuing the Mariner. Having "once turned round" out of "fear and dread," the Mariner will not turn round to the sea again—but the sea does not let him go. The verse here breaks from the typical four-line stanza into a memorable and haunting six-line pattern, a variation in style that makes the lines pop and emphasizes their importance.

> Like one, that on a lonesome road
> Doth walk in fear and dread,
> And having once turned round walks on,
> And no more turns his head;
> Because he knows a frightful fiend
> Doth close behind him tread.

A "fiend" is an evil spirit or demon, an archaic word for the devil. We remember that the Wedding Guest sees "the fiends" that possess the Mariner.

> "God save thee, ancient Mariner!
> From the fiends, that plague thee thus!—"

Furthermore, the Mariner's ship has a "fiendish look" to the three men from shore who row out to meet it.

"Dear Lord! it hath a fiendish look"
(The Pilot made reply)—
"I am a-feared—"

The fiend that pursues the Mariner is thus what the Mariner has become but does not want to know he has become or, more to the point, what he *seems* to have become—both to himself and others—once back inside the field of collective consciousness. The "fiend" is nothing more nor less than the world of symbolic imagination as seen from within the sphere of the collective consciousness on land.

Frankenstein and the Fiend

Mary Shelley's famous 1818 novel *Frankenstein; or, The Modern Prometheus* (written when she was only eighteen!) is the story of an alchemist and scientist, Victor Frankenstein, who pieces together an assortment of dead body parts, the now famous Frankenstein monster, and uses electricity to bring that dead conglomeration to life. He succeeds, but realizing the horror of what he has accomplished, Victor flees in terror from the reanimated "demoniacal corpse." Wandering alone through the streets of Ingolstadt at night, Victor's mind flashes back to the lines from *The Ancient Mariner* in which the Mariner feels pursued by a "frightful fiend."[2] According to the notes in Susan J. Wolfson's edition of *Frankenstein*, Percy Shelley "fainted on hearing these lines recited" at a private reading of *The Ancient Mariner*.[3] Victor Frankenstein *is* the Ancient Mariner. He is also Percy Shelley, Mary Shelley's husband, who was, like Victor Frankenstein, a "modern Prometheus." Percy Shelley did not literally reanimate any dead bodies, but he did use his electric genius to resurrect the phantasmagoric ideas, drives, and images lying dormant in the human psyche: "Underneath the grave, where do inhabit / The shadows of all forms that live," as Shelley writes in *Prometheus Unbound* (1820).

Any explorer "underneath the grave," not only a once-in-a-generation genius poet, faces the danger of being overwhelmed by the seductive and numinous quality of the archetypal unconscious but must face that danger in the name of creative life. Wikman, my partner, had the following dream in 1991 as she was emerging from four years in a life-and-death struggle with ovarian cancer, starting her training as a Jungian analyst, and feeling she had a new life to live.

> *I am visiting a graveyard and being guided underground by a barefoot man with a lantern who is wearing only tattered, three-quarter-length pants. He lives on the edge of the forest in a rustic cabin next to the graveyard. I take in the beauty of his hut. Then suddenly, he is my guide underneath the graves in an underground space where the poets live. As we walk along, he points to several of the transcendental poets, Whitman, Emerson, and more. Then he points to a poet-figure in the center of the underground who is holding a staff and pounding the earth above his head, which, of course, is the graveyard. Together, all the poets are chanting, "The grave cannot hold back the poets!" over and over. Suddenly, I am back aboveground on the edge of the graveyard and an open meadow. Jung meets me there, on a fence. Leaving the graveyard, we walk into the field together. He says he wants to build an engine. Then, Jung takes me to a banquet where there are many Jungian analysts gathered. A spirit alongside me says, "With your Jungian heritage, what will your politics be? Whatever you do, do not take the food that is in plastic cups! The earth cannot take them back."*

"The grave cannot hold back the poets!" This dream reveals that the poetic imagination is supreme, that LIFE-IN-DEATH and the chthonic, ancient archetype of the visionary poet lie, at least for here, at the foundation of Jungian psychology. To die and rise again she will have to stay with the divine madness and not let it collapse into literalism on the one hand or mere madness on the other. "Stay with this" is the message of her new life, of Life! The plastic forms, concepts created by consciousness, are not sufficient: they are not natural, they cannot die and be reborn, "the earth cannot take them back."

The Romantic Poets, Adonis, and Acteon

The Romantic poets were down there in the grave being overthrown by erotic beauty in the moonlight, and they were especially susceptible to the danger of not coming back up again, that is, of being overwhelmed by the *fascinosum* and overtaken by their own imagination. The LIFE-IN-DEATH they brought to life in their art often haunted them like Frankenstein's monster, like the Mariner's "frightful fiend."[4]

In *Adonais* (1821), Shelley eulogizes the poet John Keats, who died at the age of twenty-five, as Adonis, the exceedingly handsome mortal lover of the immortal Aphrodite and the archetype of the *puer aeturnus*. When Adonis was a child, Aphrodite gave him to Persephone to nurture in the underworld, and when Adonis grew up, both goddesses, heavenly and chthonic, fell in love with him. Adonis dies young, killed by a wild boar on a hunting trip, and the goddesses mourn his death eternally. In Shelley's imagination, Keats is a vulnerable, naive, innocent son-lover of the great Mother goddess.

> Where wert thou, mighty Mother, when he lay,
> When thy Son lay, pierc'd by the shaft which flies
> In darkness?

Keats is Acteon as well as Adonis, the mythic young hunter who follows his hounds into the dark recesses of the forest at night, chasing a stag far off the trodden paths in the moonlight. Deep in the wilderness, he inadvertently glimpses the goddess Diana bathing naked in a spring. Mesmerized by her ravishing beauty, he stops and gazes on her and Diana, outraged by this profanation of her virginal mystery, turns Acteon into a stag. His own hounds hunt him down and tear him to pieces.

The immature masculine psyche in Romanticism is Acteon-like, Adonis-like (and Attis-like as discussed earlier); the young poet sexually transgresses without invitation, meets the depths of the feminine-lunar mystery, and is destroyed by the beauty that fascinates him, consumed by his own runaway desire.

> He, as I guess,
> Had gazed on Nature's naked loveliness,
> Acteon-like, and now he fled astray,
> With feeble steps over the world wilderness
> And his own raging thoughts, along that rugged way,
> Pursued, like raging hounds, their father and their prey.[5]

Like the naivete of the Mariner when he drops "merrily" into the underworld, Shelley's vision of Keats is of a "beautiful child" who lacks chthonic masculinity and senex wisdom and is therefore defenseless against the dangers of the sanity-threatening fascinations of the archetypal world.

> O gentle child, beautiful as thou wert,
> Why didst thou leave the trodden paths of men
> Too soon, and with weak hands though mighty heart
> Dare the unpastur'd dragon in his den?
> Defenceless as thou wert, oh, where was then
> Wisdom the mirror'd shield, or scorn the spear?
> Or hadst thou waited the full cycle, when
> Thy spirit should have fill'd its crescent sphere,
> The monsters of life's waste had fled from thee like deer.

The problem of Attis, of Adonis, of Acteon, is the problem of being unable to either fully embrace or fully separate from the erotic field of the unconscious.[6] This is the Mariner's dilemma as well: "He, as I guess, / Had gazed on Nature's loveliness." "And now he fled astray" as "his own raging thoughts" pursued "their father and their prey"—what a perfect description of the Mariner when he returns to shore and feels himself pursued by a frightful fiend.

It takes a rare man indeed to say "hallelujah" to being symbolically killed by the divinity of the erotic imagination.

> Your faith was strong but you needed proof
> You saw her bathing on the roof
> Her beauty and the moonlight overthrew her
> She tied you to a kitchen chair
> She broke your throne, and she cut your hair
> And from your lips she drew the Hallelujah
>
> Hallelujah, Hallelujah
> Hallelujah, Hallelujah[7]

The Psychological Defenses Coleridge Used to Keep the Fiend at Arm's Length

In everyday life, we run from our fiends whenever we lack the courage or capacity to face what we are and what life is offering us. In the *Red Book*, for example, Jung confesses that he wants to run away from himself "so as not to have to live what remains unlived until now." "But," Jung continues, "you cannot flee yourself. It is with you all the time and demands fulfillment. If you pretend to be blind and dumb to this demand, you feign being blind and dumb to yourself. This way you will never reach the knowledge of the heart."[8] At sea, the Mariner turns toward himself as he eats his own flesh and drinks his own blood, and in this way attains the knowledge of the heart when he blesses the water-snakes. When he returns to shore, however, he turns away, and then the sea appears to him as a pursuing fiend that he cannot escape. The Mariner's inability to unite sea and land upon his return is an agony he carries like a new Albatross around his neck.

There are many psychological defenses that protect us from encountering ourselves: dissociation, repression, projection, intellectualization, splitting, compartmentalization, denial, addiction, and mania, to name some. But can we ever escape what we are? We can try, and yet it often seems like our fiends chase after us all the more, as paranoia for example, or possessive or compulsive behaviors, persecutory anxiety, addictions, phobias, physical symptoms with a hidden story behind them, a feeling of being at odds with ourselves, a pervasive sense that we are not living up to our potential, or simply the feeling of being a pretender.

Many patients in analysis feel (and dream) they are being punished for a crime they did not commit. Typically, their free-floating guilt and shame is the result of trauma, neglect, or abuse at a young age for which they blame themselves. Blaming oneself for the horrors one has experienced, especially as a child, is a typical defensive strategy that the psyche employs as an attempt to avoid confronting an even more threatening reality: that one's caretakers were missing, neglectful, abusive, or even malevolent. The parents must be "good" for the child to feel any sense of hope, but the cost of maintaining that necessary fiction is that the child must, therefore, be "bad." This unconscious strategy helps children cope. But as adults, these persons pay a price: without the horizontal axis of a healing relational field, this type of vicious circle tragically devours and consumes the adult personality. Psychoanalysis is an attempt to address this vicious circle by giving patients new experiences of trust by holding the opposites with them. Psychoanalysis encourages us—with a lot of understanding and support—to turn *toward* our fiends with a compassionate witness rather than run from them.

It is a significant challenge to consciously turn around and face the unconscious in its frightening forms. But if we can do this, then something unexpected almost always happens, something positive that begins to bridge split aspects of the psyche.

For example, earlier in this book we mentioned the dream of a woman in her late twenties who was going through a severe depression, including suicidal ideation, brought on by an abrupt crisis. She bolts in terror into the streets at night trying to escape a fiend chasing her—much as the Mariner turns away from his fiend, much like Victor Frankenstein running from his monster, much like Acteon trying to escape from his hounds. The inner predator running after her in the dream carries with him a bag that the woman knows is filled with women's dismembered body parts, an image of her feeling of falling to pieces. And then she does something extraordinary in the dream. She stops running, turns around, and faces her worst fears. Just then, the man walks up to her and says, "Happy birthday." As mentioned earlier, this dream corresponded with a process of symbolic death and renewal in her waking life that was quite astonishing to behold.

In his *Notebooks* and *Letters*, Coleridge often uses the word "fiend" to refer to psychosomatic (a word Coleridge invented, by the way) experiences that haunt him in his dreams. In a letter to Tom Wedgwood from September 16, 1803, Coleridge describes "*the fiend*" in his night terrors.[9] These "night-mares"—like the "Nightmare LIFE-IN-DEATH"—are no airy phantoms for Coleridge but the "foot-thick Calamities" of his life. Thus, sleep is Coleridge's hell.

In "The Pains of Sleep" (1803; 1816), Coleridge writes of a "fiendish crowd" torturing him in "a fiendish dream."

> But yester-night I prayed aloud
> In anguish and in agony,
> Up-starting from the fiendish crowd
> Of shapes and thoughts that tortured me

Therefore, during the day, Coleridge intentionally dials up all sorts of conscious defenses, such as suppression and compartmentalization, that is, "patience, employment, effort of mind, and walking," to "keep *the fiend* at Arm's length."

In the poem, the words describing the "fiendish crowd" are exclusively negative and also "not-I," as if the fiends were an otherness happening *to* Coleridge:

Anguish
Agony
Torture
Lurid
Sense of intolerable wrong
Thirst of revenge
Burning
Desire
Loathing
Wild
Hateful
Passions
Maddening
Shame
Terror
Confused
Guilt
Remorse

Woe
Fear
Punishments
Horror

On the other hand, Coleridge identifies himself in the poem with all the leavened qualities, so to speak—the ones that rise to Heaven, that are all good:

Silently
Slow
Spirit
Love
Compose
Humble
Trust
Reverential
Resignation
Supplication
Soul
Not unblest
Eternal strength and wisdom
Beloved
Love

By splitting off persecutory and critical inner objects (fiends) from consciousness, Coleridge avoids experiencing them as parts of the self. Splitting is a primitive defense that polarizes inner and outer objects into "all good" and "all bad"; it typically arises to deal with traumatic experiences in childhood. Yet split states of consciousness tend to oscillate and annihilate each other, which is the paradoxical hell of it all: the attempt to escape trauma creates its own form of madness. Thus, when Coleridge sleeps, the fiends come alive and pursue him in the form of intense visions and incomprehensible experiences of shame and guilt, as if Coleridge were being punished for a crime he did not commit.

> Such punishments, I said, were due
> To natures deepliest stained with sin,—
> For aye entempesting anew
> The unfathomable hell within,
> The horror of their deeds to view,
> To know and loathe, yet wish and do!
> Such griefs with such men well agree,
> But wherefore, wherefore fall on me?
> To be loved is all I need,
> And whom I love, I love indeed.

Coleridge is a good person, a loving person, a pious person who simply wants to be loved and to love: "to be beloved is all I need, / And whom I love, I love indeed." Why should *he* be sent to "the unfathomable hell within"?

In *Aids to Reflection* (1825), Coleridge adds religious intellectualization to his battery of defenses against the fiends that pursue him. The fiends are not *him*, and they also are not God; they *cannot be*, because God is all good and benevolent—like a good Father. Coleridge's religious "doctrine," as he calls it, assures him that "this evil ground cannot originate in the divine Will."[10] While Coleridge is honest enough to admit that he "can neither comprehend nor communicate" this doctrine, nevertheless he affirms it, most likely because—like a traumatized child who must imagine the abusive parent as "good" to feel safe enough to survive—it is safer to believe an incomprehensible religious doctrine than face an even more devastating truth: the Mariner's (and Coleridge's) fiend is the dark side of God. Rather than turning round and facing that "fiend," Coleridge (again, like his Mariner and everyone the Mariner meets on shore) interprets his dreams from within the context of the traditional Christian image of God which is all-good, all-light, while the darkness is split off.

Opium: A Defense against Pain

Coleridge openly admits to using opium during the miraculous period in his twenties that produced all the daimonic visionary poetry. Coleridge's famous poem "Kubla Khan" is, according to Coleridge himself, a vision seen in an opium-induced dream. This fact has led to a lot of scholarly speculation as to what extent the spell of Coleridge's poetry owes a debt to altered states of consciousness. Leaving aside this controversy for the moment, one thing is clear: Coleridge insists that, over the course of the three decades that he used opium, he never took it for pleasure or art's sake but only as an attempt to escape psychogenic and physical pain. In other words, opium was another way Coleridge tried to run from his fiends.

As early as December 1796, a year before he wrote *The Ancient Mariner*, Coleridge was regularly taking laudanum—a tincture containing 10 percent whole opium, the equivalent of 1 percent morphine—as treatment for a "nervous Affliction." Laudanum was not illegal in Coleridge's time and did not even require a prescription; nobody knew it was dangerously addictive. The amount of opium Coleridge reportedly dosed himself with is almost too incredible to believe. "At length," he confesses, "it became too bad. I used to take [from] 4 to 5 ounces a day of Laudanum."[11] Today, laudanum is still sometimes prescribed for the treatment of diarrhea. The recommended daily dosage, however, is no more than six milliliters or .2 ounces per day.[12] If Coleridge was really taking, as he asserts, four to five ounces a day, that means he was taking from twenty to twenty-five times today's recommended maximum dose.

Coleridge's notebooks and letters contain confessions about his opium use. On Sunday, December 23, 1804, for example, Coleridge writes that his cravings for opium (a love of "Evil" he calls it) began with a desire to escape pain: "Truth! Truth! but yet Charity! Charity! I have never loved Evil for its own sake [opium], no! nor ever sought pleasure for its own sake, but only as the means of escaping from pains that coiled round my mental powers, as a serpent around the body & wings of an Eagle! (My sole sensuality was *not* to be in pain!—)."[13] Ten years later, in a letter to Joseph Cottle dated April 26, 1814, Coleridge continues to assert that he took opium only because of his "*Terror & Cowardice* of PAIN & sudden Death, not (so help me God!) by any temptation of Pleasure, or expectation or desire of exciting pleasurable Sensations. . . . For my Case is a species of madness, only that it is a derangement, an utter impotence of the *Volition*, & not of the intellectual Faculties."[14] That same year, in a separate letter, Coleridge continues to argue that his cowardice of pain is what led to the addiction: "& this I will say & dare with trust say—that never was I led to this wicked direful practice of taking Opium or Laudanum by any desire or expectation of exciting pleasurable sensations; but purely by terror, by cowardice of pain, first of mental pain, & afterwards as my System became weakened, even of bodily Pain."[15] And finally, almost two decades after the letter above, in a letter to J. H. Green dated March 29, 1832, written two years before his death, Coleridge describes the "Poison" that has plagued his life for over three decades at this point as an "evil Being." "On Monday I had a sad trial of intestinal pain and restlessness; but thro' God's Mercy, without any craving for the Poison, which for more than 30 years has been the guilt, debasement, and misery of my Existence. I pray, that God may have mercy on me—tho' thro' unmanly impatiency of wretched sensations, that produced a disruption of my mental continuity of productive action I have for the better part of my life yearning [*sic*] towards God, yet having recourse to the evil Being—i.e. a continued act of thirty years' Self-poisoning thro' cowardice of pain, & without other motive—say rather without motive but solely thro' the goad *a tergo* [from behind] of unmanly and unchristian fear—God knows!"[16] Coleridge is clear: it was fear and cowardice of pain that led him into the asylum of opium. But the supposed cure soon became worse than the disease. Trying to escape the fiend of pain led him into the arms of the fiend of addiction, a horrible experience that "crept closer, & yet closer, till it had thrown its serpent folds round & round me, and I was no longer in my own power!" In other words, Coleridge's attempt to escape suffering by running from his inner fiends through the use of opium created even greater evil.

Turning away from suffering is a survival strategy. It never, however, leads to transformation. Psychological defenses help us cope and therefore psychoanalysis has profound respect for both the necessity of defense systems and for the necessity of exchanging them for authentic suffering. But the key that would have freed Coleridge from the bondage of opium would have been to feel and bear his real grief, real sadness, real pain, his real life, rather than trying to run from himself.

An Archangel More Than a Little Damaged

Coleridge was astonishingly brilliant. So much so that Shelley recognized him as a "cloud-encircled meteor of the air, / A hooded eagle among blinking owls."[17] But Coleridge's close friend Charles Lamb knew the other side; Coleridge, Lamb politely puts it, was "an Archangel a little damaged."[18] The damage, however, was much worse than a little. There was an unseen, dependent narcissism hiding at the bottom of Coleridge's addiction and a pervasive experience of being unseen that went unanswered his whole life beneath the radiance of his intellectual and creative luminosity. One remembers here, with compassion, the two-year-old Coleridge reaching directly for the burning coal and nobody there to help him personally mediate his relationship with the archetypal fire.

Coleridge had innumerable acquaintances and admirers, but who ever saw, let alone helped him with, "the fiends, that plague thee thus!" Everybody loved Coleridge's archangel, but few blessed his water-snakes, and only too rarely did a "stream of love" gush from the hearts of Coleridge's admirers for the painful, shameful, and abject dimensions of his body and soul. One notable exception was Dr. Gillman, who took the poet into his home to live with his family at Highgate in London in 1823 (a home that the supermodel Kate Moss purchased for twelve million dollars in 2011) where Coleridge would live out the last decade of his life—his fifties—under carefully administered low doses of opium to manage the addiction. Thanks to Dr. Gillman's compassion, Coleridge was miraculously able to not only survive but to stay almost unbelievable creative. He wrote and dictated some of his most famous philosophical works during this final stage of his life.

CHAPTER 21

"Full Plain I See the Devil Knows How to Row"

The Agonizing Conflict between Sea and Land

I have seen them riding seaward on the waves
Combing the white hair of the waves blown back
When the wind blows the water white and black.
We have lingered in the chambers of the sea
By sea-girls wreathed with seaweed red and brown
Till human voices wake us, and we drown.

—T. S. Eliot, "The Love Song of J. Alfred Prufrock"

In the prologue to Nietzsche's *Thus Spoke Zarathustra*, Zarathustra is living "in solitude as if in the sea, and the sea has borne [him] up." He is happy and fulfilled living alone with his snake, his eagle, and the sun as companions. But after ten years, at the age of forty, wisdom has accumulated, and Zarathustra is looking for "hands outstretched to take it." Therefore, he begins a "going down" to everyday life, a journey back to shore so to speak, to share his gifts with others. On the way down, Zarathustra meets an old hermit in the woods. The hermit recognizes him and recognizes that he has changed; Zarathustra has "become a child, an awakened one." What, therefore, does he seek in "the land of the sleeping"? "I am bringing gifts to men," Zarathustra responds.[1] The story of Zarathustra is an archetypal story of initiation—departure, transformation, return—in which the initiate offers the treasure of new values to the civilization he departed from. After living *his* solitude in the sea, the Mariner returns to shore, retracing its trajectory out, a circuitous journey there and back again. However, there are no hands outstretched to receive his wisdom, only rejection and incomprehension. The return phase of the journey in *The Rime of the Ancient Mariner*, as we have touched on in our discussion of the "fiend" that seems to pursue the Mariner from behind as he approaches shore, is, in my opinion, the most problematic stage in the poem, and the most painful.

The Circuitous Journey

To recap: whereas it was kirk, hill, and light-house top upon the departure, it is light-house top, hill, and kirk upon the return.

> Oh! dream of joy! is this indeed
> The light-house top I see?
> Is this the hill? Is this the kirk?
> Is this mine own countree?

As he returns home, the Mariner seems to be resurfacing from his deep dive "below" these collective landmarks, as if waking up from a dream.

> O let me be awake, my God!
> Or let me sleep alway.

As he crosses over the "harbour-bay" in the moonlight, everything is smooth as glass, "white with silent light" as the moon shines on the "rock," the "kirk" and the "steady weathercock." It may be that the "spell" of his journey is "snapt" as he looks far out to sea, but looking down into the sea all around him near the shore, the visionary world is as close as ever. The Mariner sees "crimson shadows" rise from the bay "a little distance from the prow." And, as he looks into the ship, he sees another supernatural vision, beautiful if eerie: light bodies are standing on the dead bodies of the crew and waving their hands as signals to the land, as if the supernatural world seeks not to destroy him or drown him but to bring him back to shore.

> A man all light, a seraph-man,
> On every corse there stood.
> This seraph-band, each waved his hand:
> It was a heavenly sight!
> They stood as signals to the land,
> Each one a lovely light.

This is a beatific vision of the light body, an eternal body made visible after the death of the old bodies. But all that light is soon to dissipate into fear and misunderstanding as the Mariner reenters the psychic field of collective consciousness.

Three men from shore see the lights out at sea—a Christian Hermit, a Pilot, and the Pilot's Boy—and row out to meet these lights. The Mariner sees them approaching his ship and is filled with hope. The Hermit, who "singeth loud his godly hymns / That he makes in the wood," will surely shrive his soul and wash away the Albatross's blood! Not even the two hundred dead men on board can dampen the Mariner's joy.

> The Pilot and the Pilot's boy,
> I heard them coming fast:
> Dear Lord in Heaven! it was a joy
> The dead men could not blast.

I saw a third—I heard his voice:
It is the Hermit good!
He singeth loud his godly hymns
That he makes in the wood.
He'll shrieve my soul, he'll wash away
The Albatross's blood.

Yet, as the little rowboat approaches, the men lose sight of "those lights so many and fair, / That signal made but now." Instead, as they draw closer to the Mariner's ship, the Pilot cries out to the Hermit, "Dear Lord! it hath a fiendish look—/ (The Pilot made reply) / I am a-feared."

The Trauma of Sea and Land Touching

As mentioned earlier, splitting defenses keeps us safe from experiences that threaten to overwhelm the conscious personality. If the defense collapses, however, then the "two worlds" of conscious and unconscious (sea and land) touch and the result is a flood of traumatic emotion. Sure enough, when the Mariner approaches shore, sea and land touch and the result is a powerful explosion of energy; as the little rowboat from shore drifts "close beneath the [Mariner's] ship," "sky and ocean" are "smote." A loud, rumbling sound "split[s] the bay" and the Mariner's ship goes down "like lead," recalling the Albatross that also sank "like lead" into the sea.

> The boat came closer to the ship,
> But I nor spake nor stirred;
> The boat came close beneath the ship,
> And straight a sound was heard.
>
> Under the water it rumbled on,
> Still louder and more dread:
> It reached the ship, it split the bay;
> The ship went down like lead.
>
> Stunned by that loud and dreadful sound,
> Which sky and ocean smote,
> Like one that hath been seven days drowned
> My body lay afloat;
> But swift as dreams, myself I found
> Within the Pilot's boat.

As the Mariner floats in the wreckage, "stunned" (i.e., shell-shocked, astonished, unable to react, knocked temporarily unconscious), the

three men pull him up into their boat to become the fourth, "swift as dreams." In a notebook entry from 1809, Coleridge compares the process of becoming "self-conscious" to a "shipwrecked man stunned . . . & then gradually awakened."[2] The Mariner is coming back from the land of dreams; he is waking up. But the three men from shore violently reject his awakening. As our drowned dreamer merely moves his lips to speak, holy hell breaks loose.

I moved my lips—the Pilot shrieked
And fell down in a fit;
The holy Hermit raised his eyes,
And prayed where he did sit.

I took the oars: the Pilot's boy,
Who now doth crazy go,
Laughed loud and long, and all the while
His eyes went to and fro.
"Ha! ha!" quoth he, "full plain I see
The Devil knows how to row."

What does the Mariner say that is so evil or crazy? He probably recites *The Rime of the Ancient Mariner*.

Coleridge tracks the torment of having a giant fate with the unconscious here vividly and honestly. He knows whereof he speaks; Coleridge's "eye," according to Dorothy Wordsworth, was "large and full" and "speaks every emotion of his animated mind" with "more of 'the poet's eye in a fine frenzy rolling'" than she "ever witnessed,"[3] reminding us of the visionary poet in "Kubla Khan."[4]

Beware! Beware!
His flashing eyes, his floating hair!
Weave a circle round him thrice,
And close your eyes with holy dread
For he on honey-dew hath fed,
And drunk the milk of Paradise.

The Ancient Mariner, it seems, has become the archetypal poet in "Kubla Khan." The trinity of men in the rowboat "close their eyes with holy dread" upon hearing the Mariner's "strange power of speech." But they definitely do not experience him as having fed "on honey-dew." The Pilot shrieks in terror and the Pilot's Boy "who now doth crazy go" calls the Mariner "the devil." The Hermit can only look up and pray. This is a striking scene if we let ourselves imagine it in full force: the Mariner wakes up from a sea of dreams only to be reborn—from the perspective of the trinity of men from shore "whose sails were never to the tempest given"[5]—as a Satanic lunatic. Here it is helpful to again remember that Coleridge wrote *The Rime of the Ancient Mariner* as a study on the effects of believing oneself to be under "supernatural agency" from "whatever source of delusion." The Mariner is the case study.

In this chapter, I offer four reasons for the difficulty of the Mariner's return, reasons that are generally applicable to the challenge of uniting sea and land in our own lives. These are, 1) a lack of both Eros and Logos, 2) the problem of language and communication, 3) projective identification, and 4) the absence of an effective initiatory elder.

Eros and Logos

According to Woodman, whose two late books on Romanticism are entitled *Sanity, Madness, Transformation: The Psyche in Romanticism* (2005) and *Revelation and Knowledge: Romanticism and Religious Faith* (2011), a safe return to shore from the night-sea journey requires bringing "a critical consciousness to bear upon it [the unconscious]."[6] Coleridge seems to agree; for Coleridge, the feeling of being under the power of a supernatural agency from whatever source of delusion is revelatory only when mediated by "*Reason*." "If I lose my faith in *Reason* as the perpetual revelation, I lose my faith altogether. I must deduce the objective from the subjective Revelation, or it is no longer a Revelation to me, but a beastly fear, and superstition."[7] Coleridge places a premium on "*Reason*" as the way to deal with madness. For him, reason is the saving grace against the passions and drives that threaten to overwhelm the conscious self. "When the Reason and the Will are away," Coleridge writes in a letter to his (unconsummated) lover Sara Hutchinson in 1802 detailing a series of mad mountaineering escapades, "what remains to us but Darkness & Dimness & a bewildering Shame, and Pain that is utterly Lord over us, or fantastic Pleasure, that draws the Soul along swimming through the air in many shapes, even as a Flight of Starlings in a Wind."[8]

The three men in the rowboat are obviously not capable of deducing "the objective from the subjective Revelation," and neither is the Mariner. The Mariner does not know why he shot the ALBATROSS. He blesses the water-snakes but does so "unaware." Therefore, when he returns to shore, what *could be* Revelation arouses "beastly fear" in those who hear and witness his subjective revelations; the philosopher's stone is still hidden in the shit of evil and madness.

It would be convenient if only strange people, or creative geniuses, were susceptible to this problem. However, there are mad parts to all sane people, as the Jungian analyst Schwartz-Salant insists, a point buttressed by the work of the psychoanalyst André Green (1927–2012) in his book *On Private Madness* (1986). In this book, Green describes madness as a potential that exists in all of us; madness is "a component of the human being." For Green, however, the way to deal with madness is not through Coleridgean faith in "*Reason* as the perpetual revelation" but by maintaining contact with "primordial Eros." Where Eros prevails, Green writes, the "destructive instincts" are abated and "psychosis is averted." "Madness, which is a component of the human being, is linked to the vicissitudes of primordial Eros, which are in constant conflict with the destructive instincts. When Eros prevails, it is because the passions which inhabit it become bound, and psychosis is averted. But when the destructive instincts triumph over Eros, the unbinding process is stronger than binding, and psychosis wins through."[9] Far out to sea, all, all alone, Eros prevails; a stream of love gushes from the Mariner's heart as Mary Queen sends down her grace, the vertical axis constellates, sea and sky are united, and renewal happens. But when he returns to the Trinitarian, patriarchal, Enlightenment consciousness on shore, the Mariner, as the fourth excluded from the three, becomes unbound from the erotic field; the destructive instincts triumph both in himself and others, and "psychosis wins through."

I suggest that a successful integration of the "two worlds" of sea and land requires both Logos and Eros. We need compassion for the mad parts of ourselves and each other; understanding in depth evokes compassion.

"I Moved My Lips"—: The Problem of Language and Communication

"Man's insanity is heaven's sense," as Melville points out in chapter 93 of *Moby-Dick*. Melville's famous distinction between divine and mere madness is taken from his description in *Moby-Dick* of a young black cabin boy, Pip, whose shipmates call him mad after he almost drowns at sea. But, Melville assures us, Pip sees visions of God down in the depths.

> The sea had jeeringly kept his finite body up, but drowned the infinite of his soul. Not drowned entirely, though. Rather carried down alive to wondrous depths, where strange shapes of the unwarped primal world glided to and fro before his passive eyes; and the miser-mermen, Wisdom, revealed his hoarded heaps; and among the joyous, heartless, ever-juvenile eternities, Pip saw the multitudinous, God-omnipresent, coral insects, that out of the firmament of waters heaved the colossal orbs. He saw God's foot upon the treadle of the loom, and spoke it; and therefore his shipmates called him mad. So man's insanity is heaven's sense; and wandering from all mortal reason, man

> comes at last to that celestial thought, which, to reason, is absurd and frantic; and weal or woe, feels then uncompromised, indifferent as his God.

Note that Melville does not say Pip *is* mad, only that when he speaks his shipmates (like those the Mariner shares the rowboat with) *call* him mad. The incapacity of those on land to hear Pip's visions *as visions*—not as literal facts or superstitious delusions—is the problem, not the visions per se. A successful return from the night-sea journey depends as much on the human voice as the divine or archetypal voice. If communication with others is impossible, then no matter how much one understands God's voice, sea and land are split on the horizontal axis and one is doomed to a type of isolation that is close to madness, if not the very essence of madness itself.

Jung felt isolated, in this exact sense, his entire life. Looking back on his lifelong sense of alienation from the perspective of a psychoanalyst, Jung believed that his feeling of aloneness was due primarily to the trauma of an expanded consciousness. The unique ways Jung experienced the Self, for instance his knowledge as a child that he was an everyday personality first and an eternal personality second rendered him unable to communicate his true thoughts, feelings, and experiences to other people. There was nobody around who could understand him, and therefore nobody who could accept him. "As a child I felt myself to be alone, and I am still, because I know things and must hint at things which others apparently know nothing of, and for the most part do not want to know. Loneliness does not come from having no people about one, but from being unable to communicate the things that seem important to oneself, or from holding certain views which others find inadmissible."[10] Insofar as depth psychology is "the counterweight to the conscious world," Jung knew it revealed things about the human condition that the collective "does not know about and does not want to know about."[11]

As a creative personality, Jung knew that he *must* be alone to discover something new. At the end of the *Red Book*, Jung accepts his loneliness as the necessary and inescapable price of self-knowledge: "The touchstone is being alone with oneself. This is the way."[12] But Jung also knew he had to find a way to blend divine madness with the spirit of the times if he was not to be condemned to utter isolation. That is likely the reason why Jung never published the *Red Book* but instead chose to speak to the world through the (relatively) sane voice of a medical doctor in the *Collected Works*. And even so, the longing to be understood was powerful and almost ubiquitous throughout Jung's life. As Peter Kingsley poignantly notes, only the scholar of Islamic mysticism Henri Corbin gave Jung, in Jung's own words, "not only the rarest of experiences, but the unique experience, of being completely understood."[13]

The collective refusal to understand the unconscious is so powerful that in the epilogue to the *Red Book* penned in 1959, Jung warns that, "to the superficial observer," the contents of this book "will appear like madness." Quoting Milton in his *Biographia Literaria*, Coleridge identifies with this plight which he finds also in Milton's quandary of not only wondering *how* to speak to the world but whether it is a good idea to speak at all. "Albeit, I must confess to be half in doubt, whether I should bring it forth or no, it being so contrary to the eye of the world, and the world so potent, in most men's hearts, that I shall endanger either not to be regarded or not to be understood."[14]

Projective Identification

Projective identification is a psychoanalytic concept that refers to the unconscious internalization of projections coming from outside and experiencing those projections as if they were true and real. The concept is a useful lens to look through as we seek to understand the problem of the Mariner's return—and our own.

In the 1998 book *Reefer Madness: A History of Marijuana* (not to be confused with a 1936 propaganda film with the same title), we find a story of the danger of projective identification within a context strikingly like the problems the Mariner faces as he returns to shore. This story is told by the American poet Allen Ginsberg (1926–1997); it is his own story. Evidently, Ginsberg was one of the first white collegiates in the United States to experiment with cannabis. He did so while attending Columbia University in the early '40s. One day, while walking around campus "having smoked a little grass" as part of what he thought of as an ongoing project to "resurrect a lost art or a lost knowledge or a lost consciousness," Ginsberg suddenly realized that he was the only one of all the thousands of scholars there who was in an altered state of consciousness.[15] Suddenly, pulled in by the gaze of collective psychology, as if caught in a powerful gravitational field, Ginsberg began to see himself through the eyes of those around him—a terrifying feeling! In the eyes of his contemporaries, Ginsberg felt himself no longer a noble explorer of the unconscious but simply a dope fiend: "Naturally I wondered if I were some kind of a fiend, some hateful satanic aberration of consciousness, to be the only one who had smoked this strange preparation." The "frightful fiend" was, in Ginsberg's case, the projection of society's collective madness that threatens to possess Ginsberg as if it were true and real for him alone.

Over a decade later, in 1955, Ginsberg began weekly psychotherapy sessions with a young psychiatrist at the Langley Porter Clinic in San Francisco, Dr. Philip Hicks. Hicks took the Albatross of collective guilt off Ginsberg's neck by encouraging Ginsberg to quit his conventional corporate job in advertising, pursue poetry full time, and accept his homosexuality. Effectively, Hicks gave Ginsberg permission to be himself. One sees the results in Ginsberg's epochal, iconic, and collectively obscene, heretical, and dangerous poem *Howl* (1956)—a far cry from the boy at Columbia—in which Ginsberg turns around and faces the fiends that pursued him, blesses his water-snakes, and lets his Albatross of collective projections sink "like lead" into the sea.

What Manner of Man Art Thou? The Need for an Initiatory Elder

I cannot imagine how it could ever be possible to individuate without a close, real, soulful relationship with another person. This can be a spouse, a friend, or a lover who knows the territory deeply; it does not necessarily have to be an elder or a psychotherapist, but then again, where would I have been without the elders who mentored me, especially my analysts?

It is important to find at least one sympathetic ally who can support and validate our inner experience so that we are not completely alone, for, as Diogenes (404–323 BCE) writes, the road of initiation "is a hard road, filled with darkness and gloom, but if an initiate leads you on the way, it becomes brighter than the radiance of the sun."[16]

For a time, Freud was an elder for Jung. Freud was two decades older and considered Jung to be, as he said, "my eldest son." But in 1913, after six years of intense and creative engagement, Freud became bewildered by Jung's seemingly crazy insistence that there was an archetypal-symbolic dimension to the unconscious. The relationship between the two men broke down over this, and Jung was cast out, alone, onto the wide, wide sea. The break with Freud was the beginning of Jung's night-sea journey, and on that journey, Jung had more support, on all levels, during his initiatory crisis than

Coleridge ever had. Coming after the Romantics, after Nietzsche, after Freud, all of whom traveled deeply into the psychological underworld, standing on the scientific basis of an extensive psychiatric and psychoanalytic practice, Jung was a middle-aged, internationally recognized doctor when his confrontation with the unconscious began in 1913, with a reputation as the crown prince of Freudian psychoanalysis, married to the wealthiest woman in Switzerland, and the father of multiple children. Jung also had his mediumistic lovers Sabina Spielrein and Toni Wolff, who understood and accompanied him through deep embodied erotic connections and the troubled waters of the psychotic depths and back again. Moreover, Jung discovered the alchemists as kindred spirits and later even cultivated the support of a Nobel laureate in physics, Wolfgang Pauli, as he worked on an alternative to materialism.

Coleridge had none of this. At the age of twenty-five, the age at which Jung graduated from medical school and began his work at the Burghölzli clinic in Switzerland under the world-famous psychiatrist Eugene Bleuler, and who from there coined the word "schizophrenia," Coleridge was a dropout from Cambridge, discharged from the army on the grounds of insanity, and preoccupied with a naive scheme about forming a society of poet-farmers on the banks of the Susquehanna River in the United States. Coleridge was married and had a little baby but was living psychically in dissociation around his wife and child and in poverty. He spent most of his time roaming the hills at night in moonlight reveries with Dorothy and William Wordsworth. Moreover, he was beginning to sink into the seas of opium addiction that would further cripple his personal life. Finally, when Coleridge traveled far out on the mind's oceans, there was nobody to meet him on the return who could understand and accept him, not even his closest friend and collaborator William Wordsworth, who rejected *The*

Rime of the Ancient Mariner. Coleridge had no Freud in his life, no Toni Wolff, no deep connection to others in the past who wrote positively about the apparently psychotic and heretical sides of his imagination, no Dr. Hicks; Coleridge had to deal with the projections of collective psychology within and without—the three men in the rowboat—all, all alone.

In the archetypal pattern of initiation, the Christian Hermit in *The Rime of the Ancient Mariner* should fulfill the role of initiatory elder; he should be the one who understands the Mariner's visions and mediates his return to society. The Mariner hopes for that. "Shrieve me, holy man!" the Mariner cries to the holy Hermit, begging for absolution through the ritual of Catholic confession, the sacrament of reconciliation with God. But the Hermit can barely stand in the Mariner's presence and can only utter, "What manner of man art thou?"

> And now, all in my own countree,
> I stood on the firm land!
> The Hermit stepped forth from the boat,
> And scarcely he could stand.
>
> "O shrieve me, shrieve me, holy man!"
> The Hermit crossed his brow.
> "Say quick," quoth he, "I bid thee say—
> What manner of man art thou?"

The Hermit "loves to talk with marineres / That come from a far countree," but he has never met any mariner like this one. He can only ask, "What manner of man art thou?" He is saying, in effect, "I do not understand you," or "What spirit has gotten into you? You are different from other people; you are not an ordinary man."

The Hermit's question—"What manner of man art thou?"—recalls the words of the disciples after Jesus had spoken to the winds and storms at sea and commanded them to be calm: "But the men marvelled, saying, 'What manner of man is this, that even the winds and the sea obey him!'"[17] This is a subtle but important parallel which Coleridge draws—consciously or not—between the Mariner and Jesus: the Hermit reacts to the Mariner as the disciples reacted to Jesus. As with all Messiahs, the Mariner is unrecognizable and incomprehensible to collective consciousness. The Hermit's words, placed in this context, suggest that the Hermit is, or should be, a disciple of the Mariner's, not the other way around. There is another subtle hint in the poem to this respect: the Hermit prays on moss that hides a rotted oak stump, an image pointing to the fact that the Christian "tree" or mythos is secretly in need of renewal. As mentioned earlier, it belongs to the archetypal pattern of the Messiah to be incomprehensible to others, but it does not belong to the pattern that the Messiah is incomprehensible to himself. Unlike Jesus, the Mariner has no idea what "manner of man" he is. The answer lies in understanding the meaning of his tale; in response to the Hermit's question, the Mariner is compelled to recite *The Rime of the Ancient Mariner*. But the Mariner does not understand, the Hermit does not understand, nobody in the poem understands, and thus the Mariner continues to wander the earth obsessively telling his tale over and over again.

If the Hermit in *The Rime of the Ancient Mariner* were a priest who had taken the night-sea journey himself and suffered the dark side of God, as did the fifteenth-century hermit Niklaus von Flue (1417–87), a Swiss heretic, mystic, and saint who lived dangerously and fruitfully close to madness, then things might have gone differently for the Mariner. In 1467, at the age of fifty, Brother Niklaus departed from society and made a conscious choice to leave his beloved wife and family and devote himself to the inner world. Throughout his time in the solitude of the sea, so to speak, Niklaus experienced many vivid dreams and visions. Some of these were extremely dark and unorthodox, given his Christian faith, but Niklaus's psyche was insistent on relentlessly confronting him with the shadow sides of God with the apparent goal of uniting them with his conscious values.

"If we suffer the problem of the opposites to the utmost," von Franz writes, "and accept it into ourselves, we can sometimes become a place in which the divine opposites can spontaneously come together. This is quite clearly what happened to Brother Klaus." Niklaus made the departure, was changed, and completed the return to such an extent that, unlike the Mariner, he was not a fanatic without a grip on his visions but "a sage, / . . . A physician to all men" with the power to "pour out balm" on the world. In von Franz's words, Brother Klaus was "the political savior of Switzerland" because in 1480, at the age of sixty-three, he prevented a civil war by mediating between warring factions in the cantons. Not only this; visitors from many nations and classes of society visited Niklaus's introverted hermit cell to find healing and understanding. In 1947, just a few years before Pope Pius XII declared the dogma of the Assumption *Ex Cathedra*, the pope canonized Niklaus as a saint; Niklaus became the only Swiss saint and the patron saint of Switzerland. Jung said Niklaus should be considered the patron saint of psychotherapy.

What if a figure like St. Niklaus, or Jung, had been onshore to meet the Mariner instead of the Christian Hermit? First, I believe Jung would have had empathy and understanding for the Mariner's journey instead of incomprehension ("What manner of man art thou?"), because Jung knew the territory himself. Second, and most importantly, I believe that Jung would not seek to wash the Albatross's blood from the Mariner's hands for, as Jung writes in *Answer to Job*, "the guilty man is eminently suitable and therefore chosen to become the vessel for the continuing incarnation, not the guiltless one who holds aloof from the world and refuses his tribute to life, for in him the dark God would find no room."[18] The Mariner seeks to rid himself of his guilt because he experiences the killing of the Albatross—despite all that happens at sea thereafter!—as nothing but sin and sacrilege. The guilt Jung describes above is the tragic guilt of sacrifice, and this type of guilt is different from mere sacrilege in that it is meaningful, in Jung's words, leaving room for the dark God. One never repents a sacrifice, though one suffers it horribly.

But there is no Jung to meet the Mariner onshore, and the Hermit cannot shrive his soul. Therefore, the Hermit's great question—"What manner of man art thou?"—throws the Mariner back into the sea. In response to the Hermit's question, an agony begins to burn in the Mariner's heart, compelling him to recite *The Rime of the Ancient Mariner* on the spot and continuing to compel him to recite it to those he knows must hear it.

> Forthwith this frame of mine was wrenched
> With a woeful agony,
> Which forced me to begin my tale;
> And then it left me free.
>
> Since then, at an uncertain hour,
> That agony returns:
> And till my ghastly tale is told,
> This heart within me burns.
>
> I pass, like night, from land to land;
> I have strange power of speech;
> That moment that his face I see,
> I know the man that must hear me:
> To him my tale I teach.

Jung knew the burning that Coleridge describes, and he accepted it as a sign that a "holy affliction" has been "added to you"; the holy affliction of a burning agony in the heart, the Mariner's agony, the compulsion to recite his ghastly tale, his strange power of speech—all this means that "your God is alive."[19]

"What manner of man art thou?" the holy Hermit asks the Mariner. *Gnothi Seuton*, know thyself: this maxim is the first of three carved into the entrance of the Temple of Apollo at Delphi. Self-knowledge is the Mariner's heaviest burden now that traditional religion holds nothing redemptive for him. In the preface to his *Aids to Reflection*, Coleridge praises the "art of reflection" as an art "permanent as your immortal soul."[20] Self-knowledge, in this sense, is not knowledge of the ego, not who are you, but *where* and *what* are you, and from what source you spring. "Where am I? What and for what am I? What are the duties, which arise out of the relations of my Being to itself as heir of futurity, and to the World which is its present sphere of action and impression?"[21] Knowledge and experience of the Self, Coleridge writes, leads to knowledge and experience of God. "We begin with the I KNOW MYSELF in order to end with the absolute I AM. We proceed from the SELF, in order to lose and find all self in GOD."[22] The burden of self-knowledge is the new Albatross around the Mariner's neck, the new *transitus dei* he carries in his heart after he blesses the water-snakes, and the Albatross he carries around his neck "instead of the Cross" falls "like lead into the sea." But nowhere in *The Rime of the Ancient Mariner* do we find the marriage of day and night, sun and moon, land and sea—that is, the experience of self-knowledge.

Madness, the Regressive Restoration of the Persona, and the Wedding

How can the divine madness of the sea ever be accepted by reality on land when the conventional psychology within ourselves and in others perceives those contents as mere madness or evil?[23] In Jung's understanding there are three possible outcomes to the individuation process: 1) madness, in which the spirit of the depths overcomes the spirit of the times, 2) the regressive restoration of the persona, in which the spirit of the times overcomes the spirit of the depths, and 3) a marriage between the depths of imagination and reality leading to self-knowledge or individuation.[24] In the reaction of the men from shore we see the first possibility, madness. In the Mariner's *reaction* to their reaction, we will soon see the second, the regressive restoration of the persona.

CHAPTER 22

"O Sweeter Than the Marriage-Feast, 'Tis Sweeter Far to Me, to Walk Together to the Church"

Individuation and the Regressive Restoration of the Persona

As the Hermit's question "What manner of man art thou?" rings out, compelling the Mariner to recite *The Rime of the Ancient Mariner*, the Mariner's tale of his sea journey comes to an end. But the poem is not over. Immediately, the Mariner hears two different types of music: the bride and bridesmaids singing at the wedding and the little vesper bell calling him to prayer (remember that the Albatross presided over vespers).

> What loud uproar bursts from that door!
> The wedding-guests are there:
> But in the garden-bower the bride
> And bride-maids singing are:
> And hark the little vesper bell,
> Which biddeth me to prayer!

It seems the Mariner is faced with a choice: wedding or church? He chooses the church. Why? Because the wedding, for reasons we will

explore throughout this chapter, recalls the excruciating loneliness of his night-sea journey.

O Wedding-Guest! this soul hath been
Alone on a wide wide sea:
So lonely 'twas, that God himself
Scarce seemèd there to be.

O sweeter than the marriage-feast,
'Tis sweeter far to me,

To walk together to the kirk
With a goodly company!—

To walk together to the kirk,
And all together pray,
While each to his great Father bends,
Old men, and babes, and loving friends
And youths and maidens gay.

To be "all together" at church stands in vivid and direct contrast to the bitter loneliness of being "alone on a wide, wide sea" where even "God *himself* / Scarce seemèd there to be [emphasis added]." The church is "sweeter than the marriage-feast," "sweeter far." "Sweet" means pleasing to the senses, mind, or feelings; having a pleasant disposition.[1] The phrase "to walk together to the kirk" is repeated twice in the passage above, and the word "together" is used three times in rapid succession; the feeling of community is a sweet feeling.

The Mariner belongs to those of "the visionary company," as Harold Bloom's well-known book on Romantic literature is entitled, who drop into the maternal mystery in solitude in search of a light, or consciousness—the flash of golden fire in the sea, the glittering moonlight in the Mariner's bright eye—never to be found in the kirk or light-house on land. But returning to terra firma, the Mariner seeks to rid himself of the *agon* of self-knowledge, to relieve the burning agony in his heart constellated by the Hermit's question, "what manner of man art thou," by rejoining collective consciousness. He wants to pretend that he is not of the visionary company but of the "goodly company" "whose sails were never to the tempest given," as Shelley puts it in *Adonais*, to those who altogether worship the "great Father" rather than the maternal mysteries, who collectively celebrate and affirm the status quo of tradition. The little vesper bell that calls the Mariner to prayer recalls the Albatross who presides over vespers; it is as if the Mariner wants to go back to the old days before he shot that sacred bird, before he blessed the water-snakes, before the dead body of the Albatross sank "like lead" into the sea, before Mary Queen ascended to Heaven.

There is a necessary and inevitable price to be paid on the journey toward knowledge of the self, the price of loneliness: "Alone,

alone, all, all alone, / Alone on a wide wide sea!" the Mariner cries out after the Moon rises and all the men onboard—the collective masculine consciousness—drop down dead. "As bringers of light, that is, enlargers of consciousness," Jung writes, "they [culture heroes] overcome darkness, which is to say that they overcome the earlier unconscious state. Higher consciousness, of knowledge going beyond our present-day consciousness, is equivalent to being *all alone in the world*."[2] The Mariner seeks to go back to church because the pain of feeling "all, all alone" is too great to bear. Coleridge knew this dilemma personally: solitude is necessary for the realization of "how much lies below his own consciousness," he writes, "the greater and, perhaps, nobler, certainly all the subtler, parts of one's nature must be solitary. Man exists herein to himself and to God alone—yea! In how much only to god! How much lies below his own consciousness!"[3] But that level of self-knowledge "may be among the spiritual punishments of the abandoned." "It is not impossible that this perfect (as far as in a creature can be) Self-Knowledge may be among the spiritual punishments of the abandoned, as among the joys of the redeemed Spirits."[4]

That the Mariner turns away from the wedding because he cannot bear the loneliness of the sea voyage seems a counterintuitive confession! For there are lots of people at the wedding; it is a raucous party. The association of the isolation of the night-sea journey with the wedding only makes sense if we understand the wedding not as a literal *wedding* but as a symbol. Coleridge knew that only those who "within themselves can interpret and understand the symbol" can hope to gain the "sacred power of self-intuition," as he writes in his *Biographia Literaria*."[5] As always, our capacity to tune in with poetic faith to Coleridge's poetry with mythic amplifications will help us understand and interpret the symbol of Coleridge's Wedding Feast. As the word "amplification" suggests, these comparisons turn up the volume on the symbolic signal, letting its music be heard more clearly, impacting us more directly, and increasing our sense of its *value*.

Solitude and the Mystical Wedding: Gnosticism, Taoism, Romanticism, and Depth Psychology

In *Against Heresies* (180 CE), Irenaeus, an influential member of the institutional church, reports that the heretic Gnostic initiation takes place in a bridal chamber understood as a symbolic *coniunctio* mirroring an archetypal paradigm in the heavens above. "For some of them," Irenaeus writes, "prepare a nuptial couch, and perform a sort of mystic rite (pronouncing certain expressions) with those who are being initiated, and affirm that it is a spiritual marriage which is celebrated by them, after the likeness of the conjunctions above."[6] The Gnostic Gospel of Philip describes the wedding four times as a "mystery."[7] It is this symbolic sense of the wedding that the Gnostic Gospel of Thomas draws upon when it paradoxically insists that solitude is necessary to attain the wedding. "Many are standing at the door, but it is only the solitary who will enter the Bridal Chamber."[8] The word that is translated as "solitary" in the Gospel of Thomas is *monachos* in Greek, from *monos*, or "single," from which we get the word "monk"; the monks of the Christian Middle Ages sought the sacred wedding of the *unio mystica* in solitude.

The connection between solitude and the wedding, however, is not confined to the Western or Christian tradition. Like the Mariner, the sage in the Chinese *Tao Te Ching* (600 BCE) confesses that he "drift[s] about, / like someone without a home."

> Other people are excited,
> as though they were at a parade.
> I alone don't care,

I alone am expressionless,
like an infant before it can smile.

Other people have what they need;
I alone possess nothing.
I alone drift about,
like someone without a home.
I am like an idiot, my mind is so empty.

Other people are bright;
I alone am dark.
Other people are sharper;
I alone am dull.
Other people have a purpose;
I alone don't know.
I drift like a wave on the ocean,
I blow as aimless as the wind.
I am different from ordinary people.
I drink from the Great Mother's breasts.[9]

This passage from the *Tao Te Ching* repeats the phrase "Other people . . . / I alone" seven times, a spellbinding incantation recalling the plight of the Mariner and drawing our attention again and again to the painful distinction between collective and individual. The sage is "different from other people." Why? Because he is nourished by the balance of nature and not by collective tradition. In other words, he "drinks from the Great Mother's breasts." That is what makes him feel alone in the world. So it is for Shelley, who speaks for many of the Romantics as he cries out in passionate embrace of the maternal world that Coleridge's Mariner rejects, "Mother of this unfathomable world! Favor my solemn song," in "Alastor; or, The Spirit of Solitude"[10] as his "heart ever gazes on the depth / Of thy deep mysteries."

People who orient through the symbolic power of self-intuition toward the *hierosgamos* or mystery of the sacred wedding are rare, but one finds them scattered throughout cultures and spread throughout the centuries. St. Francis, for example, the thirteenth-century Italian mystic, celebrates his "pact" with Sophia even though she wounds him, takes away his sense of self, and threatens him with madness. "If it is true that I am mad, O supreme Wisdom, the fault is yours. It dates from the day when you wounded me and I made a pact with Love. My self has been taken away and I am clothed in you."[11] Rumi also knows that belonging "to the soul of the Beloved" leaves him feeling like the Mariner, neither "of the land nor of the sea."

> What is to be done, Muslims? For I do not recognize myself. I am neither Christian, nor Jew, nor Gabr [Zoroastrian], nor Muslim. I am not of the East, nor of the West, *nor of the land, nor of the sea.* I am not of Nature's mint, nor of the circling heavens. I am not of earth, nor of water, nor of air, nor of fire. I am not of the empyrean, nor of the dust, nor of existence, nor of entity. I am not of India, nor of China, nor of Bulgaria, nor of Sasin. I am not of the kingdom of Iraqi, nor of the country of Khorasan. I am not of this world, nor of the next, nor of Paradise, nor of Hell. I am not of Adam, nor of Eve, nor of Eden or Rizwan [Heaven]. My place is the Placeless, my trace is the Traceless. 'Tis neither body nor soul, for I belong to the soul of the Beloved [emphasis added].[12]

"What is to be done?" For Rumi, the answer is: choose the wedding and consciously embrace the loneliness and disorientation—not knowing anything, not fitting in anywhere—that is intrinsic to belonging to the "the soul of the Beloved." For Coleridge's Mariner, the answer is: reject the wedding and consciously embrace collective consciousness to avoid the maddening sense of alienation that the wedding tragically requires.

The Bride

As a symbol, the bride is not any actual woman but the Beloved—the soul—a man's image of "Woman," that is, the anima as the unconscious complement to the persona. The anima is an arche-

typal phenomenon that transcends the personal experience of any individual man; she is, Jung writes, "*the archetype of life itself.*"[13]

Jung argues that there are four distinct stages of anima development in a man's life. He names these stages Eve (from the Garden of Eden), Helen (from Helen of Troy), Mary (the Virgin Mary), and Sophia (the Greek personification of wisdom).[14] There are four images of the feminine in *The Ancient Mariner* as well. At sea, the Mariner encounters three, first the Witch, a chthonic force, the death fires in the sea, then LIFE-IN-DEATH, a paradoxical nightmare of death and rebirth, and finally Mary Queen, a purely beneficent image who sends down healing rain and sleep from Heaven. These personifications of the anima are all, albeit in very different respects, purely archetypal figures, all "Goddesses throned in solitude, sublime, / Set in no place, still less in any time." The bride in *The Ancient Mariner* is the only image of the feminine on land and the only *human* image of the feminine in the entire poem. She is also the last feminine image and the first, appearing at the start and the end of the Mariner's tale, a personification of the *Beloved* not as witch, nightmare, or virgin Mother but as partner within the mystery of human relationship.

Out at sea, the nightmare LIFE-IN-DEATH's lips are red, and her hair is yellow as gold, but her skin is "white as leprosy," suggestive of isolation, horror, the land of the dead, cold, white, dead flesh. White is the absence of color, which means an absence of life, as when in states of fear the blood draws from one's face and we say, "you look white as a ghost!" The bride, in contrast, is "red as a rose."

> The bride hath paced into the hall,
> Red as a rose is she;
> Nodding their heads before her goes
> The merry minstrelsy.

The blushing bride personifies human warmth, joy, hope, and love. With the comparison of the bride to a rose, however, we also approach the deeper dimensions of the wedding. There is a long-standing connection between the rose and the wedding in Judeo-Christian and ancient traditions that is roughly parallel to the Indian Lotus. We need to know about these if we are to understand and appreciate the archetypal level of the Wedding Feast in Coleridge's poem. I offer the following five examples, ranging from the tenth century BCE to the nineteenth century.

In the tenth century BCE, the bride in the biblical Song of Songs says of herself, "I am a rose of Sharon, the rose of the valley." As in the *Ancient Mariner*, in the erotic love poetry of the Song of Songs, the bride is analogized as a rose, and she and her groom celebrate their marriage feast in a garden.

> Let my beloved come to his garden,
> and eat its choicest fruits.
>
> I came to the garden, my sister, my bride,
> I gathered my myrrh with my spice,
> I ate my honeycomb with honey
> I drank my wine with my milk.
>
> Eat, friends, drink,
> and be drunk with love!

The Rose of Sharon is "very dark but lovely." She is a sacred seductress, an embodiment of Eros married to King Solomon sexually, soulfully, and spiritually. Marrying *Her* is a return to the Garden of Paradise, for *She* transforms the entire world into a sacred experience of love.

In Apuleius's *Metamorphoses* (late second century CE), the protagonist Lucius is redeemed from his curse of being turned into an ass when he eats the roses carried by the priest of Isis in her sacred festival of ships heading out to sea. In Dante's *Divine Comedy* (1320), Beatrice reveals "the Rose Eternal" to Dante as a visible sign of the "wedding feast" to which Dante is an invited Wedding Guest.

> Into the yellow of the Rose Eternal
> That spreads, and multiplies, and breathes an odour
> Of praise unto the ever-vernal Sun,
> As one who silent is and fain would speak,
> Me Beatrice drew on, and said: "Behold
> Of the white stoles how vast the convent is!
> Behold how vast the circuit of our city!
> Behold our seats so filled to overflowing,
> That here henceforward are few people wanting!
> On that great throne whereon thine eyes are fixed
> For the crown's sake already placed upon it,
> Before thou suppest at this wedding feast."[15]

In the rose mysticism of medieval and Renaissance European alchemy, the alchemical redeemer sweats "rose-colored" blood as "the manifestation of a certain kind of Eros" that unifies the "whole and complete" human being "in the sign of the Rose."[16] One final example: in the culmination of Goethe's *Faust II* (1832), angels descend strewing roses as they lead Faust's immortal soul out of the clutches of the devil Mephistopheles. The devil tries to beat off the hovering roses, but he cannot, and he even falls in love himself under their influence.

The Garden-Bower and the Return to Paradise

The bride and bridesmaids are singing in the "garden-bower," another symbol with powerful associations in Western mythology and literature. We might recall that God was the first to plant a garden, at the beginning of all creation, east of Eden. The Garden of Eden is Paradise, a word that comes from the Greek *paradeisos*, "a park," which is derived from an Iranian source, a combination of *pairi-*, "around," and *diz*, "to make, to form (a wall)."[17] Paradise is thus neither wild nature nor the city but a garden bower, a union of nature and civilization. We might also recall that ever since God banished humanity from this Garden, we have been trying to get back in. Paradise never was and is not a place; it is a blessed state of being. A wedding taking place in a Garden is thus an image of that blessed state, a symbolic, intuitive premonition of a future world in which contraries are resolved.

Throughout the various initiatory journeys in Romanticism, the wedding is *the* symbol of the goal—Paradise regained. In his exhaustive work *Natural Supernaturalism*, Abrams offers us a treasure house of examples, but four examples from Coleridge, Wordsworth, and Novalis will perhaps suffice here to give us a feeling for the way the Romantics used the imagery of the wedding in their poetry and philosophy of nature.

In his "Dejection: An Ode," Coleridge writes of the wedding as "a new Earth and a new Heaven" created through the "Joy" that unites nature with the human being.

> [Joy] is the spirit and the power,
> Which, wedding Nature to us, gives in dower
> A new Earth and a new Heaven,
> Undreamt of by the sensual and the proud.[18]

Coleridge's reference to a new Earth and a new Heaven is an allusion to the New Jerusalem in the book of Revelation, aka the marriage of the Lamb in which the New Jerusalem is "prepared as a bride adorned for her husband."[19]

> *Let us rejoice and exult*
> *and give him the glory,*

for the marriage of the Lamb has come,
and his Bride has made herself ready.[20]

Coleridge brings the biblical apocalypse down to earth as a metaphor for the creation of a new world that takes place every day when imagination is "wedded" through love with Nature. This echoes Wordsworth's "high argument" in his "spousal verse" that the wedding of psyche and cosmos "in love and holy passion" creates the new world as "a simple produce of the common day."

For the discerning intellect of Man,
When wedded to this goodly universe
In love and holy passion, shall find these
A simple produce of the common day.
. . .
And the creation (by no lower name
Can it be called) which they with blended might
Accomplish:—this is our high argument.[21]

For Novalis as well, Nature is a "bride" who, when wedded to "a rejuvenated people," gives birth to "the new world." "Let all be changed from its Foundations! Let the new world spring from the root of humanity! . . . They will come, Nature, thy men. A rejuvenated people will make thee young again, too, and thou wilt be as its bride. . . . There will be only one beauty, and man and Nature will unite in one all-embracing divinity."[22] Perhaps nowhere in Romantic poetry, however, is the longing for Paradise as a dynamic wedding between Imagination and Nature more vividly or explicitly expressed than in Coleridge's magnificent "Kubla Khan." The archetypal (Romantic) poet has "drunk the milk of Paradise," envisioned as a sacred river of pure Imagination running through the walled garden of Xanadu.

In Xanadu did Kubla Khan
A stately pleasure-dome decree:
Where Alph, the sacred river, ran
Through caverns measureless to man
Down to a sunless sea.
So twice five miles of fertile ground
With walls and towers were girdled round;
And there were gardens bright with sinuous rills,
Where blossomed many an incense-bearing tree;
And here were forests ancient as the hills,
Enfolding sunny spots of greenery.

Such descriptions of Paradise as a symbolic state akin to the alchemical *mysterium coniunctionis* in which spirit and matter—and all contraries—are reconciled appear constantly and consistently throughout Romantic literature. Depth psychology follows suit; as Jung floats between life and death in 1944 after suffering a heart attack, he experiences otherworldly visions of the mystic *mysterium coniunctionis* as an image of profound self-knowledge. "At bottom it was I myself," Jung writes; "I was the marriage. And my beatitude was that of a blissful wedding."[23]

The Church

Like the wedding, the church in *The Ancient Mariner* is not a *church* but a symbol, in this case a symbol expressing the collective consciousness of the time and place of the poem.

Since the dawn of civilization, *Homo sapiens* has always had a church in the broad sense of the word, that is, some type of political, social, academic, tribal, religious, or corporate community organized around shared values and beliefs. The good-old-boy network, our local bar, sports teams—these are all de facto churches if we treat them as sacrosanct. And it is necessary to treat them as such to formalize the continuity of tradition, group cohesion, and the maintenance of a stable civilization. But the shadow side of any church is that "altogether" never really means *altogether*. *Extra ecclesium nulla salas*: outside the church there is no salvation; this dictum dates to the third century but is still shockingly relevant today, as one sees with just a glance at the political and culture wars filling the airwaves of mainstream and social media. One gains social cohesion at a cost, and that cost is often banishing people who do not fit the orthodoxy, who are not "one of us."

In his personal as well as professional relationships, Jung was extremely respectful of humanity's need for a church, in both a literal and broader metaphorical sense. But in his *Visions Seminars* (1930–34), Jung reveals his true feelings: the church is "an institution of make-believe." In fact, identifying with the institutional church is a barrier to self-knowledge, to individuation, to consciously living one's own life; for those fated to go through the path of individuation in the sense that Jung means it, in the sense that Coleridge describes in *The Ancient Mariner*, going back to "church" is an attempt to run from oneself and regressively restore the persona.

In words that resonate with the Mariner's conflict between wedding and church in *The Ancient Mariner*, Jung states that one needs a church only if one cannot accept one's own life. Ironically, Jung draws from the life of Christ to make his point.

> You see, Christ made desperate attempts to teach his disciples that they should not imitate him; they should live their own lives, only then would they be like him. But they did not understand it . . . they preferred to live behind him and to organize a church. So nobody has ever tried to live his own life as Christ lived his . . . with that understanding she can go out of the church. For what is the use of the church? The church is an

> institution of make-believe, the delusion that somebody has redeemed us from sin; Christ has been a substitute for living our own lives . . . inasmuch as they can accept such a life [their own], they no longer need a church of make-believe or substitution . . . [if they are] conscious enough, have suffered enough, to stand the influence of nature. She is now able to worship nature consciously.[24]

Jung often has a strange and beautiful way of sounding like an atheistic debunker and mystic all at once, and this quality shines in the passage above. Again, this passage brings to mind the dynamics in *The Ancient Mariner*: Jung's declaration that the teachings of the institutional church are a "delusion" and "a substitute for living our own lives" is an arrow shooting the Albatross; when Jung says that the goal is to "worship nature consciously," he blesses the water-snakes. Yet the Mariner does not worship nature consciously; he does so "unaware." He has no idea what "manner of man" he is. Therefore, the Mariner is not yet able to leave the church.

And yet church is not really a solution for him either. That is because it is not *true* community. It may be for others, but not for the Mariner as he really is. There is no space on the altar for the water-snakes; he cannot preach *The Rime of the Ancient Mariner* from the pulpit; nobody would know what he is talking about. Thus, the Mariner still travels "like night" from land to land, obsessively retelling his tale outside the safety of the church walls.

There is a lot of projection on Coleridge's part in this section of *The Ancient Mariner*, a palpable autobiographical connection. We remember that in an attempt to crawl back to terra firma after the visionary journeys of his twenties, Coleridge confined his erotic, numinous, and heartfelt experiences of the "one Life within us and abroad"[25] to the prison of intellectual abstraction, while his religious feeling sought shelter in the bosom of Mother Church: "My head was with Spinoza, though my whole heart remained with Paul and John."[26] Declaring "the poet is dead in me," Coleridge became the de facto intellectual voice of the Church of England. With this choice, he gained the sweetness of belonging to collective tradition but paid the price of being unable to live the truths of his inner heart.

The Recantation of Berengarius of Tours

Berengarius of Tours (ca. 999–1088), a French theologian from the Dark Ages educated at Chartres, is another example of a man tragically torn between wedding and church (a "Lynx amid moles!" according to Coleridge) who, all, all alone, followed his inner light and was rewarded for his efforts with the threat of execution and torture at the hands of the pope in Rome.

Berengarius replaced his culture's fundamentalist faith with his own sense of poetic faith. He preached that the bread and wine of the Holy Communion symbolically changes into the body and blood of Christ but not literally. In 1050, at the age of fifty, the pope excommunicated Berengarius for this view, and the church arrested him in Rome, threatening him with death if he did not recant. In fear for his life, Berengarius made a formal recantation, and the pope permitted him to return home to France. But once back home, Berengarius regretted his decision and recanted his recantation. The pope arrested him again, and once again Berengarius was forced into a Sophie's choice—the Mariner's choice—of either abandoning the truths of his heart or being thrown into the isolation of a dungeon.

The plight of Berengarius struck a poignant chord in Coleridge, so much so that he was inspired to write an emotionally charged and autobiographically tinged poem about this heretic-mystic entitled "Lines—Suggested by the Last Words of Berengarius Ob.

Anno Dom 1088" that he published in 1827, four years before his own death. I excerpt portions below.

Lines

Suggested by the Last Words of Berengarius
Ob. Anno Dom. 1088

No more 'twixt conscience staggering and the Pope
Soon shall I now before my God appear,
By him to be acquitted, as I hope;
By him to be condemned, as I fear.—

REFLECTION ON THE ABOVE
Lynx amid moles! had I stood by thy bed,
Be of good cheer, meek soul! I would have said:
I see a hope spring from that humble fear.
All are not strong alike through storms to steer
Right onward. What? though dread of threatened death
And dungeon torture made thy hand and breath
Inconstant to the truth within thy heart?
That truth, from which, through fear, thou twice
didst start,
Fear haply told thee, was a learned strife,
Or not so vital as to claim thy life:
And myriads had reached Heaven, who never knew
Where lay the difference 'twixt the false and the true!

Ye, who secure 'mid trophies not your own,
Judge him who won them when he stood alone,
And proudly talk of recreant Berengare—
O first the age, and then the man compare!
That age how dark! congenial minds how rare!
No host of friends with kindred zeal did burn!
No throbbing hearts awaited his return!
Prostrate alike when prince and peasant fell,
He only disenchanted from the spell,
Like the weak worm that gems the starless night,

Moved in the scanty circlet of his light:
And was it strange if he withdrew the ray
That did but guide the night-birds to their prey?

"Like the weak worm that gems the starless night," Berengarius is illuminated by an inner light as he extends his consciousness beyond the literal and fundamentalist ignorance of his contemporaries in the dark ages.

> That age how dark! congenial minds how rare!
> No host of friends with kindred zeal did burn!
> No throbbing hearts awaited his return!

"Was it strange if he withdrew the ray / That did but guide the night-birds to their prey?" Berengarius avoids torture at the cost of being tortured from within, to such an extent that death seems a relief. Berengarius's last words, the words that inspired Coleridge to write his poem, are, "No more 'twixt conscience staggering and the Pope."

Coleridge's Conflict between Church and Child

Berengarius's dilemma is the Mariner's dilemma and very much Coleridge's dilemma. Five years after the publication of *The Ancient Mariner*, in 1803, Coleridge had a dream in which the Mariner's suffering between wedding and church took the form of a conflict between Child and church.

> *Dozing dreamt of Hartley as at his christening—how, as he was asked who redeemed him, and was to say, "God the Son," he went on humming and hawing in one hum and haw (like a boy who knows a thing and will not make an effort to recollect) so as to irritate me greatly.*[27]

Hartley Coleridge (1796–1849) is Coleridge's firstborn son, arriving in the world less than two years before *The Ancient Mariner*

(1798), "Kubla Khan" (1797), and "Christabel" (1797). Hartley was christened on November 8, 1803, at the age of seven, and Coleridge recorded this dream on October 28, 1803, evidently anticipating his son's actual christening.[28] Yet the dream Hartley is not Hartley the actual boy; he is *the dream Hartley*, the magic image of the magic child of nature one finds in "The Nightingale: A Conversation Poem" (1798), where Hartley's eye—like the Mariner's—"did glitter" in the moonlight. Coleridge deems it wise "to make him Nature's play-mate," vowing that his "dear babe" shall grow up "familiar with these songs [of the nightingales]," that "with the night / he may associate joy." We have already seen how, in "Frost at Midnight," Coleridge projects the healing of his own childhood alienation onto the beloved image of this *puer aeternus*.

> For I was reared
> In the great city, pent 'mid cloisters dim,
> And saw nought lovely but the sky and stars.
> But thou, my babe! shalt wander like a breeze
> By lakes and sandy shores, beneath the crags
> Of ancient mountains, and beneath the clouds,
> Which image in their bulk both lakes and shores
> And mountain crags: so shalt thou see and hear
> The lovely shapes and sounds intelligible
> Of that eternal language, which thy God
> Utters, who from eternity doth teach
> Himself in all, and all things in himself.
> Great universal Teacher! he shall mould
> Thy spirit, and by giving make it ask.

Nature, the "Great universal Teacher," is Hartley's schoolmaster, not Christ's Hospital and not the institutional church, and it is especially Nature at night, in the moonlight, where Hartley will discover "that eternal language, which thy God / Utters." In the dream, Coleridge tries to bring *that* eternal Child into the church! But Hartley—unlike Berengarius and the Mariner—refuses to recant; he will not say that "God the Son" is his redeemer, and Coleridge becomes greatly irritated.[29]

In "The Pang More Sharp Than All: An Allegory," however, published in 1825 over twenty years after the Hartley dream, Coleridge intimately confesses his regret at banishing this "bright boy" from consciousness.

> Ah! he is gone, and yet will not depart!—
> Is with me still, yet I from him exiled!
> For still there lives within my secret heart
> The magic image of the magic Child,
> Which there he made up-grow by his strong art,
> As in that crystal orb—wise Merlin's feat,—
> The wondrous "World of Glass," wherein is led
> All long'd for things their beings did repeat;—
> And there he left it, like a Sylph beguiled,
> To live and yearn and languish incomplete!

The Mariner abandons himself and yet cannot abandon himself. And so did Coleridge. That is "The Pang More Sharp Than All."

A Failed Individuation Process?

Coleridge's dilemma is a humanely understandable dilemma; we all seek to, need to, present a face to the world that the world can accept so we can be accepted. We all need a persona. But what of our heresies, our madness, our deepest sexual and spiritual desires, longings, and realities? How can we ever admit them, own them, reveal them to others? This is a difficult problem, especially if we have labored intensely, and perhaps even succeeded in establishing ourselves as a professional and respectable person, or perhaps simply as being seen as likable, normal, and good. To adapt to society, we all find ways to hide our secret selves from ourselves and others. Nevertheless, a secret life still goes on living, confronting us in the form of impossible conflicts from within and without, through events that "happen to us" as we say.

"Who that thus lives with a continually divided Being," Coleridge agonizingly confesses in an 1805 notebook entry, "can remain healthy!"[30] Coleridge's vision of art is that it seeks to reconcile his—and everyone's—continually divided being. "In every work of art," Coleridge writes, "there is a reconcilement of the external with the internal, the conscious is so impressed on the unconscious as to appear in it. . . . He who combines the two is the man of genius; and for that reason he must partake of both."[31] *The Rime of the Ancient Mariner* is an example par excellence of a work of art that attempts to reconcile conscious and unconscious. Did it succeed?

The unconscious is heavily impressed on the Mariner's consciousness, but his consciousness is not sufficiently impressed on the unconscious "as to appear in it," as Coleridge says. In other words, the unconscious grips the Mariner (and Coleridge) and compels him to tell his tale, but he does not have a grip on *it*. He is, in the words of the Jungian analyst Neumann, a "hypnotized hypnotist" or, in Keats's language that we looked at earlier, a fanatic not a poet as a "sage" or "physician to all men" pouring out "balm" on a troubled world. As mentioned in part 1 of this book, depth psychology evolved in the twentieth century to address this exact crisis, the crisis of Romanticism, that the Mariner so vividly and unforgettably embodies.

Perhaps, therefore, some of us are inclined to view the stories of Berengarius, the Mariner, and Coleridge as examples of a failed individuation process. If so, I suggest we reconsider. "Ye, who secure 'mid trophies not your own, / Judge him who won them when he stood alone," Coleridge preaches to the reader of his "Lines" written to Berengarius. We are all the beneficiaries of the human sacrifices of our ancestors; the foundation on which we stand and judge them from is the foundation they built out of nothing and for which they paid with blood. Ten years before "Lines," in his *Biographia Literaria*, Coleridge had already written his own apologia to similar effect. "By what I *have* effected am I to be judged by my fellow men; what I *could* have done, is a question for my own conscience."[32] Understanding that the Mariner's dilemma is Coleridge's dilemma, we may feel compassion for Coleridge's very human need to find some stability and relatedness given the extreme, and extremely isolating, burden of self-knowledge that fate asked him to carry, a burden that went far beyond the collective consciousness of his time and place, a *transitus dei* that was too much, too early.

Wedding *and* Church

In *The Rime of the Ancient Mariner*, there is no bride in the church and there is no church for the bride. The whole situation is split: bride *or* church. The Mariner chooses the church. By way of contrast, a common critique of Jungian analysis is that it focuses exclusively on the inner union of contraries in the wedding and thus devalues the importance of a collective church. We saw this earlier in the quotation from Jung: "For what is the use of the church? The church is an institution of make-believe, the delusion that somebody has redeemed us from sin." In other words, Jungian psychology tends to choose the wedding over the church. Jung notes that "just as the person of Christ cannot be replaced by an organization, so the Bride cannot be replaced by the Church."[33]

On the other hand, there is no such thing as being the one and only member of the true church, as Jung humorously acknowledges in his ETH Lectures of 1939, the only reference to Coleridge I could discover in Jung's writings. "It is obvious that two or three form a congregation, a Church; whereas one individual is not a Church in spite of Coleridge's saying that he was a member of the only true Church and at the moment its only member!"[34] Kindred libido creates myth, and myth is always communal. Thus, the *telos* of the night-sea journey is to return with the treasure and renew the community; the purpose of the visionary company is not to go off on their own forever but to help the goodly company evolve.

By recanting his sea journey and trying to fit into the church *as it is*, the Mariner loses contact with the sacred world of the great Mother, but the church loses something as well, namely, the possibility of renewal. I suggest, therefore, that the answer to the dilemma "wedding *or* church?" is an alchemical combination of both, "wedding *and* church." This conjunction, however, cannot take place through conscious intention or will; it happens, if at all, slowly in the collective unconscious through the centuries.

The way toward a wedding of contraries in a Jungian analysis, done in deep relationship with an analyst but otherwise all, all alone, may be the way toward a new collective myth, a new church so to speak, that adequately expresses and addresses the psychological and spiritual needs of a global future. In 1949, Max Zeller, an analysand of Jung's who had spent time in a German concentration camp, told Jung of a dream that hinted at this possibility. Zeller dreamt of building a massive new temple with "incredible numbers" of other people.

> *A temple of vast dimensions was in the process of being built. As far as I could see—ahead, behind, right and left—there were incredible numbers of people building on gigantic pillars. I, too, was building on a pillar. The whole building process was in its very first beginnings, but the foundation was already there; the rest of the building was starting to go up, and I and many others were working on it.*

Jung and Zeller then had the following conversation about the dream. Jung began:

> "Ja, you know, that is the temple we all build on. We don't know the people because, believe me, they build in India and China and in Russia and all over the world. That is the new religion. You know how long it will take until it is built?"
>
> I said, "How should I know? Do you know?"
>
> He said, "I know."
>
> I asked how long it will take.
>
> He said, "About six hundred years."
>
> "Where do you know this from?" I asked.
>
> He said, "From dreams. From other people's dreams and from my own. This new religion will come together as far as we can see."[35]

As he labors in relative solitude in his analysis with Jung, Zeller's dream reveals he is unknowingly one of many people working—"altogether"—on the construction of a new religious structure, a new temple, "the new religion" as Jung interprets it. No doubt this dream compensates for feelings of isolation Zeller must have had as he worked with Jung on becoming more and more conscious of dimensions of the unconscious that others do not know about and do not want to know about. Also, the dream may have revealed a hidden source of inspiration for Zeller to become one of the founding members of the Analytical Psychology Club of Los Angeles, in 1944, after he and his wife Lore emigrated to the United States to escape Nazi Germany. Zeller had this dream five years after founding the Los Angeles group, the first of its kind in the world, where the members were required to have personal experience of Jungian analysis and whose charter declares that the club is built on the foundation of "[Jung's] attempts at an understanding of the secret workings of the soul."[36] In addition, Zeller's dream of building a new temple came one year after the founding of the first Jung Institute, in 1948 in Zurich, the first Jungian group in the world to provide formal training for analysts. Today, there are sixty-seven Jung Institutes around the world, in Africa, Asia, Australia, Europe, and North and South America, all gatherings of individuals in a collective structure built on the foundation of Jungian psychology. Important to note, however, is that the temple in Zeller's dream is not a Jung Institute! It is a symbolic image of a worldwide evolution of collective consciousness whose foundation was already laid by the time Zeller got to work.

The Romantics worked on that foundation over a century before Zeller. Most of them knew that the collective realization of the wedding—which *is* the foundation of the new church—belonged to the future. Some of them, such as Schelling, believed that this wedding was right around the corner. "In a short time," Schelling writes, "there will no longer be any difference between the world of thought and the world of reality. There will be one world. . . . But this time has not yet come. . . . The goal of the search is not yet reached."[37] If Jung's timeline is correct, however, the new temple is far from collective realization; it will arrive over five hundred years from now. One thing is clear: the temple in Zeller's dream is a metaphor for a new collective consciousness which, if it is ever to be created, will only be created by individuals who go through the process of dying to collective consciousness, who wrestle with God, and bear the loneliness inherent in that night-sea journey. The way to the wedding is through symbolic death. That is the bitter truth; it is not sweet, but it is how things work.

If "incredible numbers of people," as Zeller's dream puts it, go the way of symbolic death, then sooner or later they will meet up. Then, it will no longer be church *or* wedding, but church *and* wedding, a temple that is big enough for us as we *are*.

Coleridge worked on the foundation of the new temple in his poetry and also in his great unfinished philosophical work, his magnum opus, the *Logosophia*, the "principle Labor" and "great Object" of his life, a great Marriage of science and religion, of physics and psychology, of outer and inner. In his own words, his *Logosophia* was to contain "some 20 years incessant Thought, and at least 10 years' positive Labor" and present "a compleat and perfectly original system of Logic, Natural [Philosophy] and Theology."[38] It was to present a visionary and yet at the same time scientifically based alternative to the mechanical philosophy of the science of his time based on the unity of psyche and matter.[39] Needless to say, nobody has yet finished this book. A century after Coleridge, Jung was working on it, and many still are. But the *coniunctio*, as a collectively accepted reality, most likely belongs to a far-off future.

A Sadder and a Wiser Man . . .

The Mariner now finishes his tale, leaving the Wedding Guest "stunned / And is of sense forlorn." We might feel this way as well as we reach the end of our journey with *The Rime of the Ancient Mariner*.

At the end, both Wedding Guest and Mariner turn away from the wedding. This is a sad ending to the poem, an incomplete ending. The poem does, however, leave us with a sober note of hope; the Wedding Guest rises transformed "the morrow morn," like the Sun rising from its perennial descent into darkness, "a sadder and a wiser man."

> The Mariner, whose eye is bright,
> Whose beard with age is hoar,
> Is gone: and now the Wedding-Guest
> Turned from the bridegroom's door.
> He went like one that hath been stunned,

And is of sense forlorn:
A sadder and a wiser man,
He rose the morrow morn.

Coleridge's *Ancient Mariner* is not, therefore, a wedding song; it is a prothalamion, a song announcing a marriage yet to come.

Which some brave Muse may sing
To ages following,
Upon the bridal day, which is not long[40]

Let us end our trek through the wilderness with a note of appreciation for Coleridge, for this favorite child of God offered up as a sacrifice for the future, a true artist who drank his own blood and offered his revelations back to a world unprepared to receive them.[41] Coleridge's *Ancient Mariner* tells a story that belongs to all of us in exile and bondage in this Fallen modern world. The Mariner's journey, as well as his incomprehension, is our own. Our civilization is still on the way to the wedding.

Conclusion: An Epic Poem for the Modern World Revisited

A Fourfold Consciousness in the Fourth Industrial Revolution

In 1798 when Coleridge wrote *The Rime of the Ancient Mariner*, the industrial revolution was in full swing. Mechanical production centering on the advent of the steam engine was booming, agrarian society was shrinking, urbanization expanding, and the factory fast becoming the center of commercial and even communal life. Modernity generally praised the industrial revolution as progress, but English Romantic poets such as Blake, Wordsworth, Coleridge, Shelley, and Keats protested the loss of connection to nature and the exploitation of factory workers, especially children, low wages, and horrible living conditions.

In the early twentieth century a second industrial revolution began. This was the age of electricity, radio, cars, and telephones. Life began to move even faster, especially in Europe and North America, and become more urbanized. By 1900, 40 percent of the US population lived in cities compared to 6 percent in 1800. In the 1950s we witnessed the start of a third industrial revolution, the digital revolution responsible for today's cell phones and computers. Now we find ourselves at the beginning of a fourth.

According to a January 19, 2016, article published by the World Economic Forum, the fourth industrial revolution "can be described as the advent of cyber-physical systems . . . examples include genome editing, new forms of machine intelligence, breakthrough materials and approaches to governance that rely on cryptographic methods such as the blockchain."[1] The demonstrably exponential growth of technology in the fourth industrial revolution leads many on its cutting edge—most visibly Ray Kurzweil, an inventor, futurist, best-selling author, and a director at Google's artificial intelligence lab—to hypothesize that by 2045, "cyber-physical systems," as the WEF article puts it, will evolve so quickly that they will eclipse our capacity to keep up. What will happen then? Nobody knows. Nobody *can* know. Kurzweil borrows a metaphor from cosmology to describe this event, the singularity, an event horizon in which space-time breaks down in the presence of extreme gravity, to express how the exponential growth of technology is unknowable, uncontrollable, unpredictable, and irreversible.

Two centuries ago, Coleridge rang the alarm bell concerning the inhumane consequences of the "philosophy of mechanism" when it goes beyond being a useful scientific hypothesis and possesses us as a dogmatic truth, likening it to the Fall of Man in the modern world. But even Coleridge could not possibly have foreseen what the mechanical philosophy of nature and humanity has developed into in the twenty-first century. Today, "Man a Computer" is not a mere analogy as "Man a Machine" was in the eighteenth century. We are fast on the way toward literally and concretely becoming the machine that we previously analogized ourselves as. Kurzweil, for example, foresees a cyborg future in the next two decades or so in which human biology and artificial intelligence will merge, thus forever transforming the *being* in human beings. With an attitude of "if you can't beat 'em, join 'em," Elon Musk's company Neuralink, founded in 2016, is currently developing ultrahigh bandwidth brain-machine interfaces that seek to treat diseases like Alzheimer's and dementia as well as paralysis. But one day, the technology might become generally available as another layer of brain for anyone who wishes it, a new neocortex so to speak, used to unite the human brain with artificial intelligence. "Create the Future with Us," the Neuralink website advertises.

The Devil and Modern Man

There are metaphorical connections between the devil and modern consciousness throughout Coleridge's *Ancient Mariner* and his philosophical prose. Today, we find similar analogies in the rhetoric of some of our most sophisticated and well-informed scientists and tech entrepreneurs. Musk is as modern a Prometheus as we have on the forefront of the fourth industrial revolution, yet even he senses that an unreflective identification of technological progress with the good might be Satanic, so to speak—that is, ultimately destructive. For example, in an interview at MIT in 2014, Musk identified artificial intelligence as our "biggest existential threat" and compared the development of artificial general and super intelligence to the perilous evocation of an evil spirit. "With artificial intelligence we're summoning the demon. You know those stories where there's the guy with the pentagram, and the holy water, and he's like—Yeah, he's sure he can control the demon? Doesn't work out."[2] Echoing Musk's analogy comparing artificial intelligence and demonic possession, Stephan Hawking declared in a 2014 interview with the BBC that "the development of full artificial intelligence could spell the end of the human race. Humans, who are limited by slow biological evolution, couldn't compete and would be superseded."[3]

Are we in the middle of an amazing Promethean revolution? Or is the exponential growth of technology the Fall of Man in the modern world? No doubt if Coleridge were alive, he would view the possible loss of our humanity in the fourth industrial revolution as a Fall rather than a Promethean liberation. But if transformation requires the destruction of the status quo, then the answer to these questions is yes, both. The development of artificial general and superintelligence will be both transformational and civilization-destroying.

One of the truly bewildering challenges that we must come to grips with in reading *The Rime of the Ancient Mariner* is not that things change but *how* things change. In *The Rime of the Ancient Mariner*, the Mariner kills the Albatross to give birth to the modern soul in the Enlightenment. This development is an *opus contra naturam* and *contra deus*, a work against the status quo ante of the Christian Middle Ages. Whether one defines evil as madness, sacrilege, narcissism, or violence, shooting the innocent white bird is an evil act. In the poem, the Mariner kills God, breaks his bond with nature, and transgresses against his community. For this, he is called "the devil." His "ghastly tale" is the tale of a "hellish" crime. And yet if the Mariner only loves all God's creatures, if he only worships "the pious bird of good omen" with the rest of the crew, then the Albatross simply guides his ship back home and nothing changes: the Sun does not rise in the Enlightenment, the Mariner never encounters the repressed feminine when the Sun sets, he never blesses the water-snakes, "Mary Queen" never ascends to Heaven. Moreover, there is no *Rime of the Ancient Mariner*. The poem is a study in regret, but surely the poem itself is not something to be regretted, something that should not have been.

The Birth, Death, and Rebirth of the Modern Soul

Like the Mariner when the Sun rises to its apex, many of us now enjoy the multitude of gifts that scientific and technological progress offers us. And yet, many people also find themselves adrift and dying of thirst in a purely solar, conscious world. For those who can no longer believe in the traditional religious images as true and real, we do not have to return to the past to discover what we have lost; there is another way. We can follow the Mariner deeper into both inner and outer nature so that we might celebrate the birth, death, and, finally, rebirth of the modern soul as "a silent communion of the Spirit with the Spirit in Nature not without consciousness, tho' with the consciousness not successively unfolded!" as Coleridge puts it, or, in von Franz's words, form a relationship with "a cosmic, divine energy capable of consciousness, a quasi-conscious meaning inherent in the objective physical processes of nature."[4] The rebirth of the modern soul will build upon our religious and intellectual cultural foundations and participate in their continuing evolution by pushing faith and reason further into the weird margins where the divisions between psyche and matter dissolve in an experience of reality as a fully human form of consciousness.

Put simply, just as Coleridge's Mariner learns to pray again after he kills the Albatross and blesses the water-snakes, the modern soul might learn to pray again as well. So, if you feel a yearning for the sacred but do not participate in any organized religion, or if you feel pressed from within to expand your current religious beliefs and experiences, then "open your whole self / To sky, to earth, to sun, to moon / To one whole voice that is you," as Joy Harjo beautifully describes in "Eagle Poem." A caveat: as we have seen in our analysis of *The Ancient Mariner*, for patriarchal-solar consciousness, the new prayer requires symbolic death and a baptism in the feminine-lunar unconscious, the mystery of the "woman."[5]

According to von Franz, the death and rebirth of the modern soul means that "we will have to obey and submit ourselves to Mother Nature if we want to escape an imminent global catastrophe."[6] For patriarchal consciousness, submitting to Mother Nature—inside and out—means the conscious relinquishment of much that we as a culture have revered as true and real for centuries: namely that *we* are the good people and *they* are evil; that nature is a machine operating on the principle of causal determinism and has nothing to do with the psyche; that there is no such thing as God, Coleridge's I AM, or Jung's Self, and therefore our ego is the sole authority; that in deciding how to proceed we need no "knowledge got from birds" but can rely on our wit alone. Are we up to the challenge of dying to all that has seemed most true and real to the modern Western mind for centuries and submitting to Mother Nature inside and out? Can we stand to drink our own blood rather than the blood of our perceived enemies and celebrate a Last Supper with the deep dimensions of the unconscious mind? Can we endure the loneliness and chaos of this process as we work out the way toward a new wedding of contraries? Coleridge's Mariner shows us the way, and he also shows us how difficult the way is, at least for a European Christian man educated in the rational spirit of the Enlightenment.

Where Do New Values Come From?

Jung and Martin Luther King Jr. warned us in the 1950s and '60s that for our very survival's sake we must figuratively die to our old values and give birth to new values, to new ways of seeing, to new concepts of self and world. In April 2023, Yuval Noah Harari addressed the potentially apocalyptic consequences of AI by pointing out that we will have to develop our consciousness in parallel with our machines if we are to find a positive way forward. "I think that AI is nowhere near its full potential. But also, human beings are nowhere near our full potential. We don't really understand the full potential of our brains, of our minds. If for every dollar, for every minute, that we invest in developing AI we invest another dollar and minute in developing our own minds, and our own consciousness, I think we'll be OK."[7] Harari has been an invited speaker at the World Economic Forum in Davos, Switzerland, which also hosted a 2022 symposium entitled "Values" curated by the Bocconi University. The WEF symposium on values acknowledged that "values are essential—particularly in times of crisis,"[8] and gave voice to the opinions of many extremely intelligent, creative, and wealthy people around the world today who have their eyes on the creation of new global values for the twenty-first century.

Are the new values we so desperately need today for our very survival's sake going to be born as the brainchildren of a global elite? *The Ancient Mariner* tells a different tale, one that is confirmed by the depth psychological perspective: the death and rebirth of cultural values comes not from above but from below, through the collective unconscious understood not as an impediment to the instantiation of new myths but as a creative matrix that gives birth to them.[9] The symbolizing field, the domain of the Great Mother that Jung calls the great Dream, the ocean the Mariner sails in—these form the matrix that reveals the way forward when our intellect, willpower, and good intentions hit their limits. The relevance of Coleridge's *Rime of the Ancient Mariner* to our contemporary world is that it *shows* us what it means to develop the full potential of our own minds, our own consciousness. It does not mean to increase our intellect, make more money, acquire more power, or better adapt to the status quo but to become more conscious of what it is to be a human *being*, and to become a vessel for the consciousness that is trying to evolve inside the psyche of human beings.

How do we develop the full potential of our minds? There is an old tale of a student who came to see a rabbi and asked him, "In the olden days there were men who saw the face of God. Why don't they anymore? The rabbi replied, "Because these days no one can stoop so low." Remember, the alchemical dictum, repeated again and again in the symbolism of *The Ancient Mariner*, is that the philosopher's stone is found in the dung heap. For the modern Western mind, that dung heap is the interior world of the mythopoetic psyche that has been banished since the Enlightenment to the slimy seas of delusion, distortion, and superstition. But that is where the Mariner blesses the water-snakes and is symbolically reborn.

The New Temple and the Fourfold State of Consciousness

Relating to the great Dream was once the exclusive province of epochal cultural heroes; today that heavy burden seems to fall more and more on the shoulders of ordinary people.

My partner Wikman had the following dream in the spring of 2024 during a time of extreme challenge in her life.

> *I dreamed of an inner sanctum tabernacle that was being built that, when the four winds would blow, and even all toward the structure, this design would allow some wind in from each direction, but it would not be destroyed by any wind from any side. The curvy design with a dome vault ceiling allowed some wind in from each direction but modulated the raw force so the wind could enter and blow through but not destroy. Its shape and beauty caught me by their unique stateliness and simplicity, matching the colors and shapes of the landscape. It carried a deep feeling of serenity and held an indestructible center at the core.*

In Zeller's dream, a new temple is being constructed by vast numbers of people from all around the world. In Wikman's dream, a tabernacle, an earlier form of the temple that serves as a terrestrial dwelling place for the divine, is being built. The design of this tabernacle is special in that it can withstand the "raw force" of the fourfold nature of the wind, or spirit. It is not a tabernacle of the Trinity but of the Quaternity.

Jung writes, "One must be able to suffer God. That is the supreme task for the carriers of ideas. . . . Let us therefore be for him limitation in time and space, an earthly tabernacle."[10] Will the Western soul succeed in becoming capable of containing a fourfold consciousness as a counterbalance to the fourth industrial revolution? There is a big question mark here. What does it really mean to understand the full potential of our minds, as Harari suggests? Perhaps if enough individuals listen to and follow their dreams and not just their conscious rationality, good intentions, or willpower, then maybe the full potential of our minds as a fourfold state of consciousness that no longer excludes the feminine-lunar principle as heresy and lunacy will be added to the masculine-solar Trinity.[11] Working our way out of the *literalism* inherent in the mechanical philosophy of self and nature, a literalism that eliminates the psyche as the fourth dimension from the trinitarian nexus of space-time, energy, and causality, might prove to be one way of keeping our humanity intact as we and the world change. For example, instead of seeking to literally achieve immortality by becoming cyborgs, we might explore, and take seriously, the archetypal image of the quest for immortality *as a symbol.* Wikman's dream is not of a cyborg future but of the creation of a fourfold consciousness grounded on the earth and with an indestructible center. This dream carries with it not a fear of the demonic side of technology but a deep feeling of serenity. If the modern soul can withstand the fourfold, the people of the future may inherit from us not literal genocide but a unified field of consciousness built by everyone who has suffered and integrated their own piece of darkness.

Afterword

On a Personal Note

In hindsight, my fascination with Coleridge's poetic night-sea journey is not so surprising. The sea has always loomed large in my life and feels close to my soul, like part of my body. Growing up in Southern California, I fell in love with the ocean from a very young age, and I'm still in love. I often went bodysurfing and surfing, and I continue to spend a significant amount of time around and in the ocean. From perhaps the age of seven onward, the sea was a refuge and the place I felt closest to Nature and God. Furthermore, the theme of the solitary sea voyage has always been close to my heart. While writing my thesis on *The Ancient Mariner*, I suddenly remembered that my favorite book as a child was *The Boy Who Sailed around the World Alone*![1]

For those who are interested in the personal story behind this book, particularly my experience of coming to terms with the unconscious by way of a symbolic death that baptized me in feeling values excluded from the collective values of my upbringing, I offer the following.

College Begins at Two

I was born in 1966 to a single woman who was twenty-five years old. She felt forced by family and cultural pressure to give me up for adoption. Just weeks old, a middle-class couple in Los Angeles adopted me from a center in Long Beach and brought me home. Their values centered on hard work, money, and material success. My father was, basically, Donald Trump, not in terms of his wealth but in terms of his perspective on life: a robust extrovert, he was an industrial real estate broker and investor, with wounds from serving on a minesweeper in the Korean War that were never resolved and pockets of rage that would constantly erupt. In his last days, he told me a story that defined his attitude toward life. On a dinner date with a beautiful woman after he completed his service in the navy, he vividly remembered telling her, "All I want to be is a success." This is the value I grew up with in a word: "success." In fact, in the initial meeting with a social worker at the adoption agency, my father asked if they could adopt a boy from parents that were "tall, good-looking, and smart," these being, of course, the qualities that would help lead their adopted child to "success." After me, my parents adopted another boy, sixteen months younger. The plan was that my younger brother and I would both get either an MBA or a law degree and then go into the real estate business with our father where we would build his business into an empire. We had three options handed to us in life: lawyer, MBA, failure.

Toward that end, we both attended the Buckley School beginning at the age of two, a private school in the San Fernando Valley "where the teachers held Stanford degrees and PhDs" and the students were very often the children of Hollywood personalities and elite professionals in Los Angeles. The Buckley School was on the radar after my grandmother saw an interview on a talk show with Dr. Isabelle Buckley, who had recently written a book entitled *College Begins at Two* (1965). Since we lived in Hancock Park, which was a long distance away from the school in Sherman Oaks, we took an hour bus ride each way every day to school. Dressed in a little suit and tie, but also still in diapers, my two-year-old self boarded that bus for my first day at "college" with a paper bag containing a clean cloth diaper in the morning and a dirty one on the return ride in the afternoon.

During this time, my adopted mother, who did not stand a chance of becoming her authentic self within the collective values of the family and the times, was caught between attempting to placate my father's rage and holding a persona of family. She lived in a very dissociated state. The gravitas of my Mother's situation may have contributed to her contracting *myasthenia gravis*, which often kept her confined to her bedroom. The void in her, and the void in our home, was immense. Her capacity for attunement and tracking the interpersonal field, emotions, and even simple daily experiences was practically nonexistent. By the time my younger adopted brother and I were five and seven respectively, our saving grace was the two-week vacation that we spent on Ventura Beach every summer learning to bodysurf and surf. Surfing saved my brother and me, and we still go surfing together today, as I do with my sons. The sea became a Mother for me, and I'm extremely grateful to this day to both of my parents that they held that annual ritual that brought life to my brother and me.

High School, College, Death of My Parents, Law School

Many years later, in high school, I become a believing Christian, not because of family beliefs (quite the opposite—neither of my parents had a religious or mystical bone in their bodies) but from experiences I had in nature, and the intuition that there must be something more going on behind the scenes. There was a charismatic Christian movement that swept through Southern California in the '80s that attracted many young people, evangelical churches such as Calvary Chapel, and one of these churches was in the neighborhood. So, believing in God and thinking I should therefore go to church, I briefly attended Calvary Chapel.

Then, when my mother died of pancreatic cancer when she was sixty years old and I was twenty-two, my belief in an all-good, all-powerful Father in Heaven became untenable in the face of seeing the destruction and pain caused by my mother's cancer and encountering the shocking sadness not only of death but of witnessing close up her physical and mental disintegration. Of course, her death touched the deep Mother wound in me so profoundly that my worldview shifted. My image of God lay like a vessel of glass shattered into a hundred pieces as I fell into the depths of the type of grief that dismembers us. My childhood focus on "success," the lack of communication and emotional relatedness in my family system, and my version of Christianity at the time had no substance that would have given me a means for holding the death and disintegration of my adoptive mother. Instead, I relied on denial, splitting, compartmentalization, and emotional numbing.

Upon graduating with degrees in English literature and philosophy from University of California, San Diego in 1989, I started law school that same year at the University of San Diego. Then, right after my first year of law school, when I was twenty-three, my father, who had been ill for years with multiple myeloma, a bone marrow cancer, also died. This was a year after my mother's death. After my father's death, I really put the blinders on and devoted almost all my energies to the study of law. Before that, in the first year of law school, I put little effort in and was an average student. The next two years, after his death, I got nothing but the highest grades in my classes and participated in all the honors and extracurricular programs. I received numerous American Jurisprudence awards for attaining the highest grade in the class in individual subjects, was a finalist at the 1992 California American Trial Lawyers Association mock trial competition, won the George W. Hickman Award for Constitutional Law, and graduated with honors. I remember that I figured out at the time that if I only counted the last two years of law school, then I had the highest grades in the entire school. That is how I thought then about what was important to me. In hindsight, losing myself in work was my way of coping with my parents' death. They were gone, and their dream of attaining "success" was all I had. My brother, who was also in law school at Boalt Hall, University of California, Berkeley, and I were both completely incapable of dealing with the tragedy of losing both parents by twenty-three and twenty-one years of age, apart from going into complete denial and pretending like nothing had happened. A factual example of this is that we had no contact with extended family and there was no memorial service for either of my parents.

Just after my father's death, my natural mother who had given me up for adoption as an infant contacted me for the first time by writing me a long letter. This was another bomb going off in terms of my sense of identity. On top of everything, I convinced a woman I met in law school to marry me, in retrospect to try to salvage a sense of home and family, and this marriage instantly fell apart one year later, the summer after law school graduation.

At my law school graduation ceremony, as I was receiving all these awards, I remember a cold, hollow wind blowing through me as I thought, "The only reason you did all this was for your parents and they are not even here to see it." Nevertheless, I secured a job with a successful criminal defense and civil litigation attorney in San Diego with whom there was mutual respect and an open door to partnership. I vividly remember coming to work one day and talking with the secretary, a woman who I viewed as old (she was probably forty or so), who suddenly exclaimed, "Look at all you are doing and you're only twenty-six!" I had to agree; I really felt on top of everything. Soon, however, the parental dream of practicing law became as cold and empty as that wind. I did not think about it at the time as a depression, but that was what it was, and it was a dangerous one.

By my twenty-eighth birthday, both of my parents had died of cancer, I was married and divorced, felt empty in my profession, and had lost my faith in God. All the social supports—vocation, family, religion—had crumbled. My view of "normal" life, how things "should" go, was blown to bits. I felt like the Wedding Guest when the Ancient Mariner comes up out of nowhere and grabs him with his skinny hand. To stay with the imagery from the poem, I also felt like the Ancient Mariner, "all, all alone, alone on a wide wide sea." I was adrift at sea and everything on land was broken: broken marriage, broken heart, broken family, broken career, broken God. I was unable to deal with an extremely painful, one-sided schizoid constellation in the psyche. It would be my fate to work with this.

"Maybe You Should See a Therapist"

The *terror tremendum* of this period of my life is difficult to convey. I remember, for instance, sleeping on the floor of a torn-down house I lived in at the time, the interior taken down to the studs, shivering with fear although the house was at a normal temperature, and feeling utterly alone. Psychologically, I was in a very scary place, one that I am sure the psychiatrist I saw recognized when he prescribed for me whatever drug that was. It may have been worse than a clinical depression.

I remember my roommate in Solana Beach at the time telling me, "Tom, maybe you should see a therapist." This had never in a million years occurred to me. It was so far from anything that I would ever do. Go to therapy? Only strange people did that! I did, however, try. I made appointments with a couple different therapists including one who gave me the Beck Depression Inventory, on which I scored close to the highest possible number in the severely depressed category, but I did not get anything else out of the few sessions I had with him and did not return. I also went to a psychiatrist in San Diego who prescribed me a drug which I do not remember the name of now. It must have been something extremely strong, however, because when I took half of one of the small pills, I had to phone that doctor at night as an emergency call. I felt like I was going to die. I quit the psychiatrist and told my roommate that therapy did not work for me. He must have felt that was a bad conclusion to draw because he pushed: "Don't worry, I know a Jungian therapist, it's not for crazy people, it's different." I liked the sound of that, so I decided to schedule a session.

I remember at our first meeting the Jungian asked me if I had any dreams. I had no idea why this would be relevant at all, but, yes, I was having vivid and intense dreams. I will recount three of these dreams here that, in retrospect, I have lived with and worked on over the last three decades. In one, I am in my childhood home. The neighborhood is in chaos as the moon above turns red, starts to pulse, and explodes as everyone is running for cover. This dream has to do with the transformation of my family of origin container and the values that were inculcated in me. In another dream, I am in the jungle looking at a horrific site: all the animals had been murdered and their bodies heaped up in a mass grave. This dream clearly shows the effects of trauma on my psyche, and the need for the resurrection of an instinctual life.

The very first painting I ever made in my life was from the third dream, which I will recount here. In this dream, I am in a large house with paintings on the walls, and an unknown woman is showing me some of them as we sit on the hardwood floors together.

In the central painting, two hands appear from opposite sides of the canvas and clasp in the middle. In between them, as if contained by them, there is a black sun with a heart inside. In the blackness of the eclipse, a heart is forming like a child in the womb. This painting appears in the chapter on the eclipse of the sun in this book. The eclipse of the sun, as we have seen, plays an important role in Coleridge's *Ancient Mariner*, where it appears as a figurative image for the death of consciousness. My family of origin psychology was dying at this time, the sun or consciousness by which I lived and my sense of self along with it. But the dream of a heart growing within the darkness of the eclipse gave me the intuition (that's all it was at the time) that there *might* be a process hidden in what seemed like a void—no meaningful thought, no feeling, no connection to others.

When I would bring in my dreams, the therapist would at times take books of mythology off the shelf and show me the imagery in them. This made a deep impression on me. With the eclipse of the sun and heart-fetus painting, however, it was only much later that I would discover parallels, such as those in alchemy, that describe the eclipse of the sun as the "first step of the work," an "incubation" and a "pregnancy."

A Lawyer in Psychological Training

The following two examples will, I hope, convey something of my experience at this time as to how diametrically opposed the functions of thinking and feeling were in me. In my training as a lawyer, it was implicitly clear that we had to drum feelings out of ourselves in order to learn to "think like lawyers." For instance, on the first day of law school, the professor had us read a case that was patently and grossly unfair. I'll never forget this professor, a large woman with short dark hair and a red suit. As she asked the class what we thought of that case, one person took the bait, as I'm sure happens every year: "This was really unfair!" The response from the prof? "Fair? Where do you see the word fair in the law? You are here to think like lawyers now," etc., etc. Of course, that student felt like an idiot, which was the point, and I got the message: feeling values are stupid.

My training in psychology could not have been more different. My first ever psychology class was a "process of psychotherapy" course at Antioch University in Los Angeles. The first thing I noticed about the class was that it was 80 percent women. The second thing I noticed was that for some reason we were all sitting in a circle. I cannot remember exactly how the class developed, but within a short period of time the women were crying and sharing deeply emotional experiences. It was an outpouring of feelings. To appreciate the impact this had on me at the time, you must remember that, at the age of twenty-eight, coming from educational experiences in philosophy and law and almost totally uncommunicative when it came to emotions, I had never seen anything like it. My first day of psychology school I sat in that room totally aghast. This was a graduate program? I felt like raising my hand: "Objection, irrelevant." When were we going to learn something? What did all these feelings have to do with graduate studies?

What an *enantriodromia*. As I think about it now, it seems the psyche had a real sense of humor.

"You're a Lawyer? And You're Doing What?"

It only got worse. The encounter with the Self is a defeat for the ego, as Jung famously remarked. That language sounds so dramatic and biblical, but the transformation of ego attitudes can manifest in everyday, almost imperceptible ways. Two small but paradigmatic examples come from the time I had stopped practicing law and was pursuing a master's degree in psychology.

During one of my first psychology internships, I worked at a residential program for patients diagnosed with schizophrenia, mostly people in their twenties, young people. My job was to drive the bus and take them out to State Street in Santa Barbara so they could walk around for a bit. Of course, I did not make any money at this job. I remember meeting with one of my supervisors at that site who was just getting to know me. At one point in our meeting, he stopped talking about supervision topics and just stared at me. There was an awkward silence. From out of the blue he said, "You're a lawyer?" The look of disbelief on his face was astounding; he clearly thought I might be as crazy as the patients. "What are you doing here? Do you have some kind of religious mission or something?" he asked. I suppose that was the only way he could try to make sense of me. He did not mean that question as a compliment—rather, it was the way he might have said, "Are you on drugs?" But in a way he was right. I *was* there because of an inner sense of vocation. It certainly had nothing to do with prestige and money, that's for sure. Going from being, at twenty-six years old, an attorney who had been at the top of his class with attendant social respect and admiration and the potential to make relatively large amounts of money to driving a bus for people diagnosed with schizophrenia felt like quite a fall. It was impossible not to identify to some extent with that supervisor's negative projection and start to wonder if I was crazy after all, or if something was wrong with me. I felt like a "loser," as crazy as my supervisor thought I was. If I had not had my dreams to support me, and my analyst to support the dreams, I doubt I would have continued.

At another internship, a community mental health center in Santa Barbara that provided low-cost psychotherapy, I remember a meeting in which the center proposed charging its clientele five dollars an hour as a minimum fee instead of having no minimum fee at all. The blowback from the interns was overwhelmingly against it. How could we do such a horrible and unfair thing to charge such a high fee? This was the moment I realized that my time spent working in my new profession literally had no monetary value. What did that say about my worth? The words of one of my dad's business partners came ringing back into my head: "Money is how we keep score."

Another dimension of what happened during my night-sea journey was that a powerful connection to music and musicians came out of the great nowhere. Previously, I had not even especially liked music. I had never been the type of young person who went to concerts, or had favorite bands, or collected records. But now, I would go hear the musicians in San Diego, and I just had to learn to play guitar. I was seriously and passionately entranced. And not just with the popular music of my own culture but with blues. And not just blues but the old Delta blues: Son House, Robert Johnson, and old Texas blues like Lightnin' Hopkins. I took lessons from a local blues musician named Robin Henkel, started playing in a hack blues band in the local bar down the street in Solana Beach, and soon found myself playing with serious jazz musicians somehow. I found I had a new conflict—whether to continue with music or to train to become a Jungian analyst. I went to the Berklee College of Music in Boston for a summer program and, outside of class, I would take my guitar and play in the Boston subway and in Harvard Square. Sitting in the subway playing guitar was more death to the ego for sure, and again the inner voice boomed, "You're a lawyer? And you're doing what?" Becoming a musician was fulfilling a fate, not of Logos or power, but of Eros and feeling.

Out to Sea and Back Again

As we have seen, *nobody* understands the Ancient Mariner. Everyone he encounters onshore calls him the devil and a lunatic. At the end, the Mariner wanders "like night" and is still "all, all alone, alone on a wide, wide sea." Fortunately, during my night-sea journey I had the great privilege to have had all the support and guidance I could possibly have asked for: an analysis in which my soul was met and valued, followed by training as a Jungian analyst at the Centre for Depth Psychology according to C. G. Jung and Marie-Louise von Franz in Zurich. These were among the most profound experiences of my life. Sharing almost nothing in terms of persona with the older Swiss men and women at the "Zentrum" as it is called (they once called me "Mr. Hollywood," and no doubt wondered what this relatively young Californian was doing there), over time a reciprocity developed on the level of an *ecclesia spiritualis*, or kinship based on similar experiences of the unconscious psyche.

The Ancient Mariner is forced to submit himself to the Great Mother. So was I. His redemption at sea comes when "a stream of love gushes from [his] heart." So did mine. The community, support, and understanding that I was blessed to receive, however, stands in utter contrast to the lonely tragedy of Coleridge's night-sea journey. Unlike Coleridge, I was lucky to have many people help me deal with my wounds and dissociation and welcome me back to shore. It is my gratitude to them and my sense of sadness for Coleridge and the many others like him who were not so lucky that inspire this book.

What can I say all these years later about where the symbolic process of death and rebirth, the eclipse of the sun in my own life, was leading? What came from it? Eventually the heart, latent like an embryo in the darkness of the eclipse, was nurtured through my experiences in Jungian analysis, the creation of a family, my relationship as a father to my two boys Jake and Bennett, and my profession, which became a path with heart. Through the development of my feeling function, I was able to value the messages of the dreams, which I had always assumed were crazy nonsense, and to experience an interrelatedness of psyche and nature. The pathway of symbolic death and rebirth also led me into relationship with Monika Wikman for the last fourteen years and counting. My deepest heart has been found in my relationship with Monika, along with the fusional complexes of pain, madness, suffering, and the imperfection of love, through a bond that bridges the everyday domestic with experiences of the animal and mystical. Monika's voice and presence, as well as her own dreams, reverberate throughout this book. I feel so grateful to her for all of her gifts and, because of her and because of being with her, how far I've come to be able to love and be loved.

The individuation process, the process by which we become what we inherently are, "is only experienced," as Jung writes, "by those who have gone through the wearisome but indispensable business of coming to terms with the unconscious components of the personality."[2] From the age of two I was trained to be a "success" in terms of intelligence, money, and prestige. My depression led me into a totally different type of education, an education of the heart. And that journey continues to hold me as a foundation through another round with the black sun: at the age of fifty-eight, I have received a stage 4 cancer diagnosis.

Integration with the divine feminine and healing of the trauma body continue now at an even deeper level than I was capable of with my first black sun experience at the age of twenty-eight.[3] Dreams again lead the initiation into the depths, carrying humble hints to guide the way. And the mercy and grace of the visionary subtle body dimensions of the psyche are opening step by step with the unknown. From here I often eye our Ancient Mariner on the ship blessing the water-snakes and the turn in the psychic equation coming as the Presence of the transcendent takes hold and becomes imminent—with the rain as grace pouring down and Mary Queen of Heaven renewing the whole field (the alchemical *mundificatio*). Jung speaks about confrontation and collaboration with the unconscious at the same time as the way to work it out with the unconscious, and this has been the heart of my path in life.

Amid it all, I do feel Coleridge as a spiritual ancestor. And I am grateful to the psyche for calling me to hold deeply to my original love for literature and the Romantic poets, as well as to the complexity of Coleridge's psyche, his life, and his work. In a way, this bringing of my personal story into relationship with the archetypal dream material is what Coleridge could never do in his life; that inability to bridge sea and land is, as noted repeatedly throughout this book, the crisis of Romanticism that depth psychology evolved to address. As we touch down onshore, I hope that the reverberations from the depths of *The Rime of the Ancient Mariner* and its connection to our very personal selves have touched, at least in some small way, your own journey toward the great wedding.

Notes

Series Editor's Foreword

1. Public Image Ltd, "Albatross," released by Virgin Records on the album *Metal Box*, November 23, 1979.

2. Samuel Taylor Coleridge, *The Rime of the Ancient Mariner*, first published in 1798 in *Lyrical Ballads*.

3. William Wordsworth and Samuel Taylor Coleridge, *Lyrical Ballads: 1798 and 1802* (Oxford: Oxford University Press, 2013).

4. David Tacey, "Fay Lectures Book Series: 20th Anniversary Reviews," *Journal of Analytical Psychology* 55 (2010): 300–312.

5. Frank N. McMillan III, *Finding Jung: Frank N. McMillan Jr., a Life in Quest of the Lion* (College Station: Texas A&M Press, 2012).

Introduction

1. Ross Woodman, "Shaman, Poet, and Failed Initiate: Reflections of Romanticism and Jungian Psychology," *Studies in Romanticism* 19, no. 1 (Spring 1980): 51–82.

2. Joseph Cottle, *Reminiscences of Samuel Taylor Coleridge and Robert Southey* (New York: Wiley and Putnam, 1848), 123n, 255–56.

3. Peter Kitson, "Coleridge, the French Revolution and the Ancient Mariner: A Reassessment," *The Coleridge Bulletin New Series* 7 (1996): 47.

4. John Livingstone Lowes, *The Road to Xanadu: A Study in the Ways of Imagination* (Boston: Houghton Mifflin, 1927; Princeton, NJ: Princeton Legacy Library, 2016).

5. Samuel Taylor Coleridge, *Biographia Literaria* (London: J. M. Dent and E. P. Dutton, 1906; London: J. M. Dent & Sons Ltd., 1930), 160–61.

6. "In this condemnation of the serious parts of the Arabian Nights, I have nearly all the world, and in particular the author of the Ancient Mariner, against me, who must be allowed to be a judge of such matters, and who said, with a subtlety of philosophical conjecture which he alone possesses,

'That if I did not like them, it was because I did not dream.'" William Hazlitt, *Collected Works*, ed. A. R. Waller and Arnold Glover (London: Dent, 1903), 14.

7. Samuel Taylor Coleridge, *The Complete Works of Samuel Taylor Coleridge*, vol. 5, ed. W. G. T. Shedd (New York: Harper Brothers, 1884), 255.

8. Samuel Taylor Coleridge, *The Notebooks of Samuel Taylor Coleridge*, ed. Kathleen Coburn, vol. 2, *1804–1808* (Princeton, NJ: Princeton University Press, 1961), 2086.

9. Samuel Taylor Coleridge, *Coleridge's Notebooks: A Selection*, ed. Seamus Perry (New York: Oxford University Press, 2002), 66.

10. Richard Holmes, *Coleridge: Early Visions* (Harmondsworth, UK: Penguin, 1990), 72.

11. Jennifer Ford, *Coleridge on Dreaming: Romanticism, Dreams, and the Medical Imagination* (Cambridge: Cambridge University Press, 1998), 42.

12. "It consists of the many small dreams and the many acts of humility and submission to their hints. It is the future and picture of the new world, which we do not understand yet. We cannot know better than the unconscious and its intimations. There is a fair chance of finding what we seek in vain in our conscious world. Where else could it be?" C. G. Jung, *C. G. Jung Letters*, vol. 2, ed. Gerhard Adler and Aniela Jaffé (1953; Princeton, NJ: Princeton University Press, 2021), 591–92.

13. "To grasp its meaning, we must allow it to shape us as it shaped [the author.] Then we also understand the nature of his primordial experience. He has plunged into the healing and redeeming depths of the collective psyche, where man is not lost in the isolation of consciousness and its errors and sufferings, but where all men are caught in a common rhythm which allows the individual to communicate his feelings and strivings to mankind as a whole." Carl G. Jung, *The Collected Works of C. G. Jung*, vol. 15, ed. Herbert Read, Michael Fordham, Gerhard Adler, and William McGuire, trans. Richard F. C. Hull (1944; Princeton, NJ: Princeton University Press, 2014), 7238.

14. Samuel Taylor Coleridge, *The Rime of the Ancient Mariner Big Read*, The Arts Institute, University of Plymouth, 2020, https://www.ancientmarinerbigread.com/.

15. Philip Hoare, "Why Willem Dafoe, Iggy Pop and More Are Reading The Rime of the Ancient Mariner to Us," *The Guardian*, April 24, 2020, http://theguardian.com/books/2020/apr/24/why-willem-dafoe-iggy-pop-and-more-are-reading-the-rime-of-the-ancient-mariner-to-us.

16. Mary Norris, "The Epic Poem You Need for Quarantine," *New Yorker*, May 15, 2020, http://newyorker.com/culture/comma-queen/the-epic-poem-you-need-for-quarantine.

17. Carl G. Jung, *C. G. Jung Letters*, ed. Gerhard Adler and Aniela Jaffé, trans. Richard F. C. Hull, vol. 2, *1951–1961* (Princeton, NJ: Princeton University Press, 1975), 586.

18. Martin Luther King Jr., *Where Do We Go from Here: Chaos or Community?* (Boston, MA: Beacon Press, 2010), 142.

19. "Individuation cuts one off from personal conformity and hence from collectivity. That is the guilt which the individuant leaves behind him for the world, that is the guilt he must endeavor to redeem. He must offer a ransom in place of himself, that is, he must bring forth values which are an equivalent substitute for his absence in the collective personal sphere. Without this production of values, final individuation is immoral and—more than that—suicidal. . . . The individuant has no *a priori* claim to any kind of esteem. He has to be content with whatever esteem flows to him from outside by virtue of the values he creates. Not only has society a right, it also has a duty to condemn the individuant if he fails to create equivalent values." C. G. Jung, *The Symbolic Life: Collected Works*, vol. 18, ed. Gerhard Adler, trans. Richard F. C. Hull (Princeton, NJ: Princeton University Press, 1977), 449–54.

20. C. G. Jung, *The Collected Works of C. G. Jung*, vol. 8, ed. Gerhard Adler, trans. Richard F. C. Hull (1954; repr. Princeton, NJ: Princeton University Press, 1970), 290.

Chapter 1

1. Holmes, *Coleridge: Early Visions*, and Richard Holmes, *Coleridge: Darker Reflections, 1804–1834* (New York: Penguin, 1999).

2. Holmes, *Coleridge: Early Visions*.

3. Letter to Thomas Poole, October 16, 1797. Holmes, *Coleridge: Early Visions*, 16.

4. Letter to Thomas Poole, October 9, 1797. Samuel Taylor Coleridge, *Letters of Samuel Taylor Coleridge*, vol. 1, ed. Ernest Hartley Coleridge (London: William Heinemann, 1895), 12.

5. Samuel Taylor Coleridge, *The Collected Works of Samuel Taylor Coleridge*, ed. Kathleen Coburn, vol. 14, *Table Talk, Part II* (Princeton, NJ: Princeton University Press, 1990), 72.

6. Letter to the Reverend George Coleridge. Samuel Taylor Coleridge, *The Poems of Samuel Taylor Coleridge* (Boston, MA: C. S. Francis & Co., 1848), 167, 179.

7. Ibid., 166.

8. Carl G. Jung, *The Collected Works of C. G. Jung*, vol. 13, ed. Herbert Read, Michael Fordham, Gerhard Adler, and William McGuire, trans. Richard F. C. Hull (1954; Princeton, NJ: Princeton University Press, 2014), 6161.

9. Rose-Emily Rothenberg, "The Orphan Archetype," *Psychological Perspectives: A Quarterly Journal of Jungian Thought* 14, no. 2 (1983): 181–94.

10. Samuel Taylor Coleridge, *Aids to Reflection and the Confessions of an Inquiring Spirit* (London: George Bell and Sons, 1884), 157.

11. Coleridge, *Letters of Samuel Taylor Coleridge*, 9.

12. Coleridge, *Aids to Reflection*, 189.

13. Geoffrey Carnall, "Southey, Robert (1774–1843), Poet and Reviewer," in *Oxford Dictionary of National Biography* (Oxford: Oxford University Press, 2004), online ed., accessed August 26, 2012, oxforddnb.com.

14. Coleridge, *Letters of Samuel Taylor Coleridge*, 228–29.

15. Letter to John Thelwell, December 17, 1796. Ibid., 196–97.

16. Samuel Taylor Coleridge, *Letters, Conversations and Recollections of S. T. Coleridge*, ed. Thomas Allsop (London: Frederick Farrah, 1864), 197.

17. Molly Lefebure, *Samuel Taylor Coleridge: A Bondage of Opium* (London: Gollancz, 1974), 60.

18. To fully appreciate the stunning amount of opium that Coleridge regularly took, consider first the recommended dosages. Laudanum (now known as tincture of opium) is still prescribed for the treatment of severe diarrhea. The recommended dose today—and remember this is not for pure opium but for the same 10 percent opium tincture by weight as in Coleridge's time—is 0.3 to 0.6 milliliters, four times a day. That translates to 1.2 to 2.4 milliliters per day, or 0.04 to 0.08 ounces a day, not to exceed 6 milliliters a day. "Opium Tincture," Medscape, https://reference.medscape.com/drug/opium-tincture-342043, accessed January 17, 2022. See also "Opium Tincture Prescribing Information," Marathon Pharmaceuticals, 2009, cited in Wikipedia, "Laudanum," accessed January 17, 2022, https://en.wikipedia.org/wiki/Laudanum.

19. Samuel Taylor Coleridge, *A Choice of Coleridge's Verse*, ed. Ted Hughes (London: Faber and Faber, 1996), 9.

20. Samuel Taylor Coleridge, *Letters of Samuel Taylor Coleridge*, vol. 2, ed. Ernest Hartley Coleridge (London: William Heinemann, 1895), 694.

21. T. N. Talfourd, *The Life, Letters and Writings of Charles Lamb: A Sketch of the Life of Charles Lamb in Six Volumes*, vol. 1, ed. Percy Fitzgerald (London: E. Moxon and Co., 1876), 285.

Chapter 2

1. Henri F. Ellenberger, *The Discovery of the Unconscious: The History and Evolution of Dynamic Psychiatry* (New York: Basic Books, 1981), 199.

2. Coleridge, "On Poesy or Art," cited in S. K. Heninger Jr., "A Jungian Reading of 'Kubla Khan,'" *The Journal of Aesthetics and Art Criticism* 18, no. 3 (March 1960): 360.

3. Of interest here is the assertion made by F.W. Bateson in *English Poetry*:

> The central concept of Romanticism is the primacy of the subconscious mind. The problem, therefore, that the Romantic poet had to solve was how to establish a relationship between the instinctive energy of his own private subconscious mind, the Freudian libido, on the one hand, and the system of communal conventional sounds which constitutes language, on the other. To put it crudely, the libido does not speak English. According to the psycho-analysts, when the libido emerges into consciousness, in dreams or under the influence of drugs, it tends to express itself entirely in images, "a picture language whose meaning can only be discovered through special methods of interpretation." The Romantic poets, however, were more interested in exploiting than in interpreting the imagery of dreams and trances. They were impressed and excited by the hints it gave of a reality that was deeper and older than the communal life to which they found themselves committed by the accident of birth. Intimations of immortality are the stuff of Romantic poetry and "suggestion" is the inevitable vehicle of communication. It is impossible to translate the language of the libido literally—accurate transcriptions of dreams are either dull or ludicrous—and so the attempt was made to render the qualities of dream-experience, its strangeness, its remoteness, its inexplicability. It is significant that Romantic poetry contains a much higher proportion of negative propositions than earlier or later poetry. This is because the easiest way to define the activities of the subconscious mind is to say what they are not.

F.W. Bateson, *English Poetry: A Critical Introduction* (Oxford: Oxford University Press, 1910), 21–22.

4. Ross Woodman, *The Apocalyptic Vision in the Poetry of Shelley* (Toronto: University of Toronto, 1966).

5. Mary Shelley, *Mary Wollstonecraft Shelley*, ed. Harold Bloom (New York: Infobase Publishing, 2009), 111.

6. "Naturally, if what I say has truth in it, this will already have been dealt with by the world's poets, but the flashes of insight that come in poetry cannot absolve us from our painful task of getting step by step away from ignorance toward our goal." Donald Winnicott, "Fear of Breakdown," in *The Collected Works of D. W. Winnicott*, vol. 6, *1960–1963*, ed. Lesley Caldwell and Helen Taylor Robinson (Oxford: Oxford University Press, 2016), 523.

7. C. G. Jung, *Notes on Lectures Given at the Eidgenössische Technische Hochschule, Zürich by Prof. Dr. C. G. Jung*, 2d ed., ed. Barbara Hannah et al. (Zürich: C. G. Jung-Institute Zurich, 1959), 195.

8. Ford, *Coleridge on Dreaming: Romanticism*, 156, 157.

9. Samuel Taylor Coleridge, *Anima Poetæ: From the Unpublished Note-Books of Samuel Taylor Coleridge*, ed. Ernest Hartley Coleridge (London: William Heinemann, 1895), 64.

10. Ford, *Coleridge on Dreaming*, 33, 36, 37.

11. Samuel Taylor Coleridge, *The Collected Works of Samuel Taylor Coleridge*, vol. 14, ed. George Whalley (Princeton, NJ: Princeton University Press, 1969), 111.

12. Letter to Thomas Poole, October 16, 1797. Coleridge, *Letters of Samuel Taylor Coleridge*, 1:16.

13. Kathleen Coburn, *The Self Conscious Imagination: A Study of the Coleridge Notebooks in Celebration of the Bi-centenary of His Birth* (London: Oxford University Press, 1974), 50.

14. Samuel Taylor Coleridge, *Biographia Literaria, or, Biographical Sketches of My Literary Life and Opinions* (Princeton, NJ: Princeton University Press, 1983), lxxvi.

15. Ibid., 24.

16. Samuel Taylor Coleridge, *Bloom's Modern Critical Views: Samuel Taylor Coleridge*, ed. Harold Bloom (New York: Infobase Publishing, 2010), 113.

17. Samuel Taylor Coleridge, *The Statesman's Manual; Or, The Bible the Best Guide to Political Skill and Foresight: A Lay Sermon* (London: Gale and Fenner, 1816), xiv.

18. Coburn, *The Self Conscious Imagination*, and Kathleen Coburn, *Experience into Thought: Perspectives in the Coleridge Notebooks* (Toronto: University of Toronto Press, 1979).

19. Coburn, *Experience into Thought*, 4.

20. Samuel Taylor Coleridge, *The Notebooks of Samuel Taylor Coleridge*, vol. 5, *1827–1834 Text*, ed. Kathleen Coburn and Anthony John Harding (New York: Routledge, 2002), 5572, 5573.

21. Coleridge, *Anima Poetæ*, 64.

22. Samuel Taylor Coleridge, *The Complete Works of Samuel Taylor Coleridge in Seven Volumes*, vol. 6, ed. W. G. T. Shedd (New York: Harper & Brothers, 1884), 417.

23. Coleridge, *Biographia Literaria* (1983), 50.

24. Coleridge, "On Poesy or Art," cited in Heninger, "A Jungian Reading of 'Kubla Khan,'" 360.

25. Samuel Taylor Coleridge, *Hints Towards the Formation of a More Comprehensive Theory of Life*, ed. Seth B. Watson (London: Lea and Blanchard, 1848), 42.

26. Coleridge, *Biographia Literaria* (1983), 82.

27. Coleridge, *Anima Poetæ*, 31.

28. Coleridge, *Biographia Literaria* (1983), 114.

29. Samuel Taylor Coleridge, *Samuel Taylor Coleridge—The Major Works*, ed. H. J. Jackson (Oxford: Oxford University Press, 2009), 560.

30. Samuel Taylor Coleridge, *Specimens of the Table Talk of Samuel Taylor Coleridge*, ed. Henry Nelson Coleridge (London: J. Murray, 1852), 199.

31. Coleridge, *The Statesman's Manual*, 35.

32. Coleridge, *Biographia Literaria* (1983), 241–42.

33. Ford, *Coleridge on Dreaming*. See especially the introduction and chapter 7.

34. Ibid., 124.

35. Coleridge, *Anima Poetæ*, 204.

36. Ford, *Coleridge on Dreaming*, 184.

37. J. B. Beer, *Coleridge, the Visionary* (London: Chatto & Windus, 1959), 33.

38. Samuel Taylor Coleridge, *The Notebooks of Samuel Taylor Coleridge: Notebooks 1819–1826*, vol. 4, *Notes*, ed. Kathleen Coburn and Merton Christensen (London: Routledge, 2003), 1820.

39. Samuel Taylor Coleridge, *The Collected Works of Samuel Taylor Coleridge*, vol. 12, *Marginalia Part 1: Abbt to Byfield*, ed. George Whalley (1969; Princeton, NJ: Princeton University Press, 1980), 568.

40. Coleridge, *Biographia Literaria* (1983), 295.

41. Samuel Taylor Coleridge, *Biographia Literaria* (1906; London: J.M. Dent & Sons Ltd., 1930), 166.

42. Samuel Taylor Coleridge, *The Notebooks of Samuel Taylor Coleridge*, vol. 1, *1794–1804, Text*, ed. Kathleen Coburn (1962; New York: Routledge, 2002), 525.

Chapter 3

1. Samuel Taylor Coleridge, *Biographia Literaria* (1906; London: J.M. Dent & Sons Ltd., 1930), 159–60.

2. William Wordsworth, *The Collected Poems of William Wordsworth* (London: Wordsworth Editions, 1994), 701.

3. Emmanuel Kennedy-Xypolitas, *The Fountain of the Love of Wisdom: An Homage to Marie-Louise von Franz* (Chicago: Chiron Publications, 2006), 70.

4. For instance, Stephen M. Weissman, *His Brother's Keeper: A Psychobiography of Samuel Taylor Coleridge*, ed. George H. Pollock (1990; New York: BookSurge Publishing, 2008).

5. Samuel Taylor Coleridge, *A Choice of Coleridge's Verse*, ed. Ted Hughes (London: Faber and Faber, 1996), 6.

6. Coleridge, *Coleridge's Notebooks*, 88.

7. Ford, *Coleridge on Dreaming*, 51.

8. Edmund Burke, *A Philosophical Enquiry into the Origins of the Sublime and the Beautiful*, ed. David Womersley (New York: Penguin Classics, 1999).

9. Carl G. Jung, *The Collected Works of C. G. Jung*, vol. 9, ed. Herbert Read, Michael Fordham, Gerhard Adler, and William McGuire, trans. Richard F. C. Hull (1939; Princeton, NJ: Princeton University Press, 2014), 3629.

10. William Wordsworth, *The Prelude: A Parallel Text*, ed. Jonathan Wordsworth (New York: Penguin Classics, 1996), 21.

11. Ibid.

12. Percy Shelley, *Adonais*, lines 489–90.

13. Heninger, "A Jungian Reading of 'Kubla Khan,'" 360.

14. Ross Woodman, *Sanity, Madness, Transformation: The Psyche in Romanticism*, ed. Joel Faflak (Toronto: University of Toronto Press, 2009), 139.

15. "Coleridge is printing Xtabel, by Ld Byron's recommendation to Murray, with what he calls a vision, Kubla Khan—which said vision he repeats so enchantingly that it irradiates and brings heaven and Elysian bowers into my parlour while he sings or says it, but there is an observation 'Never tell thy dreams,' and I am almost afraid that Kubla Khan is an owl that won't bear day light, I fear lest it should be discovered by the lantern of typography and clear reducting to letters, no better than nonsense or no sense. When I was young I used to chant with extacy Mild Arcadians ever blooming, till somebody told me it was meant to be nonsense. Even yet I have a lingering attachment to it, and think it better than Windsor Forest, Dying Xtian's address &c." Charles Lamb, Letter to William Wordsworth, April 26, 1816.

16. Coleridge, *Samuel Taylor Coleridge—The Major Works*, 560.

17. Samuel Taylor Coleridge, *Coleridge: Poems*, ed. John Beer (New York: Everyman's Library, 1993), 213.

18. Lowes, *The Road to Xanadu* , 271.

19. Ford, *Coleridge on Dreaming*, 1.

20. Ibid., 92.

21. Carl G. Jung, *The Collected Works of C. G. Jung*, vol. 15, ed. Herbert Read, Michael Fordham, Gerhard Adler, and William McGuire, trans. Richard F. C. Hull (1966; Princeton, NJ: Princeton University Press, 2014), 7215.

22. Samuel Taylor Coleridge, *Bloom's Classic Critical Views: Samuel Taylor Coleridge*, ed. Harold Bloom (New York: Infobase Publishing, 2009), 36.

23. J. S. Stewart, *Heralds of God* (New York: Charles Scribner's Sons, 1946), 37.

24. Charles Lamb, *The Works of Charles Lamb*, vol. 3 (London: Edward Moxon, 1850), 29.

25. "We may further grant to those of her defenders who are lovers of poetry and yet not poets, the permission to speak in prose on her behalf: let them show not only that she is pleasant but also useful to States and to human life, and we will listen in kindly spirit; for if this can be proved we shall surely be the gainers—I mean, if there is a use in poetry as well as a delight?" Plato, *The Republic of Plato*, ed. B. Jowett (London: Oxford University Press, 1925), 323.

26. "It was agreed, that my endeavours should be directed to persons and characters supernatural, or at least romantic, yet so as to transfer from our inward nature a human interest and a semblance of truth sufficient to procure for these shadows of imagination that willing suspension of disbelief for the moment, which constitutes poetic faith." Coleridge, *Biographia Literaria*, chapter 14.

27. *Oxford English Dictionary Online*, "imagination," accessed October 12, 2021, https://www.lexico.com/definition/imagination.

28. Jon Mee, *Romanticism, Enthusiasm, and Regulation: Poetics and the Policing of Culture in the Romantic Period* (Oxford: Oxford University Press, 2003), 2.

29. Ross Woodman takes a similar position: "As distinct from psychosis, madness, understood as Plato's 'divine madness,' is the creative power of psychosis when it is dialectically processed by the imagination." Woodman, *Sanity, Madness, Transformation*, 199.

30. C. G. Jung, *Visions: Notes of the Seminar Given in 1930–1934*, ed. Claire Douglas (Princeton, NJ: Princeton University Press, 1997), 303, 307.

31. Coleridge, *Biographia Literaria* (1906), 160–61.

32. Gaston Bachelard, *The Poetics of Space* (New York: Penguin, 1964), 37.

33. James V. Baker, *The Sacred River: Coleridge's Theory of the Imagination* (Baton Rouge: Louisiana State University Press, 1957), 155.

34. Jung, *The Collected Works of C. G. Jung*, 2:1352.

35. Samuel Taylor Coleridge, "Religious Musings," in *The Complete Poems*, ed. William Keach (Princeton, NJ: Princeton University Press, 1997), 107. Coleridge's portrait of Christ draws from the well-known description of the "suffering servant" in Isaiah 53:3 who is "despised and rejected of men." "He is despised and rejected of men; a man of sorrows and acquainted with grief: and we hid as if our faces from him; he was despised, and we esteemed him not. Surely he hath born our grief and carried our sorrows: yet we did esteem him striken, smitten of God, and afflicted." *The New Oxford Annotated Bible*, ed. Michael Coogan, Marc Brettler, Carol Newsom, and Pheme Perkins (Oxford: Oxford University Press, 2018).

36. Mark 4:41 (King James Version).

37. Beer, *Coleridge, the Visionary*, 324–25.

Chapter 4

1. Wordsworth, *The Collected Poems of William Wordsworth*, 701.

2. Theodor Abt, *The Egyptian Amduat: The Book of the Hidden Chamber* (Einsiedeln, Switzerland: Daimon Verlag, 2007).

3. John Keats, *The Poetical Works of Keats* (Boston: Houghton Mifflin, 1975), 143.

4. Percy Bysshe Shelley, *The Complete Poems of Percy Bysshe Shelley* (New York: Modern Library, 1994), 492.

5. See M. H. Abrams, *Natural Supernaturalism: Tradition and Revolution in Romantic Literature* (New York: W. W. Norton & Co, 1973), and Woodman, *Sanity, Madness, Transformation* for a multiplicity of examples and reflections on this theme.

6. W. H. Auden, *The Enchafèd Flood: or, The Romantic Iconography of the Sea* (New York: Random House, 1950), 11. Also relevant here is Jung's observation that Goethe's *Faust* and Nietzsche's *Zarathustra* are exemplars of the marvels and dangers of the night-sea voyage. "[Faust is] more than a literary exercise. It is a link in the Aurea Cantena which has existed from the beginnings of philosophical alchemy and Gnosticism down to Nietzsche's *Zarathustra*. Unpopular, ambiguous, and dangerous, it is a voyage of discovery to the other pole of the world." Carl G. Jung, *Memories, Dreams, Reflections*, ed. Aniela Jaffé (New York: Vintage, 1989), 189. Mary Shelley's character Captain Walton makes similar observations in *Frankenstein* where he references Coleridge's Ancient Mariner. "It is impossible to communicate to you a conception of the trembling sensation, half pleasurable and half fearful, with which I am preparing to depart. I am going to unexplored regions, to 'the land of mist and snow,' but I shall kill no albatross; therefore do not be alarmed for my safety or if I should come back to you as worn and woeful as the 'Ancient Mariner.' You will smile at my allusion, but I will disclose a secret . . . there is something at work in my soul, which I do not understand . . . a love for the marvelous, a belief in the marvelous . . . which hurries me out of the common pathways." Mary Shelley, *Frankenstein; or, The Modern Prometheus* (1818; New York: Penguin, 1992), 19.

7. Holmes, *Coleridge: Early Visions*, 72.

8. Andreas Schweizer, *Stone by Stone: Reflections on the Psychology of C.G. Jung*, ed. Andreas Schweizer and Regine Schweizer-Vüllers (Einsiedeln, Switzerland: Daimon Verlag, 2017), 250.

9. Coleridge, *Biographia Literaria* (1906), 43.

Chapter 5

1. "I remember Him, I evoke Him, whenever I use His name, overcome by anger or by fear, whenever I involuntarily say: 'Oh God.' That happens when I meet somebody or something stronger than myself. It is an apt name given to all overpowering emotions in my own psychic system, subduing my conscious will and usurping control over myself. This is the name by which I designate all things which upset my subjective views, plans, and intentions and change the course of my life for better or worse. In accordance with tradition I call the power of fate in this positive as well as negative aspect, and inasmuch as its origin is beyond my control, 'God,' a 'personal God,' since my fate means very much myself, particularly when it approaches me in the form of conscience as a *vox Dei* with which I can even converse and argue. (We do and, at the same time, we know that we do. One is subject as well as object.)" C. G. Jung, *C. G. Jung Letters*, vol. 2, ed. Gerhard Adler & Aniela Jaffé (1953; Princeton, NJ: Princeton University Press, 2021), 525. A rudderless ship abandoned to the elements is how Jung describes the collapse of the conscious ego as the unconscious takes over the wheel. "A collapse of the conscious attitude is no small matter. It always feels like the end of the world, as though everything had tumbled back into original chaos. One feels delivered up, disorientated, like a rudderless ship that is abandoned to the moods of the elements. So at least it seems. In reality, however, one has fallen back upon the collective unconscious, which now takes over the leadership." Jung, *Collected Works* 7, 163.

2. M. L. von Franz, *Dreams: A Study on the Dreams of Jung, Descartes, Socrates and Other Historical Figures* (Boston: Shambhala, 1998), 131.

3. The North wind also figures in the alchemical imagination, but more in a paradoxical way than biblical. The cold North wind is evil, but evil plays a necessary role in the creation of the philosopher's stone. "The coral is a kind of vegetable which comes to being in the sea, and has roots and branches, and in its original state is moist. But when the wind blows North, it hardens, and turns into a red substance, which the seafarer sees under the water and cuts off; then, when it comes out of the water, it turns into a stone of a red color." Jung, *Aion*, in *Collected Works* 9, 99–100.

4. C. G. Jung, *Memories, Dreams, Reflections*, ed. Aniela Jaffé (New York: Vintage, 1989), 357. Jung, *C. G. Jung Letters*, 2:525.

5. Friedrich Nietzsche, "To the Unknown God" (1864). Nietzsche also claims that during one of his lakeside walks in Sils Maria in Switzerland, in July 1881, he saw a vision of Zarathustra that taught him the nature of revelation as "involuntary unto the extreme . . . as in a storm." He describes that experience in his *Ecce Homo*:

> Has anyone at the end of the nineteenth century a clear idea of what poets of strong ages have called *inspiration*? If not, I will describe it.—If one had the slightest residue of superstition left in one's system, one could hardly reject altogether the idea that one is merely incarnation, merely mouthpiece, merely a medium of overpowering forces. The concept of revelation—in the sense that suddenly, with indescribable certainty and subtlety, something becomes *visible*, audible, something that shakes one to the last depths and throws one down—that merely describes the facts. One hears, one does not seek; one accepts, one does not ask who gives; like lightning, a thought flashes up, with necessity, without hesitation regarding its form—I never had any choice.
>
> A rapture whose tremendous tension occasionally discharges itself in a flood of tears—now the pace quickens involuntarily, now it becomes slow; one is altogether beside oneself, with the distinct consciousness of subtle shudders and of one's skin creeping down to one's toes; depth of happiness in which even what is most painful and gloomy does not seem something opposite but rather conditioned, provoked, a *necessary* color in such a superabundance of light; an instinct for rhythmic relationships that arches over wide spaces of forms—length, the need for a rhythm with wide arches, is almost the measure of the force of inspiration, a kind of compensation for its pressure and tension.
>
> Everything happens involuntarily in the highest degree but in a gale of feeling of freedom, of absoluteness, of power, of divinity.—The involuntariness of image and metaphor is strangest of all; one no longer has any notion of what is an image or a metaphor; everything offers itself as the nearest, most obvious, simplest expression. It actually seems, to allude to something Zarathustra says, as if the things themselves approached and offered themselves as metaphors ("Here all things come caressingly to your discourse and flatter you; for they want to ride on your back. On every metaphor you ride to every truth. . . . Here the words and wordshrines of all being open up before you; here all being wishes to become word, all becoming wishes to learn from you how to speak").
>
> This is my experience of inspiration; I do not doubt that one has to go back thousands of years in order to find anyone who could say to me, "it is mine as well."

Friedrich Nietzsche, *Ecce Homo*, trans. Walter Kaufman (New York: Vintage, 1989), 300–301.

6. Friedrich Nietzsche, *The Will to Power*, ed. Walter Kaufman (New York: Vintage Books, 1968), 435. Of note with respect to contemporary dimensions of psychotherapy: Nietzsche's prescription of art to save us

from the illness of reality is a rare case. Typically, it is the reverse. Most theories of psychotherapy are designed to protect reality from the dangers of art, or imagination. But Nietzsche's perspective is very close to Jung's method of practice when it comes to not building ego consciousness and social adaptation but to dealing with the outbreak of the individuation process. Thus, Jung tended to believe that Jungian analysis was only for the second half of life.

7. Coleridge, *Samuel Taylor Coleridge—The Major Works*, 125.

Chapter 6

1. William Shakespeare, *The Oxford Shakespeare: Macbeth*, ed. Nicholas Brooke (Oxford: Oxford University Press, 2008), act 5, scene 5, lines 25–27.

2. Lowes, *The Road to Xanadu*, 35.

3. D. H. Lawrence, *D. H. Lawrence and Italy: Sketches from Etruscan Places, Sea and Sardina, Twilight in Italy*, ed. Simonetta de Filippis, Paul Eggert, and Mara Kalnis (New York: Penguin Classics, 2008), 8.

4. Friedrich Nietzsche, *Thus Spoke Zarathustra: A Book for Everyone and No One*, ed. and trans. R. J. Hollingdale (New York: Penguin Classics, 1961), 129.

5. Shelley, *Adonais*, stanza 52.

6. "The *Iconologia* of Cesare Ripa," accessed July 5, 2021, www.levity.com/alchemy/iconol04.html.

Chapter 7

1. Facts about the wandering albatross are taken from Carl Safina, *Eye of the Albatross: Visions of Hope and Survival* (New York: Henry Holt and Co., 2002).

2. "As in Goethe's *Faust*, here too it is the feminine element (Eve) that knows about the secret which can work against the total destruction of mankind, or man's despair in the face of such a development." Jung, *Letters*, 2:386–87.

3. "In the Scriptures they [i.e., the histories] are the living *educts* of the Imagination; of that reconciling and mediatory power, which, incorporating the Reason in Images of Sense, and organizing (as it were) the flux of the Senses by the permanence and self-circling energies of the Reason, gives birth to a system of symbols, harmonious in themselves and consubstantial with the truths of which they are the *conductors*. . . . Now an Allegory is but a translation of abstract notions into a picture-language which is itself nothing but an abstraction from objects of the senses; the principle being

more worthless even than its phantom proxy, both alike unsubstantial, and the former shapeless to boot. On the other hand a Symbol . . . is characterized by a translucence of the Eternal through and in the Temporal. It always partakes of the Reality which it renders intelligible; and while it enunciates the whole, abides itself as a living part in that Unity, of which it is the representative. The others are but empty echoes which the fancy arbitrarily associates with apparitions of matter, less beautiful but not less shadowy than the sloping orchard or hill-side pasture-field seen in the transparent lake below." Coleridge, *The Statesman's Manual*, 6:28–31.

4. Matthew 3:13, 16–17 (King James Version).

5. Herman Melville, *Moby-Dick, or The White Whale* (New York: Penguin Classics, 2002), 204.

6. Ibid., 1.

7. Coleridge, *The Collected Works*, 12:558.

8. Coleridge, "Dejection: An Ode."

9. Coleridge, "Constancy to an Ideal Object."

10. C. G. Jung, *The Undiscovered Self* (London: Routledge, 2002), 17.

11. John Hart, *Is Ideology Becoming America's Official Religion?*, *Forbes*, November 30, 2017, accessed August 24, 2022, https://www.forbes.com/sites/johnhart/2017/11/30/is-ideology-becoming-americas-official-religion/?sh=7f577736164b.

12. See, for example, Thomas Singer and Samuel Kimbles, *The Cultural Complex: Contemporary Jungian Perspectives on Psyche and Society* (New York: Routledge, 2004), the main thesis of which, in my opinion, is an extension into sociopolitical life of Donald Kalshed's *The Inner World of Trauma: Archetypal Defenses of the Personal Spirit* (New York: Routledge, 1996).

13. William Wordsworth, *The Major Works*, ed. Stephen Gill (Oxford: Oxford University Press, 2008), 375.

14. Theodor Abt, "Introduction," *Psychological Perspectives* 46, no. 1 (Spring 2008): 27.

15. C. G. Jung, *The Red Book: Liber Novus*, ed. Sonu Shamdasani, trans. Mark Kyburz and John Peck (New York: W. W. Norton, 2009), 334.

Chapter 8

1. Arthur Schopenhauer, *The Horrors and Absurdities of Religion* (London: Penguin, 2009), 65.

2. Safina, *Eye of the Albatross*, 79ff. See also the website for the Tasmanian Albatross Fund, www.tasmanianalbatrossfund.com.au/a-human-history/, which recounts the journal entry of Matthew Flinders, one of the

first of the Europeans to discover Albatross Island in 1798: "There were vast numbers of albatrosses on that isle to which their name is given, which were tending their young in the beginning of December; and being unacquainted with the power or disposition of man, did not fear him: we taught them their first lesson of experience."

3. Ross Pomeroy, "Scientists Have Learned from Cases of Animal Cruelty," *RealClear Science*, January 23, 2012, accessed October 3, 2022, https://www.realclearscience.com/blog/2012/01/scientists-can-be-cruel.html#:~:text=Ren%C3%A9%20Descartes,-Descartes%20believed%20that&text=In%20the%201600s%2C%20Descartes%20put,tell%20onlookers%20not%20to%20worry. See also Richard Dawkins, "Richard Dawkins on Vivisection: 'But Can They Suffer?,'" accessed October 3, 2022, https://boingboing.net/2011/06/30/richard-dawkins-on-v.html.

4. Matthew 27:45, 27:51, 27:52 (New Oxford Annotated Bible).

5. "He destroys that form, he grinds it under his heel, and then darkness falls, as if the white bird had meant a source of light. Complete darkness ensues, which is exactly what one would expect, for in extinguishing the light of the Holy Ghost, he has eliminated the spiritual element altogether . . . the sin against the Holy Ghost has been committed and the Indian is cursed, like Ahasuerus who rejected his Lord and has to wander until he finds the white bird again. This woman has evidently surrendered to the powers of evil, to a sort of devil who is the eternal enemy of the spirit." Jung, *Visions*, 119.

6. Immanuel Kant, *An Answer to the Question: What Is Enlightenment?* (London: Penguin, 2009).

7. Thomas Paine, *Age of Reason: Being an Investigation of True and Fabulous Theology* (New York: Willey Book Company, 1794), 238, 5.

8. Ibid.

9. Gary Laderman and Luis Leon, eds., *Religion and American Cultures: Tradition, Diversity, and Popular Expression*, 2d ed., 4 volumes (Santa Barbara, CA: ABC-CLIO, 2014), 1402.

10. Francis Bacon, *The New Organon* (1620).

11. Coleridge's early philosophical views were significantly influenced by Priestley's. Coleridge admired Priestley's support for the French Revolution as well as his toleration of religious dissenters. Coleridge was less likely, however, to have condoned Priestley's use of the air pump in his scientific experiments to demonstrate, "rather gruesomely, the effect of the absence of air on birds and small animals." Peter Stiles, "The Appeal of Integration: The Influence of Joseph Priestley on the Development of the Visual Arts and Fiction in the Late Eighteenth and Early Nineteenth Centuries," in "Religion, Literature and the Arts Project 1996 Conference

Proceedings," 1996, 281, accessed October 14, 2021, https://openjournals.library.sydney.edu.au.

12. William Blake, *Jerusalem*, Section 52, "To the Deists."

13. Abrams, *Natural Supernaturalism*.

14. Samuel Taylor Coleridge, "Aphorisms on Spiritual Religion," in *Aids to Reflection*, 189.

15. Samuel Taylor Coleridge, *Coleridge: A Collection of Critical Essays*, ed. Kathleen Coburn (New York: Prentice-Hall, 1967), 140.

16. Coleridge, *The Statesman's Manual*, 28.

17. Samuel Taylor Coleridge, *Collected Letters: 1815–1819*, ed. Earl Leslie Griggs (London: Clarendon, 1959), 575.

18. Coleridge, *Coleridge: A Collection of Critical Essays*, 137.

19. Ibid., 140.

20. Jacques Clinchamps de Malfilâtre, "Le Soleil fixe au milieu des planets," in *Solar Poetry and the Subject of the Enlightenment*, ed. Didier Coste (Lafayette, IN: Purdue University Press, 1990), 232–38.

21. Sophocles, *The Three Theban Plays: Antigone; Oedipus the King; Oedipus at Colonus*, trans. Robert Fagles (New York: Penguin Classics, 2000), 155, lines 433–35.

22. Coleridge, *Biographia Literaria* (1983), chapter 13.

Chapter 9

1. Andrew Solomon, *The Noonday Demon: An Atlas of Depression* (New York: Scribner, 2001).

2. "I am a son of Earth and starry sky. I am parched with thirst and am dying; but quickly grant me cold water from the Lake of Memory to drink." In the Orphic myth, Mnemosyne, a goddess, gives the deceased soul water from the Lake of Memory to quench its thirst. Fritz Graf and Sarah Iles Johnston, *Ritual Texts for the Afterlife: Orpheus and the Bacchic Gold Tablets* (New York: Routledge, 2007), 4–5.

3. "The Valley Spirit never dies.
It is named the Mysterious Female.
And the Doorway of the Mysterious Female
is the base from which Heaven and Earth sprang.
It is there within us all the while;
Draw upon it as you will, it never runs dry."

Laozi, *The Way and Its Power: Lao Tzu's Tao Te Ching and Its Place in Chinese Thought*, trans. Arthur Waley (New York: Grove Press, 1958), 149.

4. Coleridge, *Collected Letters*, 3:575. "*A fall* of some sort or other—the creation, as it were, of the non-absolute—as the fundamental postulate of the

moral history of man. Without this hypothesis, man is unintelligible, with it, every phenomenon is explicable. The mystery itself is too profound for human insight." Coleridge, *Complete Works*, 6:303.

5. Cited by Elliott B. Gose Jr., "Coleridge and the Luminous Gloom: An Analysis of the 'Symbolical Language' in 'The Rime of the Ancient Mariner,'" *PMLA* 75, no. 3 (June 1960): 238–44.

6. T. S. Eliot, *The Waste Land and Other Poems* (New York: Vintage, 2021), 57.

Chapter 10

1. Samuel Taylor Coleridge, *The Literary Remains of Samuel Taylor Coleridge* (Freeditorial Press: Hoboken, NJ: 2024), 238.

2. "The union of consciousness (Sol) with its feminine counterpart the unconscious (Luna) has undesirable results to begin with: it produces poisonous animals such as the dragon, serpent, scorpion, basilisk, and toad . . . the first to appear are the cold-blooded animals . . . The first progeny of the *matrimonium luminarium* are all, therefore, rather unpleasant." Carl G. Jung, *Collected Works*, vol. 14, *Mysterium Coniunctionis*, trans. Gerhard Adler and R. F. C. Hull (Princeton, NJ: Princeton University Press, 1977), 144.

3. "What the west represses in its view of nature is the chthonian, which means 'of the earth'—but earth's bowels, not its surface. . . . I adopt it as a substitute for Dionysian, which has become contaminated with vulgar pleasantries. The Dionysian is no picnic. It is the chthonian realities which Apollo evades, the blind grinding of subterranean force, the long slow suck, the muck and ooze. It is the dehumanizing brutality of biology and geology, the Darwinian waste and bloodshed, the squalor and rot we must block from consciousness to retain our Apollonian integrity as persons. . . . The daemonism of chthonian nature is the west's dirty little secret." Camille Paglia, *Sexual Personae: Art and Decadence from Nefertiti to Emily Dickinson* (New York, NY: Vintage Books,1990), 5–6.

4. "Alchemical projections," Jung writes, "represent collective contents that stand in painful contrast—or rather compensatory relation—to our highest rational convictions and values." Jung, *Collected Works*, 13:238.

5. "Their 'philosophy' was, indeed, nothing but projected psychology. For as we have said, their ignorance of the real nature of chemical matter favoured the tendency to projection. Never do human beings speculate more, or have more opinions, than about things which they do not understand." Jung, *Collected Works*, 14:519.

6. See, for example, Woodman, *Romanticism, Alchemy, and Psychology*.

7. Jung, *Collected Works*, 14:554.

8. Coleridge, *Anima Poetæ*, 204.

9. Johann Daniel Myliu, *Rosarium Philosophorum of the De Alchemia Opuscula* (1550; New York: Theophania, 2011).

10. John Read, *Prelude to Chemistry: An Outline of Alchemy* (Cambridge, Mass.: MIT Press, 1996), 130.

11. Muhammad Ibn Umail, *Corpus Alchemicum Arabicum Vol. 1B (CALA 1B): Book of the Explanation of the Symbols*, ed. Theodor Abt (Zurich: Living Human Heritage, 2010).

12. Jung, *Collected Works*, 8:53–54.

13. "Madness is not simply a bodily disease. It is the sleep of the spirit with certain conditions of wakefulness; that is to say, lucid intervals. During this sleep, or recession of the spirit, the lower or bestial states of life rise up into action and prominence. It is an awful thing to be eternally tempted by the perverted senses. The reason may resist—it does resist—for a long time; but too often, at length, it yields for a moment, and the man is mad for ever. An act of the will is, in many instances, precedent to complete insanity. I think it was Bishop Butler who said, that he was all his life struggling against the devilish suggestions of his senses, which would have maddened him, if he had relaxed the stern wakefulness of his reason for a single moment." Coleridge, *The Collected Works of Samuel Taylor Coleridge*. 14:144–45.

14. "The weird sisters, hand in hand, / Posters of the sea and land, / Thus do go about, about." William Shakespeare, *The Oxford Shakespeare: Macbeth*, ed. Nicholas Brooke (Oxford: Oxford University Press, 2008), act 1, scene 3, lines 32–34. "I'll drain him dry as hay. / Sleep shall neither night nor day / Hang upon his pent-house lid; / He shall live a man forbid. / Weary seven nights nine times nine / Shall he dwindle, peak and pine. / Though his bark cannot be lost, / Yet it shall be tempest-tost." Ibid., act 1, scene 3, lines 19–27.

15. Samuel Taylor Coleridge, *The Notebooks of Samuel Taylor Coleridge*, vol. 3, *1808–1819*, ed. Kathleen Coburn (London: Routledge, 1973), 3312.

16. Coleridge, *A Choice of Coleridge's Verse*, 6.

17. "Our gold is not the common gold. But thou hast inquired concerning the greenness deeming the bronze to be a leprous body on account of the greenness it has on it. Therefore I say unto thee that whatever is perfect in the bronze is that greenness only, because that greenness is straightaway changed by our magistery into our most true gold." Myliu, *Rosarium Philosophorum*.

18. Coleridge, *Collected Letters*, 1:643.

19. "It is a most instructive part of my Life the fact, that I have been always preyed on by some Dread, and perhaps all my faulty actions have been the consequence of some Dread or other on my mind / from fear of Pain, or

Shame, not from prospect of Pleasure /—So in my childhood & Boyhood the horror of being detected with a sorehead; afterwards imaginary fears of having the Itch in my Blood—/ then a short-lived Fit of Fears from sex—then horror of DUNS, & a state of struggling with madness from an incapability of hoping that I should be able to marry Mary Evans (and this strange passion of fervent tho' wholly imaginative and imaginary Love uncombinable by my utmost efforts with any regular Hope—/ possibly from deficiency of bodily feeling, of tactual ideas connected with the image) had all the effects of direct Fear, & I have lain for hours together awake at night, groaning and praying—Then came that stormy time / and for a few months America really inspired Hope, & I became an exalted Being—then came Rob. Southey's alienation / my marriage—constant dread in my mind respecting Mrs. Coleridge's Temper, &c—and finally stimulants in the fear & prevention of violent Bowl-attacks from mental agitation / then almost epileptic night-horrors in my sleep / & since then every error I have committed, has been the immediate effect of the Dread of these bad most shocking Dreams—any thing to prevent them." Coleridge's "Dread," however, is also at times linked not to a fear of being overwhelmed by bodily states but to fear of a "*deficiency* of bodily feeling [emphasis added]." Ibid., 2398.

Chapter 11

1. Jung, *Visions*, 1213.

2. Thomas Mann, *The Thomas Mann Reader*, Joseph Warner Angell, Ed. (New York: Knopf, 1950), 440. See also Jung's feeling about this matter: "The historical condition is always whole, it is sacred, taboo; many generations have believed in it and whoever tries to destroy it is considered a criminal; so you are akin to the criminal, you are in a way destroying what the ages have built up . . . so this mark which our patient bears is like the mark of a criminal, an innovator, one who commits the crime of being unhistorical . . . Mrs. Sigg: The theologian Fischer says that the mark made on Cain was the mark of the cross." Jung, *Visions*, 1040.

3. "Filled with disgust and remorse for having destroyed something so great and beautiful, I turned to flee, impelled by the fear that the murder might be discovered. But a tremendous downfall of rain began, and I knew that it would wipe out all traces of the dead. I had escaped the danger of discovery; life could go on, but an unbearable feeling of guilt remained.

"When I awoke from the dream, I turned it over in my mind, but was unable to understand it. I tried therefore to fall asleep again, but a voice within me said, 'You must understand the dream, and must do so at once!'

The inner urgency mounted until the terrible moment came when the voice said, 'If you do not understand the dream, you must shoot yourself!' In the drawer of my night table lay a loaded revolver, and I became frightened. Then I began pondering once again, and suddenly the meaning of the dream dawned on me. 'Why, that is the problem that is being played out in the world.' Siegfried, I thought, represents what the Germans want to achieve, heroically to impose their will, have their own way. 'Where there is a will there is a way!' I had wanted to do the same. But now that was no longer possible. The dream showed that the attitude embodied by Siegfried, the hero, no longer suited me. Therefore it had to be killed.

"After the deed I felt an overpowering compassion, as though I myself had been shot: a sign of my secret identity with Siegfried, as well as of the grief a man feels when he is forced to sacrifice his ideal and his conscious attitudes. This identity and my heroic idealism had to be abandoned, for there are higher things than the ego's will, and to these one must bow." Carl G. Jung, *Memories, Dreams, Reflections*, ed. Aniela Jaffe (New York: Vintage, 1989), 220.

4. Jung, *Collected Works* 15:72.

5. John J. Crawley. "Saint Christopher Martyr Third Century," accessed October 10, 2014, https://en.wikipedia.org/wiki/Saint_Christopher#cite_note-Crawley-12.

6. "How shall we comfort ourselves, the murderers of all murderers? What was holiest and mightiest of all that the world has yet owned has bled to death under our knives: who will wipe this blood off us? What water is there for us to clean ourselves? What festivals of atonement, what sacred games shall we have to invent? Is not the greatness of this deed too great for us? Must we ourselves not become gods simply to appear worthy of it?" Friedrich Nietzsche, *The Gay Science: With a Prelude in Rhymes and an Appendix of Songs*, trans. Walter Kaufman (New York: Vintage, 1974), 181.

7. Friedrich Nietzsche, "Among Birds of Prey," in *The Complete Works of Friedrich Nietzsche*, vol. 9, ed. Alan D. Schrift (Stanford, CA: Stanford University Press, 2021), 347. In *The Gay Science*, Nietzsche expands upon his idea of the heaviest burden:

> *The greatest weight.* What, if some day or night a demon were to steal after you into your loneliest loneliness and say to you: "This life as you now live it and have lived it, you will have to live it once more and innumerable times more: and there will be nothing new in it, but every pain and every joy and every thought and sigh and everything unutterably small or great in your life will have to return to you, all in the same succession and sequence—even this spider and this moonlight between the trees, and even this moment and I myself. The

eternal hourglass of existence is turned upside down again and again, and you with it, speck of dust!"

Would you not throw yourself down and gnash your teeth and curse the demon who spoke thus? Or have you once experienced a tremendous moment when you would have answered him: "You are a god and never have I heard anything more divine." If this thought gained possession of you, it would change you as you are or perhaps crush you. The question in each and every thing, "Do you desire this once more and innumerable times more?" would lie upon your actions as the greatest weight. Or how well disposed would you have to become to yourself and to life *to crave nothing more reverently* than this ultimate eternal confirmation and seal?

Nietzsche, *The Gay Science*, 273–74.

8. "When you see your matter going black, rejoice," the alchemists repeated over and over; "you are at the beginning of the work." Myliu, *Rosarium Philosophorum*.

Chapter 12

Percy Bysshe Shelley, *Prometheus Unbound*, in *The Complete Poems of Percy Bysshe Shelley*, act 1, scene 1, lines 195–203. Here the voice of Earth speaks, of Demeter, revealing the life in the underworld, the collective unconscious.

1. "*What, you are stepping westward?*"—"*Yea.*" /—'Twould be a *wildish* destiny." William Wordsworth, *Selected Poetry*, ed. Stephen Gill and Duncan Wu (Oxford: Oxford University Press, 2008), 146.

2. These are the first and last words—the only words—the Mariner ever speaks to the crew, a fact that gives us a subtle feeling for this character's solitary preoccupations.

3. William Hazlitt, "My First Acquaintance with Poets," in *Selected Writings*, ed. John Cook (Oxford: Oxford University Press, 2009), 211.

4. "If one lives close to the earth, if one lives with the blood, there are some things which one simply cannot do or imagine. For instance, to make a straight line through nature, like a railway that disfigures a whole countryside, is an offense to nature—not to the forest or the mountain, they do not lament, but to our own nature. It violates the blood, because our blood knows no straight line." Jung, *Visions*, 237.

5. "The old philosophers called this blackness the Raven's Head or black sun. . . . In this state the sun is surrounded by the anima media natura and is therefore black. It is a state of incubation or pregnancy. Great importance was attached to the blackness as the starting point of the work." Jung, *Collected Works*, 14:512.

6. Marie-Louise von Franz, *Aurora Consurgens: A Document Attributed to Thomas Aquinas on the Problem of Opposites in Alchemy: A Companion Work to C. G. Jung's Mysterium Coniunctionis* (Toronto: Inner City Books, 2000), 256.

7. "I am the mediatrix of the elements, making one to agree with another; that which is warm, I make cold, and the reverse; that which is dry I make moist, and the reverse; that which is hard I make soft, and the reverse. I am the end and my beloved is the beginning. I am the whole work and all science is hidden in me." The feminine dimension of the philosopher's stone speaking for herself. Von Franz, *Aurora Consurgens*, 143. In his book *The White Goddess*, the mythologist Robert Graves asserts that Coleridge's daimonic Female is "as faithful a record of the White Goddess as exists." Even the leprous skin is faithful to the archetypal image: "Coleridge's mention of leprosy is strangely exact." Graves reports that it is possible that the island of Samothrace, famous for its mysteries of the White Goddess and the Cabeiri, takes its name from "scaly leprosy"—"Samo" means white and the Old Goidelic word for leprosy was "Samothrusc." Robert Graves, *The White Goddess: A Historical Grammar of Poetic Myth*, ed. Grevel Lindop (New York: Farrar, Straus and Giroux, 1997), 424.

8. Von Franz, *Aurora Consurgens*, 358.

9. Romans 8:5–7.

10. Von Franz, *Aurora Consurgens*, 225.

11. Ibid., 261.

12. Andrew Robinson, "Einstein Said That—Didn't He?," *Nature*, May 3, 2018, 30.

13. Jung, *Collected Works*, vol. 5, *Symbols of Transformation*, ed. Gerhard Adler, trans. R. F. C. Hull (Princeton, NJ: Princeton University Press, 1977), par. 299.

14. Coleridge, *The Notebooks of Samuel Taylor Coleridge*, 1:979.

15. See Orly Bareket, Rotem Kahalon, Nurit Shnabel, and Peter Glick, *The Madonna-Whore Dichotomy: Men Who Perceive Women's Nurturance and Sexuality as Mutually Exclusive Endorse Patriarchy and Show Lower Relationship Satisfaction*, Springer Science+Business Media, 2018, accessed June 30, 2022, https://socsci3.tau.ac.il/nurit-shnebel/wp-content/uploads/2018/02/The-Madonna-Whore-Dichotomy_-Men-Who-Perceive-Womens-Nurturance-and-Sex. . . . pdf.

16. Pamela Davenport, *Romantic but Hardly Romantic: Sarah Fricker's Life as Coleridge's Wife*, July 29, 2017, accessed June 14, 2024, https://wordsworth.org.uk/blog/2017/07/29/romantic-but-hardly-romantic-sarah-frickers-life-as-coleridges-wife/#.

17. Adam Roberts, "Sarah Hutchinson, Coleridge's 'Asra,'" November 1, 2017, https://wordsworth.org.uk/blog/2017/11/01/sara-hutchinson/.

18. Lefebure, *Samuel Taylor Coleridge*, 371–73.

19. Coleridge, *Coleridge's Notebooks*, 19.

20. Sigmund Freud, *The Uncanny*, trans. David McLintock (New York: Penguin Classics, 2003), 121.

21. Coleridge, *Biographia Literaria*, chapter 13, part 1.

22. Anthony Faulkes, *Edda* (London: Viking Society for Northern Research, 2005), 17.

23. "With its ecstatic abandon and berserker frenzies of emotion, Wotanism, in its orgiastic as well as its mantic form, lacks the clear eye of the higher knowledge, which was lost through the 'upper castration' performed by Erda." Erich Neumann, *The Origins and History of Consciousness* (Princeton, NJ: Princeton University Press, 1973), 379–80. This theme is also present in *Oedipus Rex*; the prophet Tiresias is blind but has inner sight, while Oedipus is sighted but inwardly blind. In *Oedipus at Colonus*, Oedipus's daughters Antigone and Ismene become the guides of the blind old man. The young feminine leads Oedipus, once so certain that he needed "no knowledge got from birds" to solve the riddle of the sphinx, toward the apotheosis of his death: "We couldn't see the man—he was gone—nowhere! And the king, alone, shielding his eyes, both hands spread out against his face as if some terrible wonder flashed before his eyes and he, he could not bear to look." Sophocles, *The Three Theban Plays*, 381.

24. "I had not a dispute but a disquisition with Dilke, upon various subjects; several things dove-tailed in my mind, and at once it struck me what quality went to form a Man of Achievement, especially in Literature, and which Shakespeare possessed so enormously—I mean Negative Capability, that is, when a man is capable of being in uncertainties, mysteries, doubts, without any irritable reaching after fact and reason—Coleridge, for instance, would let go by a fine isolated verisimilitude caught from the Penetralium of mystery, from being incapable of remaining content with half-knowledge. This pursued through volumes would perhaps take us no further than this, that with a great poet the sense of Beauty overcomes every other consideration, or rather obliterates all consideration." Keats, *The Complete Poetical Works and Letters of John Keats*, 277.

25. Nathan Schwartz-Salant, *The Mystery of Human Relationship* (New York: Routledge, 1998).

26. Ovid, *Fasti*, book 4, in *Roman Poetry C1st BC to C1st AD*, trans. Boyle (Cambridge, Mass.: Harvard University Press, 1931), 222ff.

27. Coleridge, *Letters of Samuel Taylor Coleridge*, 2:714.
To William Godwin . . . Dear Godwin I fear, your Tragedy 1 will find me in a very unfit state of mind to sit in Judgement on it. I have been, during the last 8 months, undergoing a process of intellectual exsiccation. In my long Illness I had compelled into hours of Delight many a sleepless, painful ____________________ 1 This was Abbas, King of Persia, which was not accepted for presentation at Drury Lane. hour of Darkness by chasing down metaphysical Game—and since then I have continued the Hunt, till I found myself unaware at the Root of Pure Mathematics—and up that tall smooth Tree, whose few poor Branches are all at it's [*sic*] very summit, am I climbing by pure adhesive strength of arms and thighs—still slipping down, still renewing my ascent.—You would not know me—! all sounds of similitude keep at such a distance from each other in my mind, that I have forgotten how to make a rhyme—I look at the Mountains (that visible God Almighty that looks in at all my windows) I look at the Mountains only for the Curves of their outlines; the Stars, as I behold them, form themselves into Triangles—and my hands are scarred with scratches from a Cat, whose back I was rubbing in the Dark in order to see whether the sparks from it were refrangible by a Prism. The Poet is dead in me—my imagination (or rather the Somewhat that had been imaginative) lies, like a Cold Snuff on the circular Rim of a Brass Candle-stick, without even a stink of Tallow to remind you that it was once cloathed & mitred with Flame. That is past by!—I was once a Volume of Gold Leaf, rising & riding on every breath of Fancy—but I have beaten myself back into weight & density, & now I sink in quicksilver, yea, remain squat and square on the earth amid the hurricane, that makes Oaks and Straws join in one Dance, fifty yards high in the Element. However, I will do what I can—Taste & Feeling have I none, but what I have, give I unto thee.—But I repeat, that I am unfit to decide on any but works of severe Logic. I write now to beg, that, if you have not sent your Tragedy, you may remember to send Antonio with it, which I have not yet seen—& likewise my Campbell's Pleasures of Hope, which Wordsworth wishes to see. Have you seen the second Volume of the Lyrical Ballads, & the Preface prefixed to the First?—I should judge of a man's Heart, and Intellect precisely according to the degree & intensity of the admiration, with which he read those poems—Perhaps, instead of Heart I should have said Taste, but when I think of The Brothers, of Ruth, and of Michael, I recur to the expression, & am enforced to say Heart. If I

die, and the Booksellers will give you any thing for my Life, be sure to say—"Wordsworth descended on him, like the Υω+Ƭθ σ+ˆεατόΥ from Heaven; by shewing to him what true Poetry was, he made him know, that he himself was no Poet." In your next Letter you will perhaps give me some hints respecting your prose Plans.—. God bless you & S. T. Coleridge I have inoculated my youngest child, Derwent, with the Cowpoxhe passed thro' it without any sickness.—I myself am the Slave of Rheumatism—indeed, tho' in a certain sense I am recovered from my Sickness, yet I have by no means recovered it. I congratulate you on the settlement of Davy in London.—I hope, that his enchanting manners will not draw too many Idlers round him, to harrass & vex his mornings.— . . . 1 P.S.—What is a fair Price—what might an Author of reputation fairly ask from a Bookseller for one Edition, of a 1000 Copies, of a five Shilling Book?—

28. Ibid., 2:694.

29. Charles Lamb letter to William Wordsworth, April 26, 1816. "I think his essentials not touched: he is very bad, but then he wonderfully picks up another day, and his face when he repeats his verses hath its ancient glory, an Archangel a little damaged."

30. C. G. Jung, *Jung on Alchemy*, ed. Nathan Schwartz-Salant (Princeton, NJ: Princeton University Press, 1995), 30. The Cybele-Attis myth seems to describe some of the problems along the way to the *mysterium coniunctionis* of opposites. Jung zeroes in on this myth to describe how the Father and Mother worlds seek reconciliation in the psyche of the alchemist. That mystery, in its Christian version, includes the still irreconcilable qualities of good and evil (Christ and the devil), as well as male and female, psyche and matter, human and divine, all of which are at the heart of *The Ancient Mariner*. As in alchemy, Coleridge's *Ancient Mariner* was an undercurrent to Coleridge's conscious Christianity, the figure of his Ancient Mariner being a version of the feminine-masculine alchemical redeemer, a "son of Tiamat." Jung writes, "Thus the filius philosophorum is not just the reflected image, in unsuitable material, of the son of God; on the contrary, this son of Tiamat reflects the features of the primordial maternal figure. Although he is decidedly hermaphroditic he has a masculine name—a sign that the chthonic underworld, having been rejected by the spirit and identified with evil, has a tendency to compromise. There is no mistaking the fact that he is a concession to the spiritual and masculine principle, even though he carries in himself the weight of the earth and the whole fabulous nature of primordial animality." Jung, *Collected Works*, vol. 12, *Psychology and Alchemy*, ed. Gerhard Adler, trans. R. F. C. Hull (Princeton, NJ: Princeton University Press, 1980), 61.

Chapter 13

1. "The Flower of Coleridge," *Art and Popular Culture*, accessed January 27, 2022, http://www.artandpopularculture.com/The_Flower_of_Coleridge.

2. Jung, *Collected Works*, 18:809.

3. "But I ask you, when do men fall on their brothers with mighty weapons and bloody acts? They do such if they do not know that their brother is themselves. They themselves are sacrificers, but they mutually do the service of sacrifice. They must all sacrifice each other since the time has not yet come when man puts the bloody knife into himself in order to sacrifice the one he kills in his brother. . . . The time is still not ripe. But through this blood sacrifice it should ripen. So long as it is possible to murder the brother instead of oneself, the time is not ripe. Frightful things must happen until men grow ripe. But anything else will not ripen humanity. Hence all this that takes place in these days must also be, so that the renewal can come." Jung, *The Red Book*, 239. Jung also addresses the psychological meaning of drinking blood in a ritual setting in his *Visions* seminars. Jung, *Visions*, 457, 95, 992.

4. Barbara Hannah, *Encounters with the Soul: Active Imagination as Developed by C. G. Jung* (New York: Chiron, 2015), 8.

5. Umail, *Corpus Alchemicum Arabicum*. Jung, *Collected Works*, 14:375

6. Jung, *Collected Works*, 14:362.

7. Ibid., 14:364.

8. "Whoever is not able to love himself is unworthy of loving other people and people kick him out of the house. And they are quite right. It is very difficult to love oneself, as it is very difficult to really love other people. But in as much as you can love yourself you can love other people; the proof is whether you can love yourself, whether you can stand yourself. This is exceedingly difficult; there is no meal worse than one's own flesh.

"Try to eat it in a ritual way, try to celebrate communion with yourself, eat your own flesh and drink your own blood—see how the thing tastes. You will marvel. Then you see what you are to your friend and relation; just as bad as you seem to yourself are you to them. Of course they are all blindfolded, . . . so they may not see the poison they eat in loving you; but if you know this, you can understand how important it is to be alone sometimes. It is the only way in which you can establish decent relations to other people. Otherwise, it is always a question, not of give and take, but of stealing." C. G. Jung, *Nietzsche's Zarathustra: Notes of the Seminar Given in 1934–1939*, ed. James L Jarrett (Princeton, NJ: Princeton University Press, 1988), 800.

9. "Because the carnal mind is enmity against God; for it is not subject to the law of God, nor indeed can be. So then, those who are in the flesh cannot please God. But you are not in the flesh but in the Spirit, if indeed

the Spirit of God dwells in you. Now if anyone does not have the Spirit of Christ, he is not His." Romans 8:7–9. "Ye adulterers and adulteresses, know ye not that friendship with the world is enmity with God? Whosoever therefore will be a friend of the world is the enemy of God." James 4:4.

10. Woodman, *Sanity, Madness, Transformation*, 48.

Chapter 14

1. "In schizophrenia that is not the case; the vessel is so badly broken that the pieces cannot be joined together again, it will remain in pieces. But in the beginning it is very much the same thing [as a normal process of dissociation in a state of emotion, normal because it does not last, it is put together again] and is also due as a rule to a too narrow mental condition . . . or something else happens which doesn't fit into suburbia, something unlikely, not foreseen, and then they go crazy because their own idea of the world has been knocked to pieces . . . if somebody has really exploded and is lying scattered on the road, sure enough there is no coming together again. And that is surely due, as I said, to a certain peculiar narrowness of mind and outlook which does not grant infinite possibilities to the deity, a mind which thinks God can be only good and therefore the world must be good because He has made it, and anything evil is only a mistake. Such foolish ideas." Jung, *Visions*, 1297.

2. Monika Wikman, *Pregnant Darkness: Alchemy and the Rebirth of Consciousness* (Berwick, Maine: Nicolas-Hays, 2004).

3. Abt, *Corpus Alchemicum Arabicum*, 33.

Chapter 15

John Keats, "The Fall of Hyperion: A Dream," in *John Keats: The Complete Poems*, ed. John Barnard (New York: Penguin Classics, 1977), 435.

1. Veronica Goodchild, *Eros and Chaos: The Sacred Mysteries and the Dark Side of Love* (Berwick, ME: Nicolas-Hays, 2001), 196.

2. Monika Wikman, *Pregnant Darkness: Alchemy and the Rebirth of Consciousness* (Berwick, Maine: Nicolas-Hays, 2004), 19.

3. Orpheus, *The Hymns of Orpheus*, trans. Thomas Taylor (Philadelphia: University of Pennsylvania Press, 1999).

4. When Jung describes the birth of depth psychology, he unintentionally translates *The Rime of the Ancient Mariner* into his uniquely beautiful blend of psychological-poetic prose. "Since the stars have fallen from heaven and our highest symbols have paled, a secret life holds sway in the unconscious. It is for this reason that we have a psychology today, and for this reason that we speak of the unconscious. All this discussion would be superfluous in an age or culture that possessed symbols. For these are

spirit from above; and at such a time, also, spirit is above. It would be a foolish and senseless undertaking for such people to wish to experience or investigate an unconscious that contains nothing but the silent, undisturbed sway of nature. But our unconscious conceals natural spirit, which is to say, spirit turned to water; and this spirit disturbs it. Heaven has become empty space to us, a fair memory of things that once were. But our heart glows, and a secret unrest gnaws at the roots of our being." Jung, *Collected Works*, 9:23.

5. Esther Harding, *The Parental Image* (Toronto: Inner City Books, 2003), 134.

6. Blaise Pascal, *Pensées and Other Writings*, ed. Anthony Levi, trans. Honor Levi (Oxford: Oxford University Press, 2008).

7. J. L. Haney, *Bibliography of Samuel Taylor Coleridge* (Philadelphia: For Private Circulation, 1903), 51. Letter to Benjamin Flower, December 11, 1796. Coleridge, *Letters of Samuel Taylor Coleridge*, 1:267.

Chapter 16

1. Coleridge, *Letters of Samuel Taylor Coleridge*, 1:352.

2. "At this moment my eyes were dwelling on the lovely Lace-work of those fair fair Elm-trees, so richly so softly black between me and the deep red Clouds & Light of the Horizon, with their intersticies of twilight Air made visible—and I received the solution of my difficulty, flashlike, in the word, BEAUTY! In the intuition of the Beautiful! This too is spiritual—and [by] the Goodness of God this is the short-hand, Hieroglyphic of Truth—the mediator between Truth and Feeling, the Head and the Heart—The sense [of] Beauty is implicit knowledge—a silent communion of the Spirit with the Spirit in Nature not without consciousness, tho' with the consciousness not successively unfolded! . . . —To a spiritual Woman it is Music—the intelligible Language of Memory, Hope, Desiderium / the rhythm of the Soul's movements." Raimonda Modiano, *Coleridge & the Concept of Nature* (London: Palgrave Macmillan, 1985), 29.

3. In alchemy, the "shining oil" is a symbol of the feminine soul, the *aqua divina*, the *aqua sapientiae*. Von Franz, *Aurora Consurgens*, 226.

4. "So this would be a true symbol, it would be the light of vision, of understanding, a form in which the magic fire could be contained; no longer the chthonic witchcraft of a merely emotional nature, but the pure light of truth." Jung, *Visions*, 696.

5. As Blake says, "Everything that lives is holy, life delights in life." William Blake, *The Four Zoas*, in, *William Blake: The Poetical Works*, ed. John Sampson (Oxford: Oxford University Press, 1908), 551.

6. "Thus the higher, the spiritual, the masculine inclines to the lower, the earthly, the feminine; and accordingly, the mother, who was anterior to the world of the father, accommodates herself to the male principle and, with the aid of the human spirit (alchemy or 'the philosophy'), produces a son not the antithesis of Christ but rather his chthonic counterpart, not a divine man but a fabulous being conforming to the nature of the primordial mother. And just as the redemption of man the microcosm is the task of the 'upper' son, so the 'lower' son has the function of a salvator macrocosmi." Jung, *Collected Works*, 12:23, par. 26.

7. Jung, *Visions*, 550.

8. "The End of Paganism," https://penelope.uchicago.edu/~grout/encyclopaedia_romana/greece/paganism/paganism.html#:~:text=There%20was%20no%20official%20proscription,or%20any%20city%20was%20permitted.

9. "She puts her arms about the serpent and says, 'You are beautiful to me,' not horrid or terrifying, but beautiful. She accepts the serpent, which shows that she is making friends with the element which threatened her before with complete destruction." Jung, *Visions*, 600.

10. See Abrams, *Natural Supernaturalism*.

11. "The most refined abstractions of logic conduct to a view of life, which, though startling to the apprehension, is, in fact, that which the habitual sense of its repeated combinations has extinguished in us. It strips, as it were, the painted curtain from this scene of things. I confess that I am one of those who am unable to refuse my assent to the conclusions of those philosophers who assert that nothing exists but as it is perceived. It is a decision against which all our persuasions struggle, and we must be long convicted before we can be convinced that the solid universe of external things is 'such stuff as dreams are made of.'" Percy Bysshe Shelley, *The Complete Works of Percy Bysshe Shelley: Prose*, vol. 6, ed. Roger Ingpen and Walter E. Peck (New York: Gordian Press, 1965), 194.

12. "Life, & the world, or whatever we call that which we are & feel, is an astonishing thing. The mist of familiarity obscures from us the wonder of our being. . . . Life, the great miracle, we admire not, because it is so miraculous. It is well that we are thus shielded by the familiarity of what is at once so certain and so unfathomable, from an astonishment which would otherwise absorb and overawe the function of that which is its object." Ibid., 193.

13. William Wordsworth, "Lines Composed a Few Miles above Tintern Abbey, On Revisiting the Banks of the Wye during a Tour, July 13, 1798."

14. William Wordsworth, "The Solitary," in *Prospectus*, reprinted in the 1814 preface to *The Excursion*.

15. "Some kinder casuists are pleased to say
In nameless print—that I have no devotion;
But set those persons down with me to pray,
And you shall see who has the properest notion
Of getting into heaven the shortest way;
My altars are the mountains and the ocean,
Earth, air, stars,—all that springs from the great Whole,
Who hath produced, and will receive the soul.

16. "So Man looks out in tree & herb & fish & bird & beast
Collecting up the scatter'd portions of his immortal body
Into the Elemental forms of everything that grows. . . .
And in the cries of birth & in the groans of death his voice
Is heard throughout the Universe: wherever a grass grows
Or a leaf buds, The Eternal Man is seen, is heard, is felt,
And all his sorrows, till he reassumes his ancient bliss.

17. William Blake letter to Trusler, August 29, 1799.

18. Shelley, *Adonais*, stanza 55.

19. "It is just this confrontation of object and subject, their mingling and identification, the resultant insight into the mysterious unity of ego and actuality, destiny and character, doing and happening, and thus into the mystery of reality as an operation of psyche—it is just this confrontation that is the alpha and omega of all psychoanalytic knowledge." Thomas Mann, "Freud and the Future," in *Essays of Three Decades* (New York: Alfred A. Knopf, 1976), 412.

20. Sonu Shamdasani, *Jung and the Making of Modern Psychology: The Dream of a Science* (Cambridge: Cambridge University Press, 2003), 167. Connections between Romanticism and psychoanalysis have been recognized by many. See, for example, Lionel Trilling in his chapter, "Freud and Literature" in *The Liberal Imagination*, where he notes that, "What we must deal with is nothing less than a whole Zeitgeist, a direction of thought. For psychoanalysis is one of the culminations of the Romanticist literature of the nineteenth century. If there is perhaps a contradiction in the idea of a science standing upon the shoulders of a literature which avows itself inimical to science in so many ways, the contradiction will be resolved if we remember that this literature, despite its avowals, was itself scientific in at least the sense of being passionately devoted to a research into the self." Lionel Trilling, *The Liberal Imagination* (New York: The New York Review of Books Classics, 2008), 35.

21. Jung, *Collected Works*, 9:23.

22. Marlo and Kline list some of the important therapeutic effects of synchronistic events in the therapeutic relationship. "Utilizing synchronic-

ity in therapy can be associated with several positive therapeutic effects. First, it is helpful in focusing therapy on core issues and in highlighting the salience and meaning of such issues. Second, it validates the patient's subjective experience, which, in turn, promotes psychological growth. Third, it can facilitate a connection between the patient and therapist and deepen their work. Finally, by perceiving events and relationships as synchronistic, it conveys that life events, including the patient's symptoms and predicaments, are inherently meaningful and purposeful. It may, therefore, directly address the despair, pain, and meaninglessness that frequently lead people to seek psychotherapy." H. Marlo and J. S. Kline, "Synchronicity and Psychotherapy: Unconscious Communication in the Psychotherapeutic Relationship," *Psychotherapy: Theory, Research, Practice, Training* 35, no. 1 (1998): 13–22.

23. "As a totality, the self is by definition always a complexio oppositorum, and the more consciousness insists on its own luminous nature and lays claim to moral authority, the more the self will appear as something dark and menacing." Jung, *Collected Works*, 11:443.

24. Woodman makes the point directly. "In the mythopoetic achievement of the Romantics . . . dwells . . . the birth of a modern consciousness which the twenty-first century must finally learn to inhabit if human life is to continue, not without God, but with a conscious understanding of the human." Woodman, *Sanity, Madness, Transformation*, xx.

Chapter 17

1. Ronald Douglas Gray, *Goethe the Alchemist: A Study of Alchemical Symbolism in Goethe's Literary and Scientific Works* (Cambridge: Cambridge University Press, 2010), 19.

2. "But when this wave is raised from the water by the wind and made pregnant in its nature, and has received within itself the reproductive power of the feminine, it retains the light scattered from on high together with the fragrance of the spirit, and that is Nous given shape in various forms. This [light] is a perfect God, who is brought down from the unbegotten light on high and from the spirit into man's nature as into a temple, by the power of nature and the movement of the wind. It is engendered from the water and commingled and mixed with the bodies as if it were the salt of all created things, and a light of the darkness struggling to be freed from the bodies, and not able to find a way out. For some very small spark of the light is mingled with the fragrance from above. . . . Therefore every thought and care of the light from above is how and in what way the Nous may be delivered from the death of the sinful and dark body, from the father below, who

is the wind which raised up the waves in tumult and terror, and begot Nous his own perfect son, who is yet not his own son in substance. For he was a ray of light from on high, from that perfect light overpowered in the dark and terrible, bitter polluted water, and a shining spirit carried away over the water." Hippolytus, *Elenchos*, vol. 5, 19, 14ff. Quoted in Jung, *Collected Works*, 14:244.

3. "In the Beginning God created the Universal Spirit or the Universal Agent of Nature, the Soul of the Universe. This is the first emanation of Divine Light; it is a unity and immortal, capable of manifesting itself, when moved or agitated, into Light and Fire. It is multipliable and yet is and remains but one. It is Omnipresent and yet occupies no visible space or room, except when manifested or multiplied in its third principle, Fire. It has the power of becoming material and of returning again to universality." Jeffrey Raff, *The Wedding of Sophia: The Divine Feminine in Psychoidal Alchemy* (Lake Worth, Fla.: Nicolas-Hays), 46.

4. Hildegard von Bingen, *Scivias*, trans. Mother Columba Hart and Jane Bishop (Mahwah, NJ: Paulist Press, 1990), *De Operitione Dei*, part 1, vision 1.

Iterumque vocem de cello	And again I heard a voice from heaven
Me sic docentem audivi, et dixit:	Instructing me. And it said:
Scribe ergo secundum me in modum hunc.	Write, therefore, what I tell you in this manner.
Et vidi velut in medio australis aeris	And I saw amid the southern airs,
Pulcram mirificamque inmisterio dei	in the mystery of God a beautiful, wondrous
Imaginem quasi hominis formam,	figure with a human form,
Cuius facies tante pulcritudinis et claritatis erat,	whose face was so lovely and bright
Ut facilius solem quam ipsam inspicere possem.	that it would be easier to look at the sun;
Et curculus amplus aureique coloris	and a broad circlet the color of gold
Caput eiusdam faciei circumdederat	surrounded her head and face.
Et imago hec dicebat:	And the figure spoke thus:
Ego summa et ignea vis	I am the great and fiery power
Que omnes viventes scintillas accendi	who has kindled every living spark

et nulla mortalia efflavi	and extinguished nothing mortal—
sed illa diiudico ut sunt.	for I judge these things as they are.
Circueuntem circulum	In circling circles
Cum superioribus pennies meis,	with my upper wings
Id est cum sapientia,	(that is, with Wisdom)
Circumvolans recte ipsum ordinavi.	I fly around, ordaining all things rightly.

5. "These sparks Khunrath explains as 'radii atque scintillae' of the 'anima catholica,' the world-soul, which is identical to the spirit of God . . . They were seeds of light broadcast into the chaos, which Khunrath calls, 'mundi future seminarium' (the seed plot of a world to come). One such spark is the human mind. The arcane substance—the watery earth or earthy water (limus: mud) of the World Essence—is 'universally animated' by the 'fiery spark of the soul of the world,' in accordance with the Wisdom of Solomon 1:7: 'For the Spirit of the Lord filleth the world.' In the 'Water of the Art,' in 'our Water,' which is also the chaos, there are to be found the 'fiery sparks of the soul of the world as pure Formae Rerum essentiales.' . . . numinosity entails luminosity . . . Khunrath writes: 'There be . . . Scintillae Animae Mundi igneae, Luminis nimirum Naturae, fiery sparks of the world soul, i.e. of the light of nature . . . dispersed or sprinkled in and throughout the structure of the great world into all fruits of the elements everywhere.' The sparks come from the 'Ruach Elohim,' the Spirit of God." C. G. Jung, "On the Nature of the Psyche," in *Collected Works*, 8:190.

6. Exodus 3:14 (English Standard Version).

7. Coleridge was also inclined to intuitions such as Brand's that there might be something of value in the "fallen" human body. Taking the alchemical dictum *in stercore invenitur* quite literally, as Brand also did, Coleridge writes of being enraptured by his own urine: "What a beautiful Thing urine is, in a Pot, brown, yellow, transpicuous, the Image, diamond shaped of the Candle in it, especially, as it now appeared, I have emptied the Snuffers into it & the Snuff floating about, painting all-shaped Shadows on the Bottom." As he stares into his chamber pot as if it were an alchemical flask, Coleridge falls into a revelation of beauty in the putrid. He is mesmerized by "the Image" of a diamond-shaped candle appearing on the surface as shadows of ashes paint the bottom. What an alchemist! Coleridge, *Coleridge's Notebooks*, 52.

8. "Robert Boyle," Science History Institute, accessed February 5, 2023, https://www.sciencehistory.org/historical-profile/robert-boyle#:~:text

=Indeed%20he%20practiced%20alchemy%20until,universe%20according%20to%20definite%20laws.

9. William Y-Worth, *Chymicus Rationalis . . . In Which Is Contained, A Philosophical Description of the Astrum Lunare Microcosmicum, or Phospheros* (London, 1692). Cited in "The Preparation of Phosphorus," accessed January 17, 2022, www.levity.com/alchemy/phosphor.html.

10. In 2013, for example, Rupert Sheldrake's talk based on his book *The Science Delusion* for a TEDx event at Whitechapel, London, called "Challenging Existing Paradigms" explicitly challenged the materialist belief system and was banned by TEDx. "TED 'Bans' the Science Delusion," accessed February 11, 2023, https://www.sheldrake.org/reactions/tedx-whitechapel-the-banned-talk.

11. Coleridge, *Letters of Samuel Taylor Coleridge*, 1:352.

12. Abrams, *Natural Supernaturalism*, 269.

13. Albert Einstein, *Relativity: The Special and General Theory—A Clear Explanation That Anyone Can Understand* (New York: Wings Books, 1988), 292.

14. Scientific research is based on the idea "that everything that takes place is determined by laws of nature, and therefore this holds for the actions of people. For this reason, a research scientist will hardly be inclined to believe that events could be influenced by a prayer, i.e. by a wish addressed to a supernatural being. However, it must be admitted that our actual knowledge of these laws is only imperfect and fragmentary, so that, actually, the belief in the existence of basic all-embracing laws in nature also rests on a sort of faith. All the same this faith has been largely justified so far by the success of scientific research. But, on the other hand, everyone who is seriously involved in the pursuit of science becomes convinced that a spirit is manifest in the laws of the universe—a spirit vastly superior to that of man, and one in the face of which we with our modest powers must feel humble. In this way the pursuit of science leads to a religious feeling of a special sort, which is indeed quite different from the religiosity of someone more naive." Albert Einstein, *Albert Einstein: The Human Side* (Princeton, NJ: Princeton University Press, 2013), 32–33.

"But whoever has undergone the intense experience of successful advance made in this domain is moved by profound reverence for the rationality made manifest in existence. By way of the understanding he achieves a far-reaching emancipation from the shackles of personal hopes and desires, and thereby attains that humble attitude of mind towards the grandeur of reason incarnate in existence which, in its profoundest depths, is inaccessible to man. This attitude, however, appears to me to be religious in the highest sense of the word. Thus it seems to me that science not only purifies the religious impulse of the dross of its anthropomorphism, but also contributes to a religious spiritualization of our understanding of life." Albert Einstein, "Science and Religion," *Nature* 146 (1940): 605–7.

"I maintain that the cosmic religious feeling is the strongest and noblest motive for scientific research. . . . In my view, it is the most important function of art and science to awaken this feeling and keep it alive in those who are receptive to it." Albert Einstein, "Religion and Science," *New York Times*, November 9, 1930, 1.

15. Jung writes to Wolfgang Pauli on October 14, 1935, "The radioactive nucleus is an excellent symbol for the source of energy of the collective unconscious, the ultimate external stratum of which appears as individual consciousness. As a symbol, it indicates that consciousness does not grow out of any activity that is inherent to it; rather, it is constantly being produced by an energy that comes from the depths of the unconscious and has thus been depicted in the form of rays since time immemorial. The center is thus represented by the Greek Gnostics as *Spinther* (the spark) or as *Phos archetypon* (the archetypal light)." C. G. Jung and Wolfgang Pauli, *Atom and Archetype: The Pauli/Jung Letters 1932–1958*, ed. C. A. Meier (Princeton, NJ: Princeton University Press, 2001), 14.

16. Ray Kurzweil, "Do You Believe in God?," Singularity University, https://www.youtube.com/watch?v=-JvfdmPp3d8. Kurzweil's reaction is not scientifically idiosyncratic. Einstein, for example, writes of "cosmic religious feeling" as the motive force behind all creative scientific inquiry "My feeling is religious insofar as I am imbued with the insufficiency of the human mind to understand more deeply the harmony of the universe which we try to formulate as 'laws of nature.'" Peter Galison, Gerald James Holton, and Silvan S. Schweber, *Einstein for the 21st Century: His Legacy in Science, Art, and Modern Culture* (Princeton, NJ: Princeton University Press, 2008), 37.

17. Coleridge, *Biographia Literaria* (1983), 183.

18. Ibid., 129.

19. Coleridge, "Definition of Miracle," in *The Complete Works of Samuel Taylor Coleridge*, 5:544.

20. Coleridge, *The Notebooks of Samuel Taylor Coleridge*, 3:3325.

21. "I seem to myself to behold in the quiet objects, on which I am gazing, more than an arbitrary illustration, more than a mere simile, the work of my own fancy. I feel an awe, as if there were before my eyes the same power as that of the reason—the same power in a lower dignity, and therefore a symbol established in the truth of things. I feel it alike, whether I contemplate a single tree or flower, or meditate on vegetation throughout the world, as one of the

great organs of the life of nature." Kathleen Coburn, *Coleridge: A Collection of Critical Essays* (New York: Prentice-Hall, 1977), 177.

22. Samuel Taylor Coleridge, *The Complete Works of Samuel Taylor Coleridge*, vol. 2, ed. W. G. T. Shedd (New York: 1853), 469.

Chapter 18

1. Philo, *Questions and Answers on Exodus*, trans. Ralph Marcus (Cambridge, Mass: Harvard University Press, 1953), 15. In the *Red Book*, Jung also identifies psychological qualities in terms of gender: The "celestial soul . . . appearing in the form of a bird" is masculine, "the daimon of sexuality," which appears as a serpent, is feminine. "The daimon of sexuality approaches our soul as a serpent. She is half human soul and is called thought-desire. The daimon of spirituality descends into our soul as the white bird. He is half human soul and is called desire-thought." Jung, *The Red Book*, 354.

2. "That it is by a negation and voluntary Act of *no*-thinking that we think of earth, air, water, &c as dead—It is necessary for our limited powers of consciousness that we should be brought to this negative state, & that should pass into Custom—but likewise necessary that at times we should awake & step forward—& this is effected by Poetry & Religion /—. The Extenders of Consciousness—Sorrow, Sickness, Poetry, Religion." Coleridge, *Notebooks*, vol. 3, 3630.

3. "From this state hast thou fallen! Such shouldst thou still become, thyself all permeable to a holier power! . . . But what the plant is on its own and unconsciously—that must thou make thyself to become." Abrams, *Natural Supernaturalism*, 270.

4. "The same Providence that visited Jacob by Signs, Visions, and guiding Impulses, formed him with an original aptitude for & susceptibility of the same.—N.B. By feminine qualities I mean nothing detractory—no participation in the Effeminate. In the best and greatest of men, most eminently—and less so, yet still present in all but such [as] are below the average worth of Men, there is a feminine Ingredient.—There is a Woman in the Man—tho' not perhaps the Man in the Woman—Adam therefore loved Eve—and it is the Feminine in us even now, that makes every Adam love his Eve, and crave for an Eve—Why, I have inserted the dubious 'perhaps'—why, it should be less accordant with truth to say, that in every good Woman there is the Man as an Under-song, than to say that in every true and manly Man there is a translucent Under-tint of the Woman—this would furnish matter for a very interesting little Essay on sexual Psychology." Coleridge, *Samuel Taylor Coleridge—The Major Works*, 560.

5. Isabell Naumann, "Assumption: History of Doctrine," https://udayton.edu/imri/mary/a/assumption-history-of-doctrine.php.

6. "The power of art," Coleridge writes, "reveals itself in the balance or reconcilement of opposite or discordant qualities." Samuel Taylor Coleridge, *Biographia Literaria: The Collected Works of Samuel Taylor Coleridge*, ed. James Engell and Jackson Bate (Princeton, NJ: Princeton University Press, 1985), 2:5. "Art might be defined as of a middle quality between a thought and a thing." Samuel Taylor Coleridge, "On Poesy or Art," in *The Literary Remains of Samuel Taylor Coleridge*.

7. "The illustration in Pandora points to the great secret which the alchemists dimly felt was implicit in the Assumption. The proverbial darkness of sublunary matter has always been associated with the 'prince of this world,' the devil. He is the metaphysical figure who is excluded from the Trinity but who, as the counterpart of Christ, is the sine qua non of the drama of redemption. . . . Dorn, however, saw in the quaternity the absolute opposite of the Trinity namely, the feminine principle, which seemed to him 'of the devil,' for which reason he called the devil the 'four horned serpent.' . . . Dorn puts into words what is merely hinted at in the Pandora illustration." Jung, *Collected Works*, 14:188.

8. "One could have known for a long time that there was a deep longing in the masses for an intercessor and mediatrix who would at last take her place alongside the Holy Trinity and be received as the 'Queen of heaven and Bride at the heavenly court.' For more than a thousand years it has been taken for granted that the Mother of God dwelt there. I consider it to be the most important religious event since the Reformation." Jung, *Collected Works*, 11:264. In *Mysterium Coniunctionis*, Jung follows this train of thought. The Assumption "is exactly what the adepts recognized as being the secret of their coniunctio. . . . The correspondence is indeed so great that the old Masters could legitimately have declared that the new dogma has written the Hermetic secret in the skies." Jung, *Collected Works*, 14:466.

9. Referring to the lower half of the *Pandora* image, Jung comments, "This is without doubt the *anima mundi* who has been freed from the shackles of matter, the *filius macrocosmi*, or Mercurius-Anthropos, who, because of his double nature, is not only spiritual and physical but unites in himself the morally highest and lowest." Jung, *Collected Works*, 12:396.

10. Jung, *Collected Works*, 12:365, fig. 232.

11. Jung, *Collected Works*, 14:419–20.

12. "The new dogma," Jung comments, "expresses a renewed hope for the fulfillment of that yearning for peace which stirs deep down in the soul, and for a resolution of the threatening tension between the opposites." Jung, *Collected Works*, 11:465.

13. "As a symbol of the monistic union of matter and soul," Pauli writes in a 1953 letter to Jung concerning the dogma of the Assumption, "this *assumptio* has an even deeper meaning for me."

14. For an amazing contemporary image of this symbolism, see Anselm Kiefer's painting *Quaternity* (1973).

15. "Therefore the Hebrew prophetess cried without restraint, 'One becomes two, two becomes three, and out of the third comes the One as the fourth.' . . . The one joins the three as the fourth and thus produces the synthesis of the four in a unity." "The *Assumptio Mariae* paves the way not only for the divinity of the *Theotokos* (i.e., her ultimate recognition as a goddess), but also for the quaternity. At the same time, matter is included in the metaphysical realm, together with the corrupting principle of the cosmos, evil." Jung, *Collected Works*, 11:171.

16. It is abundantly clear from *The Rime of the Ancient Mariner* that, as Jung puts it, "the one that joins to the three has a difficult form." Andreas Schweizer and Regine Schweizer-Vüllers, *Stone by Stone: Reflections on the Psychology of C. G. Jung* (Einsiedeln: Daimon-Verlag, 2017), 180.

17. Jung, "A Psychological Approach to the Dogma of the Trinity," in *Collected Works*, 11:121.

18. Jung, *Collected Works*, 13:228.

19. Jung, *Collected Works*, 11:314.

20. According to Jung in his essay "The Spirit Mercurius," "The multiple aspects of Mercurius may be summarized as follows:

(1) Mercurius consists of all conceivable opposites. He is thus quite obviously a duality, but is named a unity in spite of the fact that his innumerable inner contradictions can dramatically fly apart into an equal number of disparate and apparently independent figures.
(2) He is both material and spiritual.
(3) He is the process by which the lower and material is transformed into the higher and spiritual, and vice versa.
(4) He is the devil, a redeeming psychopomp, an evasive trickster, and God's reflection in physical nature.
(5) He is also the reflection of a mystical experience of the artifex that coincides with the opus alchymicum.
(6) As such, he represents on the one hand the self and on the other the individuation process and, because of the limitless number of his names, also the collective unconscious.

Jung, "The Spirit Mercurius," in *Collected Works*, 13:237.

21. Ibid., 13:245.

22. "The real subject of Hermetic philosophy is the *coniunctio oppositorum* . . . This is precisely the figure we meet in the Apocalypse as the son of

the sun-woman . . . the bringing together of the light and the dark." "The nuptial union in the *thalamus* (bridal-chamber) signifies the *hierosgamos*, and this in turn is the first step towards incarnation, towards the birth of the saviour who, since antiquity, was thought of as the *filius solis et lunae*, the *filius sapientiae*, and the equivalent of Christ. When, therefore, a longing for the exaltation of the Mother of God passes through the people, this tendency, if thought to its logical conclusion, means the desire for the birth of a saviour, a peacemaker, a '*mediator pacem faciens inter inimicos*' [a mediator making peace between enemies]. Although he is already born in the pleroma, his birth in time can only be accomplished when it is perceived, recognized, and declared by man." Jung, *Collected Works*, 11:454, 462.

23. "Evil today has become a visible Great Power. One half of humanity battens and grows strong on a doctrine fabricated by human ratiocination; the other half sickens from the lack of a myth commensurate with the situation. The Christian nations have come to a sorry pass; their Christianity slumbers and has neglected to develop its myth further in the course of the centuries. Those who gave expression to the dark stirrings of growth in mythic ideas were refused a hearing; Gioacchino da Fiore, Meister Eckhart, Jacob Boehme, and many others have remained obscurantists for the majority. The only ray of light is Pius XII and his dogma. But people do not even know what I am referring to when I say this. They do not realize that a myth is dead if it no longer lives and grows." Jung, *Memories, Dreams, Reflections*, 331.

24. "Filling the conscious mind with ideal conceptions is a characteristic of Western theosophy, but not the confrontation with the shadow and the world of darkness. One does not become enlightened by imagining figures of light, but by making the darkness conscious. The later procedure, however, is disagreeable and therefore not popular." Jung, "The Philosophical Tree," in *Collected Works*, 13:265.

25. Anthony Storr, ed., *The Essential Jung* (Princeton, NJ: Princeton University Press, 1983), 322.

26. Ibid., 322–23. "The dogmatization of the *Assumptio Mariae* points to the *hierosgamos* [holy wedding] in the pleroma, and this in turn implies . . . the future birth of the divine child, who, in accordance with the divine trend towards incarnation, will choose as his birthplace the empirical man. The metaphysical process is known to the psychology of the unconscious as the individuation process. . . . The birth of the saviour who, since antiquity, was thought of as the *filius solis et lunae*, the *filius sapientiae*, and the equivalent of Christ. When, therefore, a longing for the exaltation of the Mother of God passes through the people, this tendency, if thought to its logical conclusion, means the desire for the birth of a saviour,

a peacemaker, a 'mediator *pacem faciens inter inimicos.*' Although he is already born in the pleroma, his birth in time can only be accomplished when it is perceived, recognized, and declared by man." Jung, *Collected Works*, 11:461.

27. See Woodman, "Blake's Fourfold Body," in *Sanity, Madness, Transformation*, 86–109, and Anne K. Mellor, "The Human Form Divine and the Structure of Blake's Jerusalem," *Studies in English Literature, 1500–1900* 11, no. 4 (1971): 595–620.

28. "On the occasion of the entry of the Mother of God into the heavenly bridal-chamber, he [the Protestant] should bend to the great task of reinterpreting all the Christian traditions. . . . This is a case, if there ever was one, where psychological understanding is needed, because the mythologem coming to light is so obvious that we must be deliberately blinding ourselves if we cannot see its symbolic nature and interpret it in symbolic terms." Jung, *Collected Works*, 11:467. "She is 'a woman clothed with the sun.' Note the simple statement 'a woman'—an ordinary woman, not a goddess and not an eternal virgin immaculately conceived. No special precautions exempting her from complete womanhood are noticeable, except the cosmic and naturalistic attributes which mark her as *an anima mundi* and peer of the primordial cosmic man, or Anthropos. She is the feminine Anthropos, the counterpart of the masculine principle." Jung, *Collected Works*, 11:439.

29. "And there appeared a great wonder in heaven: a woman clothed with the sun, and the moon under her feet, and upon her head a crown of twelve stars." Book of Revelation 12:1 (King James Version). The woman is pregnant and about to give birth, "travailing in birth, and pained to be delivered." Book of Revelation 12:2.

30. I expand on this dream and its connection to the Romantic imagination in my review of Woodman's book *Sanity, Madness, Transformation*. Thomas Elsner, "The Voice That in Madness Is Wanting," *Jung Journal* 2, no. 3 (Summer 2008): 98–122.

31. "The series of eight incarnations of the 'true prophet' is distinguished by the special position of the eighth, namely Christ. The eighth prophet is not merely the last of the series; he corresponds to the first and is at the same time the fulfillment of the seven, and signifies the entry into a new order. I have shown in *Psychology and Alchemy* (pars. 200ff) with the help of a modern dream, that whereas the seven form an uninterrupted series, the step to the eighth involves hesitation or uncertainty and is a repetition of the same phenomenon that occurs with three and four (the Axiom of Maria). It is very remarkable that we meet it again in the Taoist series of 'eight immortals' (hsien-yen): the seven are great sages or saints who dwell

in heaven or on the earth, but the eighth is a girl who sweeps up the fallen flowers at the southern gate of heaven. The parallel to this is Grimm's tale of the seven ravens: there the seven brothers have one sister. One is reminded in this connection of Sophia, of whom Irenaeus says: 'This mother they also call the Ogdoad, Sophia, Terra, Jerusalem, Holy Spirit, and, with a masculine reference, Lord.' She is 'below and outside the Pleroma.' The same thought occurs in connection with the seven planets in Celsus's description of the 'diagram of the Ophites,' attacked by Origen." Jung, *Collected Works*, 14:400–401.

"In the introduction to his diagram Celsus reports on the idea, found among the Persians and in the Mithraic mysteries, of a stairway with seven doors and an eighth door at the top. The first door was Saturn and was correlated with lead, and so on. The seventh door was gold and signified the sun. The colours are also mentioned. The stairway represents the 'passage of the soul' (animae transitus). The eighth door corresponds to the sphere of the fixed stars." Jung, *Collected Works*, 14:403. "This may be a cogent reason why the eighth is feminine: it is the mother of a new series [the week, the musical octave]. In Clement's line of prophets the eighth is Christ. As the first and second Adam he rounds off the series of seven, just as, according to Gregory the Great, he, 'coming in the flesh, joined the Pleiades, for he had within himself, at once and for ever, the works of the sevenfold Holy Spirit.'" Jung, *Collected Works*, 14:404.

32. Coleridge, "On Poesy or Art." See Heninger, "A Jungian Reading of 'Kubla Khan,'" 360.

33. "The dogmatization of the *Assumptio Mariae* points to the hieros gamos in the pleroma, and this in turn implies, as we have said, the future birth of the divine child, who, in accordance with the divine trend towards incarnation, will choose as his birthplace the empirical man. The metaphysical process is known to the psychology of the unconscious as the individuation process." Jung, *Collected Works*, 11:467.

Chapter 19

1. "At this moment my eyes were dwelling on the lovely Lace-work of those fair fair Elm-trees, so richly so softly black between me and the deep red Clouds & Light of the Horizon, with their intersticies of twilight Air made visible—and I received the solution of my difficulty, flashlike, in the word, BEAUTY! In the intuition of the Beautiful! This too is spiritual—and [by] the Goodness of God this is the short-hand, Hieroglyphic of Truth—the mediator between Truth and Feeling, the Head and the Heart—The sense [of] Beauty is implicit knowledge—a silent communion of the Spirit

with the Spirit in Nature not without consciousness, tho' with the consciousness not successively unfolded! . . . —To a spiritual Woman it is Music—the intelligible Language of Memory, Hope, Desiderium / the rhythm of the Soul's movements." Modiano, *Coleridge and the Concept of Nature*, 29.

Chapter 20

1. Samuel Taylor Coleridge, *Collected Letters of Samuel Taylor Coleridge*, ed. E. L. Griggs (Oxford: Oxford University Press, 1956–71), 545.

2. Mary Shelley, *Frankenstein; or, The Modern Prometheus*, vol. 1 (London: Lackington, Hughes, Harding, Mavor & Jones, 1818), 103.

3. Mary Shelley, *Frankenstein: A Longman Cultural Edition*, ed. Susan J. Wolfson (Harlow, UK: Longman, 2002).

4. Shelley, *Prometheus Unbound*, in *The Complete Poems of Percy Bysshe Shelley*, act 1, scene 1, lines 195–203. Here the voice of Earth speaks of Demeter, revealing the life in the underworld, the collective unconscious.

For know there are two worlds of life and death:
One that which thou beholdest; but the other
Is underneath the grave, where do inhabit
The shadows of all forms that think and live
Till death unite them and they part no more;
Dreams and the light imaginings of men,
And all that faith creates or love desires,
Terrible, strange, sublime and beauteous shapes.
There thou art, and dost hang, a writhing shade.

5. Percy Bysshe Shelley, *Adonais: An Elegy on the Death of John Keats*, in *Shelley: Poems and Prose*, ed. Jack Donovan (New York: Penguin Classics, 2017), 31, lines 274–79.

6. Schwartz-Salant, *The Mystery of Human Relationship.*

7. Leonard Cohen, "Hallelujah" (1984).

8. Jung, *The Red Book*, 233.

9. "While I am awake, by patience, employment, effort of mind, and walking I can keep *the fiend* at Arm's length; but the Night is my Hell, Sleep my tormenting Angel. Three nights out of four I fall asleep, struggling to lie awake—and my frequent Night-screams have almost made me a nuisance in my own House. Dreams with me are no Shadows, but the very Substances and foot-thick Calamities of my life." R. B. Litchfield, *Tom Wedgwood: The First Photographer: An Account of His Life, His Discovery and His Friendship with Samuel Taylor Coleridge* (New York: Kessinger Publishing, 2010), 147.

10. "A moral evil is an evil that has its origin in a will. An evil common to all must have a ground common to all. But the actual existence of moral evil we are bound in conscience to admit; and that there is an evil common to all is a fact; and this evil must therefore have a common ground. Now this evil ground cannot originate in the divine Will: it must therefore be referred to the will of man. And this evil ground we call original sin. It is a mystery, that is, a fact, which we see, but cannot explain; and the doctrine a truth which we apprehend, but can neither comprehend nor communicate." Coleridge, *Aids to Reflection*, in *The Collected Works of Samuel Taylor Coleridge*, 9:288.

11. Ibid., 3:490.

12. The Global Library of Women's Medicine: An Expert Resource for Medical Professionals, "Opium Tincture, Deodorized (Laudanum): Indications and Dosages," accessed January 21, 2022, https://glowm.com/resources/glowm/cd/pages/drugs/o006.html.

13. Coleridge, *The Notebooks of Samuel Taylor Coleridge*, vol. 2.

14. Samuel Taylor Coleridge, *Collected Letters of Samuel Taylor Coleridge*, vol. 3, *1807–1814*, ed. Earl Leslie Griggs (Oxford: Clarendon Press, 1959), 476–77.

15. Letter to J. J. Morgan, May 15, 1814. Ibid., 491.

16. Ibid., 6:894–95.

17. Percy Bysshe Shelley, "Letter to Maria Gisborne, 1820," in *The Poems of Shelley*, ed. Jack Donovan and Kelvin Everest (New York: Routledge, 2011), 1:207.

18. Letter to Wordsworth, April 26, 1816. Charles Lamb and Mary Anne Lamb, *Letters of Charles and Mary Lamb*, vol. 3, *1809–1817*, ed. E. W. Marrs (Ithaca, NY: Cornell University Press, 1978).

Chapter 21

1. Nietzsche, *Thus Spoke Zarathustra*, 3–7.

2. "The moment, when the Soul begins to be sufficiently self-conscious, to ask concerning itself, & its relation, is the moment of its *intellectual* arrival into the World—Its *Being*—enigmatic as it must seem—is posterior to its *existence*—. Suppose the shipwrecked man stunned, & for many weeks in a state of Idiotcy or utter loss of Thought and Memory—& then gradually awakened." Coleridge, *The Notebooks of Samuel Taylor Coleridge*, 3:3594.

3. Holmes, *Coleridge: Early Visions*, 150.

4. "Third comes the kind of madness that is possession by the Muses, which takes a tender virgin soul and awakens it to a Bacchic frenzy of songs

and poetry that glorifies the achievements of the past and teaches them to future generations. If anyone comes to the gates of poetry and expects to become an adequate poet by acquiring expert knowledge of the subject without the Muses' madness, he will fail, and his self-controlled verses will be eclipsed by the poetry of men who have been driven out of their minds."

5. "The breath whose might I have invoked in song
Descends on me; my spirit's bark is driven,
Far from the shore, far from the trembling throng
Whose sails were never to the tempest given;
The massy earth and sphered skies are riven!
I am borne darkly, fearfully, afar;
Whilst, burning through the inmost veil of Heaven,
The soul of Adonais, like a star,
Beacons from the abode where the Eternal are.

Shelley, *Adonais*, in *Shelley's Poetry and Prose.*

6. "The crisis of Romanticism lay in consciousness. The problem lay not in what Shelley calls, 'the mind in creation,' . . . The problem lay in bringing a critical consciousness to bear upon it." Woodman, *Sanity, Madness, Transformation*, 38.

7. Letter to J. J. Green, March 29, 1832. Coleridge, *Collected Letters*, 6:895.

8. Earl Leslie Griggs, *Wordsworth and Coleridge* (Princeton, NJ: Princeton University Press, 1939), 155.

9. Quoted in Schwartz-Salant, *The Mystery of Human Relationship: Alchemy and the Transformation of the Self*, 36.

10. Jung, *Memories, Dreams, Reflections*, 356.

11. "All my writings may be considered tasks that assailed me from within myself. They represent a compensation for our times, and I have been impelled to say what no one wants to hear. . . . I knew that what I said would be unwelcome, for it is difficult for people of our times to accept the counterweight to the conscious world." Ibid., 222.

12. Jung, *The Red Book*, 330.

13. Peter Kingsley, *Catafalque: Carl Jung and the End of Humanity* (London: Catafalque Press, 2021), 8. In his autobiography, Jung describes the loneliness inherent in the confrontation with the unconscious in more general terms. "The images of the unconscious place a heavy burden on a man. Failure to understand them, or a shirking of responsibility, deprives him of his wholeness and imposes a painful fragmentariness on his life." Jung, *Memories, Dreams, Reflections*, 193.

14. Coleridge, *Biographia Literaria* (1906), 74.

15. [Ginsberg]:

"There was this trip laid on it that there were dope fiends. Anybody who had that altered consciousness was a sort of fiend. That was the *official* terminology and conception. Now a fiend—that's a very strange category of human being. Even the Nazis didn't have fiends; they had Jews, but they didn't have human beings who were actual fiends. What is a fiend?" Ginsberg leaped up and grabbed a massive unabridged dictionary from the wall, them shuffled to the 'F' section.

"It's a horrific category, indicating some kind of strange reality, or almost science-fiction distortion of reality. It has a very funny association. Let's see the origin of the word. Hmmm—fiend. 1. Satan; the Devil. Any evil spirit. A diabolically cruel or wicked person. So it had to do with the devil and with the diabolic. So it's a kind of Catholic concept of some unremediable extreme evil, fixed, eternal evil. The origin is from the Icelandic—to hate. Ohhh. Well, okay, so that was dope fiends; that means the Narcotics Department was cultivating—were using—a word which has as its root the word 'hatred.' One who smoked marijuana in the forties would naturally be affected by this giant official government propaganda, which was reproduced in every media at great length.

". . . In 1947, walking on the Columbia campus after having smoked a little grass, I knew I was the only person in that entire several acres of 20,000 intelligent scholars who was in this particular state of consciousness. Naturally I wondered if I were some kind of a satanic fiend, some hateful satanic aberration of consciousness, to be the only one who had smoked this strange preparation. . . . It was like being part of a cosmic conspiracy or Gnostic conspiracy to resurrect a lost art or a lost knowledge or a lost consciousness. One was very aware of all that, but at the same time, being human, naturally doubting one's role. Is this the right thing to do? Have I made a pact with the devil? What's going on here?" Larry "Ratso" Sloman, *Reefer Madness: A History of Marijuana* (New York: St. Martin's Griffin, 1998), 176–77.

16. Heraclitus, *The Art and Thought of Heraclitus*, ed. Charles H. Kahn (Cambridge: Cambridge University Press, 1981), 95.

17. Matthew 8:27 (King James Version).

18. Jung, *The Collected Works of C. G. Jung*, 11:460.

19. "The life of the divine child, which you have eaten, will feel like glowing coals within you. It will burn inside you like a terrible, inextinguishable fire. But despite all the torment, you cannot let it be, since it will not let you be. From this you will understand that your God is alive and that your soul has begun wandering on remorseless paths. You feel that the

fire in the sun has erupted in you. Something new has been added to you, a holy affliction. . . . Finally the fear of the inescapable seizes you, for it comes after you slowly and invincibly. There is no escape. So it is that you come to know what a real God is." Jung, *The Red Book*, 291.

20. "If you are not a thinking man, to what purpose are you a man at all? In like manner, there is one knowledge, which it is every man's interest and duty to acquire, namely, SELF-KNOWLEDGE: or to what end was man alone, of all animals, endued by the Creator with the faculty of self-consciousness? Truly said the pagan moralist, E coelo descendit gnothi Seauton [from heaven descended "Know thyself"] . . . Self-knowledge is the key to this casket [of the treasures of knowledge]; and by reflection alone can it be obtained . . . by reflection you may draw from the fleeting facts of your worldly trade, art or profession, a science permanent as your immortal soul; and make even these subsidiary and preparative to the reception of spiritual truth 'doing as the dyers do, who having first dipt their silks in colours of less value, then give them the last tincture of crimson in grain.'" Coleridge, *Aids to Reflection*, 27.

21. Samuel Taylor Coleridge, *Coleridge's Writings*, vol. 4, *On Religion and Psychology*, ed. J. Beer (London: Palgrave Macmillan, 2002), 150.

22. Coleridge, *Biographia Literaria* (1983), 283.

23. "Shelley, that is, approached poetry in the same spirit that Jung in the 1930's approached alchemy: to discover in it the projected life of the soul that scientific materialism had reduced to a delusion. Shelley, like Jung after him, went within himself to discover the psychic reality of delusion as it manifested in the realm of metaphor and myth." Woodman, *Sanity, Madness, Transformation*, 160.

24. C. G. Jung, "The Relations between the Ego and the Unconscious," in *Collected Works of C. G. Jung*, vol. 7, *Two Essays on Analytical Psychology*, ed. Gerhard Adler, trans. R. F. C. Hull (Princeton, NJ: Princeton University Press, 1967). "The regressive restoration of the persona is a possible course only for the man who owes the critical failure of his life to his own inflatedness. With diminished personality, he turns back to the measure he can fill. But in every other case resignation and self-belittlement are an evasion, which in the long run can be kept up only at the cost of neurotic sickliness." Ibid.168.

Chapter 22

1. "Old English *swete*, Mercian *swoete*, 'pleasing to the senses, mind or feelings; having a pleasant disposition,' from Proto-Germanic **swotja-* (source also of Old Saxon *swoti*, Old Frisian *swet*, Swedish *söt*, Danish *sød*,

Middle Dutch *soete*, Dutch *zoet*, Old High German *swuozi*, German *süß*), from PIE root **swād-* 'sweet, pleasant' (source also of Sanskrit *svadus* 'sweet'; Greek *hedys* 'sweet, pleasant, agreeable,' *hedone* 'pleasure'; Latin *suavis* 'pleasant' (not especially of taste), *suadere* 'to advise,' properly 'to make something pleasant to')." *Online Etymological Dictionary*, accessed May 2, 2023, https://www.etymonline.com/word/sweet.

2. Jung, *Collected Works*, 9:169.

3. Coleridge, *The Notebooks of Samuel Taylor Coleridge*, 1:1554.

4. Mark Storey, *The Problem of Poetry in the Romantic Period* (London: Palgrave Macmillan. 2000), 41.

5. "They and only they can acquire the philosophic imagination, the sacred power of self-intuition, who within themselves can interpret and understand the symbol, that the wings of the air sylph are forming within the skin of the caterpillar, those only who feel in their own spirits the same instinct which impels the chrysalis of the horned fly to leave room in the involucrum for antennae yet to come. They know and feel that the potential works in them, even as the actual works on them!" Coleridge, *Biographia Literaria* (1906), 139.

6. Saint Irenaeus of Lyons, *Against Heresies*, ed. Alexander Roberts and James Donaldson (New York: Ex Fontibus, 2020), 96.

7. The Gospel of Philip, 64:31–65:1; 67:27–30; 71:3–15; 85:22–86:19.

8. Jean-Yves Leloup, *The Gospel of Thomas: The Gnostic Wisdom of Jesus* (Rochester, Vt.: Inner Traditions, 2005), no. 75.

9. Laozi, *Tao Te Ching*, chapter 20.

10. "Mother of this unfathomable world!
Favor my solemn song, for I have loved
Thee ever, and thee only; I have watched
Thy shadow, and the darkness of thy steps,
And my heart ever gazes on the depth
Of thy deep mysteries.

Percy Bysshe Shelley, *The Major Works*, ed. Zachary Leader and Michael O'Neill (Oxford: Oxford University Press, 2009), 92.

11. Francis of Assisi, *The Canticle of Love*.

12. Reynold Nicholson, *Divani Shamsi Tabriz* (San Francisco: Rainbow Bridge, 1973), 79.

13. Jung, *Collected Works*, 9:32.

14. Jung, "The Psychology of the Transference," *Collected Works*, 16:174.

15. Dante, *The Divine Comedy*, trans. Henry Wadsworth Longfellow, 1867.

16. "On no account is it a question here of a future Christ or *salvator microcosmi*, but rather of the alchemical *salvator macrocosmi* representing the still unconscious idea of the whole and complete man, who shall bring

about what the sacrificial death of Christ has obviously left unfinished, namely the deliverance of the world from evil. Like Christ he will sweat a redeeming blood but . . . it is 'rose-colored,' not natural or ordinary blood, but symbolic blood, a psychic substance, the manifestation of a certain kind of Eros which unifies the individual as well as the multitude in the sign of the Rose and makes them whole." C. G. Jung, *Alchemical Studies: The Collected Works of C. G. Jung*, ed. Gerhard Adler, trans. R. F. C. Hull (Princeton, NJ: Princeton University Press, 1968), 295.

17. *Online Etymological Dictionary*, "Paradise," retrieved May 5, 2023, https://www.etymonline.com/word/paradise.

18. Abrams, *Natural Supernaturalism*, 29.

19. Revelation 21:2 (English Standard Version).

20. Revelation 19:6–8 (English Standard Version).

21. Abrams, *Natural Supernaturalism*, 27.

22. Ibid., 30.

23. Jung, *Memories, Dreams, Reflections*, 293. Interestingly, the Quaternity was prominent in Jung's experience of the inner wedding; it was on April 4, 1944 (or 4/4/44!), that Jung returned from his near-death experience: "The exact day I was allowed to sit up on the edge of my bed for the first time since the beginning of my illness."

24. Jung, *Visions*, 586.

25. Samuel Taylor Coleridge, "The Eolian Harp," in *The Complete Poems*, ed. William Keach (London: Penguin Books, 1997), 87.

26. Coleridge, *Biographia Literaria* (1983), 1:201.

27. Coleridge, quoted in Lowes, *The Road to Xanadu*, 69.

28. Coleridge, *Notebooks*, 1:1620.

29. As I was training as a Jungian analyst in Switzerland in April of 2001, I had a dream in which my unconscious presented me with a choice between the church and the Child.

> *I dreamt I was talking with Marie-Louise von Franz. We were looking at a certain poem, which was at the same time music—classical music by Haydn. This poem, von Franz said, had at least five or six layers of meaning. But now, if one is going to interpret those deeper layers, that must mean that either you are someone the church will pay to teach them these things, or that you are like a Child.*

I was not familiar with European orchestral music at the time of this dream and, although I had heard of Haydn, I could not have told you anything about him. So the dream was puzzling to me. But life drew my attention back to the dream a few days later through a synchronicity when our group attended an evening concert at the church in Niklausen, a village close to our seminars. The performance was *The Seven Last Words of Christ* (1787), a composition by Joseph Haydn consisting of seven sections of music accompanied by readings from the gospel. In other words, I was about to hear a poem that was also music, written by Haydn, taking place in a church.

Still today this dream and the synchronicity surrounding it continues to draw my attention to the many ways in which my life has felt the tension between the inner path of renewal (becoming "like a Child") and adaptation to collectivity (being paid by the church).

Unfortunately, Hartley was saddled throughout his life by his father's projection of the divine child.

LONG time a child, and still a child, when years
Had painted manhood on my cheek, was I,—
For yet I lived like one not born to die;
A thriftless prodigal of smiles and tears,
No hope I needed, and I knew no fears.
But sleep, though sweet, is only sleep, and waking,
I waked to sleep no more, at once o'ertaking
The vanguard of my age, with all arrears
Of duty on my back. Nor child, nor man,
Nor youth, nor sage, I find my head is gray,
For I have lost the race I never ran:
A rathe December blights my lagging May;
And still I am a child, tho' I be old,
Time is my debtor for my years untold.

Hartley Coleridge, "Long Time a Child," in *Poets of the English Language* (New York: Viking Press, 1950).

30. Coleridge, *Coleridge's Notebooks*, 88.

31. Heninger, "A Jungian Reading of 'Kubla Khan,'" 360.

32. Coleridge, *Biographia Literaria* (1983), 1:222.

33. Jung, *Collected Works*, 11:465. Jung alludes here to a tension in Catholic tradition over whether Mary is the bride of Christ or the church is the bride of Christ. The bride of Christ is often used to refer to the community of believers—the church.

34. Jung, *Notes on Lectures*, 195.

35. Max Zeller, *The Dream: The Vision of the Night* (Santa Fe, N.Mex.: Fisher King Press, 2015), 2.

36. C. G. Jung, "Letter Jan 30, 1953 to Society of Analytical Psychology of Southern California," accessed January 17, 2021, http://www.junginla.org/about/.

37. Friedrich Wilhelm Joseph von Schelling, *The Ages of the World*, trans. Frederick de Wolfe Bolman Jr. (New York: 1942), 90–92.

38. Coleridge, *Collected Letters*, 4:736.

39. Modiano, "Coleridge and Natural Philosophy."

40. Spenser, *Prothalamion*, 1596, lines 159–62.

41. The remarks of J. S. Mill in this respect are still as relevant today as when he made them in 1838. "The time is yet far distant when, in the estimation of Coleridge, and of his influence upon the intellect of our time, anything like unanimity can be looked for. As a poet, Coleridge has taken his place. But as a philosopher, the class of thinkers has scarcely yet arisen by whom he is to be judged. The limited philosophical public of this country is as yet too exclusively divided between those to whom Coleridge and the views which we promulgated or defended are everything, and those to whom they are nothing." J. S. Mill and F. R. Leavis, introduction to *Mill on Bentham and Coleridge* (Cambridge: Cambridge University Press, 1980).

Conclusion

1. Nicholas Davis, "What Is the Fourth Industrial Revolution?," World Economic Forum, January 19, 2016, accessed January 19, 2022, http://www.webforum.org/agenda/2016/01/what-is-the-fourth-industrial-revolution.

2. Elon Musk, "One-on-One with Elon Musk," interview at MIT, 2014, accessed July 5, 2021, https://aeroastro.mit.edu/videos/centennial-symposium-one-one-one-elon-musk.

3. Rory Cellen-Jones, "Stephen Hawking Warns Artificial Intelligence Could End Mankind," BBC News, December 2, 2014, accessed January 17, 2022, https://www.bbc.com/news/technology-30290540.

4. Von Franz, *Aurora Consurgens*, 166–67.

5. "*Ouranos ano, Ouranos kato* [heavens above, heavens below]—this symbolism reveals the whole mystery of the 'woman': she contains in her darkness the sun of 'masculine' consciousness, which rises as a child out of the nocturnal sea of the unconscious, and as an old man sinks into it again. She adds dark to the light, symbolizes the *hierogamy* of opposites, and reconciles nature with spirit." Jung, *Collected Works*, 11:439.

6. Theodor Abt, *Book of the Explanation of the Symbols, CALA IA* (Einsiedeln, Switzerland: Daimon Verlag, 2006), 133.

7. "AI Could Be the End of Democracy—Yuval Noah Harari on the Threat of Artificial Intelligence," Piers Morgan Uncensored, April 19, 2023, accessed May 8, 2023, https://www.youtube.com/watch?v=JV9tzdYT5FU.

8. World Economic Forum, "Values," 2022, accessed June 5, 2022, https://intelligence.weforum.org/topics/a1Gb0000000LGrDEAW?tab=publications.

9. "The central ideas of Christianity are rooted in Gnostic philosophy, which, in accordance with psychological laws, simply had to grow up at a time when the classical religions had become obsolete. It was founded on

the perception of symbols thrown up by the unconscious individuation process which always sets in when the collective dominants of human life fall into decay. At such a time there is bound to be a considerable number of individuals who are possessed by archetypes of a numinous nature that force their way to the surface in order to form new dominants. This state of possession shows itself almost without exception in the fact that the possessed identify themselves with the archetypal contents of their unconscious, and, because they do not realize that the role which is being thrust upon them is the effect of new contents still to be understood, they exemplify these concretely in their own lives, thus becoming prophets and reformers." Jung, *Collected Works*, 12:35, par. 41.

10. Jung, *Letters*, 1:65.

11. "What is the great Dream?" "It consists," Jung writes, "of the many small dreams and the many acts of humility and submission to their hints." Jung, *Letters*, 2:586.

Afterword

1. Robin Lee Graham and Derek L. T. Gill, *The Boy Who Sailed around the World Alone* (New York: Golden Press, 1973).

2. Jung, *On the Nature of the Psyche*, in *Collected Works* 8:290.

3. For those astrologically inclined, the first black sun occurred during a Saturn return, and the second black sun has occurred with a Pluto-Sun opposition culminating at the same time as a second Saturn return.

Bibliography

Abrams, M. H. *Natural Supernaturalism: Tradition and Revolution in Romantic Literature*. New York: W. W. Norton & Co, 1973.

Abt, Theodor. *Book of the Explanation of the Symbols, CALA IA*. Einsiedeln, Switzerland: Daimon Verlag, 2006.

———. *The Egyptian Amduat: The Book of the Hidden Chamber*. Einsiedeln, Switzerland: Daimon Verlag, 2007.

Auden, W. H. *The Enchafèd Flood: Or, The Romantic Iconography of the Sea*. New York: Random House, 1950.

Bachelard, Gaston. *The Poetics of Space*. New York: Penguin, 1964.

Baker, James V. *The Sacred River: Coleridge's Theory of the Imagination*. Baton Rouge: Louisiana State University Press, 1957.

Bareket, Orly, Rotem Kahalon, Nurit Shnabel, and Peter Glick. *The Madonna-Whore Dichotomy: Men Who Perceive Women's Nurturance and Sexuality as Mutually Exclusive Endorse Patriarchy and Show Lower Relationship Satisfaction*. Berlin: Springer Science + Business Media, 2018.

Bateson, F. W. *English Poetry: A Critical Introduction*. Oxford: Oxford University Press, 1910.

Beer, J. B. *Coleridge, the Visionary*. London: Chatto & Windus, 1959.

Blake, William. *The Four Zoas*. In *William Blake: The Poetical Works*, edited by John Sampson. Oxford: Oxford University Press, 1908.

Burke, Edmund. *A Philosophical Enquiry into the Origins of the Sublime and the Beautiful*. Edited by David Womersley. New York: Penguin Classics, 1999.

Carnall, Geoffrey. "Southey, Robert (1774–1843), Poet and Reviewer." *Oxford Dictionary of National Biography*. Oxford: Oxford University Press, 2004.

Cellen-Jones, Rory. "Stephen Hawking Warns Artificial Intelligence Could End Mankind." BBC News, December 2, 2014. https://www.bbc.com/news/technology-30290540

Coburn, Kathleen. *Coleridge: A Collection of Critical Essays*. New York: Prentice-Hall, 1977.

———. *Experience into Thought: Perspectives in the Coleridge Notebooks.* Toronto: University of Toronto Press, 1979.

———. *The Self Conscious Imagination: A Study of the Coleridge Notebooks in Celebration of the Bi-centenary of His Birth 21 October 1772.* London: Oxford University Press, 1974.

Coleridge, Samuel Taylor. *Aids to Reflection.* Edited by Henry Nelson Coleridge. Oxford: Palala Press, 2016.

———. *Aids to Reflection and the Confessions of an Inquiring Spirit.* London: George Bell and Sons, 1884.

———. *Anima Poetæ: From the Unpublished Note-Books of Samuel Taylor Coleridge.* Edited by Ernest Hartley Coleridge. London: William Heinemann, 1895.

———. *Biographia Literaria.* 1906. Reprint, London: J.M. Dent & Sons Ltd., 1930.

———. *Biographia Literaria.* Vol. 1, edited by James Engell and Walter Jackson Bate. Princeton, NJ: Princeton University Press, 1983.

———. *Biographia Literaria: Or, Biographical Sketches of My Literary Life and Opinions.* Princeton, NJ: Princeton University Press, 1983.

———. *Bloom's Classic Critical Views: Samuel Taylor Coleridge.* Edited by Harold Bloom. New York: Infobase Publishing, 2009.

———. *A Choice of Coleridge's Verse.* Edited by Ted Hughes. London: Faber and Faber, 1996.

———. *Coleridge: A Collection of Critical Essays.* Edited by Kathleen Coburn. New York: Prentice-Hall, 1967.

———. *Coleridge: Poems.* Edited by John Beer. New York: Everyman's Library, 1993.

———. *Coleridge's Notebooks: A Selection.* Edited by Seamus Perry. New York: Oxford University Press, 2002.

———. *Coleridge's Writings.* Vol. 4, *On Religion and Psychology,* edited by J. Beer. London: Palgrave Macmillan, 2002.

———. *Collected Letters.* Vol. 1, *1785–1800,* edited by Earl Leslie Griggs. 1956. Reprint, Oxford: Oxford University Press, 2002.

———. *Collected Letters.* Vol. 3, *1815–1819,* edited by Earl Leslie Griggs. London: Clarendon, 1959.

———. *Collected Letters of Samuel Taylor Coleridge.* Vol. 3, *1807–1814,* edited by Earl Leslie Griggs. Oxford: Clarendon Press, 1959.

———. *The Collected Works of Samuel Taylor Coleridge.* Edited by R. J. White. Princeton, NJ: Princeton University Press, 1972.

———. *The Collected Works of Samuel Taylor Coleridge.* Vol. 9, edited by Kathleen Coburn. Princeton, NJ: Princeton University Press, 1993.

———. *The Collected Works of Samuel Taylor Coleridge*. Vol. 12, *Marginalia: Part 1, Abbt to Byfield*, edited by George Whalley. 1969. Reprint, Princeton, NJ: Princeton University Press, 1980.

———. *The Collected Works of Samuel Taylor Coleridge*. Vol. 12, *Marginalia: Part 3, Irving to Oxlee*, edited by H. J. Jackson and George Whalley. Princeton, NJ: Princeton University Press, 1992.

———. *The Collected Works of Samuel Taylor Coleridge*. Vol. 14, edited by George Whalley. Princeton, NJ: Princeton University Press, 1969.

———. *The Collected Works of Samuel Taylor Coleridge*. Vol. 14, *Table Talk, Part II*, edited by Kathleen Coburn. Princeton, NJ: Princeton University Press, 1990.

———. *The Collected Works of Samuel Taylor Coleridge*. Vol. 14, *Table Talk, Part II*, edited by Kathleen Coburn and B. Winer. Princeton, NJ: Princeton University Press, 2019.

———. *The Complete Works of Samuel Taylor Coleridge*. Vol. 2, edited by W. G. T. Shedd. New York: Harper Brothers, 1853.

———. *The Complete Works of Samuel Taylor Coleridge*. Vol. 5, edited by W. G. T. Shedd. New York: Harper Brothers, 1884.

———. *The Complete Works of Samuel Taylor Coleridge*. Vol. 6, *Table Talk*, edited by W. G. T. Shedd. New York: Harper Brothers, 1884.

———. *Hints towards the Formation of a More Comprehensive Theory of Life*. Edited by Seth B. Watson. London: Lea and Blanchard, 1848.

———. *Letters, Conversations and Recollections of S. T. Coleridge*. Edited by Thomas Allsop. London: Frederick Farrah, 1864.

———. *Letters of Samuel Taylor Coleridge*. Vol. 1, edited by Ernest Hartley Coleridge. London: William Heinemann, 1895.

———. *Letters of Samuel Taylor Coleridge*. Vol. 2, edited by Ernest Hartley Coleridge. London: William Heinemann, 1895.

———. *The Notebooks of Samuel Taylor Coleridge*. Edited by Kathleen Coburn. 4 vols. Princeton, NJ: Princeton University Press, 1973.

———. *The Notebooks of Samuel Taylor Coleridge*. Vol. 1, *1794–1804*, edited by Kathleen Coburn. New York: Pantheon, 1957.

———. *The Notebooks of Samuel Taylor Coleridge*. Vol. 1, *1794–1804*, edited by Kathleen Coburn. 1962. Reprint, New York: Routledge, 2002.

———. *The Notebooks of Samuel Taylor Coleridge*. Vol. 2, edited by Kathleen Coburn. Princeton, NJ: Princeton University Press, 1980.

———. *The Notebooks of Samuel Taylor Coleridge*. Vol. 2, *1804–1808*, edited by Kathleen Coburn. Princeton, NJ: Princeton University Press, 1961.

———. *The Notebooks of Samuel Taylor Coleridge*. Vol. 3, edited by Kathleen Coburn. London: Routledge and Kegan Paul, 1973.

———. *The Notebooks of Samuel Taylor Coleridge: Notebooks 1819–1826*. Vol. 4, *Notes*, edited by Kathleen Coburn and Merton Christensen. London: Routledge, 2003.

———. *The Notebooks of Samuel Taylor Coleridge*. Vol. 5, *1827–1834 Text*, edited by Kathleen Coburn and Anthony John Harding. New York: Routledge, 2002.

———. *The Poems of Samuel Taylor Coleridge*. Boston: C.S. Francis & Co., 1848.

———. "On Poesy or Art." In *The Literary Remains of Samuel Taylor Coleridge*, edited by H. N. Coleridge. London: William Pickering, 1836.

———. *The Rime of the Ancient Mariner Big Read*. Plymouth, UK: The Arts Institute, University of Plymouth, 2020. https://www.ancientmarinerbigread.com/.

———. *Samuel Taylor Coleridge—The Major Works*. Edited by H. J. Jackson. Oxford: Oxford University Press, 2009.

———. *Specimens of the Table Talk of Samuel Taylor Coleridge*. Edited by Henry Nelson Coleridge. London: J. Murray, 1852.

———. *The Statesman's Manual; Or, The Bible the Best Guide to Political Skill and Foresight: A Lay Sermon*. London: Gale and Fenner, 1816.

Cottle, Joseph. *Reminiscences of Samuel Taylor Coleridge and Robert Southey*. New York: Wiley and Putnam, 1848.

Dante Alighieri, *The Divine Comedy*. Translated by Henry Wadsworth Longfellow. New York: Houghton Mifflin, 1913.

Davis, Nicholas. "What Is the Fourth Industrial Revolution?" World Economic Forum, January 19, 2016. https://www.weforum.org/agenda/2016/01/what-is-the-fourth-industrial-revolution/#:~:text=The%20Fourth%20Industrial%20Revolution%20can,capabilities%20for%20people%20and%20machines

Einstein, Albert. *Albert Einstein: The Human Side*. Princeton, NJ: Princeton University Press, 2013.

———. *Relativity: The Special and General Theory: A Clear Explanation That Anyone Can Understand*. New York: Wings Books, 1988.

———. "Religion and Science." *New York Times*, November 9, 1930.

Eliot, T. S. *The Waste Land and Other Poems*. New York: Vintage, 2021.

Ellenberger, Henri. *The Discovery of the Unconscious: The History and Evolution of Dynamic Psychiatry*. New York: Basic Books, 1981.

Elsner, Thomas. "The Voice that in Madness is Wanting." *Jung Journal* 2, no. 3 (Summer 2008).

Ford, Jennifer. *Coleridge on Dreaming: Romanticism, Dreams and the Medical Imagination*. Cambridge: Cambridge University Press, 1998.

Francis of Assisi. *Canticle of the Sun of Saint Francis of Assisi*. New York: Leopold Classic Library, 2015.

Freud, Sigmund. *The Uncanny*. Translated by David McLintock. New York: Penguin Classics, 2003.

Galison, Peter, Gerald James Holton, and Silvan S. Schweber. *Einstein for the 21st Century: His Legacy in Science, Art, and Modern Culture*. Princeton, NJ: Princeton University Press, 2008.

Goodchild, Veronica. *Eros and Chaos: The Sacred Mysteries and the Dark Side of Love*. Berwick, Maine: Nicolas-Hays, 2001.

Gose, Elliott B., Jr. "Coleridge and the Luminous Gloom: An Analysis of the 'Symbolical Language' in 'The Rime of the Ancient Mariner.'" *PMLA* 75, no. 3 (1960).

Graf, Fritz, and Sarah Iles Johnston. *Ritual Texts for the Afterlife: Orpheus and the Bacchic Gold Tablets*. New York: Routledge, 2007.

Graham, Robin Lee, and Derek L. T. Gill. *The Boy Who Sailed around the World Alone*. New York: Golden Press, 1973.

Gray, Ronald Douglas. *Goethe the Alchemist: A Study of Alchemical Symbolism in Goethe's Literary and Scientific Works*. Cambridge: Cambridge University Press, 2010.

Haney, J. L. *Bibliography of Samuel Taylor Coleridge*. Philadelphia: For Private Circulation, 1903.

Hannah, Barbara. *Encounters with the Soul: Active Imagination as Developed by C. G. Jung*. New York: Chiron, 2015.

Harari, Yuval Noah. "AI Could Be the End of Democracy—Yuval Noah Harari on the Threat of Artificial Intelligence." Piers Morgan Uncensored, April 19, 2023. https://www.youtube.com/watch?v=JV9tzdYT5FU

Harding, Esther. *The Parental Image*. Toronto: Inner City Books, 2003.

Hart, John. "Is Ideology Becoming America's Official Religion?" *Forbes*, November 30, 2017.

Hazlitt, William. *Collected Works*. Edited by A. R. Waller and Arnold Glover. London: Dent, 1903.

———. *Selected Writings*. Edited by John Cook. Oxford: Oxford University Press, 2009.

Heninger, S. K., Jr. "A Jungian Reading of 'Kubla Khan.'" *The Journal of Aesthetics and Art Criticism* 18, no. 3 (March 1960).

Heraclitus. *The Art and Thought of Heraclitus*. Edited by Charles H. Kahn. Cambridge: Cambridge University Press, 1981.

Hoare, Philip. "Why Willem Dafoe, Iggy Pop and More Are Reading The Rime of the Ancient Mariner to Us." *The Guardian*, April 24, 2020.

Holmes, Richard. *Coleridge: Darker Reflections, 1804–1834*. New York: Penguin, 1999.

———. *Coleridge: Early Visions, 1772–1804.* Harmondsworth, UK: Penguin, 1990.

Ibn Umail, Muhammad. *Corpus Alchemicum Arabicum Vol. 1B (CALA 1B): Book of the Explanation of the Symbols.* Edited by Theodor Abt. Zurich: Living Human Heritage, 2010.

Irenaeus. *Against Heresies.* New York: Beloved Publishing LLC, 2014.

Jung, C. G. *C. G. Jung Letters.* Vol. 2, edited by Gerhard Adler and Aniela Jaffé. 1953. Reprint, Princeton, NJ: Princeton University Press, 2021.

———. *The Collected Works of C. G. Jung.* Vol. 2, edited by Gerhard Adler. Translated by Richard F. C. Hull. Princeton, NJ: Princeton University Press, 1973.

———. *The Collected Works of C. G. Jung.* Vol. 5, edited by Gerhard Adler. Translated by R. F. C. Hull. 1952. Reprint, Princeton, NJ: Princeton University Press, 1977.

———. *The Collected Works of C. G. Jung.* Vol. 7, edited by Gerhard Adler. Translated by R. F. C. Hull. 1967. Reprint, Princeton, NJ: Princeton University Press, 1972.

———. *The Collected Works of C. G. Jung.* Vol. 8, edited by Gerhard Adler. Translated by R. F. C. Hull. 1954. Reprint, Princeton, NJ: Princeton University Press, 1970.

———. *The Collected Works of C. G. Jung.* Vol. 9, edited by Herbert Read, Michael Fordham, Gerhard Adler, and William McGuire. Translated by Richard F. C. Hull. 1939. Reprint, Princeton, NJ: Princeton University Press, 2014.

———. *The Collected Works of C. G. Jung.* Vol. 11, edited by Herbert Read and Gerhard Adler. Translated by R. F. C. Hull. 1970. Reprint, Princeton, NJ: Princeton University Press, 1975.

———. *The Collected Works of C. G. Jung.* Vol. 12, edited by Gerhard Adler. Translated by R. F. C. Hull. 1944. Reprint, Princeton, NJ: Princeton University Press, 1980.

———. *The Collected Works of C. G. Jung.* Vol. 13, edited by Herbert Read, Michael Fordham, Gerhard Adler, and William McGuire. Translated by Richard F. C. Hull. 1954. Reprint, Princeton, NJ: Princeton University Press, 2014.

———. *The Collected Works of C. G. Jung.* Vol. 14, edited by Gerhard Adler. Translated by R. F. C. Hull. 1955. Reprint, Princeton, NJ: Princeton University Press, 1977.

———. *The Collected Works of C. G. Jung.* Vol. 15, edited by Herbert Read, Michael Fordham, Gerhard Adler, and William McGuire. Translated by Richard F. C. Hull. 1944. Reprint, Princeton, NJ: Princeton University Press, 2014.

———. *The Collected Works of C. G. Jung.* Vol 16, edited by Gerhard Adler. Translated by R. F. C. Hull. 1966. Reprint, Princeton, NJ: Princeton University Press, 1985.

———. *The Collected Works of C. G. Jung.* Vol. 18, edited by Gerhard Adler. Translated by R. F. C. Hull. 1957. Reprint, Princeton, NJ: Princeton University Press, 1977.

———. *The Essential Jung.* Edited by Anthony Storr. Princeton, NJ: Princeton University Press, 1983.

———. *Jung on Alchemy.* Edited by Nathan Schwartz-Salant. Princeton, NJ: Princeton University Press, 1995.

———. *Memories, Dreams, Reflections.* Edited by Aniela Jaffé. New York: Vintage, 1989.

———. *Notes on Lectures Given at the Eidgenössische Technische Hochschule, Zürich by Prof. Dr. C. G. Jung.* Edited by Barbara Hannah. 2d ed. Zurich: C. G. Jung-Institute Zurich, 1959.

———. *The Red Book: Liber Novus.* Edited by Sonu Shamdasani. Translated by Mark Kyburz and John Peck. New York: W. W. Norton, 2009.

———. *Visions: Notes of the Seminar Given in 1930–1934.* Edited by Claire Douglas. Princeton, NJ: Princeton University Press, 1997.

Jung, C. G., and Wolfgang Pauli. *Atom and Archetype: The Pauli/Jung Letters, 1932–1958.* Edited by C. A. Meier. 2001. Reprint, Princeton, NJ: Princeton University Press, 2014.

Kant, Immanuel. *An Answer to the Question: What Is Enlightenment?* London: Penguin, 2009.

Keats, John. *The Complete Poetical Works and Letters of John Keats.* Cambridge, Mass: Houghton, Mifflin and Company, 1899.

———. *John Keats: The Complete Poems.* Edited by John Barnard. New York: Penguin Classics, 1977.

———. *The Poetical Works of Keats.* Boston: Houghton Mifflin, 1975.

Kennedy-Xypolitas, Emmanuel. *The Fountain of the Love of Wisdom: An Homage to Marie-Louise von Franz.* Chicago: Chiron Publications, 2006.

King, Martin Luther, Jr. *Where Do We Go from Here: Chaos or Community?* Boston: Beacon Press, 2010.

Kingsley, Peter. *Catafalque: Carl Jung and the End of Humanity.* London: Catafalque Press, 2021.

Kitson, Peter. "Coleridge, the French Revolution and the Ancient Mariner: A Reassessment." *The Coleridge Bulletin New Series* 7 (1996).

Kotowicz, Zbigniew. *R. D. Laing and the Paths of Anti-Psychiatry.* New York: Routledge, 1997.

Laderman, Gary, and Luis Leon, eds. *Religion and American Cultures: Tradition, Diversity, and Popular Expression*. 2d ed. 4 vols. Santa Barbara, CA: ABC-CLIO, 2014.

Lamb, Charles. *The Works of Charles Lamb*. Vol. 3. London: Edward Moxon, 1850.

Lamb, Charles, and Mary Anne Lamb. *Letters of Charles and Mary Lamb*. Vol. 3, *1809–1817*, edited by E. W. Marrs. Ithaca, NY: Cornell University Press, 1978.

Laozi. *Tao Te Ching*. Translated by Stephen Mitchell. New York: Harper Perennial, 1994.

———. *The Way and Its Power: Lao Tzu's Tao Te Ching and Its Place in Chinese Thought*. Translated by Arthur Waley. New York: Grove Press, 1958.

Lawrence, D. H. *D. H. Lawrence and Italy: Sketches from Etruscan Places, Sea and Sardinia, Twilight in Italy*. Edited by Simonetta de Filippis, Paul Eggert, and Mara Kalnis. New York: Penguin Classics, 2008.

Lefebure, Molly. *Samuel Taylor Coleridge: A Bondage of Opium*. London: Gollancz, 1974.

Leloup, Jean-Yves. *The Gospel of Philip*. Translated by Joseph Rowe. New York: Inner Traditions, 2004.

———. *The Gospel of Thomas: The Gnostic Wisdom of Jesus*. Rochester, Vt.: Inner Traditions, 2005.

Lowes, John Livingstone. *The Road to Xanadu: A Study in the Ways of Imagination*. 1927. Reprint, Princeton, NJ: Princeton Legacy Library, 2016.

Malfilâtre, Jacques Clinchamps. "Le Soleil fixe au milieu des planets." In *Solar Poetry and the Subject of the Enlightenment*, edited by Didier Coste. Lafayette, Ind.: Purdue University Press, 1990.

Mann, Thomas. *The Thomas Mann Reader*. Edited by Joseph Warner Angell. New York: Knopf, 1950, 440.

Marlo, H., and J. S. Kline. "Synchronicity and Psychotherapy: Unconscious Communication in the Psychotherapeutic Relationship." *Psychotherapy: Theory, Research, Practice, Training* 35, no. 1 (1998).

Medscape. "Opium Tincture." Accessed January 17, 2022. https://reference.medscape.com/drug/opium-tincture-342043.

Mee, Jon. *Romanticism, Enthusiasm, and Regulation: Poetics and the Policing of Culture in the Romantic Period*. Oxford: Oxford University Press, 2003.

Mellor, Anne K. "The Human Form Divine and the Structure of Blake's Jerusalem." *Studies in English Literature, 1500–1900* 11, no. 4 (1971).

Melville, Herman. *Moby-Dick, or, The White Whale*. New York: Penguin Classics, 2002.

Mill, J. S. *Mill on Bentham and Coleridge*. Edited by F. R. Leavis. Cambridge: Cambridge University Press, 1980.

Modiano, Raimonda. "Coleridge and Natural Philosophy." In *Coleridge and the Concept of Nature*. London: Palgrave Macmillan, 1985.

Musk, Elon. *One-on-One with Elon Musk*. Cambridge, Mass.: MIT Press, 2014.

Myliu, Johann Daniel. *Rosarium Philosophorum of the De Alchemia Opuscula*. 1550. Reprint, New York: Theophania, 2011.

Neumann, Erich. *The Origins and History of Consciousness*. Princeton, NJ: Princeton University Press, 1973.

New Oxford Annotated Bible. Edited by Michael Coogan, Marc Brettler, Carol Newsom, and Pheme Perkins. Oxford: Oxford University Press, 2018.

Nicholson, Reynold. *Divani Shamsi Tabriz*. San Francisco: Rainbow Bridge, 1973.

Nietzsche, Friedrich. *The Gay Science: With a Prelude in Rhymes and an Appendix of Songs*. Translated by Walter Kaufman. New York: Vintage, 1974.

———. *Thus Spoke Zarathustra: A Book for Everyone and No One*. Edited and translated by R. J. Hollingdale. New York: Penguin Classics, 1961.

———. *The Will to Power*. Edited by Walter Kaufman. New York: Vintage Books, 1968.

Norris, Mary. "The Epic Poem You Need for Quarantine." *The New Yorker*, May 15, 2020.

Orpheus. *The Hymns of Orpheus*. Translated by Thomas Taylor. Philadelphia: University of Pennsylvania Press, 1999.

Pagila, Camille. *Sexual Personae: Art and Decadence from Nefertiti to Emily Dickinson*. New York: Vintage Books, 1990.

Paine, Thomas. *The Age of Reason: Parts I & II*. Edited by Moncure Daniel Conway. New York: Merchant Books, 2010.

Pascal, Blaise. *Pensées and Other Writings*. Edited by Anthony Levi. Translated by Honor Levi. Oxford: Oxford University Press, 2008.

Philo. *Questions and Answers on Exodus*. Translated by Ralph Marcus. Cambridge, Mass.: Harvard University Press, 1953.

Plato. *The Republic of Plato*. Edited by B. Jowett. London: Oxford University Press, 1925, 323.

Pomeroy, Ross. "Scientists Have Learned from Cases of Animal Cruelty." *RealClear Science*, January 23, 2012.

Raff, Jeffrey. *The Wedding of Sophia: The Divine Feminine in Psychoidal Alchemy*. Lake Worth, Fla.: Nicolas-Hays, 2003.

Robinson, Andrew. "Einstein Said That—Didn't He?" *Nature*, May 3, 2018.

Rothenberg, Rose-Emily. "The Orphan Archetype." *Psychological Perspectives: A Quarterly Journal of Jungian Thought* 14, no. 2 (1983).

Safina, Carl. *Eye of the Albatross: Visions of Hope and Survival*. New York: Henry Holt and Co., 2002.

Schopenhauer, Arthur. *The Horrors and Absurdities of Religion*. London: Penguin, 2009.

Schwartz-Salant, Nathan. *The Mystery of Human Relationship*. New York: Routledge, 1998.

Schweizer, Andreas. *Stone by Stone: Reflections on the Psychology of C.G. Jung*. Edited by Andreas Schweizer and Regine Schweizer-Vüllers. Einsiedeln, Switzerland: Daimon Verlag, 2017.

Shakespeare, William. *The Oxford Shakespeare: Macbeth*. Edited by Nicholas Brooke. Oxford: Oxford University Press, 2008.

Shamdasani, Sonu. *Jung and the Making of Modern Psychology: The Dream of a Science*. Cambridge: Cambridge University Press, 2003.

Shelley, Mary. *Frankenstein: A Longman Cultural Edition*. Edited by Susan J. Wolfson. Harlow, UK: Longman, 2002.

———. *Frankenstein; or, The Modern Prometheus*. 1818. Reprint, New York: Penguin, 1992.

———. *Mary Wollstonecraft Shelley*. Edited by Harold Bloom. New York: Infobase Publishing, 2009.

Shelley, Percy Bysshe. *The Complete Poems of Percy Bysshe Shelley*. New York: Modern Library, 1994.

———. *The Major Works*. Edited by Zachary Leader and Michael O'Neill. Oxford: Oxford University Press, 2009.

———. *The Poems of Shelley*. Edited by Jack Donovan and Kelvin Everest. New York: Routledge, 2011.

———. *Shelley: Poems and Prose*. Edited by Jack Donovan. New York: Penguin Classics, 2017.

———. *Shelley's Poetry and Prose*. Edited by Donald H. Reiman and Sharon B. Powers. New York: Norton, 1977.

Singer, Thomas, and Samuel Kimbles. *The Cultural Complex: Contemporary Jungian Perspectives on Psyche and Society*. New York: Routledge, 2004.

Sloman, Larry "Ratso." *Reefer Madness: A History of Marijuana*. New York: St. Martin's Griffin, 1998.

Solomon, Andrew. *The Noonday Demon: An Atlas of Depression*. New York: Scribner, 2001.

Sophocles. *The Three Theban Plays: Antigone; Oedipus the King; Oedipus at Colonus*. Translated by Robert Fagles. New York: Penguin Classics, 2000.

Spenser, Edmund. *Prothalamion & Epithalamion.* New York: Houghton Mifflin & Co., 1902.

Stewart, J. S. *Heralds of God.* New York: Charles Scribner's Sons, 1946.

Stiles, Peter. "The Appeal of Integration: The Influence of Joseph Priestley on the Development of the Visual Arts and Fiction in the Late Eighteenth and Early Nineteenth Centuries." Religion, Literature and the Arts Project 1996 Conference Proceedings, 1996.

Storey, Mark. *The Problem of Poetry in the Romantic Period.* London: Palgrave Macmillan, 2000.

Talfourd, T. N. *The Life, Letters and Writings of Charles Lamb: A Sketch of the Life of Charles Lamb in Six Volumes.* Vol. 1, edited by Percy Fitzgerald. London: E. Moxon and Co., 1876.

Trilling, Lionel. *The Liberal Imagination.* New York: The New York Review of Books Classics, 2008.

Von Bingen, Hildegard. *Scivias.* Translated by Mother Columba Hart and Jane Bishop. Mahwah, NJ: Paulist Press, 1990.

Von Franz, M.-L. *Aurora Consurgens: A Document Attributed to Thomas Aquinas on the Problem of Opposites in Alchemy: A Companion Work to C. G. Jung's Mysterium Coniunctionis.* Toronto: Inner City Books, 2000.

———. *Dreams: A Study on the Dreams of Jung, Descartes, Socrates and Other Historical Figures.* Boston: Shambhala, 1998.

Von Schelling, Friedrich Wilhelm Joseph. *The Ages of the World.* Translated by Frederick de Wolfe Bolman Jr. New York: AMS Press, 1942.

Weissman, Stephen M. *His Brother's Keeper: A Psychobiography of Samuel Taylor Coleridge.* Edited by George H. Pollock. 1990. Reprint, New York: BookSurge Publishing, 2008.

Wikman, Monika. *Pregnant Darkness: Alchemy and the Rebirth of Consciousness.* Berwick, Maine: Nicolas-Hays, 2004.

Winnicott, Donald. "Fear of Breakdown." In *The Collected Works of D. W. Winnicott*, Vol. 6, *1960–1963*, edited by Lesley Caldwell and Helen Taylor Robinson. Oxford: Oxford University Press, 2016.

Woodman, Ross. *The Apocalyptic Vision in the Poetry of Shelley.* Toronto: University of Toronto Press, 1966.

———. *Sanity, Madness, Transformation: The Psyche in Romanticism.* Edited by Joel Faflak. Toronto: University of Toronto Press, 2009.

———. "Shaman, Poet, and Failed Initiate: Reflections of Romanticism and Jungian Psychology." *Studies in Romanticism* 19, no. 1 (Spring 1980): 51–82.

Wordsworth, William. *The Collected Poems of William Wordsworth.* London: Wordsworth Editions, 1994.

———. *The Major Works*. Edited by Stephen Gill. Oxford: Oxford University Press, 2008.

———. *The Prelude: A Parallel Text*. Edited by Jonathan Wordsworth. New York: Penguin Classics, 1996.

———. *Selected Poetry*. Edited by Stephen Gill and Duncan Wu. Oxford: Oxford University Press, 2008.

World Economic Forum. "Values." 2022.

Zeller, Max. *The Dream: The Vision of the Night*. Santa Fe, N.Mex.: Fisher King Press, 2015.

Index

Note: page numbers in italics refer to figures.

Abrams, M. H., 250–51, 364

albatross: Antarctic, characteristics of, 117–18; in dream during Jungian analysis, 261–62; European sailors' routine abuse of, 137; "gooney birds" as sailors' name for, 125, 137

Albatross: as angel of imagination healing trauma, 113; and animal guides in folklore and myth, 118; and birds as sacred, saving presence, 114–17; circling of, 121; in dream during Jungian analysis, 261–62, 263; dropping from Mariner's neck, 255–56, 262, 309; dwelling in mist, fog, smoke and Moon-shine, 127; hung around Mariner's neck, 17, 176–79, *178*, *179*, 180, 181, *182*, 186, 191; Mariner's bearing of, as *transitus dei*, 177–79, 186, 191; as mere bird, in crew's mundane view, 129; parallels to Melville's *Moby-Dick*, 124–26; as personification of symbolic, 121; splitting of ice by, 112–13, 114; and white bird symbolism in psychotherapy, 118–21, *120*

Albatross, Mariner's shooting of, 16, 160; as act of hubris, 154–55, 238; as act of Satanic self-idolatry, 153–54, 155; Amenhotep IV's destruction of gods and, 180; as analogous to scientific revolution, 149–51, 277–78; and cost of breaking with convention, 145, 147–49; crew's changes of opinion about, 16–17, 140–42, 176, 181; and emergence of Mariner's "I," 143, 146–47, 158, 235, 298; as Fall of Man through materialism, 152–53, 277–78; as "hellish thing," 135, 143, 158; interpretations of, 5, 156–57; and Mariner as holy criminal, 186; Mariner's perception as sacrilege, 137, 309, 348–49; and modern humans' relationship to animals, 137–39; and narcissistic personality disorder, 155; parallels in Jung, 368; reason for, as unstated, 135; references to, at end of *Rime*'s subsequent parts, 135–36; as sacrifice of idol necessary for evolution of consciousness, 132, 140–44, 152, 158, 298, 309, 385; and science's rejection of empathy, 269; as symbolic slaying of Christ/Christianity, 139–40, *141*, *142*, 143; and transformation of Mariner into modern men, 143–44, 158; voices linking to Mariner's suffering, 18, 308–309

"Albatross" (Public Image Ltd), xi–xii

alchemy: assumption of Mary Queen in, *287*, 287–89, 441n7, 441n9; Boyle and, 268; Coleridge on

alchemy (continued)
psychological relevance of, 52–53, 169–70; color system in, 199, 425n5; as description of encounters with unconscious, 168–69, 421n6; and discovery of phosphorus, 266–68, *267*; eclipse symbolism in, 227; gold's metaphorical meaning in, 170, 264–65; historical practice of, 169; and imagery of Romanticism, 169; images of eating and drinking of self in, 221; as link between Romanticism and depth psychology, 170–71; *mysterium coniunctionis* in, 366; on new redeemer who will unite the whole human being, 363, 451–52n16; North wind in, 415n3; parallels to Romanticism, 264–65; pelican flask in, 221; philosopher's stone in, 221, 233, 388–89, 426n7; as "proto-science" for Jungian depth psychology, 3, 169; *Rime* and, 3–4; and *Rime*'s solar wasteland, 168; rose symbolism in, 363, 451–52n16; Sophia (wisdom) in, 206; and union of Mother and Father worlds, 429n30; white bird symbolism in, 132
Amduat, 14–15, 88, 164
Amenhotep IV (Akhenaten), 180
Ancient Mariner Big Read, The (2020), 11–12
anima: as archetype of eros and life, 105, 361; Coleridge on, 51, 67; Jung on, 361; as symbolic bride, 360–63
animals: dead, author's dream about, 139, 397; modern humans' treatment as objects, 137–39
Apuleius, 238, 362–63
archetypes in Jung, 49, 69, 71, 82
art: Coleridge on psychological function of, 286, 304, 374; Nietzsche on, 104, 416–17n6; visionary, Jung on collective Psyche as source of, 11, 406nn12–13
artificial intelligence, as existential threat, 384
Asra. *See* Hutchinson, Sara (aka Asra)
Attis myth. *See* Cybele-Attis myth
Aurora Consurgens (attr. Aquinas), 200–201

Bacon, Francis, 147–49, *148*
Berengarius of Tours, 369–71
Biographia Literaria (Coleridge): on consciousness and world as forms of same power, 274–76; as effort to come to terms with poetic imagination, 42; on imagination, 72–73, 170; on Milton, 341; on reptilian limbic brain, 97–98; on *Rime*, 8–9, 72; on symbols and power of self-intuition, 356, 451n4; on what he did *vs.* what he could have done, 375
bird, white: in alchemical symbolism, 132; in Christian symbolism, 121–23, *122*, *123*; in Melville's *Moby-Dick*, 124–26; as symbol in psychotherapy, 118–21, *120*; in Wright's *Experiment on a Bird*, *149*, 149–51
black sun: author's cancer diagnosis and, 403–404; author's depression and, 226–28, 397–98; author's dream of, and related painting, 226–28, *227*, 397–98; as symbol in alchemy, 227–28
Blake, William, 73, *250*, 256
blood, drinking of. *See* Last Supper of one's own flesh and blood
Böhme, Jakob, 127–28
Brand, Hennig, 266–68
Bride, in *Rime*, as symbol of anima, 360–63

Campbell, Joseph, 101–2
chance: DEATH and LIFE-IN-DEATH's dice game and, 17, 201–202; and Jung on synchronic-

ity, 203; and world of oracles *vs.* rational cause and effect, 201–204
Christianity: as asylum for Coleridge from daimonic imagination, 41–42; crippling guilt in, 299–300; as "make-believe" for Jung, 367–68, 375; mythology of birth, death, and rebirth of modern soul as replacement for, 385–87; projection of guilt from, as source of hate and bigotry, 300. *See also* religious beliefs
Christopher (Saint), 186, *189*
church, Mariner's choice between wedding and, 19–20, 352–53; church, symbolism of, 19–20, 353–56, 366–69; *vs.* ideal of church *and* wedding, 375–79; parallels to Coleridge's own life, 368–69; and vespers' evocation of Albatross, 355; wedding, symbolism of, 356–63
Coleridge, Berkeley (son), 209
Coleridge, Hartley (son), 66, 209, 371–73, 453n29
Coleridge, Samuel T.: on anguish as God's corrective power, 237; brilliance of, 328; on deep feeling necessary for deep thinking, 244, 271; on dreaming psyche and reality, 216–17; exploration of psychic inner world, xiii–xiv, xiv, 6, 46–54; eyes of, and poet's eye in "Kubla Khan," 336; on his alienation from God, 237; marriage of, 28, 34, 38–39, 42, 208–10; odd manner of walking, 195–96; as possessed by mysterious power, 195–96; on psychological relevance of alchemy, 52–53, 169–70; on reasoning power (logos) necessary to process revelations from unconscious, 337–38; world unprepared to receive revelations of, 381
Coleridge's life: army, joining and discharge, 33–34; at Cambridge University, 33, 34; childhood injury from hot coal, 32–33, 329; as Christian, 121; church membership changes, 284; death of second son, 209; epitaph, written by himself, 43; experience of silver light shooting from body, 68; fame for power of thought, 40; father's death, 26–27; first love, 209–10; flooding of home, 209; French Revolution, hopes for, 33, 35–36, 93–95; friends' failure to help psychological pain, 329; friendship with Wordsworths, 39; Gillman family, residence with, 43, 329; happy early childhood, 24–26; ill health, 43; interest in "Dreams, Visions, Ghosts, Witchcraft, &c," 68; as isolated, imaginative, bookish child, 24–25; isolation at boarding school, 27–32, 111–12; later-life conservative politics, 214; laudanum addiction, 39, 40–41, 43, 326, 327–28, 408n18; overview of, 344; Pantisocracy community plans, 34, 93–94; parents, 24; relation to his poetry, 23; sources on, 23; voluminous reading as small child, 24–25; youthful naive optimism, 93–95
Coleridge's poetry: as dream worked on by conscious mind, 9–10; images of children separated from mother in, 205–206; as living water seeking to heal wasteland, 165; mix of thought and feeling in, 37–38; period of greatest productivity, 39; retreat from daimonic intensity of, 41–42, 213–15, 368, 428–29n27
Coleridge's psychological typology, 37–38; alternate periods of strong feeling and repression, 37–38; conflict between Church and inner child, 371–73; Cybele-Attis typology and, 213–14; dreams of, as schizoid defenses against life, 25–26; early life, and Wotan archetype, 212–13;

Coleridge's psychological typology (continued)
failure to integrate unconscious into conscious, 374; fear of/attraction to erotic imagination, 210–12, 213–15; illnesses caused by emotional trauma, 31; and individuation process, 374; inferiority-superiority complex, 26; inferior relationship to reality, 37; as introverted, intuitive type, 37; loneliness, 26, 43; messianic complex, 82; mother complex, 27–32, 210; narcissism, 26, 215, 328–29; "ominous" dimensions, early awareness of, 32–33; orphan complex, 30; rebellion against authority, 32–33; repetition of childhood trauma, 33–34; repressed Feminine in, 174–75; resentment, contempt, and vanity, 25–26; retreat from daimonic intensity of poetry, 41–42, 213–15, 368, 428–29n27; separation from mother, effects of, 28, 205–206; use of eloquence to mask feelings, 38; weakness resulting from early trauma, 30

Coleridge's works: *Aids to Reflection*, 214–15, 325–26, 350, 450n20; "Apologia pro Vita Sua," 65; "Christabel," 39, 40, 66, 175, 204, 205; "Constancy to an Ideal Object," 30–31, 128–29; *The Constitution of Church and State*, 214–15; "Dejection: An Ode," 104–5, 128, 214, 243–44, 364–65; *The Destiny of Nations*, 10, 205–6; "France: An Ode" ["The Recantation: An Ode"], 35–36, 95; "Frost at Midnight," 28–29, 66, 111–12, 206, 372; later-life religious writings, 121, 214–15; *Lay Sermons*, 214–15; *Lectures on Revealed Religion*, 121; "Lines—Suggested by the Last Words of Berengarius Ob," 369–71, 374–75; "Lines Written at Shurton Bars, September 1795," 89–90; *Logosophia*, 379; "Monody on the Death of Chatterton," 65, 68, 101–2; "The Nightengale," 66, 372; *Notebooks*, 10, 175–76, 244, 335, 422–23n19, 432n2, 447n2; "Ode to the Departing Year," 239–40; "The Pains of Sleep," 172, 323–24; "The Pang More Sharp Than All," 42, 373; *On Poesy or Art*, 286; "Recollections of Love," 209; "Religious Musings," 83; *Sibylline Leaves*, 16; *The Statesman's Manual*, 121, 417–18n3; *Table Talk*, 156; "To the Author of the Ancient Mariner," 7–8; visionary poetry, roots of Jungian depth psychology in, 3; "The Wanderings of Cain," 205–206. *See also Biographia Literaria* (Coleridge); "Kubla Kahn" (Coleridge); *Lyrical Ballads* (Wordsworth and Coleridge); *Rime of the Ancient Mariner* (Coleridge)

Coleridge, Sarah Fricker (wife), 28, 34, 208, 209

complexes: of Coleridge, 26–32, 82, 210; dream figures as personifications of, 47–48; Jung's theory of, 81–82

consciousness: Coleridge on, 10–11, 167, 274–76; as modern scientific mystery, 273–76; split states, causes and effects of, 324–26

conscious-unconscious bipolarity: Coleridge and, 62, 64; Romantics' awareness of, 64, 69; Wedding Guest and Mariner as image of, 62–65. *See also* unconscious's integration into conscious life (individuation)

creative people: collective shadow projections carried by, 181–83; emergence of gifts through wounds, 31–32

crew of ship: changing views on Albatross, 16–17, 140–42, 176, 181;

death of, and Mariner's individuation process, 173, 233–34, 235–37; men of light standing over bodies of, 18, 332; reanimation of, 18, 306–307
Cybele-Attis myth, 213–15, 429n30

DEATH: and alchemical symbolism, 199; arrival at Mariner's ship, 17, 193–95, 196–97; winning of ship's crew in dice game, 201–202. *See also* ship bearing DEATH and LIFE-IN-DEATH
death and rebirth, symbolic: and creation of new collective unconscious, 378; as cultural necessity, Jung on, 13–14, 59, 91, 220; in Egyptian *Amduat*, 88; individuation as, 14, 96–98; Mariner's journey as, 4–5, 14, 60, 88–89, 90–91, 159, 386–88; modern tendency to resist, 91; myths of, 90–91; rise and set of sun as image of, 88; as transformative, 90–91
Degas, Edgar, 181–83
Delphi, Temple of Apollo at, 349–50
depression: Mariner's journey as descent into, 89–91; and psychological transformation, 90–91
Descartes, René, 99–100, 138, 145
Doré, Gustave, 100, 140, *141*, *245*, 245–46, *246*
dreams: of Coleridge, 25–26, 211–12, 214; Coleridge on, 9–11, 25, 47–48, 52, 216–17; in Jungian analysis, 76–81, 300–302, *301*, 322, 397–98; Jung on, 11, 76–81, 377, 406nn12–13

Ebn Ebn Thalud, 211–12, 214
eclipses: LIFE-IN-DEATH's eclipse of sun, 226; psychological significance of, 225–28
Eden/Paradise: garden-bower of *Rime's* wedding as, 363–64; as metaphor, 364–66
ego consciousness, obliteration in Jungian individuation: and birth of new consciousness, 225–28; danger of, 235; as life-in-death, 235–37
Einstein, Albert, 203, 272–73, 438–39n14, 438n14, 439n16
Eleusinian mystery rites, 105
Eliot, T. S., 165, 226–27, 330
Elsner, Thomas (author): affinity for Coleridge and *Rime*, 391, 402, 404; cancer diagnosis, 403–4; childhood and schooling, 391–93; Christian beliefs adopted and lost, 393–94; contacted by birth mother, 395; depression and Jungian analysis, 118–20, 226–28, 397–98, 403; dreams, 217–19, 226–28, *227*, 285, 303–404, 397–98, 452–53n29; dreams and divine feminine as guide for, 403–404; early marriage and divorce, 395; *The Eighth Planet*, 302–304, *303*; law school and legal practice, 394–96; and music in individuation process, xv, 401–402; parents, 392, 393, 394; partner (Monika Wikman), xv–xvi, 227, 317–18, 389, 390, 403; supporters of individuation process, 402; training in Jungian analysis, 2, 402; turn from law to study of psychology, 398–402
Enlightenment, 144–47; and cost of breaking with convention, 144–46; disparagement of imagination, 147–50; and disruption of European cultural and religious values, 92–93; and French Revolution, 93–94; as liberation of thought from religion and social convention, 144–47; Prometheus as patron saint of, 152; rejection of divination, 202–203
eros: anima as archetype of, 105; of Coleridge, 208; dominance over Mariner at sea, 338–39; star and crescent symbol and, 231

erotic unconscious: Coleridge's fear of/attraction to, 210–12, 213–15; as Great Mother, 215
European values, scientific revolution and, 92–93
evil: acceptance as part of self, 248–49, 298, 300, 385; in Christian thought, 298, 299; dream about, in Jungian therapy, 300–302, *301*; as great power in modern world, Jung on, 443n23; Mariner's shooting of Albatross as embrace of, 298, 309, 385; necessity of including in complete image of God, 298. *See also* God, dark side of (archetypal unconscious); repressed content; water snakes, Mariner's blessing of
eye, right: Coleridge's dream woman's attack on, 211, 214; as image of rational nature, 212–13; Wotan's gouging-out of, 212

Fall of Man: Coleridge on modern materialism as, 152, 153, 262, 276, 383; Mariner's shooting of Albatross as, 152–53, 277–78
Feminine principle: in Christian symbolism, 199–201; four images of, in *Rime*, 361; glittering eye of Mariner and, 66–69; LIFE-IN-DEATH as, 197–99; Mariner's fear of, 201; as nightmare for solar/rational Masculine, 198–99, 201; symbolic link to emotion and nature, 196, 199–201
fourfold structure. *See* Quaternity
French Revolution, 33, 34, 35–36, 93, 94–95
Freud, Sigmund, 44, 208, 211, 259, 343

garden-bower of wedding, 363–64
Ginsberg, Allen, 342–43, 449n15
Gnosticism, 255–56, 357
God: death of, and human as new locus of symbolic, 234, 431–32n4; expiation of guilt from killing of, 190–91; Mariner's alienation from, 17; modern people's "weightless" existence without, 186–88; as name for overpowering aspects of psychic system, 99, 415n1; necessity of including feminine and evil in complete image of, 298; Nietzsche on murder of, 188–90, 424n6
God, dark side of (archetypal unconscious): church's rejection of, in *Rime*, 368; Coleridge's failure to recognize, 325–26, 447n10; Mariner's discovery of, 262–63. *See also* evil
Goethe, Johann Wolfgang von, 169, 204, 208, 363, 414n6
guilt: childhood trauma and, 321; as first step in individuation, 183; from killing God, expiation of, 190–91; split states of consciousness and, 324–26

Harjo, Joy, 115–17, 129, 386
"hatching" (mystical union), in individuation process, 96, 97
Hermit: as failed guide for individuation, 345–47, 349; Mariner's hope for absolution from, 333–34, 346; oak-stump of, as image of decayed Christian mythos, 347; reaction to Mariner, and disciples' reaction to Jesus, 84, 346
Hildegard of Bingen, 265–66, 435–37nn2–5
holy criminal: carrying of collective shadow projections, 181; Jesus as, 186; Jung on, 423n2; Mariner as, 186
Hutchinson, Sara (aka Asra), 28, 104, 172, 209, 337–38

Ibn Umail, Muhammad, 132, 170
Iconology of Cesare Ripa, 112–13
imagination: acceptance as symbolic truth, in Jung, 75, 131–32; Coleridge on, 25–26, 48, 72–73, 121, 127–29, 170, 276, 417–18n3; Coleridge's early psychoanalytic interpret of, 72; Coleridge's mother complex and, 30–31; Coleridge's retreat from intensity of, 40–42, 368; Enlightenment disparagement of, 147–50; fundamentalist's interpretation as God, 129; life without, as inanimate chaos, 131; modern lack of faith in reality of, 126, 127, 129; moonlight's awakening of, 65; ocean's power to unleash, 126–27; poetic faith in truth and reality of, 124–27; as powerful force with practical consequences, 131; Romantics on, 73–74; as second world creator, in Jung, 48; values as product of, 129–30; visionary, Plato on, 71–72; visionary, Romantics' defense of, 72–74; and vision of fanatic *vs.* poet/messiah, 74, 86
individuation: as central to Jung's theory, xiv; Christianity as obstacle to, 367; Coleridge on, 50; Coleridge's inability to complete, xiv–xv; Coleridge's lack of guide for, 344–45, 374–75; cutoff from collectivity resulting from, 407n19; definition of, 14; guide for, as necessity, 343; guilt as first step in, 183; Jung on stages of, 95–97; Jung's supports for, 343–44; killing of guiding star as necessary for, 309–10; Mariner's inability to complete, xv, 373–75; Mariner's lack of guide for, 345–49; and Mary's Assumption, 304, 445n33; necessary creation of substitute values, 407n19; Niklaus von Flue as model of, 347–48; and psychological function of art for Coleridge, 304; *Rime* as representation of, xiv; as symbolic death and rebirth, 14; three potential outcomes, Jung on, 350–51, 450n24; *transitus dei* and, 183–90
Industrial Revolution, Fourth, 382–85, 390
intellect separated from feeling, and human turned to devils, 138
introversion, as first stage of individuation, 96–97
introversion and extroversion, Coleridge's anticipation of Jung's theory of, 48
Islam, crescent moon and star symbolism in, 230–31, *231*

Jesus: baptism of, and white bird symbolism, 123, *123*; carrying of cross as *transitus dei*, 186, *187*; as holy criminal, 186; Jung on teachings of, 367–68; Mariner's parallels to, 83–84; St. Christopher's carrying of, 186, *189*
Jung, Carl: on acceptance of lower nature's sacredness, 248–49; on alchemical redeemer to unite human being, 363, 451–52n16; on alchemy as "proto-science" for depth psychology, 169; on anima, 361; *Answer to Job*, 348–49; on bipolarity inherent in self, 62; career and family life of, 343; on Christianity as "make-believe," 367–68, 375; and Coleridge, 46, 375–76; on collective unconscious, 439n15; on conscious worship of nature as goal, 368; on creative person's emotional storms, 102; on Cybele-Attis myth, 215, 429n30; on danger of encountering unconscious, 448n13;

Jung, Carl (continued)
on death of Christian myth, 443n23; on dreams of killing sacred object, 140, 183, 309, 419n5, 423–24n3; on eclipse symbolism in alchemy, 227; encounter with unconscious, 3, 98; on enlightenment through conscious recognition of darkness, 300, 443n24; on evil as great power in modern world, 443n23; and faith in truth and reality of imagination, 124; on Feminine/chthonic counterpart of Christ, 248–49, 433n6; forward to Werblowsky's *Lucifer and Prometheus*, 298; on gender of psychological qualities, 440n1; and German romantics, 46; on God as name for overpowering aspects of psychic system, 99, 415n1; heart attack, and visions of self-knowledge, 366, 452n23; on Hermetic philosophy, 442–43n22; on human blood/nature as nonlinear, 196; on imagination, 75; on individuation, stages of, 95–97; isolation due to knowledge of unconscious, 340–41, 448n11; on killing one's idols, 132; letter to Keller, 95–96; on living waters within unconscious, 259–60; on loneliness as cost of journey toward knowledge of the self, 356; on loss of faith in religious symbols, 259–60; on Mary Queen, assumption of, 286–89, 292, 302, 441nn7–9, 442n15, 443–44n26, 444n28; mediumistic lovers of, 344; on Mercurius, 442n20; as model for initiatory individuation guide, 348–49; *Mysterium Coniunctionis*, 222; on new values, establishment of, 190, 377, 378, 387, 454–55n9; on opposites, uniting within the self, 220; patient living on the moon, 60, 109; on Plato's *Timeus*, 296–98; *Psychology and Alchemy*, 286–87; *The Red Book*, 3, 62, 98, 120–21, 132, 341, 440n1; on regression, 171, 172–73; supports for his individuation process, 343–44; on symbolic death and rebirth, 13–14, 59, 91, 220; on synchronicity, 203, 261, 291–92, 293; on taking back projections, 220–21, 222, 430n3; on true prophet, eight incarnations of, 444–45n31; on unconscious's reflection of affective posture, 81; *Visions Seminars*, 75, 140, 177–79, 222–23, 249; on war, of projected inner psychic conflicts and, 222, 430n3; white bird as symbol of soul in, 120–21
Jungian depth psychology: addressing crisis of Romanticism as goal of, 46, 54, 224, 263, 374; Coleridge's anticipation of, xiv, 6, 46–54; on compensatory dynamics, 170–71; embrace of evil as necessary for evolution of consciousness, 298, 385; killing of guiding star as necessary for individuation, 309; marriage of conscious and unconscious as goal of, 45, 223, 228; on *mysterium coniunctionis* and self-knowledge, 366; Romanticism and, 3, 44, 45, 170–71, 258–59, 378, 409n3, 434n20; underemphasis on community, 375–76

Keats, John: "La Belle Dame Sans Merci," 69; on Coleridge, 213, 427n24; *Endymion*, 231; "The Fall of Hyperion," 74, 91, 229; on imagination, 74; on "Negative Capability," 213, 427n24; "Ode to a Nightingale," 257–58; "Ode to Psyche," 151, 238–39; sacred union of imagination and nature in, 257–58; in Shelley's *Adonais*, 318–20
"Kubla Kahn" (Coleridge): and access to facts about inner nature, 72,

413n26; and Coleridge's daimonic imagination, 40–41, 412n15; Coleridge's laudanum use and, 40–41; delay in publishing, 41; glittering eye of poet in, 66, 336; influences on Coleridge during writing of, 39, 40; on marriage of imagination and Nature, 365; sacred river in, 244; "Vision in a Dream" subtitle, 9

Kurzweil, Ray, 273–74, 275, 383, 439n16

Lamb, Charles, 43, 69–71, 328

land of mist and snow, 107–109; as image of schizoid defenses of conscious self, 109–10; and symbolism of icy landscapes, 110–12

Last Supper of one's own flesh and blood: author's post-9/11 dream about, 217–19, 222; as Black Mass, in Christian view, 222–23; destruction of Christian age as goal of, 223, 430–31n9; images of, in alchemy, 221; in Jung, as image of introjecting shadow impulses, 220–21, 222, 430n8; in Jung, as reunion of lower and higher nature, 223; as means of becoming our own redeemer, 300

LIFE-IN-DEATH: and alchemical symbolism, 199, 206–207, 425n5; appearance of, 228, 361; arrival at Mariner's ship, 17, 193–95, 196–97; and Christian symbolism of Feminine *vs.* Masculine, 199–201; coldness of, 203–4; and Coleridge's erotic imagination, 210–12, 213–15; and Coleridge's mother complex, 210; dice game with DEATH, 203; and eclipse of sun, 226; as Feminine principle from within Mariner, 197–99, 280–81, 440n4; and madonna-whore dichotomy, 208–10; obliteration of ego consciousness in individuation and, 235–37; as personification of Coleridge's poetic imagination, 212; portrayals as naked woman, 206–207, *207*; sexual overtones of, 207–208; three whistles summoning crescent moon, 229; transformation into Mary Queen, 279–80; winning of Mariner in dice game, 17, 201–202. *See also* ship bearing DEATH and LIFE-IN-DEATH

LIFE-IN-DEATH, Mariner's absorption into: and disappearance of all Masculine things, 238; and new revelation uniting sacred and earthly natures, 238; with rise of crescent moon with star, 231–32; and seven days of suffering, 238, 241; as symbolic death/humiliation, 280–81, 440n2; and torment of individuation process, 233–34, 235–38

Lyrical Ballads (Wordsworth and Coleridge), xiii, xiii–xiv, 7, 15–16

madness as eruption of bestial states, Coleridge on, 172, 422n13

Madonna-whore dichotomy in Coleridge, 208–10

mandalas, 294

Mann, Thomas, 181–83, 258–59, 434n19

Mariner: as avatar, 88; biting of arm and drinking of blood, 194, 196, 216, 217–19, 223–24, 320–21; as Christian shadow, 85; as compensatory image to Christ, 299; compulsion to tell tale, 19, 20, 190–91, 349–50, 449–50n19; departure from land, 87–88, 89–91, 92–95; failure to integrate unconscious into conscious, 374; as fourth of Quaternity,

Mariner (continued)
295–96, 299; glittering eye of, 65–69, 83, 308; as image of Coleridge's messianic complex, 82; as image of unconscious mind, 77, 81; inability to understand his own meaning, 85–86; and incomprehensibility of messiahs, 85; journey of, as search for primordial mother, 32; as Mercurius, 299; as Merlin, 298–99; parallels to Jesus, 83–84, 413n35; path to redemption, in Christian terms, 298; penance of, 308–9, 348–49; as personification of Coleridge's traumas, 62; as personification of modern consciousness, 152–55, 247, 280; as post-Christian Messiah for modern world, 82–83, 85–86, 190–91, 299; similar figures in dreams in psychoanalysis, 76–81; "strange power" of speech of, 69–71; supernatural delusions, source of, 195; symbolic death of, 14, 60; and vision of fanatic *vs.* poet/messiah, 74, 86; as "wandering Jew," 20, 84–85, 181. *See also* Albatross, Mariner's shooting of; death and rebirth, symbolic, Mariner's journey as

Mariner's "I"/individuality: and echoes of Coleridge's loneliness, 29; emergence with shooting of Albatross, 143, 146–47, 158, 235, 298; as Satanic *principium individuationis* in Christian terms, 298; and torment of individuation process, 233–34, 235–38, 355–56

Mariner's journey: as circular, 314, 331; as failed individuation process, xv, 373–75; as story of death and rebirth of modern soul, 4–5, 88–89, 386–88

Mariner's rescue by Pilot, Pilot's boy, and Hermit: and Mariner "seven days drowned," 304; Mariner's hope for absolution from Hermit, 333–34, 346; Mariner's joy at first sight of, 332; Quaternity imagery in, 295–96, 334–35; seraph-men of light summoning help, 18, 332; terror of rescuers, 336–37, 338

Mariner's return to land: and abandonment of new values, 190–91; and *agon* of self-knowledge, 309–10, 350, 355–56; and difficulty of integrating unconscious mind, 315; and failure of *eros* to triumph over destructive instinct, 338–39; fiendish look of ship and Mariner, 334; "frightful fiend" of unconscious pursuing him, 315–17, 320, 321; inability to accept killing of Albatross as necessary sacrifice, 309–10; and isolation of those knowing unconscious, 340–41; lack of language to express unconscious, 339–41; lack of reasoning power to process revelations, 337–38; ominous shapes lingering in otherwise quiet water, 332; and possible outcomes of Jungian individuation, 350; and problem of return in initiatory sequence, 315; projective identification and, 341–43; rejection by Hermit, as failed re-integration to society, 349; as resurfacing from deep inward dive, 331; sinking of ship, evocation of Albatross in, 334; snapping of spell that revealed visionary truths, 314, 331–32; and trauma of conscious contact with unconscious, 334–37. *See also* church, Mariner's choice between wedding and; return, as stage of initiatory sequence

Mariner's transformation after 7th day, 241–43; and BEAUTY as mediator between Head and Heart, 307, 445–46n1; collective male consciousness still cursing Mariner, 307; discovery/creation of new God, 262–63; dream of rain leading to rain (synchronicity), 290–93; and flashes of golden fire now in the sky, 305; as fourth, completing Quaternity, 295–96, 299; and LIFE-IN-DEATH's transformation into Mary Queen, 279–81; Mariner's failure to understand and integrate, 263; parallels in Romantic poetry, 250–58; rain as symbol of Mariner's inner balance, 292, 305; as redemption from the Fall, 243; as replacement of Masculine with Feminine, 279–81; as sacred union of imagination and nature, 255–56; and 7 + 1 symbolism, 303–304; storm, symbolism of, 305, 306; "stream of love" from within as source of, 243–44; as symbolic death and rebirth, 262–63, 305, 308; and turn from seeing to hearing/feeling, 307; as "unaware," 368; as union of conscious and unconscious minds, 263, 307, 445–46n1. *See also* water snakes

Mary Queen, assumption of, *282*, *283*; in alchemical symbolism, *287*, 287–89, 295, 441n7, 441n9; author's dream about, 285; and balance of male and female, 293–94; in Catholic tradition, 281–84, 302; as central symbol of Coleridge's art, 304; in Eastern Orthodoxy, 281; as full human form of consciousness, 302; as identical to Jung's individuation, 304; as image of conscious-unconscious union, 304; Jung on symbolism of, 286–89, 292, 302, 441n7–9, 442n15, 443–44n26; and Lourdes miracles, 284; as mediatrix between human and divine, 286; in *Rime*, symbolism of, 279–81, 289, 290, 295; and Trinity transformed into Quaternity, 293–94; as Western equivalent to union of yang and yin, 292

materialism, mechanical: as Antichrist, 152; Coleridge's rejection of, 48, 270–73, 274–75, 383; consciousness and, 273–76; Einstein on, 272–73, 438n14; as Fall of Man for Coleridge, 152, 153, 272, 276, 383; Jung's rejection of, 48, 270; modern condemnation of those rejecting, 270–71, 277–78, 438n10; modern critique of, 276–78

matter, spiritualization of: in alchemy, 289; Jung's synchronicity and, 293

Melville, Herman, 79, 124–26, 127, 339–40

Mercurius, 299, 442n20

Mithraism cult, 183, *184*, *185*

modern consciousness: birth of, Coleridge on, 153; denigration of imagination, 127; destruction necessary for rebirth of, 386–87; evil's necessary role in achievement of, 158; expansion necessary for new world, 263, 435n24; loss of symbols and, 431–32n4; Mariner entry into, with shooting of Albatross, 143–44, 158; Mariner's *transitus* as *transitus* of, 179; mythology of birth, death, and rebirth of, 385–87; narcissism of, 155; replacement of religion with political beliefs, 130–31; Satanic self-idolatry characteristic of, 153–55; Trinity's lack of salience for, 294; "weightless" existence of purely egocentric life, 186–88. *See also* values, new global

modern world: parallels to solar wasteland in *Rime*, 385–86; range of existential threats in, 13

moon, in *Rime*: as feminine eye of unconscious, 66, 67–68; with star, symbolism of, 229, 230–34, 235–37
mother: effects of Coleridge's separation from, 28, 205–206; erotic unconscious as Great Mother, 215; and healthy balance of psyche and soma, 204; negative, *Rime*'s LIFE-IN-DEATH as, 30–31; neglect by, and clinical experience of coldness, 204–205
mother complex: of Coleridge, 27–32, 210; dreams conveying encapsulation within, 80–81; Jung on, 30
Mother Nature. *See* Nature
Musk, Elon, 383–84

narcissistic personality disorder, Mariner and, 155
Nature: conscious worship of, as goal in Jung, 368; Eden/Paradise as metaphor for marriage of imagination and, 364–66; lower, accepting sacredness of, as "problem of today," 248–49; Mariner's finding of God in, 255–56; symbolic link to Feminine principle, 196, 199–201; union of imagination and, as goal in Romanticism, 255–58, 364–66
Nature, Coleridge and, 28–29
Neumann, Eric, 86, 213, 374
Neuralink, 383–84
New Jerusalem, in Revelations, 364–65
Newton, Isaac, 268–69
Nietzsche, Friedrich: on art as escape from reality, 104, 416–17n6; and collective shadow projections carried by transgressors of norm, 181–83; *The Gay Science*, 188–90, 424–25nn6–7; and icy isolation of rebellious consciousness, 110; on murder of God, 188–90, 424n6; *Thus Spoke Zarathustra*, 330–31, 414n6; on Unknown God driving inner storms, 103–104, 415–16n5; on Zarathustra's *transitus dei*, 188–90, 424–25n7
Niklaus von Flue, 347–48
Noah's Ark, and white bird symbolism, *122*, 123
North wind, symbolism of, 99–100, 415n3

ocean: in Coleridge, as inner depth from which dreams emerge, 10–11; as metaphor for unconscious, 45; power to unleash imagination, 126–27; in *Rime,* reflection of moon on, as "bright eye," 66; symbolism in Western literature, 92. *See also* "Vast, Great and Whole"
Orpheus and Eurydice, 105–106
Orphic burial rites, 164, 420n2

Paine, Thomas, 145–46, 151
Pandora (Reusner), *287*, 287–89, 295, 441n7, 441n9
Pantisocracy community, plans for, 34–35, 93, 94
Pauli, Wolfgang, 293, 344
Penrose, Roger, 277
Persephone, myth of, 105
Philo of Alexandria, 279, 293
philosopher's stone, 221, 233, 388–89, 426n7
phosphorus, discovery of, 266–69, *267*
Plato, 71–72, 296–98
projections: failing to recognize unconscious and, 220; Jung on taking back of, 220–21, 222, 430n3; as source of hate and bigotry, 300
projective identification, 341–43
Prometheus, 33, 132, 140–44, 152, 158
psychoanalysis, Jungian: accepting internal fiends with compassion in, 321–22; active imagination technique in, 80; author's experi-

ence in, 118–20, *120*; faith in truth of imagination in, 75–76; initial dream as indication of problem and solution, 119; and psychology as source of experience, 259; suicidal ideation replaced with symbolic death in, 78; welcoming symbolic imagination with faith in, 132
psycho-analytic, Coleridge's invention of term, 4, 48
psychosomatic, Coleridge's invention of term, 48, 322

quantum physics, 203
Quaternity: Assumption of Mary Queen and, 293–94; as basis of new global values, 389–90; and feminine/evil in complete image of God, 298; as image of wholeness, 294; in Jung's experience of self-knowledge, 452n23; and Mariner as fourth, 295–96, 299, 334–35; of mind and reality, 294–95; symbolism of, 303–304

Rainmaker, Chinese, Jung's story of, 291–92
rain or dew in *Rime*: as image of spiritualization of matter, 289; Mariner's dream of rain before rain (synchronicity), 290–93; as symbol of Mariner's inner balance, 292, 305
religious beliefs: Enlightenment as liberation from, 144–47; freedom experienced by those escaping from, 146–47; Mariner's shooting of Albatross as escape from, 143; modern replacement with political beliefs, 130–31; replacing with faith in symbolic imagination as step forward, 131–32. *See also* Christianity
repressed content: as chthonian, 421n3; of Coleridge, as Feminine, 174–75; as covered with "slime from the deep," 171–72, 173; as dimension of self required for wholeness, 173; emergence in mental or physical symptoms, 321; terror of facing, as dependent on attitude, 173. *See also* evil; unconscious
reptiles, as symbol, 168
return, as stage of initiatory sequence: community renewal as goal of, 376–78; Mariner's failure to complete, 315, 376; Nietzsche's Zarathustra and, 330–31. *See also* Mariner's return to land
Rime of the Ancient Mariner (Coleridge): author's encounter with, 1–2; as bridge between alchemy and depth psychology, 3–4; as call for transformation of consciousness, 15; Coleridge on meaning of, 8–9, 194–95, 337; and Coleridge's daimonic imagination, 40–41; Coleridge's "Lines Written at Shurton Bars" and, 89–90; Coleridge's personal psychology and, 15, 40; connections between modern consciousness and Satan in, 383–84; and Cybele-Attis mythologem, 215; as effort to reconcile conscious and unconscious, 374; and Egyptian *Amduat*, 14–15; elusive meaning of, 7–8; as journey of individuation, xiv; moral of, 156–57; as mythic night-sea journey, 87; origin of idea, and composition, 15–16, 65; parallels to Jungian analysis, 6; as prothalamion for wedding yet to come, 380–81; resonance with modern foreboding, 12; scholarship on, 8; and scientific opposition to religious feeling for nature, 269; as search for feminine spirit (anima) lost to conscious life, 105–106;

Rime of the Ancient Mariner (Coleridge) (continued)
as self-portrait of collective unconscious, 3–4; as story of death and rebirth of modern soul, 4–5, 88–89, 386–88; symbolism of, as doorway to something new, 6; synopsis of, 16–20; as underworld journey, 14–15; versions of, 9, 16, 199; written in time of association with Wordsworths, 39
Romanticism: author's engagement with, 2–3; crescent moon with star symbolism in, 231; crisis of, as problem addressed by depth psychology, 46, 54, 224, 263, 374; cultural disruptions of scientific revolution and, 92–93; death of God as precondition of, 151; defense of poetry, 72–74; and depth psychology, differences of, 44–45, 409n3; emotional storms as subject in, 102–103; encounters with archetypal unconscious, 318–20; as foundation for depth psychology, 378; on humans as *homo imaginatus*, 129; immature masculine psyche in, 319; inability to reconcile conscious and unconscious, 45; inward journey as descent into unconscious mind, 88–89; Mariner's blessing of water snakes and, 250–58; parallels in alchemy, 169, 170–71, 264–65; parallels in depth psychology, 170–71, 258–59, 434n20; roots of depth psychology in, 3, 44, 378; sacred union of imagination and nature in, 255–58, 364–66; and scientific opposition to religious feeling for nature, 269; and search for lost divinity, 239–40; and transition to post-Christian religion, 238–39; view of nature as heretical, 258
Rosarium Philosophorum, 170, 289
roses, symbolism of, 361–63
Rumi, 359

sacrifice *vs.* sacrilege, in killing of Albatross, 309, 348–49
Schwartz-Salant, Nathan, 215, 233–34, 338
science: Coleridge's interest in, 271–72; opposition to religious feeling for nature, 269; treatment of animals as objects, 137–38. *See also* materialism
self-idolatry: Mariner's shooting of Albatross as, 153–54, 155; modern consciousness and, 153–55
September 11th terrorist attacks, 217–19
7 + 1 systems, 303–4, 444–45n31
Shelley, Mary, 152, 306, 316, 414n6
Shelley, Percy B.: *Adonais*, 89, 102–3, 318–20; on afterlife, 193; "Alastor," 358; atheism of, 251–52; on Coleridge's brilliance, 328; *A Defense of Poetry*, 73; on emotional storms, 102–103; failure to integrate unconscious into conscious life, 45; and "frightful fiend" pursuing Mariner, 316–17; on imagination, 73; journey within himself, 450n23; *On Life*, 253; Mariner-like acceptance of opposites within nature, 252; "Mont Blanc," 252–53; on nature of God, 251–52; *The Necessity of Atheism*, 251–52; *Prometheus Unbound*, 91, 193, 316–17; *Queen Mab*, 251–52; sacred union of imagination and nature in, 252–53, 433nn11–12; on white radiance of Eternity, 111
ship bearing DEATH and LIFE-IN-DEATH, 193–97, 225–28
ship of Mariner, homeward voyage: arrival at home port, 18–19; and

conflict between Sun and Moon, 308; force propelling, 18, 307–308; as metaphor for Christian Church, 247–48; nature and supernatural as powerfully alive during, 263; ocean's "bright eye" parallel to Mariner's, 308; two voices describing Mariner's crime and penance, 18, 308–309
slimy things in slimy sea, 17, 97, 168, 171, 174, 233–35
snake/serpent: Coleridge's description of unconscious as, 62, 175; tension between Christ and, within Coleridge, 62, 175–76. *See also* uroboros; water snakes, Mariner's blessing of
solar wasteland, ship's doldrums in, 16–17; as image of pure light of Enlightenment devoid of Feminine/imagination, 160–65; loss of God/Albatross's protective wing as cause of, 164; as Masculine space devoid of Feminine water, 163–65, 174; parallels in alchemy, 166–68, 171; parallels in modern civilization, 385–86; parallels in therapeutic regression, 166–68, 171–73; parallels in world mythology, 164–65; repressed content of, as Feminine, 174–75; and wind as image of imagination as impulse, 161–63; and witches curse in Shakespeare's *Macbeth*, 174
Sophia (wisdom), 206, 265, 359
Sophocles, 154–55, 427n23
Southey, Robert, 28, 34, 94, 209
STORM-BLAST driving ship off course, 99–106
storms, emotional: artists' susceptibility to, 102; and descent into unconscious, 102–104; pursuit of, to avoid stultifying normal life, 104–105; in Romantic poetry, 102–103; as starting point for journey toward wholeness, 102
"stream of love" from within Mariner, 243–44
sun: at noon, power to halt ships progress, 161, 307–308; rise and set of, as symbolic death and rebirth, 88. *See also* solar wasteland, ship's doldrums in
symbols: Coleridge on reality of, in physical world, 275–76, 439–40n21; Coleridge's Jungian insights on, 51–52; from collective unconscious, accepting truth of, 131–32. *See also* unconscious, collective
synchronicity, 203, 261, 290–93, 434–35n22, 452–53n29

Tao Te Ching, 164–65, 357–58, 420n3
Teresa of Avila (saint), 110–11
thought, freedom of, 144–45
3 + 1 systems. *See* Quaternity
The Thunder: Perfect Mind (Gnostic fragment), 200
Tiamat, sons of, 429n30
Tiepolo, Giovanni Battista, *282*
transformation: dissolving of old consciousness as first step in, 228; need for analytic vessel for unfolding of, 228; as symbol death, 260–62; typical resistance to, 166–67; work required to recognize meaning of symbols in, 263
transitus dei: Albatross hung around Mariner's neck as, 177–79, 186, 191; cases of carrying of new living God, 186; in cult of Mithraism, 183, *184*, *185*; and death of Pan at dawn of Christianity, 184–86; and Jesus carrying cross, 186, *187*; of Mariner, as that of modern consciousness, 179; and modern people's "weightless" existence without God to carry, 186–88; Nietzsche's Zarathustra's

transitus dei (continued)
carrying of self-knowledge in, 188–90, 424–25n7; and tragic guilt as first stage of individuation, 183
Transitus Mariae, 281
Trinity: as no longer salient for modern mind, 294; transformation into Quaternity with assumption of Mary Queen, 293

unconscious: archaic and anarchic content of, 96–98; Coleridge on damage done by hiding of, 374; Coleridge's anticipation of depth psychology on, 46–54; Coleridge's repression of, 323, 324–26; Coleridge's suffering from dreams prompted by, 322–24, 446n9; Coleridge's unaided exploration of, xiv–xv; danger of being overwhelmed by, 316–18; defenses against integration of, 321; descent into, as second stage of Jung's individuation, 96–98; dreams' exposure of existence, 76; exposure of, as terrifying experience, 60; facing, as goal of psychoanalysis, 321–22; Freud and Jung's dispute over, 343; Freud on discovery of, 44; as "frightful fiend" pursuing Mariner, 316, 320, 321; as hidden from most modern people, 60; hiding of, as necessary for functioning in society, 373–74; impossibility of escaping, 321; Mariner as image of, 77, 81; Romantic poets and, 44, 318–20, 446n4; as sublime, 63; terror of facing, as dependent on attitude, 173; urge to run from, Jung on, 320. *See also* repressed content; "Vast, Great and Whole"
unconscious, collective: Coleridge on, 50–51; Coleridge's work toward new myth based on, 379, 454n41; conveyance through dreams of things we need to know, 76–81; as dark side of God, Coleridge's failure to recognize, 325–26, 447n10; as Great Dream referenced by visionary art, 11, 406nn12–13; Mariner as messiah bringing new values from, 85; masculine resistance to symbolic death at hands of, 320; power to generate rebirth, 317–18; prompting of symbolic death and rebirth during crises, 77–79; Romanticism's laying of foundation for new myth of, 378; Romantics' search within, for lost divinity, 239–40; as source of new myth for modern age, 376–78, 388–89, 454–55n9
unconscious's integration into conscious life (individuation): Assumption of Mary as image of, 302; British Romantics' failure in, 45, 54; as Coleridge's unrealized goal, 45, 54; as goal of Jungian depth psychology, 45, 223, 228; as key to peace and ending racism, sexism, and homophobia, 223; Last Supper of one's own flesh and blood and, 223; Logos and Eros required for, 339; Mariner's rejection by Hermit as failure of, 349; *Rime*'s slimy things and, 168; unpleasant animals arising from, Jung on, 21n2
uroboros, 221, 313–14

values, new global: collective unconscious as source of, 388–89, 454–55n9; expiation of guilt from killing God through creation of, 190–91; global elite's effort to shape, 388; mythology of birth, death, and rebirth of modern consciousness as, 385–87; Quaternity as basis of, 389–90

"Vast, Great and Whole": Coleridge's access to, provided by dreaming/ imagination, 10–11, 25–26; Coleridge's characterizations of, 10–11, 35–37; Coleridge's inability to escape yearning for, 42; Coleridge's life-long orientation toward, 37–38; Coleridge's search for, 35–37, 41–42
von Franz, Marie-Louis, 60, 100, 200–201, 347–48, 386, 452–53n29

wandering Jew, 20, 84–85, 181
water snakes, Mariner's blessing of, 17–18; as acceptance of lower nature's sacredness, 245–49; and beauty's mediation between head and heart, 244; as contrary to Christian, Enlightenment values, 249; and new revelation of sacred, 190; parallels in Jungian depth psychology, 258–62, 263, 368; parallels in Romantic poetry, 250–58; as recognition of unity of consciousness and Nature, 275, 276; as redemptive revelation of God in nature, 212; and transformation of Mariner's consciousness, 241–43; as "unaware," 368
water snakes' trails, as flash of golden fire, 18, 243; alchemy and, 264–65, 269–70; bioluminescence and, 269; Doré's image of, *246*; and Mariner's transformative revelation, 97, 240, 243; Pentecost imagery and, 247; and promise of new world for modern man, 263; sparks of light in Gnosticism and, 265–66, 435–37nn2–5; as sparks of reborn sun, 244–45
wedding. *See* church, Mariner's choice between wedding and
Wedding Guest: fear of madness, 60; fear that Mariner is a ghost, 59–60; impact of Mariner's tale on, 19–20; with Mariner, as image of conscious-unconscious bipolarity, 62–65; and Mariner as fourth member of Quaternity, 295–96; Mariner as guide into world of unconscious for, 60–61; Mariner's selection and transfixing of, 57–59, 64–65; as "sadder and wiser" man after hearing Mariner, 379–80; turn from wedding, 19–20
wicked whisper heard by Mariner, 236–37
Wikman, Monika, xv–xvi, 227, 317–18, 389, 390, 403
Woodman, Ross, 2–3, 223–24, 302, 337, 450n23
Wordsworth, Dorothy, 28, 39, 336
Wordsworth, William: Coleridge and, 15, 39, 43, 153, 208–209, 271, 344; on conscious-unconscious bipolarity in self, 64; on glimpses of "immortal sea," 87; on hellish depths of Mind of Man, 239–40; integration of Christian and Enlightenment thought, 254–55; on marriage of imagination and Nature, 365; "Ode: Intimations of Immortality," 239; *The Prelude*, 91, 106, 239–40; *The Recluse*, 254–55; sacred union of imagination and nature in, 255–56; on spirit pervading nature, 253–54; "Tintern Abbey," 253–54. *See also Lyrical Ballads* (Wordsworth and Coleridge)
World Economic Forum, 382–83, 387–88
Wotan myth, 212–13, 306, 427n23
Wright, Joseph (Wright of Derby): *The Alchymist . . . Discovers Phosphorus*, 266, *267*; *An Experiment on a Bird in the Air Pump*, *149*, 149–51, 269

Zeller, Max, 376–78, 389